COUNTR

CW00735235

GUIDE TO
RURAL
ENGLAND

THE NORTH WEST OF ENGLAND

By David Gerrard

Published by:
Travel Publishing Ltd
7a Apollo House, Calleva Park
Aldermaston, Berks, RG7 8TN
ISBN 1-904-43446-0
© Travel Publishing Ltd

Country Living is a registered trademark of The National
Magazine Company Limited.

First Published: *2003*   *Second Edition:*   *2006*

COUNTRY LIVING GUIDES:

East Anglia	Scotland
Heart of England	The South of England
Ireland	The South East of England
The North East of England	The West Country
The North West of England	Wales

PLEASE NOTE:

All advertisements in this publication have been accepted in good faith by Travel
Publishing and they have not necessarily been endorsed by *Country Living*
Magazine.

All information is included by the publishers in good faith and is believed to be
correct at the time of going to press. No responsibility can be accepted for errors.

Editor: David Gerrard

Printing by: Scotprint, Haddington

Location Maps:© Maps in Minutes ™ (2006)   © Crown Copyright, Ordnance Survey 2006

Walks: Walks have been reproduced with kind permission of the internet
walking site www.walkingworld.com

Walk Maps: Reproduced from Ordnance Survey mapping on behalf of the
Controller of Her Majesty's Stationery Office, © Crown Copyright.
Licence Number MC 100035812

Cover Design: Lines & Words, Aldermaston

Cover Photo: Ashness Bridge overlooking Derwent Water, Lake District
© www.britainonview.com

Text Photos: Text photos have been kindly supplied by the Pictures of Britain photo
library © www.picturesofbritain.co.uk

Foreword

Britain is an explorer's paradise – the variety of landscape, wildlife and cultural attractions promises days of energetic walking and breathtaking sights, or quiet contemplation amid awe-inspiring nature.

Each month, *Country Living Magazine* celebrates the richness and diversity of our countryside with features on rural Britain and the traditions that have their roots there. So it is with great pleasure that I introduce you to the *Country Living Magazine Guide to Rural England* series. Packed with information about unusual and unique aspects of our countryside, the guides aim to point both fair-weather and intrepid travellers in the right direction.

This book provides a fascinating tour of the North West of England, from the sandstone villages of the Eden Valley in Cumbria to the rugged and varied terrain of the Forest of Bowland in Lancashire. One of the main attractions of this area is the Lake District. Venture out on one of the walking trails or explore the area by mountain bike. To take things at a more leisurely pace, enjoy a boat ride on one of the beautiful lakes or visit the historic houses and castles.

Each chapter also provides insights into local heritage and history, and easy-to-read facts about places to visit, stay, eat, drink and shop.

I hope this guide will help make your visit a rewarding experience and that you will return inspired, refreshed and ready to head off on your next countryside adventure.

Susy Smith

Susy Smith
Editor, Country Living magazine

PS To subscribe to *Country Living Magazine* each month, call 01858 438844

Introduction

This is the second edition of *The Country Living Guide to Rural England - the North West* which has been fully updated. In this respect we would like to thank the many Tourist Information Centres in Lancashire, Cheshire,Cumbria, Greater Manchester, Merseyside and the Isle of Man for helping us update the editorial content. The guide is edited by David Gerrard who has published nearly 40 titles covering a wide range of travel, leisure and local history topics including previous editions of the *Country Living* Rural Guide series. David has ensured that this edition is packed with vivid descriptions, historical stories, amusing anecdotes and interesting facts on hundreds of places in the traditional countryside of North West England

Cumbria includes the Lake District famous for its impressive mountain scenery, green rolling hills, fast flowing rivers, deep lush forests and, of course, the enchanting lakes themselves. Readers who wish to explore the rural retreats of the North West however, should definitely *not* ignore the hundreds of scenic attractions and interesting places to be found elsewhere in the rest of this region

The coloured advertising panels within each chapter provide further information on places to see, stay, eat, drink, shop and even exercise! We have also selected a number of walks from *www.walkingworld.com* (full details of this website may be found to the rear of this guide) which we highly recommend if you wish to appreciate fully the beauty and charm of the varied rural landscapes of the North West.

The guide however is not simply an "armchair tour". Its prime aim is to encourage the reader to visit the places described and discover much more about the wonderful towns, villages and countryside of the North West of England. Whether you decide to explore this region by wheeled transport or by foot we are sure you will find it a very uplifting experience.

We are always interested in receiving comments on places covered (or not covered) in our guides so please do not hesitate to use the reader reaction form provided at the rear of this guide to give us your considered comments. This will help us refine and improve the content of the next edition. We also welcome any general comments which will help improve the overall presentation of the guides themselves.

Finally, for more information on the full range of travel guides published by Travel Publishing please refer to the details and order form at the rear of this guide or log on to our website at www.travelpublishing.co.uk

Travel Publishing

Locator Map

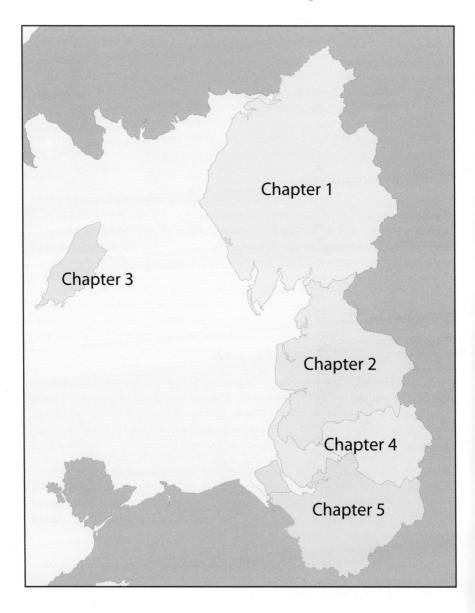

Contents

1 CUMBRIA & THE LAKE DISTRICT

Lake Windermere

Visitors from all over the world are drawn in their millions to the Lake District with its irresistible combination of enchanting lakes, picturesque villages and some of the most dramatic scenery in England. The highest mountain in the country, Scafell Pike (3,205ft), the largest and deepest lakes, Windermere and Wast Water respectively, are all found here, along with hundreds of other mountains, another 14 lakes (although apart from Bassenthwaite they are called 'meres' or 'waters'), challenging crags and lovely wooded valleys. Despite the huge influx of visitors, most do not venture far from the main tourist 'honey-pots' so it's still easy to find the peaceful glades and windswept, isolated fells celebrated by the Lake Poets, Wordsworth, Coleridge and Southey. Between them, this lyrical trio transformed the pervading 18th century perception of the most northwesterly corner of England as an intimidating wilderness into an appreciation of its majestic scenery.

Almost exactly one third of the county's 2,636 square miles lies within the boundaries of the Lake District National Park, created in 1951 to protect the area from "inappropriate development and to provide access to the land for public enjoyment". Its 22,292 square kilometres include a wonderfully varied landscape, and the opportunities for enjoying the great outdoors are almost boundless. For many people travelling from the south into Cumbria, their first experience of the county is the area around Kendal and Kirkby Lonsdale. These ancient settlements both provide an excellent introduction to the history, people, and economy of Cumbria.

The southeastern corner of the extensive Lake District National Park is Cumbria's best known and most popular area, with the main resort towns of Windermere, Bowness-on-Windermere and Ambleside, and, of course, Lake Windermere itself. They are certainly busy with tourists during the summer months but their charm and attraction remain for all to see. Also, with the unpredictability of Lakeland weather, they provide a whole host of indoor amusements to appeal to all ages.

The whole area opened up to tourism as a result of the Victorians' growing interest in the natural landscape and their engineering ability in providing a railway service. So these villages, once little more than places where the fell farmers congregated to buy and sell their livestock and exchange gossip, grew into inland resorts with fine Victorian and Edwardian villas, houses, and municipal buildings.

Lying between the lakes and mountains of the Lake District and the sandy estuaries of Morecambe Bay, the Cartmel and Furness Peninsulas are areas of gentle moorland, craggy headlands, scattered woodlands, and vast expanses of sand. It was once a stronghold of the Cistercian monks, whose influence can still be seen in the buildings and fabric of the landscape. This is Cumbria's ecclesiastical centre and there were several monasteries here. The rapid growth of Barrow-in-Furness, which will be forever linked with the shipbuilding industry, changed the face of much of the area, but as the iron industry declined so did the town.

The arrival of the railways in the mid-19th century saw the development of genteel resorts such as Grange-over-Sands overlooking the treacherous sands of Morecambe Bay. Grange is still an elegant little town and has been spared the indignity of vast amusement parks and rows of slot machines, retaining its character as a quiet and pleasant holiday centre.

The North Cumbrian coast, from Workington in the south to the Solway Firth in the north, is one of the least known parts of this beautiful county but it certainly has a lot to offer. It is an area rich in heritage, with a network of quiet country lanes, small villages, old ports, and seaside resorts. The coast's largest town, Workington, on the site of a Roman fort, was once a large port, prospering on coal, iron and shipping. It later became famous for fine-quality steel, and though its importance has declined, it is still the country's largest producer of railway lines. Further up the coast is Maryport, again a port originally built by the Romans.

A short distance inland lies Cockermouth on the edge of the Lake District National Park, a pretty market town with some elegant Georgian buildings. However, most visitors will be more interested to see and hear about the town's most famous son, the poet William Wordsworth, who was born here in 1770.

The northernmost stretch of coastline, around the Solway Firth, is an area of tiny villages with fortified towers standing as mute witness to the border struggles of long ago. These villages were the haunt of

Boat Trip on Ullswater

LOCATOR MAP

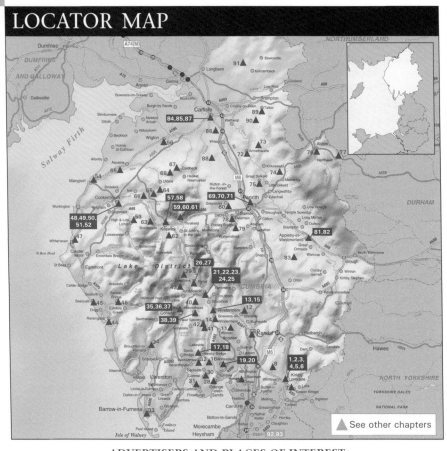

ADVERTISERS AND PLACES OF INTEREST

ADVERTISERS AND PLACES OF INTEREST

smugglers, wildfowlers, and half-net fishermen. What is particularly special about this coastline is its rich birdlife. The north Cumbrian coast was also the setting for Sir Walter Scott's novel *Redgauntlet*, and the fortified farmhouse by the roadside beyond Port Carlisle is said to be the 'White Ladies' of the novel.

The River Eden, one of the few large rivers in England that flows northwards, rises on the high limestone fells above Mallerstang Common, near the North Yorkshire border, and runs to the outskirts of Carlisle where it turns sharply east and flows into the Solway Firth. For much of its course, the river is accompanied by the famous Settle to Carlisle Railway, a spectacularly scenic route saved from extinction in the 1960s by the efforts of local enthusiasts.

For more than 350 years the area around Carlisle was known as the Debatable Lands, a lawless region where the feared Border Reivers sacked and plundered at will. Every winter, when their own food stocks were almost depleted, armed gangs from across the border would ride southwards to seize the cattle and sheep of their more prosperous neighbours. Stealing and murdering, they wreaked havoc in this area and almost every village would have had a fortified structure, usually a pele tower, where the inhabitants and their animals could hide safely.

This is also the county of Hadrian's Wall, the most important monument built in Britain by the Romans; many stretches of the wall are still visible, and Birdoswald and other centres give an excellent insight into Roman border life.

Parma Violet

52 Main Street, Kirkby Lonsdale, Cumbria LA6 2AJ
Tel/Fax: 015242 72585
e-mail: info@parmaviolet.co.uk
website: www.parmaviolet.co.uk

Parma Violet, together with many other specialist shops and cafes, is located on the Main Street of the wonderfully quaint Victorian market town of Kirkby Lonsdale, less than half an hour's drive from the Lake District. It was dreamt of long before it was born and when its door finally opened, Parma Violet was at last able to reveal its carefully sourced eclectic mix of gifts, toys, home and garden products, cards, jewellery and vintage items.

From collectable children's Ladybird books and Lola Rose jewellery to French enamel soap dishes and beautiful heart-shaped 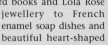  willow wreaths, Parma Violet really does have everything you are looking for to breathe life into any home. The shop has something to suit every budget and whether you come away with a beautiful shell to place in your bathroom, or a magnificent painted antique mirror for your hallway, your experience is sure to be a real treat If you are not able to visit the shop in person some items are also available to buy through mail order. You can expect lovely packaging and a little extra something as standard with every order placed.

KIRKBY LONSDALE

One fine day in 1875 John Ruskin came to Kirkby Lonsdale and stood on the stone terrace overlooking the valley of the River Lune. It was, he declared, "one of the loveliest scenes in England, therefore in the world." He was equally enthusiastic about the busy little market town - "I do not know in all my country," he continued, "a place more naturally divine than Kirkby Lonsdale."

Ruskin had been inspired to visit the town after seeing Turner's painting of that view, and Turner himself had come in 1816 on the recommendation of William Wordsworth. All three of them made a point of going to see the **Devil's Bridge** over the Lune, a handsome, lofty structure of three fluted arches reputedly built by Satan himself in three days. According to legend an old woman, unable to cross the deep river with her cattle, had asked the Devil to build her a bridge. He agreed but demanded in return the soul of the first creature to

Market Day, Kirkby Lonsdale

cross but his evil plan was thwarted by Cumbrian cunning. The old woman threw a bun across the bridge which was retrieved by her dog and thus she cheated the Devil of a human soul.

Kirkby's Main Street is a picturesque jumble of houses spanning several centuries, with intriguing passages and alleyways skittering off in all directions, all of them worth exploring. It's still a pleasure to stroll along the narrow

WYCK HOUSE

4 Main Street, Kirkby Lonsdale, Cumbria LA6 2AE
Tel/Fax: 015242 71953
website: www.studioarts.co.uk/wyckhouse.htm
e-mail: wyckhouse@studioarts.co.uk

Located just 50 yards from Kirkby Lonsdale's market square, **Wyck House** is a warm and friendly family-run guest house, the home of Pat and Brian Bradley. The quality accommodation comprises spacious double or twin rooms, all of them en suite and equipped with remote control colour TV and hospitality tray. A hearty English breakfast with lots of choice is included in the tariff. The house is non-smoking and pets are not accepted. Situated between the Yorkshire Dales and the English Lake District, Kirkby Lonsdale is an appealing little town with many well-appointed public houses and restaurants all within easy walking distance of Wyck House.

MANSERGH HALL FARM SHOP

Mansergh Hall, Kirkby Lonsdale, via Carnforth,
Lancashire LA6 2EN
Tel: 015242 71397 Fax: 015242 72219
e-mail: info@manserghhall.co.uk
website: www.manserghhall.co.uk

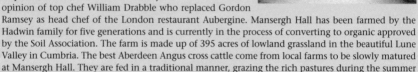

"The meat from **Mansergh Hall Farm Shop** is absolutely exquisite, full of flavour and incredibly tender." Such was the opinion of top chef William Drabble who replaced Gordon Ramsey as head chef of the London restaurant Aubergine. Mansergh Hall has been farmed by the Hadwin family for five generations and is currently in the process of converting to organic approved by the Soil Association. The farm is made up of 395 acres of lowland grassland in the beautiful Lune Valley in Cumbria. The best Aberdeen Angus cross cattle come from local farms to be slowly matured at Mansergh Hall. They are fed in a traditional manner, grazing the rich pastures during the summer months; in winter, they are housed, and fed home grown swedes, rolled barley and beet pulp.

The farm sells top quality beef, pork and lamb, and its awards include the prestigious Best Home Cured Bacon prize at the North West Fine Foods Producer of the Year Awards 2003. The farm also makes its own delicious range of sausages. The most popular varieties are Cumberland and Granny's sausage. Made to a recipe first used at Mansergh Hall in the early 1900s, Granny's is a superb blend of pork, sage and marjoram which received an enthusiastic recommendation from *The Times Magazine*.

bath house

Georgian House, 1 New Road, Kirkby Lonsdale, Cumbria LA6 2AB
Tel/Fax: 015242 73189
e-mail: enquiries@thebathhouseshop.com
website: www.thebathhouseshop.com

The Bath House is a beautiful lifestyle shop with a light and airy atmosphere, packed with life's little essentials and luxuries, including decorative tin ware for the kitchen, locally made blankets, ceramics, bathroom accessories, gifts for the gardener, and children's toys, from the very best of British and Scandinavian design-led companies.

Treat yourself to Bath House's superb own-brand bath and bodycare products, developed and manufactured in the U.K. to the company's own specifications, and all expertly hand-finished by Bath House's experienced staff in Sedbergh. Hand-wrapped soaps, heavenly bathing sugars, luxurious bath soaks and vitamin-rich creams that are so deliciously packaged, you'll find them impossible to resist. A fragrant haven for shoppers, choose from the sophisticated Kew Gardens ranges, with natural botanical extracts, Bathing Therapy's sumptuous bathing sugars, or Bath House Baby's delightful gift boxes.

This 'mini department store' is easy to find, located on the corner adjacent to the market square in Kirkby Lonsdale, which is quickly becoming known as the Oxford Street of the Dales. Whether you are looking for a perfect gift or a even a treat for yourself, there's a fabulous selection for new babies, birthdays and weddings. With a great selection of cards and gift wraps from Sedbergh-based sister company Picture Palace Cards, you'll find everything you need at The Bath House shop.

THE CARIAD COFFEE HOUSE & TEA ROOM

7 Market Square, Kirkby Lonsdale, Cumbria LA6 2AN
Tel: 015242 73271
website: www.thecariad.co.uk &

The Cariad is a coffee house with a difference. After your country walk, enjoy traditional home-cooked food using local Cumbrian produce and soak up the relaxed ambience. As the food is made on the premises, it is free from artificial preservatives and additives. The bread is made to their own recipe using Carr's of Carlisle flour without added enzymes, improvers or bleach. The potato hash and home-made chutneys are popular, as is the chunky sticky toffee pudding with thick butterscotch sauce, and the seasonal fruit crumbles. The fruit scones are so popular that owners Paul and Eirian now write on the board outside what time they are out of the oven! The Cariad also offers organic seasonal salads, traditional Sunday roasts, and is licensed. There is a roaring fire during winter months and dogs are welcome.

BOW WOW

18, Market Street (telephone: 015242 72900).
Tel: 015242 72900 website: www.bowwowshop.co.uk

While in Kirkby Lonsdale, why not also visit Paul and Eirians recently opened dog shop. It is perhaps the only shop of its kind in Cumbria where – an unusual twist – you can treat your dog and yourself under the same roof.
The shop offers hand-made dog-shaped cushions, dog coats, and unusual artwork exclusive to **Bow Wow**, as well as an innovative combination of owners' funky leather belts and wristbands with matching dog collars.

streets bearing names such as Jingling Lane, past the 16th century weavers' cottages in Fairbank, across the **Swine Market** with its 600-year-old cross where traders have displayed their wares every Thursday for more than 700 years, past ancient hostelries to the even more venerable **St Mary's Church** with its noble Norman doorway and massive pillars. In the churchyard, a late Georgian gazebo looks across to the enchanting view of the Lune Valley painted by Turner.

The town has three times been national winner of the 'Britain in Bloom' competition and also attracts thousands of visitors for its **Victorian Fair**, held on the first full weekend in September, and again in December for the Yuletide procession through streets ablaze with coloured lights and decorated Christmas trees.

AROUND KIRKBY LONSDALE

HALE

7 miles W of Kirkby Lonsdale off the A6

This tiny village surrounded by woodland and close to the Lancashire border is home to the **Lakeland Wildlife Oasis** where a wide range of animals and birds can be seen and a hands-on exhibition tells the evolutionary story. Visitors can drape a snake around their neck, exchange inquisitive glances with a ruffled lemur or a meerkat squatting on its haunches, and admire creatures rarely seen in captivity such as flying foxes and poison arrow frogs. The tropical hall is the home of numerous free-flying birds, bats and butterflies, and other exhibits range from leaf-cutter ants to pygmy marmosets. The Oasis was established in 1991 by Dave and Jo Marsden, who were

HIPPING HALL

Cowan Bridge, Kirkby Lonsdale,
Cumbria LA6 2JJ
Tel: 015242 71187 Fax: 015242 72452
e-mail: info@hippinghall.com
website: www.hippinghall.com

Hipping Hall is a magnificent, instantly welcoming 17th century building set in three acres of beautifully landscaped gardens. The Hall has been transformed into a wonderful modern country house hotel and restaurant by the new owners, the Wildsmith family. Great care has been taken to retain the historic nature of the building whilst injecting a contemporary feel with the use of striking colours and bold fabrics.

The bedrooms at Hipping have been designed to contrast with the rich interiors of the downstairs public rooms. Shades of white combine with a variety of patterns and textures to create a refreshing sense of calm. Each bedroom has its own unique appeal but contains a luxury hand-built bed made up with the finest cotton linen. The en-suite bathrooms have been designed with the latest modern fittings and stunning natural stone tiles.

The double height medieval banqueting hall complete with minstrels gallery, log fire and oak beams is the setting for a unique dining experience. Food at Hipping is under the direction of former Young Chef of the Year, Jason 'Bruno' Birkbeck, who creates menus in his own style blending traditional cuisine with modern ideas. Hipping Hall is open to non-resident diners every evening and Sunday lunch. Light lunches and afternoon teas are served throughout the week.

keepers at Chester Zoo before setting up this popular family attraction, which is open throughout the year.

BEETHAM

8 miles W of Kirkby Lonsdale on the A6

Approached through a pergola of rambling roses, the **Church of St Michael and All Angels** dates from Saxon times and, during restoration work in the 1830s, a hoard of around 100 coins, minted in Norman times, was discovered inside the building at the base of a pillar. Although badly damaged during the Civil War, when its windows were smashed and effigies broken, a glass fragment of Henry IV in an ermine robe has survived the centuries. The village is also home to an unusual 19th century **Post Office** with a distinctive black and white studded door.

Just outside the village lies **Heron Corn Mill**, a restored and working watermill with fully operational grinding machinery. A fine example of a traditional corn mill which operated for trade in the Westmorland farming area, the mill ceased trading as recently as the 1950s. Visitors to the mill can see an exhibition about its history and view the milling process. Also here is the **Museum of Paper Making**, which was established in 1988 to commemorate 500 years of papermaking in England.

ARNSIDE

10 miles W of Kirkby Lonsdale off the B5282

This quiet town on the Kent Estuary, with its short but elegant promenade, was once a busy port with its own shipbuilding and sea-salt refining industry. As the estuary silted up during the 19th century, a process accelerated by the construction of the striking 50-arch railway viaduct, so the port declined. Today, it is a favourite

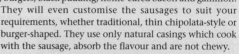

KITRIDDING FARM SHOP

Kitridding Farm, Lupton, via Carnforth, Lancashire LA6 2QA
Tel/Fax: 015395 67484
e-mail: christine@kitridding.co.uk
website: www.kitridding.co.uk

The Lambert family have been farming at Kitridding Farm in the lovely Lune Valley for more than half a century. As with many other upland farms, they chose to diversify by marketing their own beef and lamb, at first through local Farmer's Markets and mail order. Then in May 2002 they opened their own **Kitridding Farm Shop** on the farm. As well as preparing fresh cuts of their own beef, lamb and pork – cut to customers' requirements – the Lamberts also create a wide range of home-made gourmet sausages based on traditional recipes and techniques, burgers, black pudding, home-cured bacon and gammon.

They will even customise the sausages to suit your requirements, whether traditional, thin chipolata-style or burger-shaped. They use only natural casings which cook with the sausage, absorb the flavour and are not chewy.

The shop also stocks an extensive selection of local produce – chicken, bacon, cheese, free range eggs, hand-made butter, preserves, puddings and sauces, and much, much more. The shop is open from 10am to 6pm, Friday, and from 10am to 5pm on Saturday. As we go to press, the Lamberts are finalising plans for a Tea Room and local crafts area which is scheduled to open mid to late 2006.

LAKELAND WILDLIFE OASIS

Hale, Milnthorpe, Cumbria LA7 7BW
Tel: 015395 63027
e-mail: mail@wildlifeoasis.co.uk
website: www.wildlifeoasis.co.uk

Opened in 1991 the **Lakeland Wildlife Oasis** quickly established itself as one of the Lake District's premier visitor attractions. "Half zoo, half museum and totally fascinating", the Oasis takes visitors on a tour through the world of wildlife using its own unique blend of live animals and imaginative hands-on exhibits. The centre is half undercover and so is an ideal place to visit in any weather.

Exhibits include sea life, a butterfly house, and a tropical hall with free flying bats and birds as well as reptiles, amphibians and small mammals. Many of the animals here are rarely seen in captivity and many are threatened with extinction and kept as part of a national or international breeding programme. Amongst the more interesting outdoor exhibits are the ever popular meerkats, lemurs, a monkey house, the only fossas in the north of England and a large walk-through aviary. Some animals are allowed to wander freely amongst the visitors and there are regular "meet the animals" sessions.

Other attractions are the well-stocked gift shop and the Creature Comforts Café although picnic facilities are available for those who wish to bring their own food. The Wildlife Oasis is located on the A6 just five minutes drive north of junction 35 on the M6 and is open every day of the year (except Christmas Day and Boxing Day).

retirement destination and a peaceful holiday resort.

Around Arnside itself there is a wonderful choice of country walks, particularly over and around **Arnside Knott**. This limestone headland, now a nature reserve rich in old woods and wild flowers, is part of the Arnside and Silverdale Area of Outstanding Natural Beauty. Knott comes from the Saxon word meaning 'rounded hill', which, in this case, rises 521 feet above sea level and gives extensive views of the Lakeland fells, the Pennines, and the southern Cumbrian coast. There is a beautiful path around the headland and along the shoreline past Blackstone Point.

Inland, and found down a quiet lane, is **Arnside Tower**, one of the many pele towers that were built in the area in the 14th century. This particular tower dates from the 1370s and it may have been part of the chain of towers designed to form a ring of protection around Morecambe Bay.

KENDAL

A survey a few years back by Strathclyde University revealed that the highest

Sunset at Arnside

quality of life of any town in England was to be found in Kendal, the 'capital' of South Lakeland. That assessment came as no surprise to the residents of this lively, bustling town which was once one of the most important woollen textile centres of northern England. The Kendal woollen industry was founded in 1331 by John Kemp, a Flemish weaver, and it flourished and sustained the town for almost 600 years until the development of competition from the huge West Riding of Yorkshire mills during the Industrial Revolution of the 19th century. The town's motto 'Wool is my Bread' reveals the extent to which the economy of Kendal depended on the wool from the flocks of Herdwick sheep that roamed the surrounding fells. The fame of the cloth was so great that Shakespeare refers to archers clad in Kendal Green cloth in his play *Henry IV*. These archers were the famous **Kendal Bowmen** whose lethal longbows were made from local yew trees culled from the nearby limestone crags. It was these men who clinched the English victories at Agincourt and Crécy and fought so decisively against the Scots at the Battle of Flodden Field in 1513.

Kendal has royal connections too. The Parr family lived at **Kendal Castle** until 1483 - their most famous descendant was Catherine Parr, the last of Henry VIII's six wives. Today, the castle's gaunt ruins stand high on a hill overlooking the town, with most of the castle wall and one of the towers still standing, and two underground vaults still complete. Castle Hill is a popular place for walking and picnicking and in summer the hillside is smothered with wild flowers. From the hilltop there are spectacular views and a panorama panel here assists in identifying the distant fells.

Anyone wandering around the town cannot help but notice the numerous alleyways, locally known as yards, that are such a distinctive feature of Kendal. An integral part of the old town, they are

ABBOT HALL ART GALLERY AND MUSEUM

Kendal, Cumbria LA9 5AL
Tel: 01539 722464 Fax: 01539 722494

Abbot Hall Art Gallery forms part of a complex within Abbot Hall park and includes work by John Ruskin and the celebrated portrait painter, George Romney, who was born nearby at Dalton-in-Furness in 1734. The permanent collection also includes a wide range of 18th, 19th and 20th century British paintings and watercolours, and the Gallery hosts regular touring exhibitions.

A short walk from the Brewery Arts Centre is the **Museum of Lakeland Life and Industry** which is themed around traditional rural trades of the region, such as blacksmithing, wheelwrighting, agricultural activities, weaving and printing. Here, too, are recreated cottage interiors, elegantly furnished period rooms and a reconstruction of the study in which the celebrated author, Arthur Ransome, wrote the children's classic *Swallows and Amazons*.

At the other end of the town, near the railway station, is the **Museum of Natural History and Archaeology**, founded in 1796 and one of the oldest museums in the country. Based on the collection first exhibited by William Todhunter in the late 18th century, the Museum takes visitors on a journey from prehistoric times, a trip which includes an interactive exhibit which tells the story of Kendal Castle. The famous fellwalker and writer, Alfred Wainwright, whose handwritten guides to the Lakeland hills will be found in the backpack of any serious walker, was honorary clerk here between 1945 and 1974. Many of his original drawings are on display.

a reminder that the people of Kendal used to live under a constant threat of raids by the Scots. The yards were a line of defence against these attacks, an area that could be secured by sealing the one small entrance, with the families and livestock safe inside.

Shoppers are spoilt for choice in Kendal. In addition to all the familiar High Street names, the **Westmorland Shopping Centre, Blackhall Yard** and **Elephant Yard**, all in the heart of the town, and the **K Village Factory Shopping** complex on the outskirts, make it easy to shop until you drop. One local product well worth sampling is **Kendal Mint Cake**, a tasty, sugary confection which is cherished by climbers and walkers for its instant infusion of energy. Another once-popular local medication, **Kendal Black Drop**, is no longer available. 'A more than commonly strong mixture of opium and alcohol', Kendal Black Drop was a favourite tipple of the poets Samuel Taylor Coleridge and Thomas de Quincey.

Kendal's excellent sporting facilities include the **Kendal Leisure Centre**, which offers a one-week tourist pass, Kendal Wall, which is one of the highest indoor climbing facilities in the country, Kendal ski slope, two local golf courses and a driving range. Drama, music and the visual arts are presented in a regularly changing programme of exhibitions, live music, theatre productions and craft workshops at the **Brewery Arts Centre**. The Centre also houses Kendal's cinema which presents a mixture of mainstream, classic and art house films.

A number of interesting museums and galleries are also located in Kendal. The **Museum of Lakeland Life and Industry**, which is themed around traditional rural trades of the region, and

Long Sleddale, near Kendal

Abbot Hall Art Gallery form part of a complex within Abbot Hall park. The museum, in re-created farmhouse rooms, contains a wide variety of exhibits, including Arthur Ransome memorabilia, craft workshops, a Victorian street scene, artefacts from the Arts and Crafts movement, nautical displays and Captain Flint's Locker, a pirate activity area for children and families. The gallery, in an elegant Georgian villa, houses a collection of society portraits by the locally born George Romney and watercolour scenes by Ruskin and Turner, while the 20th century and contemporary scene is represented by Walter Sickert, Ben Nicholson, Lucien Freud and Bridget Riley. The **Museum of Natural History and Archaeology**, founded in 1796, is one of the oldest museums in the country. Based on the collection first exhibited by William Todhunter in the late 18th century, the museum takes visitors on a journey from prehistoric times, a trip which includes an interactive exhibit which tells the story of Kendal Castle.

The famous fellwalker and writer, Alfred Wainwright, whose handwritten guides to the Lakeland hills will be found in the backpack of any serious walker, was honorary clerk here between 1945 and 1974. Many of his original drawings are on display. In the summer of 2004 a small exhibition will open chronicling the life of a local eccentric called Millican Dalton. Affectionately known as the **Cave Man of Borrowdale**, he lived for 50 years in a cave blasted from the slate of Castle Crag near Keswick and propounded his views on Quaker pacifism, vegetarianism and the outdoor life. He achieved notoriety between the two World Wars by offering women the chance to go on expeditions involving camping, river crafting and shooting rapids.

Adjacent to the elegant Georgian Abbot Hall and Museum is the 13th century **Parish Church** of Kendal, 'the Church of the Angels', one of the widest in England, with five aisles and a peal of 10 bells.

Perhaps the most unusual attraction in Kendal is the **Quaker Tapestry Exhibition** at the Friends Meeting House in the centre of the town. This unique exhibition of 77 panels of community embroidery explores Quaker history from the 17th century to the present day. These colourful, beautifully crafted tapestries are the work of some 4,000 people, aged between four and 90, from 15 countries. A Quaker costume display, embroidery demonstrations, workshops and courses, and a large-screen colour video combine to provide a fascinating insight into the Quaker movement and its development.

AROUND KENDAL

BURNESIDE
2 miles N of Kendal off the A591

There has been a settlement here since the Stone Age and the remains of a stone

CROOK HALL

Crook, nr Kendal, Cumbria LA8 8LF
Tel/Fax: 01539 821352
e-mail: metcalfe@crookhall.fsnet.co.uk
website: www.crookhallfarm.co.uk

Set in beautiful countryside between Kendal and Lake Windermere, **Crook Hall** is an historic farmhouse on a working sheep farm. It's approached by a winding lane half a mile long which opens up a breathtaking view of the valley below. The spacious farmhouse dates from the 16th century, with later additions, and retains several original features including magnificent oak panelling in the guest lounge, old beams and a period staircase. The poet William Wordsworth was once a frequent visitor to the farm. It's now the home of the Metcalfe family who welcome bed & breakfast visitors to this charming old property, approx 15 minutes from Junction 36 of the M6.

The spacious en suite bedrooms are all individually decorated and include one with a four-poster bed and glorious views across fields and woodland. All rooms are equipped with TV and radio, alarm clock, hair dryer and hospitality tray. Guests also have the use of the comfortable TV lounge and breakfast room. For evening meals, there are several good country inns within easy reach. Crook Hall is non-smoking; pets cannot be accommodated, and debit or credit cards are not accepted. A warm welcome awaits.

THE RAILWAY HOTEL

The Banks, Staveley, nr Kendal,
Cumbria LA8 9NB
Tel: 01539 821385

The little town of Staveley lies a few miles east of Windermere, beside the A591, and it's here you will find **The Railway Hotel**. It's an impressive 19th century building with a black-and-white exterior and a cosy traditional interior. As we go to press, the new mine hosts,

Mark and Sarah Moore, are completing a major programme of refurbishment and all of the premises, including the accommodation will be finished to the highest standards. By the time you read this, Mark will again be offering customers the same kind of quality cuisine for which he was well-known at his previous establishment. "We aim to make the Railway Hotel *the* place to eat in the area," he says. Freshly cooked and locally sourced, the food will be available throughout the day. Located right in the heart of the town, the hotel has its own extensive car parking.

circle can be seen close by on **Potter Fell**. By the 15th century, Burneside was a settled agricultural area and a rich variety of mills sprang up along the River Sprint - fulling, corn, cotton, wool, bobbin, and the original rag paper mill at **Cowan Head**.

The River Sprint, which meets the River Kent just south of the village, has its own remarkably beautiful Longsleddale Valley which curves past Garnett Bridge deep into the high fell country. A bridle path climbs from the head of the valley into Kentmere, another spectacularly beautiful walk.

SEDGWICK
4 miles S of Kendal off the A590

At Raines Hall Farm, the **Lakeland Maize Maze** is the area's first. Designed by Adrian Fisher, the world's leading maze designer, the maze is cut into a nine-acre field of maize with miles of paths

creating a devilish puzzle. There's also a Headlong Maze and an Arrow Maze as well as pedal tractors, sandpit, picnic area, giant draughts and a variety of farmyard animals.

LEVENS
5 miles S of Kendal off the A590

At the southern tip of Scout Scar, overlooking the Lyth Valley and the lower reaches of the River Kent, stands **Levens Hall** with its unique topiary gardens. The superb Elizabethan mansion (described as 'one of the wonders of Lakeland') developed from a 14th century pele tower and the gardens were first laid out in 1694. They were the work of Colonel James Grahame, a keen gardener, who purchased the hall in 1688 and employed a Frenchman, Guillaume Beaumont, to create the amazing topiary work (Beaumont also redesigned the gardens at Hampton

Court for James II). The topiary is by no means the only attraction in the grounds, which also include a Fountain Garden created in 1994 to mark the tercentenary of the gardens. The interior of the house is equally rewarding - a wealth of period furniture, fine panelling and plasterwork, a dining room with walls covered in goatskin, and paintings by Rubens, Lely and Cuyp. A major location for the BBC TV serial *Wives and Daughters*, the Hall's other attractions include a collection of working steam engines, a tea room, gift shop and plant centre.

Only a couple of miles north of Levens Hall, just off the A591, is another stately old residence, **Sizergh Castle**, the impressive home of the Strickland family since 1239 although the property is now administered by the National Trust. Originally a pele tower built to withstand border raiders, the house has been added to and altered over the intervening centuries to provide the family, as times became less violent, with a more comfortable home. Now boasting intricately carved chimney mantels, fine oak panelling, and a collection of portraits of the Stuart royal family, the castle stands in well laid out gardens and 1,500 acres of grounds which provide superb views over the Lakeland fells.

Sizergh Castle

MILNTHORPE
7 miles S of Kendal on the A6

About two miles south of Milnthorpe, on the A6, **Lakeland Wildlife Oasis** offers visitors the chance to enjoy a fascinating journey through the animal kingdom "from magic molecules to mischievous monkeys", The indoor and outdoor exhibits include sea life, butterfly and tropical halls, a host of hands-on displays and many rare and unusual species.

BRIGSTEER
3 miles SW of Kendal off A591

This tiny hamlet lies under the limestone escarpment of Scout Scar. From this pretty settlement, the road leads into the National Trust property of **Brigsteer Woods** where, as the climate is milder here due to its sheltered position, there are wild daffodils in the spring.

SEDBERGH

In 1974 Sedbergh was brusquely removed from the West Riding of Yorkshire and became part of Cumbria. However, it still lies within the Yorkshire Dales National Park and the surrounding scenery certainly belongs to the Dales with the mighty **Howgill Hills** - great pear-shaped drumlins shaped by glaciers - soaring to more than 2,200 feet (670 metres). **Winder Hill**, which provides a dramatic backdrop to the little market town, is half that height, but with its sleek grassy flanks and domed top, seems much loftier. Four valleys and four mountain streams meet here and for centuries Sedbergh (pronounced Sedber) has been an important centre for cross-Pennine travellers. During the golden age of stage coach travel, the town became a staging post on the route between Lancaster and Newcastle-upon-Tyne. The complete journey between Lancaster and Newcastle took from 4am to 7pm: 15 hours to cover a distance of about 120 miles, an average speed of eight miles per hour. At the **King's Arms Hotel**, the four horses would be swiftly changed before the equipage rattled off again across the moors to Teesdale, Durham and Newcastle.

In those days, the stage-coach would have been used frequently by the boys attending Sedbergh's famous **Public School**. Its founder was Roger Lupton, a Howgill boy who rose to become Provost of Eton: he established the school because he felt that one was desperately needed "in the north country amongst the people rude in knowledge". In later years, Wordsworth's son studied here and Coleridge's son, Hartley, became a master. The school's extensive grounds, through which visitors are welcome to wander, seem to place the old-world town within a park.

That impression is reinforced by following the path beside the River Rawthay to **Brigflatts**. Close to where George Fox stayed overnight with his friend Richard Robinson is the oldest **Quaker Meeting House** in the north of England. Built in 1675, and still with its original oak interior, this beautiful, simple building has changed little over the years.

This area is filled with Quaker history and **Firbank Knott**, on nearby Firbank Fell, can be said to be the birthplace of Quakerism for it was here, in 1652, that the visionary George Fox gave his great sermon to inspire a huge gathering from the whole of the north of England. This meeting was to lead to the development of the **Quaker Movement**. The simple boulder on the fell, from which Fox delivered his momentous words, is marked by a plaque and is now known as **Fox's Pulpit**.

Sedbergh seems a very friendly town. At **St Andrew's Church**, for example, Protestants and Roman Catholics take turns to use the building for their own services, an arrangement believed to be rare in England.

To the east of the town, on a small wooded hill top, lies **Castlehaw**, the remains of an ancient motte-and-bailey castle. Built by the Normans in the 11th century, the castle guarded the valleys of the River Rawthey and the River Lune against the marauding Scots. Also just outside town, on the A683 Garsdale road, is **Farfield Mill** Heritage and Arts Centre, where spinners, weavers, potters, woodcarvers and other craftspeople use traditional skills to produce high-quality goods, all of it for sale in the shop.

AROUND SEDBERGH

DENT
4 miles SE of Sedbergh off the A684

This charming village, the only one in Dentdale - one of Cumbria's finest dales - has a delightful cobbled main street with tall cottages lining the road. Visitors to this tranquil place will find it hard to believe that, in the 18th century, Dent was of greater importance than nearby Sedbergh. The impressive **St Andrew's Church** is Norman in origin though it

Cobbled Street in Dent

underwent an almost complete rebuilding in the early 15th century. Inside can be seen the Jacobean three-decker pulpit that is still in use and also the local marble which paves the chancel.

Farming has, for many years, dominated the local economy but knitting, particularly in the village, has also played an important part. During the 17th and 18th centuries, the women and children, on whom this work fell, became known as the '**Terrible Knitters of Dent**' which, today, sounds uncomplimentary but the local use of the word terrible meant quite the opposite (like 'wicked' today!).

Dent's most famous son is undoubtedly the 'Father of Geology', **Adam Sedgwick**. Born the son of the local vicar in 1785, Sedgwick went on to become the Woodwardian Professor of Geology at Cambridge University and also a friend of Queen Victoria and Prince Albert. The fountain of pinkish Shap granite in the village centre is Dent's memorial to this great geologist. Dent stone, with no iron pyrites likely to cause sparks, was popular for millstones used in gunpowder works. The little

valley of Dentdale winds from the village up past old farms and hamlets to **Lea Yeat** where a steep lane hairpins up to Dent Station, almost five miles from the village. This is a marvellous place to begin a ramble into Dentdale or over the Whernside. In the shadow of Whernside itself, **Whernside Manor** is a famous house with associations with the slave trade. Dent railway station is the highest in Britain, over 1,100 feet above sea level, and it lies on the famous Settle-Carlisle railway line.

GARSDALE
6 miles E of Sedbergh on the A684

Lying just north of Dentdale, Garsdale is both a dale and a village, both overlooked by the dramatic **Baugh Fell**. The River Clough follows down the dale from Garsdale Head, the watershed into Wensleydale, where a row of Midland Railway cottages lies alongside the former junction station on the Settle-Carlisle line. This is now a surprisingly busy little place during the summer months when, from time to time, preserved steam locomotives pause to take on water from a moorland spring.

WINDERMERE

'Birthwaite' village no longer features on any map, thanks to the Kendal and Windermere Railway Company which built a branch line to it in 1847. With an eye on tourist traffic, and considering the name Birthwaite had little appeal, they named the station Windermere even though the lake is over a mile distant. In the early days carriages and,

CEDAR MANOR HOTEL & RESTAURANT

Ambleside Road, Windermere,
Cumbria LA23 1AX
Tel: 015394 43192 Fax: 015394 45970
e-mail: info@cedarmanor.co.uk
website: www.cedarmanor.co.uk

Cedar Manor Hotel & Restaurant stands within easy walking distance of Windermere and the lake, surrounded by breaktaking scenery and with a wealth of leisure facilities such as sailing, windsurfing, golf and pony trekking all close at hand. This grand old hotel was built in 1854 as a private country retreat and takes its name from a majestic Indian Cedar tree, said to be 200 years old, which overlooks the mature private gardens with their fine specimen maples and beautiful flower borders.

The hotel is privately owned and the resident proprietors pride themselves on offering the warmest of welcomes to all their guests and guarantee their personal attention to make your stay an enjoyable and refreshing experience to be savoured to the full. Guests can settle down in the lounge and enjoy the soothing view across the gardens, play board games, read or savour a quiet drink from the bar which is well-stocked with aperitifs, local bottled beers and choice wines.

Dining at the Cedar Manor is a delight. The interesting and varied menu offers dishes such as Cumbrian fell-bred beef or Shetland salmon, along with a tasty vegetarian option as well. All dishes are prepared using only the freshest seasonal produce available. Don't forget to leave room for one of the sumptuous puddings or a selection of English cheeses. Coffee and liqueurs may be enjoyed either at your table or in the bar.

Breakfast too is highly satisfying with a choice that includes a Cumberland Grill, American style pancakes with bacon and maple syrup, and grilled Manx kippers.

The guest bedrooms at the Cedar Manor have all been individually designed to a very high standard and each has its own distinct character whilst remaining in harmony with the overall tasteful style of the rest of the hotel. There's a choice of bedrooms ranging from a full suite to four-poster rooms, a twin and exquisite double rooms. Some enjoy fine views of the Langdale Pikes and all are decorated in keeping with the style and tradition of a fine Victorian house. Each room benefits from full en suite facilities, TV and telephone. And if you want to bring a pet along, there are two rooms in the Coach House where pets are allowed.

in later years, buses linked the station with the landing stages in the village of Bowness on the shores of the lake. As the village burgeoned into a prosperous Victorian resort, it became popularly, and then officially, known by the name of its station, while Windermere water was given the redundant prefix of Lake.

The Victorian heritage still predominates in the many large houses here, originally built as country retreats for Manchester businessmen - the railway made it possible for them to reach this idyllic countryside in just over two hours. Hotels, boarding houses, comfortable villas and shops sprang up around the

The Swan, Lake Windermere

station and spread rapidly down the hill towards the lake until Birthwaite and Bowness were linked together.

Windermere's railway is still operating, albeit now as a single track branch line. The **Lakes Line** is now the only surviving Railtrack line to run into the heart of the Lake District. Diesel railcars provide a busy shuttle service to and from the main line at Oxenholme. The route, through Kendal, Burneside and Staveley, is a delight and provides a very pleasant alternative to the often crowded A591.

Within a few yards of Windermere Station, just across the busy main road, is a footpath that leads through the woods to one of the finest viewpoints in Lakeland, **Orrest Head**. This spectacular vantage point provides a 360-degree panoramic view that takes in the ten-mile length of Windermere, the Cumbrian hills and even the fells of the Yorkshire Pennines. In Victorian times, visitors wandered through such ravishing scenery carrying, not cameras,

but small, tinted mirrors mounted in elaborate frames. Arriving at a picturesque spot, they placed themselves with their back to the view, held the mirrors above them and so observed the view framed as in a painting. The image they saw recalled the romantic landscapes of Claude Lorraine: the mirrors accordingly were known as **Claude Glasses**.

AROUND WINDERMERE

Bowness-on-Windermere
1½ miles S of Windermere

It is from this attractive, but seasonally very busy town right on the edge of Windermere that most of the lake cruises operate. Lasting between 45 and 90 minutes, the cruises operate daily and provide connections to the Lakeside & Haverthwaite Steam Railway, the **Fell Foot Country Park** and the **Visitor Centre** at Brockhole - this centre (also easily reached by road) is idyllically situated in 30 acres of gardens and grounds and has two floors of interactive exhibitions. There are evening wine/champagne cruises during the summer months, and rowing boats and self-drive motor boats are also available for hire all year round.

Not only is **Windermere** the largest lake in Cumbria but it is, at 11 miles long, the largest in England. Across from Bowness, the lake is almost divided in two by **Belle Island**, which is believed to have been inhabited by the Romans. During the Civil War, it was owned by Colonel Phillipson (the Royalist supporter who disgraced himself by riding into Kendal Parish Church) and his family had to withstand an 80-day siege, successfully, while the Colonel was away on another campaign. In 1774, the island was bought by a Mr English, who constructed the round house which, at the time, caused such consternation that

he sold the property and the island to Isabella Curwen, who planted the surrounding trees.

Fishermen, too, find great enjoyment practising their skills on this well-stocked lake. Once considered a great delicacy in the 17th and 18th centuries, the char, a deep-water trout, is still found here - though catching it is a special art.

Away from the marinas and car parks is the old village where **St Martin's Church** is of particular interest. It has a magnificent east window filled with 14th and 15th century glass, and an unusual 300-year-old carved wooden figure of St Martin depicted sharing his cloak with a beggar.

On the lake shore just to the north of the village is the **Windermere Steamboat Centre**. Housed here is a unique collection of Lake Windermere's nautical heritage. The exhibits, mainly Victorian and Edwardian craft, include

---

MAGUIRE METCALFE

20 Lake Road, Bowness on Windermere, Cumbria LA23 3AP
Tel/Fax: 015394 47291
e-mail: enquiries@maguiremetcalfe.co.uk
website: maguiremetcalfe.co.uk

Anyone convinced that gorgeous shops only exist in London should pay a visit to **Maguire Metcalfe** in Bowness-on-Windermere. This fascinating shop offers a delicious mix of lovely things from quirky faux fur shrugs to magical crystal door handles. Owners Glynnis Maguire and Helen Metcalfe have collected together a real treasure trove, with new surprises wherever you look. "English eccentrics will love our stripy boot socks and our range of useful home goodies will have every domestic goddess in a spin! We have something to satisfy your every whim."

The shop's range of baby clothes means that little ones in the Lakes have never looked so stylish, and adults too can indulge themselves, enjoying the fabulous clothing and accessories on offer. Finding quirky vintage furniture is a speciality of the duo including items such as a red polka dot footstool. Amongst the bathroom goodies on sale are the Miso Pretty bath and beauty products, and the uplifting 'Wash Away Your Sins' soap. No wonder the *English Home* magazine listed Maguire Metcalfe amongst its '100 Favourite Shops'.

WINDERMERE STEAMBOATS & MUSEUM

Rayrigg Road, Windermere, Cumbria LA23 1BN
Tel: 01539 445565
website: www.steamboat.co.uk

The **Windermere Steamboat Museum** is a unique collection of Victorian and Edwardian steam launches which includes the *SL Dolly*, the oldest mechanically powered boat in the world. *Dolly* celebrated her 150th birthday in 2000 and still has her original engine in working order despite its having lain on the bed of Ullswater for more than 60 years before being recovered. Some of the launches are still in working order and occasional cruises are possible. Private charters of an Edwardian steam launch can also be arranged. Facilities include a model boat pond, shop, tea room and picnic area.

Dolly, the oldest mechanically powered boat in the world, and Beatrix Potter's rowing boat. The Swallows and Amazons exhibition features guided tours of *Esperance*, Arthur Ransome's inspiration for Captain Flint's houseboat. The museum grounds also include a model boat pond, shop, tea room and picnic area.

Just down the road from the Steamboat Museum is the Old Laundry Visitor Centre, the home of **The World of Beatrix Potter**, one of the most popular visitor attractions in the country. Here visitors can enjoy fascinating re-creations of the Lakeland author's books, complete with the sounds, sights and even smells of the countryside. 2002 saw the centenary of the publication of the first *Tale of Peter Rabbit*, and to mark the occasion the Peter Rabbit Centenary springs to life every 15 minutes and features some previously unpublished illustrations from the stories.

About a mile-and-a-half south of Bowness, **Blackwell** is a treasure trove of the Arts and Crafts Movement. Completed in 1900, it is the largest and most important surviving masterpiece of the architect MH Baillie Scott (1865-1945). Inspired by Lakeland flora and fauna, he designed every last detail of this outstanding house,

Bowness-on-Windermere

creating a symphony of art nouveau stained glass, oak panelling, intricate plasterwork and fanciful metalwork. From the gardens there are wonderful views of Windermere and the Coniston fells.

WINSTER
3 miles S of Windermere on the A5074

This charming hamlet has an old post office, originally built in the early 17th century as a cottage, that is much photographed. South from the village runs the Winster Valley, which provided Wordsworth with one of his favourite walks. It was at **Low Ludderburn**, a couple of miles to the south, that Arthur Ransome settled in 1925 and here that he wrote his classic children's novel *Swallows and Amazons*.

While living here, Ransome discovered the peaceful churchyard at **Rusland** and decided that was where he wanted to be

buried. And when he died in 1967 that is indeed where he was interred, joined later by his second wife Eugenia.

NEWBY BRIDGE
8 miles S of Windermere on the A592

The bridge here crosses the River Leven which runs from the southern tip of Windermere to Morecambe Bay. According to geologists, the mass of end moraines seen here show clearly that the village lay at the southernmost point of Windermere since they were deposited by the glacier while it paused having carved out the lake. Today, however, the village is some distance from the water's edge, which can be reached on foot, by car, or by taking the steam train on the Lakeside & Haverthwaite Railway. As the village lies at the junction of two major south Cumbrian roads, it is also a popular tourist destination.

AIREY'S FARM SHOP

Snowdrop Villa, Ayside, Grange-over-Sands, Cumbria LA11 6JE
Tel: 015395 31237
e-mail: aireysfarmshop@hotmail.com
website: www.aireysfarmshop.co.uk

Finding "meat like it used to taste" is one very good reason for paying a visit to **Airey's Farm Shop** at Ayside in the Lake District National Park. The shop is owned and run by the Airey family whose aim is to produce quality meat with the flavour of years gone by. Accordingly, they offer meat from rare and traditional breeds, such as Lakeland Herdwick lamb, as well as modern day breeds. The animals are raised on their own farms as naturally as possible, or on local Cumbrian farms with the same standard of animal welfare as their own.

The Aireys identify four essentials for producing good meat with tenderness and flavour: the breed

of animal – rare and traditional ones tend to carry more fat and marbling which gives better flavour; correct finishing, to the right conformation and fat cover; stress-free animals at slaughter – the Airey's have their own private slaughterhouse on the premises; and maturing of meat – the flavour is enhanced when the meat is left to hang. The shop sells beef, pork, lamb, bacon, ham and also makes its own range of sausages on the premises. The shop is open from 10am to 5pm (Monday); 9am to 5.30pm (Tuesday to Friday), and from 9am to 12.30pm on Saturday.

One mile north of the village, **Fell Foot Park** (National Trust) is a delightful 18-acre site of landscaped gardens and woodland laid out in late-Victorian times. Rowing boats can be hired at the piers from which there are regular ferries across to Lakeside, and pleasure cruises operate during the summer school holidays.

LAKESIDE
10 miles S of Windermere off the A590

Located at the southwestern tip of Windermere, Lakeside sits beneath gentle wooded hills. It's the northern terminus of the **Lakeside & Haverthwaite Railway**, a four-mile route through the beautiful Leven valley which was once part of a line stretching to Ulverston and Barrow-in-Furness. Throughout the season, hard-working steam locomotives chug along the track, their departure times set to coincide with boat arrivals from Bowness - a joint boat and train return ticket is available. The locomotives in use include 42073 and 42085, ex-LMR Fairburn 0-6-4 tank engines, and 5643, an ex-GWR 0-6-0

THE BOATHOUSE HOTEL

Lakeside, Newby Bridge, Cumbria LA12 8AS
Tel: 01395 31381 e-mail: enquiries@boathousehotel.co.uk
Fax: 015395 31129 website: www.boathousehotel.co.uk

Located just 150 yards from the famous Windermere Steamers jetty, **The Boathouse Hotel** is a family-run business offering an inviting combination of warm family atmosphere, delicious home-cooked food and comfortable en suite bedrooms, some with lake views. No need to use a car here – just stroll down to the jetty and board the steamers that serve all points on the lake. The hotel is a popular venue for various functions since its versatile facilities enable it to cater for all kinds of events, whether it be a family celebration, business meeting or a Lakeside wedding with all the luxury trimmings.

THE AQUARIUM OF THE LAKES

Lakeside, Newby Bridge, Cumbria LA12 8AS
Tel: 01539 530153
website: www.aquariumofthelakes.co.uk

The **Aquarium of the Lakes** boasts the largest collection of freshwater fish in the UK. Over 30 displays allow you to discover the world of both the fish and the wildlife which dwell in and alongside the water. A walk-through tunnel along a re-created lake bed provides great views of char, perch and diving ducks, whilst in the Morecambe Bay displays, visitors come face to face with sharks and rays from around the local coast. A dramatic waterfall leads down to a moorland stream with salmon.

The mischievous otters on the riverbank are a special favourite with children and for the more earnest visitor there are educational displays on anything from leeches to lobsters. "The Quay" shop stocks a good range of quality gifts and souvenirs, and the "Café at the Quay" offers light refreshments and a good view of the lake.

WITHERSLACK HALL EQUESTRIAN CENTRE

Witherslack Hall Farm, Witherslack,
Grange-over-Sands, Cumbria LA11 6SD
Tel: 015395 52244 Fax: 015395 52593
e-mail: info@whec.co.uk
website: www.lakelandriding.co.uk

Located on a private estate in the beautiful Winster Valley, Witherslack Hall Equestrian Centre has stables arranged round a cobbled yard with the schooling ménage housed in magnificent Victorian farm buildings. The Centre has facilities for disabled riders and full livery facilities. Beginners, novices and experienced riders are all welcome. Gareth and Lynne offer private and group lessons, rides of one-hour, one-and-a-half hours, two-hour, half day or full day

which includes a packed lunch and soft drink. Fully qualified staff do their very best to make these outings both enjoyable and safe.

The varied rides pass through ancient woodland, a small private fell, along quiet country lanes and through farmland. The group might stop at the village pub for a hot toddy on a cold winter's day, or relax outside the pub on a warm summer's evening before meandering back to the centre as evening falls. The centre specialises in children's holidays, a wonderful break during which they can eat, sleep and breath ponies! Adults, too, are welcome to stay for bed & breakfast at the farmhouse.

HALECAT GARDEN NURSERY

Halecat House, Witherslack, Grange-over-Sands,
Cumbria LA11 6RT
Tel: 015395 52536 Fax: 015395 52096
website: www.halecat.co.uk

Halecat Garden Nursery is hidden away in the grounds of Halecat House in the pleasant village of Witherslack,

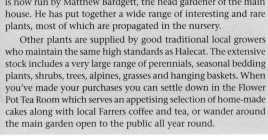

just one mile off the A590. The business began in a small way selling plants propagated in the gardens of the main house. As it grew, it gradually took over the kitchen garden, making way for stock beds which still provide most of the plants on sale. The nursery is now run by Matthew Bardgett, the head gardener of the main house. He has put together a wide range of interesting and rare plants, most of which are propagated in the nursery.

Other plants are supplied by good traditional local growers who maintain the same high standards as Halecat. The extensive stock includes a very large range of perennials, seasonal bedding plants, shrubs, trees, alpines, grasses and hanging baskets. When you've made your purchases you can settle down in the Flower Pot Tea Room which serves an appetising selection of home-made cakes along with local Farrers coffee and tea, or wander around the main garden open to the public all year round.

tank. Also present on display or under steam (when not occasionally required elsewhere) is FR20, built for the Furness Railway and Britain's oldest working standard gauge steam locomotive (see also under Haverthwaite).

Nearby lies Britain's only freshwater aquarium, the **Aquarium of the Lakes** with the largest collection of freshwater fish in the UK and also a number of playful otters and diving ducks. A unique attraction for visitors is to walk along a re-creation of Windermere's lake bed in an underwater tunnel.

A mile or so north of Lakeside, **Stott Park Bobbin Mill** (English Heritage) is a must for anyone interested in the area's industrial heritage. One of the best preserved in the country, it's a genuine working 19th century mill and stands in a lovely woodland setting at the southern end of the Lake. Visitors can join the inclusive 45-minute tour, watch wooden bobbins being made as they were 200 years ago, and browse over the informative exhibition.

Edward Leigh Groves bequeathed the mansion and the estate 'for the better development of the health, education and social welfare services of the County of Westmoreland'. Some time later, the Lakeland Horticultural Society took over responsibility for the garden, which is still run by volunteers of that society, whose primary aim is to promote 'knowledge on the cultivation of plants, shrubs and trees, especially those suited to Lakeland conditions'. Highlights include the borders in the walled garden, the many specimen trees, the summer-autumn heathers and the National Collections of astilbes and hydrangeas.

TROUTBECK
3 miles N of Windermere off the A592

Designated a conservation area, Troutbeck has no recognisable centre, as the houses and cottages are grouped around a number of wells and springs which, until recently, were the only form of water supply. Dating from the 16th, 17th, and 18th centuries, the houses

WITHERSLACK
9 miles S of Windermere off the A590

On the edge of the village is the **Latterbarrow Reserve** of the Cumbrian Wildlife Trust, a relatively small reserve that is home to some 200 species of flowering plants and ferns. Further from the village is **Witherslack Hall**, once the summer residence of the Earls of Derby and now a school.

TROUTBECK BRIDGE
1 mile N of Windermere on the A591

Just north of this little village in the valley of Trout Beck lies the Royal Horticultural Society's four-acre garden at **Holehird**. In 1945,

Troutbeck

retain many of their original features, including mullioned windows, heavy cylindrical chimneys, and, in some cases, exposed spinning galleries, and are of great interest to lovers of vernacular architecture. **Troutbeck Church**, too, is worthy of a visit as there is a fine east window, dating from 1873, that is the combined work of Edward Burne-Jones, Ford Maddox Brown, and William Morris.

However, perhaps the best known building at Troutbeck is **Townend** (National Trust), another enchanting example of Lake District vernacular architecture. Built in 1626, the stone and slate house contains some fine carved woodwork, books, furniture and domestic implements collected by the Browne family, wealthy farmers who lived here for more than 300 years until 1944. Open from April to October, the house runs a regular 'living history' programme, so if you visit on a Thursday you can meet Mr George Browne - circa 1900. Another notable resident of Troutbeck was the '**Troutbeck Giant**' - Thomas Hogarth, uncle of the painter William Hogarth.

KENTMERE
8 miles NE of Windermere off the A591

This hamlet, as its name implies, lies in part of the valley that was once a lake; drained to provide precious bottom pasture land. A large mill pond remains to provide a head of water on the River Kent for use at a paper mill. Inside **St Cuthbert's Church** is a bronze memorial to Bernard Gilpin, who was born at Kentmere Hall in 1517 and went on to become Archdeacon of Durham Cathedral. Known as The Apostle of the North, Gilpin was also a leader of the Reformation and, in 1558, he travelled to London to face charges of heresy against the Roman Catholic

Church. During the journey, Gilpin fell and broke his leg but, fortunately, while he was recovering Catholic Queen Mary died and was succeeded by Protestant Queen Elizabeth. The new queen restored Gilpin to favour and saved him from being burnt at the stake.

The beautiful valley of the River Kent is best explored on foot. A public footpath runs up its western side, past **Kentmere Hall**, a fortified pele tower that is now a private farmhouse. Following the river southwards, the **Dales Way** runs down into Kendal and on into the Yorkshire Dales.

BROCKHOLE
3 miles NW of Windermere off the A591

The **Lake District Visitor Centre** at Brockhole provides enough activities for a full family day out. Lake cruises depart from the jetty here for 45-minute circular trips and groups of more than 20 can even organise their own private boat. The gardens and grounds were the work of Thomas H Mawson, a Lancastrian who trained in London and set up in business in Windermere in 1885. He soon became fashionable and landscaped the gardens of many wealthy industrialists. Within the beautifully landscaped grounds at Brockhole, visitors can join an organised walk accompanied by one of the gardening team, leave their children in the well-equipped adventure playground, enjoy a lakeside picnic or visit the rare breeds of sheep. A wide variety of events takes place during the season - among them a Medieval Living Weekend, a Taste of Cumbria Food Fair, a Christmas Craft Fair and much more. Brockhole itself is a fine Victorian mansion, originally built for a Manchester silk merchant.

AMBLESIDE

4 miles NW of Windermere on the A591

Standing less than a mile from the head of Lake Windermere, Ambleside is one of the busiest of the Lakeland towns, a popular centre for walkers and tourists, with glorious walks and drives radiating from the town in all directions. Ambleside offers a huge choice of pubs, restaurants, cafés, hotels and guest houses, as well as art galleries, a two-screen cinema and a mix of traditional family-run shops supplemented by a modern range of retailers in the new

The Bridge House, Ambleside

Market Cross Centre. Because of its many shops specialising in outdoor clothing, the town was recently described as 'the anorak capital of the world' and it would certainly be hard to find a wider selection anywhere of climbing, camping and walking gear.

Many of Ambleside's buildings are constructed in the distinctive grey green stone of the area which merges attractively with the green of the fields and fells all around. The centre of the town is now a conservation area and perhaps the most picturesque building here is **The Bridge House**, a tiny cottage perched on a packhorse bridge across Stock Ghyll. Today it's a National Trust shop and information centre, but during the 1850s it was the home of Mr and Mrs Rigg and their six children. The main

AMBLESIDE LODGE

Rothay Road, Ambleside, Cumbria LA22 0EJ
Tel: 015394 31681
e-mail: hmd@ambleside-lodge.com
website: www.ambleside-lodge.com

Standing in 2.5 acres of garden and just a short walk from Lake Windermere, **Ambleside Lodge** is an elegant Lakeland home built around 1875 which has been sympathetically modernised and now offers a high standard of bed & breakfast accommodation. All the guest bedrooms have en suite facilities, colour TV and hospitality tray, and enjoy delightful views. For real indulgence, book one of the Premier suites or king size four-poster rooms with Jacuzzi spa baths. Leisure facilities include membership of a private club just five minutes drive from the Lodge which offers a swimming pool, sauna, steamroom, gymnasium and beauty salon.

LUCY'S OF AMBLESIDE

Church Street, Ambleside, Cumbria LA22 0BU
Tel: 015394 32288
e-mail: info@lucysofambleside.co.uk
website: www.lucysofambleside.co.uk

Lucy's of Ambleside is not just one business but four – plus a cookery school.

First, there's Lucy's Specialist Grocers which tempts customers with a stunning array of everything from cheese to chocolates. A food lover's paradise, this is a great place to come and browse for everything good to eat, to give or to keep. The shop is open every day from 9am to late.

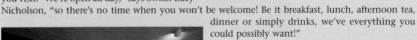

Then there's Lucy's on a Plate, a lively and enjoyable café by day and a uniquely atmospheric restaurant by night. The cuisine is designed to suit all tastes and ages, and the ever-changing menu offers fresh delights each time you visit. "We're open all day," says owner Lucy Nicholson, "so there's no time when you won't be welcome! Be it breakfast, lunch, afternoon tea, dinner or simply drinks, we've everything you could possibly want!"

Part of the restaurant, 'Lucy's Bite on the Side', is a delightful private dining room, ideal for special parties.There is also a lovely conservatory and walled courtyard.

Lucy's Inside Out is the outside catering wing of the enterprise. If you would prefer to spend time relaxing with your guests rather than getting stressed in the kitchen, Lucy's will prepare everything for you and bring a taste of the bistro into the

comfort of your own home or chosen venue. "Hatches, matches and dispatches a speciality" – and all meals are catered for, whether small and intimate, or large and loud.

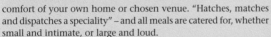

Lucy Four is a wine bar and bistro, and "is the original 'party demon' for a devil of a good time. Plan to spend an evening there, be it for a drink, for a bite, or for a feast…It's a fiendish find for everyone!" The bar is open from 5pm to 11pm.

Finally, there's LucyCooks, a cookery school opening in 2006. "Whether you're nine or 90," says Lucy, "we'll be offering a whole range of one day courses designed to suit everyone from novice to Nigella."

There's no doubt that once you've encountered this fabulous combination of delicatessen, café and restaurant, outside catering, and wine bar and bistro. You'll agree with Lucy's slogan:

"Once discovered, never forgotten!"

THE ARMITT MUSEUM

Rydal Road, Ambleside, Cumbria LA22 9PL
Tel: 01539 431212
e-mail: info@armitt.com
website: www.armitt.com

A short walk from the mill brings you to **The Armitt**, an attractive building which contains a gallery, museum and library dedicated to the area's history since Roman times and to its most famous literary luminaries, John Ruskin and Beatrix Potter. Visitors can "talk" to John Ruskin, watch a 19th century lantern slide show, and marvel at Beatrix Potter's pre-Mrs Tiggywinkle watercolours - exquisite scientific studies of fungi and mosses.

Other exhibits include a lock of Ruskin's hair, a life mask of Harriet Martineau, the political writer and author of an early *Guide to the Lakes*, and a fascinating collection of photographs by Herbert Bell (1856-1946), an Ambleside chemist who became an accomplished photographer, concentrating on lakeland scenes. The Armitt hosts regular exhibitions, lectures and concerts, and also has its own shop selling items produced exclusively for sale only at the museum.

room of this one-up, one-down residence measures just 13 feet by six feet, so living chez Rigg was decidedly cosy. Close by, at **Adrian Sankey's Glass Works**, visitors can watch craftsmen transform molten material into glass in the age-old way and also purchase the elegant results.

A short walk from the mill brings the visitor to the **Armitt Museum** and Library dedicated to the area's history since Roman times and to its most famous literary luminaries, John Ruskin and Beatrix Potter. Among the highlights are Beatrix Potter's early watercolours - exquisite studies of fungi and mosses - and a fascinating collection of photographs by Herbert Bell, an

Ambleside chemist who became an accomplished photographer.

The popular panoramic view of Ambleside, looking north from the path up **Loughrigg Fell**, reveals the town cradled within the apron of the massive Fairfield Horseshoe which rises to nearly 3,000 feet. Within the townscape itself, the most impressive feature is the rocket-like spire, 180 feet high, of **St Mary's Church**. The church was completed in 1854 to a design by Sir George Gilbert Scott, the architect of London's St Pancras Station and the Albert Memorial. Inside the church is a chapel devoted to the memory of William Wordsworth and an interesting 1940s mural depicting the

CROW HOW COUNTRY HOUSE

Rydal Road, Ambleside, Cumbria LA22 9PN
Tel: 015394 32193 e-mail: stay@crowhowhotel.co.uk
Fax: 015394 31770 website: www.crowhowhotel.co.uk

Crow How Country House hotel occupies a lovely secluded position in the beautiful Rydal Valley just half a mile from Ambleside. This grand Victorian house offers quality en suite accommodation in nine individually furnished bedrooms. All enjoy spectacular views, and have colour TV and hospitality tray. The owners, the Doano family, pride themselves on their food – the Cumbrian breakfasts and dinners are freshly prepared from the highest quality ingredients. Crow How is licensed and there's a comfortable residents' lounge. The hotel is non-smoking; well-behaved dogs are accepted.

LOG HOUSE RESTAURANT & B&B

Lake Road, Ambleside, Cumbria LA22 0DN
Tel: 015394 31077
website: www.loghouse.co.uk

Located midway between Ambleside town and the shore of Windermere, just five minutes walk from both, the **Log House Restaurant & B&B** was once the home of the famous local artist Alfred Heaton Cooper. After his student days in London, Alfred returned briefly to the north to retrace Turner's journey through the famous beauty spots of Yorkshire. He then set off to the Norwegian fjords to make his living selling landscapes to the European tourists who went there in great numbers.

Alfred married a local girl but, unable to make a living there, he returned to England and eventually settled in the Lake District where wealthy tourists promised a better income. His decision to have the red-roofed log cabin shipped from Norway caused quite a stir locally. It was first erected in Coniston village as a studio and later moved to Ambleside which attracted more visitors. Alfred's wife ran the studio while he tramped the Lakeland fells painting scenes that inspired him and would appeal to visitors. Today, his paintings sell for several thousand pounds and many thousands of reproductions are sold at the Grasmere gallery that bears his name.

Over the years, Alfred's delightfully idiosyncratic cabin has played many different roles – as artist's studio, as a shop of various kinds, and even as a tearoom. It is now home to Steven Edmonson and Karen Needham's outstanding restaurant and B&B establishment. With its excellent cuisine and three luxury bedrooms, the Log House is the perfect place for a gourmet weekend. Award-winning chefs Shaun Edmondson and John Durbin have created an enticing menu which is available every lunchtime (noon until 2pm) and evening (6.30pm to 9pm). The à la carte menu offers dishes such as local smoked salmon or a twice-baked goats' cheese soufflé amongst the starters; wild mushroom and asparagus risotto or Dover sole with Morecambe Bay potted shrimps amongst the main dishes. In the evening, there's an equally alluring table d'hôte menu to choose from. Service is courteous and efficient, and the prices reflect great value for money – especially if you come on a dinner, bed & breakfast basis.

The three luxury bedrooms enjoy southerly views to Loughrigg Fell, are strictly non-smoking and are equipped with LCD TV with DVD, video and radio, as well as coffee and tea-making facilities. Two of the bedrooms have the original Log House wooden beams. Please note that at weekends and public holidays, accommodation is offered for a minimum of two nights.

ancient ceremony of rush-bearing. The ceremony, dating back to the days when the floor of the church was covered by rushes, is still held on the first Saturday in July. Some 400 children process through the town bearing colourful decorated rushes and singing the specially commissioned Ambleside Rushbearer's Hymn.

A few weeks later, the famous **Ambleside Sports** take place, an event distinguished by the variety of local traditional sports it features. In addition to carriage-driving, ferret or pigeon racing, and tugs of war, the Sports include Cumberland and Westmorland wrestling (a little like Sumo wrestling but without the rolls of fat), muscle-wrenching fell racing, and hound trailing.

Another experience not to be missed while staying at Ambleside is a boat cruise on Lake Windermere to Bowness. There are daily departures from the pier at **Waterhead**, about a mile south of the town. At Bowness, there are connections to other lakeland attractions and, during the summer months, evening wine cruises. Rowing boats and self-drive motor boats can also be hired. Just to the west of the pier is **Borrans Park**, a pleasant lakeside park with plenty of picnic spots, and to the west of the park, the site of Galava Roman Fort. There is little to be seen of the fort but the setting is enchanting. Also well worth a visit is nearby **Stagshaw Garden** (NT), a spring woodland garden which contains a fine collection of shrubs, including some impressive rhododendrons, azaleas and camellias. Parking is very limited and vehicular access is hazardous, so it's best to park at Waterhead car park and walk.

Perhaps the most unusual visitor attraction in Ambleside is the **Homes of Football**, described by the *Sunday Times* as a national treasure. It began as a

travelling exhibition of football photographs and memorabilia but now has a permanent home in Lake Road. Photographer Stuart Clarke recorded games and grounds at every kind of venue from the Premier League down to amateur village teams. There are now 60,000 photographs on file and a massive selection on show, framed and for sale. Some of the memorabilia retail for £200 or more but a free picture postcard of your favourite soccer ground is included in the modest entrance fee.

From Ambleside town centre, a steep road climbs sharply up to the dramatic **Kirkstone Pass** and over to Ullswater. The pass is so called because of the rock at the top which looks like a church steeple. Rising to some 1,489 feet above sea level, the road is the highest in the Lake District and, though today's vehicles make light work of the climb, for centuries the Pass presented a formidable obstacle. The severest incline, known as **The Struggle**, necessitated passengers stepping out of their coach and making their way on foot, leaving the horses to make the steep haul with just the empty coach.

RYDAL
6 miles NW of Windermere on the A591

In 1813, following the deaths of their young children Catherine and Thomas, William and Mary Wordsworth were too grief stricken to stay on at the Old Rectory in Grasmere. They moved a couple of miles down the road to **Rydal Mount**, a handsome house overlooking tiny **Rydal Water**. By now, the poet was well-established and comparatively prosperous. A salaried position as Westmorland's Distributor of Stamps (a tax official), supplemented his earnings from poetry. Although Wordsworth only ever rented the house, it is now owned by his descendants and has been open

VILLA COLOMBINA

Grasmere, Cumbria LA22 9SH
Tel/Fax: 015394 35268

Located on the edge of the delightful and historic village of Grasmere, **Villa Colombina** offers authentic Italian cuisine in a Lakeland setting. Pass through its porticoed entrance and you immediately feel the buzz of a lively, popular restaurant where good food is the first priority. While studying the menu, settle down in one of the comfortable armchairs and enjoy a pre-prandial drink.

The choice is extensive. The starters range from baked giant mushrooms filled with goat's cheese and sundried tomatoes, through fresh mussels, a classic minestrone soup and the Villa Colombina's

own vegetarian antipasto. Then you are faced with a choice between pizzas, pasta dishes, risottos, chicken offerings such as saltimbocca, and steaks. Desserts include the traditional Italian sweets, tiramisu and panacotta, as well as almond lemon polenta cake, sticky toffee pudding and a selection of continental and English cheeses. The restaurant is licensed for those having a meal and offers a choice of beers, ales, ciders and house wine by the glass. There's also a wide choice of soft drinks, teas, coffees, juices and children's drinks. The Villa Colombina is non-smoking and has its own off-road car parking.

BARNEY'S NEWSBOX

Broadgate, Grasmere, Cumbria LA22 9TA
Tel: 015394 35627 Fax: 015394 35008
website: www.barneys-newsbox.co.uk

Barney's Newsbox started as a small village newsagent back in 1985 and has grown to become, amongst other things, the largest jigsaw shop in the UK. It's still a busy newsagents stocking local newspapers, maps, guide books, greeting cards and confectionery local to the lakes, but also offers a wide range of other items such as gifts, novelty items, T-shirts, and sweat shirts. Barney's is also well-known for its range of model cars, hand-made cars and car kits, with thousands of them available in stock.

Barney's has two entrances: one takes you into the newsagents; the other, named Call The Wild, is

devoted to the theme of wildlife with a huge range of items such as ceramics, children's toys, teddy bears, wildlife toys, clothing, music and more. Owners William Livesey and Linda Perren have devoted most of the top floor to its incredible range of jigsaws. There are more than 4,000 different puzzles to choose from, including a range of Lake District jigsaws, some of them from their own designs. There are jigsaws for children and ones for the real expert – the largest is composed of 18,000 pieces. A catalogue is available and Barney's also operates a mail order service.

Rydal Water

Cottage where Wordsworth lived in dire poverty from 1799 to 1808, obliged to line the walls with newspaper for warmth. The great poet shared this very basic accommodation with his wife Mary, his sister Dorothy, his sister-in-law Alice and, as almost permanent guests, Coleridge and De Quincey. (Sir Walter Scott also stayed, although he often sneaked off to the Swan Hotel for a dram since the Wordsworths were virtually teetotallers.) Located on the outskirts of the village, Dove Cottage has been preserved intact: next door is an award-winning museum dedicated to Wordsworth's life and works.

to the public since 1970. The interior has seen little change and retains a lived-in atmosphere. It contains first editions of the poet's work and many personal possessions, among them the only surviving portrait of his beloved sister, Dorothy. William was a keen gardener and the four-acre garden remains very much as he designed it.

GRASMERE
7 miles NW of Windermere on the A591

In 1769 Thomas Gray described Grasmere as "a little unsuspected paradise". Thirty years later, Wordsworth himself called it "the loveliest spot that man hath ever found". Certainly, Grasmere enjoys one of the finest settings in all Lakeland, its small lake nestling in a natural scenic amphitheatre beside the compact, rough-stone village.

For lovers of Wordsworth's poetry, Grasmere is the pre-eminent place of pilgrimage. They come to visit **Dove**

Dove Cottage, Rydal Mount, another of the poet's homes near Grasmere, and his birthplace, Wordsworth House at Cockermouth, are all owned by the **Wordsworth Trust**, which offers a discount ticket covering entrance to all three properties.

In 1808, the poet moved to **The Rectory** (private) opposite St Oswald's Church. In his long poem, *The Excursion*, he describes the house and its lovely garden beside the River Rothay. The church, too, is remembered in the same poem:

Not raised in nice proportions was the pile,
But large and massy, for duration built,
With pillars crowded and the roof upheld
By naked rafters intricately crossed,
Like leafless underboughs in some thick wood.

In 1850, the Poet Laureate was buried beneath yew trees he himself had planted in **St Oswald's** churchyard. He was joined here by his sister Dorothy, in 1885, and his wife Mary, in 1889.

Grasmere

Distance:	3.7 mile (5.9 kilometres)
Typical time:	180 mins
Height gain:	305 metres
Map:	Explorer OL 7
Walk:	ww.walkingworld.com ID:1390
Contributor:	Jim Grindle

Access Information:

Grasmere is north of Ambleside on the A591 Ambleside/Keswick road. There are three large car parks in the village and some smaller ones. Buses from Ambleside to Keswick call in the village.

Description:

A lane gives way to a track rising gradually above the Vale of Grasmere. There are a number of seats and other resting-places from which to admire the views so that the walk can be savoured by the slowest walker. The tarn itself is an attractive, quiet spot (although Wainwright didn't like it much.) The descent is clear but steeper than the way up and the return is across the beautiful meadows surrounding Grasmere Village.

Additional Information

In the churchyard at Grasmere are the graves of William Wordsworth and his wife. On the main road is Dove Cottage, their home for a number of years and worth a visit. Much of the open land in the area is owned by the National Trust.

Features:

Hills or Fells, Mountains, River, Lake/Loch, Toilets, Museum, Church, National Trust/NTS, Wildlife, Flowers, Great Views, Food Shop, Good for Kids, Public Transport, Tea Shop

Walk Directions:

1 Start from the Information Centre where you can check the weather forecast before setting off. Turn right as you leave the Centre and walk up to the junction by the church. Turn right and go past the main car park to the junction with the main road. Turn left there to find the new crossing point.

2 Go over and turn right. Just ahead of you a lane branches off from the main road. Follow signs for Dove Cottage. Take the lane which is a left fork. Past Dove Cottage the lane rises and you come across an open marshy area. At the top the lane forks.

3 Take the left fork and then watch for a track on the left, signposted to Alcock Tarn.

4 The seat is another good indicator. In a few moments the track splits and you will see a gate a little below you.

5 Go through the gate with its National Trust sign onto the track that leads up to the tarn. One track joins from below but there is no other track off. You will know when you are near the tarn because it has a wall around it.

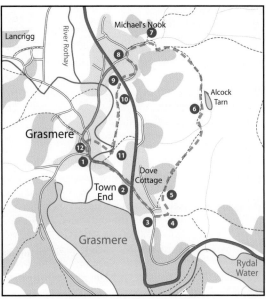

6 The walk continues on the left of the tarn to a stile in the wall at the far end. Beyond the wall, the track is rougher but still clear. Zigzags lead down until the path is squeezed between a wall on the left and a beck on the right. Don't despair - there is a bridge, on the other side of which is a gate.

7 Cross the bridge and go through the gate onto a tarmac drive. This drops to a junction with a lane. Turn left and just out of sight of this shot you will come to another lane on the left.

8 Turn left at this junction and follow the lane down to the main road, where the Church of Our Lady of the Wayside stands on the corner.

9 Just to the right on the main road is a crossing point. Go over but don't take the footpath by it. Turn left to a gate 50m away. Go along the enclosed track into the field at the end and then follow the field edge on the right to the first of a sequence of gates.

10 You can always see the next gate and the yellow arrows accurately show the direction. You will reach the Millennium Bridge (non-wobbly). Only the most recent maps will show this bridge.

11 Cross the bridge and at the far side, turn left. This path will bring you out at the north side of the church, in the centre of the village.

12 Turn left and take the first turning on the right for the information centre.

Located opposite the village green the **Heaton Cooper Studio** has a changing exhibition of paintings, prints and sculptures from four generations of the Heaton Cooper family from Alfred Heaton Cooper (1863-1929) to present day members.

In Grasmere town cemetery is the grave of **William Archibald Spooner**, sometime Warden of New College, Oxford. He gave his name to Spoonerisms, in which the initial letters of two words are transposed, with amusing results. Here are a few of his gems, some genuine, others perhaps apocryphal:

Kinquering Kongs their titles take.
You have hissed all my mystery lessons.
You have deliberately tasted two worms and you can leave Oxford by the town drain.
Yes indeed: the Lord is a shoving leopard.

He spent many holidays in Grasmere with his wife at her house, How Foot.

Like Ambleside, Grasmere is famous for its **Sports**, first recorded in 1852, which still take place in late August. The most

Grasmere

THE GRANGE HOTEL

Station Square, Grange-over-Sands,
Cumbria LA11 6EJ
Tel: 015395 33666
Fax: 015395 35064
e-mail: info@grange-hotel.co.uk
website: www.grange-hotel.co.uk

The famous travel writer Bill Bryson
declared Grange-over-Sands one of his
top six UK holiday destinations and
undoubtedly the best way to enjoy a
stay at this gracious Victorian resort
with its mile-long promenade is to
book into the magnificent **Grange
Hotel**. Built in classical Italianate style
in 1866, the Grange has long been
established as one of the Lake District's premier hotels. It occupies a superb position with panoramic
views, has 50 well-appointed bedrooms, stylish décor throughout, enjoys a glowing reputation for its
outstanding cuisine, and is noted for its warm hospitality.

Owners Hugh and Jenny Rushton pride themselves on the hotel's cuisine. Only the very best of
fresh, local produce is used with freshly-baked breads just part of the bountiful hot and cold breakfast
buffet. But the highlight of the day will surely be a sumptuous candlelit five-course table d'hôte dinner
served in the elegant Carriages Restaurant where the wine list features the finest produce from vineyards
around the globe. If you prefer something lighter, the Lounge Bar Menu has something for everyone
– from delicious home-made soups to vegetarian tortilla wraps. There are also menu options for children
and for those with special dietary requirements.

The accommodation at the Grange maintains the elevated standards evident throughout the hotel.
Each of the 50 en suite bedrooms is provided with satellite TV, direct dial telephone, hairdryer and
hospitality tray. And if you want to feel really pampered, you can upgrade to one of the superior or
executive rooms.

Other amenities at the Grange include the cosy lounge bar, the terrace with its breathtaking views,

and the impressive Health & Leisure Suite.
Open every day from 7am to 10pm, the suite
boasts a spacious heated pool equipped with
optional jets; a roomy 12-person Jacuzzi; a
sauna and steam room; fast-tan solarium and
a well-equipped gym. Fully qualified beauty
therapists are on hand to provide a wide range
of popular health and beauty treatments. These
include aromatherapy, waxing, deluxe
manicures and pedicures, as well as an
extensive range of face and body treatments
tailored to your particular requirements.

And when you're ready to explore this
lovely part of south Cumbria, the options are
numerous: Levens Hall with its unique topiary
garden and historic house is close by; Holker
Hall with its famous car museum; the Beatrix
Potter Experience in Ambleside and the
amazing South Lakes Animal Park are all within
easy reach.

LANCRIGG VEGETARIAN COUNTRY HOUSE HOTEL

Easedale, Grasmere, Cumbria LA22 9QN
Tel: 015394 35317   Fax: 015394 35058
e-mail: info@lancrigg.co.uk   website: www.lancrigg.co.uk

Described by the artist William Heaton Cooper as "a perfect example of a gracious country house in precisely the right place", **Lancrigg Vegetarian Country House Hotel** was originally a Westmorland farmhouse. Then in 1839, William Wordsworth encouraged his friend Elizabeth Fletcher to buy the house which was to become a regular meeting place for the Lakeland poets and for other literary giants such as Charles Dickens who stayed here on his visits north. Since 1985 this historic old property has been owned by Robert and Janet Whittington who have always aimed to maintain Lancrigg's original charm in the context of a modern hotel.

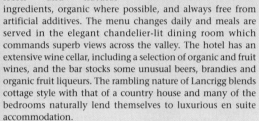

The vegetarian cuisine is based on the finest quality fresh and natural ingredients, organic where possible, and always free from artificial additives. The menu changes daily and meals are served in the elegant chandelier-lit dining room which commands superb views across the valley. The hotel has an extensive wine cellar, including a selection of organic and fruit wines, and the bar stocks some unusual beers, brandies and organic fruit liqueurs. The rambling nature of Lancrigg blends cottage style with that of a country house and many of the bedrooms naturally lend themselves to luxurious en suite accommodation.

celebrated event in the Lake District, they attract some 10,000 visitors and feature many pursuits unique to Cumbria such as Cumberland and Westmorland wrestling as well as the more understandable, though arduous, fell running.

Collectors of curiosities who happen to be travelling north on the A591 from Grasmere should look out for the vintage black and yellow AA telephone box on the right hand side of the road. Still functioning, **Box 487** has been accorded Grade II listed building status by the Department of the Environment.

GRANGE-OVER-SANDS

Grange, as it's known locally, is an attractive little town set in a natural sun-trap on the north shore of Morecambe Bay. Much of its Victorian charm can be credited to the **Furness Railway Company**, which developed the town after building the Lancaster to Whitehaven line in 1857. The railway provided a safe alternative to this hazardous journey. At Grange the company built an elegant mile-long promenade (now traffic free) and set out the colourful ornamental gardens. Prosperous merchants built grand country homes here and it wasn't long before local residents began referring to their town as the 'Torquay of the North'.

The route to Grange, across the sands of **Morecambe Bay**, is a treacherous one, though it was used not only by the Romans but also by the monks of Furness Abbey and, later, even by stage coaches looking to shorten their journey time. Avoiding the quicksands of the bay,

CARTMEL STICKY TOFFEE PUDDING CO. LTD

The Square, Cartmel, Cumbria LA11 6QB
Tel: 015395 58300 Fax: 015395 58507
e-mail: stpudcartmel@fsbdial.co.uk
website: www.stickytoffeepudding.co.uk

The Johns family have been making sticky toffee puddings since 1984, first in their restaurant in Grange and from 1989 here in Cartmel Village Shop on the Square. In the small kitchen at the rear of the shop they made many of the dishes they had served in the restaurant but now produced them as take home products. As demand for Sticky Toffee Pudding increased, they gradually stopped making their other products. **Cartmel Sticky Toffee Pudding Co. Ltd** uses only the very best ingredients for this traditional Cumbrian pudding which has caused something of a storm nationwide enjoying press coverage in various national papers and TV, including the ultimate accolade of being celebrated as one of Rick Stein's *Food Heroes*. The shop also sells its own sticky toffee pudding sauce – delicious with ice cream, barbecued bananas or baked apples – as well as an extensive range of high quality comestibles from other producers.

If for some reason you can't make it to this charming little village, the puddings are available in individual delicatessens nationwide, as well as at Harvey Nichols, Selfridges and Fortnum & Mason food halls, and even in Waitrose supermarkets. Requests for puddings to be sent to friends and relatives who have not yet enjoyed the experience of a sticky toffee pudding, or for repeat orders has ensured a continuous growth of the company's mail order side of the business which now covers a large part of Europe.

At the other end of Cartmel village, adjacent to the Priory gates, awaits a different kind of treasure chest. The vision for the recently opened Priory Shop was conceived and realised by the same talented family and their dedicated team of workers. The main inspiration of the shop is an exclusive range of original home decorations, from popular Selfridge's lines such as Gisella Graham and Sia; gifts with a gardening theme, luxury chocolates and ice cream, traditional confectionery, local Bath House toiletries and beautiful cards and wrapping paper.

which have taken many lives over the centuries, is a difficult task. Back in the 16th century, the Duchy of Lancaster appointed an official guide to escort travellers over the shifting sands and also provided him with a house at Grange. The town still has an official guide who takes groups on a three-hour walk across the bay. The sands are extremely dangerous since "the tide comes in with the merciless speed of a galloping horse" - a crossing should never be attempted without the help of a qualified guide.

Away from the hotels, shops, and cafés of the town there are some lovely walks and none is more pleasant than the path behind Grange which climbs through magnificent limestone woodlands rich in wild flowers. The path finally leads to the 727-foot **Hampsfell Summit** and **The Hospice**, a little stone tower from which there are unforgettable views over the bay and, in the opposite direction, the craggy peaks of the Lake District.

Grange is also the starting point of the **Cistercian Way**, an exceptionally interesting 33-mile long footpath through Furness to Barrow which takes in, naturally, many Cistercian sites.

AROUND GRANGE-OVER-SANDS

LINDALE
2 miles NE of Grange-over-Sands off the A590

This small village was the birthplace of a man who defied the scepticism of his contemporaries and built the first successful iron ship. 'Iron Mad' John Wilkinson also built the first cast iron barges and later created the castings for the famous Iron Bridge at Coalbrookdale. After his death in 1808 he was buried in an iron coffin (naturally) in an unmarked grave, and the lofty **Wilkinson Obelisk** to his memory that stands near the village crossroads is also

cast in iron. The admirers who erected it however omitted to provide the iron column with a lightning conductor. A few years later it was struck to the ground by a lightning bolt. The obelisk lay neglected in shrubbery for some years but has now been restored and towers above the village once again. Just outside Lindale, at **Castle Head**, is the imposing house that Wilkinson built by the River Winster.

CARTMEL
2 miles W of Grange-over-Sands off the B5278

One of the prettiest villages in the Peninsula, Cartmel is a delightful cluster of houses and cottages set around a square from which lead winding streets and arches into back yards. The village is dominated by the famous **Cartmel Priory**, founded in 1188 by Augustinian canons. Like all monastic institutions, the priory was disbanded in 1537 and several of its members were executed for participating in the Pilgrimage of Grace. Today, substantial remains of the 12th century Gatehouse (National Trust) survive, but the rest of the Priory was cannibalised to build many of the village's cottages and houses. After the Dissolution, only the south aisle of the **Church of St Mary and St Michael** was still standing but, in 1620, George Preston of Holker began restoring the entire building and the richly carved black oak screens and stall canopies date from this restoration. St Mary & St Michael's has recently been described as "the most beautiful church in the northwest". Inside, in the southwest corner of the church, is a door known as **Cromwell's Door**. The holes in it are said to have been made by indignant parishioners firing at Parliamentarian soldiers who had stabled their horses in the nave.

Cartmel is also famous for its attractive **Racecourse**, set beside the River Eea, on

Cartmel Priory

Cumbria's premier stately house, **Holker Hall** is one of the homes of the Cavendish family, the Dukes of Devonshire. An intriguing blend of 16th century, Georgian and Victorian architecture, it's a visitor-friendly place with no restraining ropes keeping visitors at a distance, there's a fire burning in the hearth and a lived-in, family atmosphere. There's also an impressive cantilevered staircase, a library with some 3,500 leather bound books (plus a few dummy covers designed to hide electricity sockets), and an embroidered panel said to be the work of Mary, Queen of Scots.

Each year, Holker's 25 acres of award-winning gardens host the **Holker Garden Festival**, which has been hailed as the 'Chelsea of the North'. The gardens are the pride of Lord and Lady Cavendish, who developed the present layout from the original 'contrived natural landscape' of Lord George Cavendish 200 years ago. The Great Holker Lime and the stunning spring display of rhododendrons are among the delights not to be missed. Here, too, are a wonderful rose garden, an azalea walk and a restored Victorian rockery. Lord and Lady Cavendish put their pride into words: "If you gain from your visit a small fraction of the pleasure that we ourselves get from them, then the work of generations of gardeners will not have been in vain."

which meetings are held in May, July and August. Located close to the village, the course must be one of the most picturesque in the country and it is certainly one of the smallest. A holiday atmosphere descends on the village for race days and, though the competition is fierce, it is a wonderful and relaxing day out.

FLOOKBURGH

3 miles SW of Grange-over-Sands on the B5277

An ancient Charter Borough, Flookburgh is still the principal fishing village on Morecambe Bay. Roads from the square lead down to the shore where fishermen still land their catches of cockles, shrimps and (less often nowadays) flukes, the tasty small flat fish from which the village takes its name.

At the **Lakeland Miniature Village** are 120 buildings hand-made from local Coniston slate by Edward Robinson and accurate down to the last detail. In 2005, an oriental teahouse was opened here and overlooks the owner's oriental garden.

SOUTHERN LAKELAND NURSERIES

Cark in Cartmel, Grange-over-Sands, Cumbria LA11 7JZ
Tel: 015395 58237 Fax: 015395 58112
website: www.southlakesgardencentre.co.uk

For more than half a century, **Southern Lakeland Nurseries** has been serving gardeners all across the northwest and now offers what is probably the most extensive array of garden products to be found in the region. It's located in the village of Cark-in-Cartmel, just four miles from Grange-over-Sands and close to Holker Hall, and is run by Michael and Victoria Taylor – it was Michael's father who established the business all those years ago. Many of the plants on sale are carefully grown at the nursery where half an acre of glass protects thousands of houseplants, outdoor and bedding plants.

A large area is devoted to garden accessories including tools, planters, pots, hanging baskets and all the usual garden requirements. As the Nurseries' motto puts it: "From seeds to trees – and almost everything in between!" In the autumn months, bulbs feature large at the centre, while pot plants and flowers are available all year round. The Nurseries' Interflora service enables flowers to be sent worldwide. You'll find that the staff are happy to help with your requirements and advice is freely given. Open seven days a week, all year round, the nurseries have ample free parking and good access for the disabled.

The Holker Hall estate contains a wide variety of other attractions - formal gardens, water features, a 125-acre deer park, picnic and children's play areas, a gift shop and café. Also within the grounds is the **Lakeland Motor Museum** which, as well as boasting a completely restored 1920s garage, has more than 100 vehicles on show among well over 20,000 well-presented exhibits.

ULVERSTON

It was way back in 1280 that Edward I granted Ulverston its market charter; more than seven centuries later, colourful stalls still crowd the narrow streets and cobbled market square every Thursday. It's a picturesque scene but a walk up nearby **Hoad Hill** is rewarded with an even more striking view of the town. The great expanse of Morecambe Bay with a backdrop of the Pennines stretches to the south, the bulk of Ingleborough lies to the east, Coniston Old Man and the Langdale Pikes lie to the west and north. Crowning the hill is a 100ft-high **Replica of the Eddystone Lighthouse**, raised here in 1850 to commemorate one of Ulverston's most distinguished sons, Sir John Barrow. Explorer, diplomat and author, he served as a Lord of the Admiralty for more than 40 years, his naval reforms contributing greatly to England's success in the Napoleonic Wars.

An even more famous son of Ulverston was Stanley Jefferson, born at number 3, Argyle Street on June 16th, 1890. Stanley is far better known to the world as Stan Laurel. His 30-year career in more than 100 comedy films with Oliver Hardy is celebrated in the town's **Laurel and Hardy Museum** in King Street. The museum was founded in 1976 by the late Bill Cubin, who devoted his life to the

LAKELAND'S WOODLAND HERITAGE EXHIBITION
@ GEORGE BARKER AND SONS- TIMBER MERCHANTS.

Contact details: George Barker & Sons Ltd
Riverside Sawmills, Backbarrow, Ulverston,
Cumbria LA12 8TA
Tel: 015395 31236   Fax: 015395 30801
e-mail info@timbergardenfurniture.com
website www.timbergardenfurniture.com

Located on the edge of the river Leven and surrounded by
the splendor of the Lake District hills George Barker and
Sons have been trading as a family firm since 1858.

The company has always worked with timber in one way
or another and their current production, which can be
viewed from a special viewing gallery, is based around the
garden leisure industry and includes furniture, decking and garden rooms. The company also retails a
range of hot tubs, sauna and other garden leisure accessories.

The Lakeland Woodland Heritage Exhibition is an informative and
entertaining interpretation of the history of the Lakeland woodland and
of the company's long association with it. The display covers the many
wood based crafts such as swill basket making, charcoal burning, besom
making and other allied trades which abounded in the locality during the
Industrial Revolution many of which continue to this day.

- Discover the most unusual use for a swill basket....can you guess?
- What on earth is a Bool machine and what was it used for?
- What do BBQs and gunpowder have in common?
- What is coppicing and why was it so important to the survival of the local forests?
- Discover the history of Backbarrow village as an important base for the production of cotton and iron ore during the industrial revolution.
- Can you see the wood from the trees?

Entry to the exhibition is free of charge and opening hours are 10 am to 5pm Monday to Saturday all
year round.

Gift shop & Café: (Opening hours as per the Exhibition)

Next to the exhibition there is a cosy coffee shop serving a selection of fresh coffees and teas along
with a range of delicious hot and cold snacks, cakes
and biscuits. The daily specials board should keep your
taste buds tingling and coming back for more.

While you enjoy your refreshments you can also
browse othe selection of quality gift items many of
which are sourced locally and include some award
winning chutneys as well as hand made pottery, wood
turning and greetings cards.

There are also a number of items which are directly
linked to the themes of the exhibition as well as some
souvenir type gifts.

famous duo and collected an extraordinary variety of memorabilia, believed to be the largest in the world. Everything is here, including letters, photographs, personal items, and even furniture belonging to the couple. There's also a small cinema showing the duo's films and documentaries about them throughout the day.

The oldest building in the town is the **Church of St Mary** which, in parts, dates from 1111. Though it was restored and rebuilt in the mid-19th century and the chancel was added in 1903, it has retained its splendid Norman door and some magnificent stained glass, including a window designed by the painter Sir Joshua Reynolds.

Ulverston also boasts England's shortest, widest and deepest **Canal**. Visitors can follow the towpath walk alongside which runs dead straight for just over a mile to Morecambe Bay. Built by the famous engineer John Rennie and opened in 1796, the canal ushered in a half-century of great prosperity for Ulverston as an inland port. At its peak, some 600 large ships a year berthed here but those good times came to an abrupt end in 1856 with the arrival of the railway. The railway company's directors bought the canal and promptly closed it.

A superb example of an early Victorian Gothic mansion, **Conishead Priory** (free) is now home to an International Buddhist Centre with a unique and striking Temple. Fascinating guided tours of the house and Temple are available on request, and visitors can stroll through the beautiful grounds and woodlands extending to Morecambe Bay. There's also a gift shop and conservatory café.

The town's other attractions include **The Lakes Glass Centre**, which features the high-quality Heron Glass and Cumbria Crystal. Also at the Centre is the **Gateway to Furness Exhibition**, providing a colourful snapshot of the history of the Furness Peninsula. There's more history at the **Ulverston Heritage Centre**, which also has a gift shop selling souvenirs and crafts made in Cumbria, while modern entertainment is provided at the Coronation Hall theatre complex and the traditional Roxy Cinema.

The open area to the north of the town, known as **The Gill**, is the starting point for the 70-mile Cumbria Way. The route of the Cumbria Way was originally devised by the Lake District area of the Ramblers Association in the mid-1970s and provides an exhilarating journey through a wonderful mix of natural splendour and fascinating heritage. The first section is the 15-mile walk to Coniston.

AROUND ULVERSTON

HAVERTHWAITE
5 miles NE of Ulverston off the A590

Haverthwaite is the southern terminus of the Lakeside & Haverthwaite Railway, a branch of the Furness railway originally built to transport passengers and goods to the steamers on Lake Windermere. It was one of the first attempts at mass tourism in the Lake District. Passenger numbers peaked in the 1920s, but the general decline of rail travel in the 1960s led to the railway's closure in 1967. However, a group of dedicated rail enthusiasts rescued this scenic stretch, restored its engines and rolling stock to working order and now provide a full service of steam trains throughout the season.

SWARTHMOOR
1 mile S of Ulverston off the A590

Swarthmoor Hall was built in around 1586 by George Fell, a wealthy landowner. It was his son, Judge Thomas Fell, who married Margaret Askew, who, in turn, became a follower of George Fox after hearing him preach in 1652. At that time, many people were suspicious of Fox's beliefs but Margaret was able to persuade her husband to use his position to give Fox protection and shelter, and the hall became the first settled centre of the Quaker Movement. Missionaries were organised from here and the library was stocked with both Quaker and anti-Quaker literature. Judge Fell died in 1658 and, 11 years later, Margaret married George Fox. The hall is open during the summer and it gives a fascinating insight into the history of the early Quakers.

BARDSEA

2 miles S of Ulverston off the A5087

The village stands on a lovely green knoll overlooking the sea and, as well as having a charming, unhurried air about it, there are some excellent walks from here along the coast either from its Country Park or through the woodland.

Just up the coast, to the north, lies **Conishead Priory**, once the site of a leper colony that was established by Augustinian canons in the 12th century. The monks from the priory used to act as guides across the dangerous Cartmel Sands to Lancashire. After the Dissolution, a superb private house was built on the site and the guide service was continued by the Duchy of Lancaster. In 1821, Colonel Braddyll demolished the house and built in its place the ornate Gothic mansion that stands here today. He was also responsible for the atmospheric ruined folly on **Chapel Island** that is clearly visible in the estuary.

Latterly, the Priory has been a private house, a hydropathic hotel, a military hospital and a rest home for Durham miners; it is now owned by the Tibet

Buddhist Manjushri Mahayana Buddhist Centre, which was established here in 1977. During the summer months, visitors are welcome to the house, which is open for tours, and there is a delightful woodland trail to follow through the grounds. A new Buddhist temple was opened in 1998, based on a traditional design which symbolises the pure world (Mandala) of a Buddha.

GREAT URSWICK

3 miles S of Ulverston off the A590

The ancient village **Church of St Mary and St Michael** is noted for its unusual and lively woodcarvings that were created by the Chipping Campden Guild of Carvers. As well as the figure of a pilgrim to the left of the chancel arch, there are some smaller carvings in the choir stall of winged children playing musical instruments. Also worthy of a second look is the 9th century wooden cross which bears a runic inscription.

Lying between Great Urswick and Bardsea and overlooking Morecambe Bay is **Birkrigg Common**, a lovely area of open land. Here, on the east side of the common, is the **Druid's Circle**, with two concentric circles made up of 31 stones up to three feet high.

LINDAL-IN-FURNESS

3 miles SW of Ulverston on the A590

The **Colony Country Store** combines the aromatic character of an old-fashioned country general stores with the cost-cutting advantages of a Factory Shop. There's a huge range of textiles, glassware, ceramics and decorative accessories for the home, but the Colony is also Europe's leading manufacturer of scented candles, supplying millions of scented and dinner candles every year to prestigious stores around the world.

BARROW-IN-FURNESS

Undoubtedly the best introduction to Barrow is to pay a visit to the **Dock Museum**, an impressive glass and steel structure which hangs suspended above a Victorian graving dock. Audio-visual displays and a series of exhibits describe how Barrow grew from a tiny hamlet in the early 1800s to become the largest iron and steel centre in the world and also a major shipbuilding force in just 40 years. The museum has some spectacular models of ships of every kind, an art gallery hosting both permanent and travelling exhibitions, and a high tech interactive film show where characters from Barrow's history come to life to tell the town's story. It was James (later Sir James) Ramsden who established the first Barrow Iron Ship Company in 1870, taking advantage of local steel production skills. In 1896, the firm was acquired by **Vickers**, a name forever linked with Barrow, and for a number of years was the largest armaments works in the world. Sir James was also the general manager of the Furness Railway and the town's first mayor. At the Ramsden Square roundabout is a statue to Sir James, and at the next roundabout is a statue of HW Schneider, one of the men who developed the Furness iron mines and was involved in the Barrow Haematite Steel Company.

Barrow is the western starting point of the **Cistercian Way**, a 33-mile-walk to Grange-over-Sands through wonderfully unspoilt countryside.

AROUND BARROW-IN-FURNESS

GLEASTON
3 miles E of Barrow-in-Furness off the A5087

This village is typical of the small,

THE DOCK MUSEUM

North Road, Barrow-in-Furness, Cumbria LA14 2PW
Tel: 01229 894444
e-mail: dockmuseum@barrowbc.gov.uk
website: www.dockmuseum.org.uk

The Dock Museum is a spectacular modern museum built over an orginal Victorian dock. Its displays trace the fascinating history of Barrow showing how it grew from a tiny 19th century hamlet to the biggest iron and steel centre in the world and a major shipbuilding force in just 40 years.

One permanent exhibition entitled "Shipbuilders to the World" looks at the development of shipbuilding in Barrow Shipyard from the launch of its first iron steamship in 1873 to the present day. It includes exciting interactive displays, a range of model ships and access to many images from the museum's nationally important collection of glass negatives.

The Dock Museum has a fully landscaped waterfront site, with paths linking to the Cumbria Coastal Way, an adventure playground and picnic area. A wide range of tempting snacks and hot meals are available in the Strollers Coffee Shop. The museum has no admission charge and car parking is also free.

peaceful villages and hamlets that can be found in this part of the peninsula. Here, standing close by the ruins of **Gleaston Castle**, can be found **Gleaston Water Mill**. The present buildings date from 1774, with the massive original wooden gearing still in place. The machinery is operational most days - an 18ft water-wheel and an 11ft wooden pit wheel serviced by an intriguing water course. Evening tours with supper are available by prior arrangement. Also on site is the Pig's Whisper Country Store with thousands of piggy collectables and a teashop selling homemade meals and scones.

FOULNEY ISLAND
5 miles E of Barrow-in-Furness off the A5087

The island, like its smaller neighbour Roa Island, is joined to the mainland by a causeway. The site of the local lifeboat station, the island is small and sheltered from the Irish Sea by Walney Island.

PIEL ISLAND
5 miles SE of Barrow-in-Furness via foot ferry from Roa island.

Though this tiny island was probably visited by both the Celts and the Romans, its first recorded name is Scandinavian - Fotheray - from the Old Norse meaning 'fodder island'. In 1127 the islands were given to the Savignac Monks by King Stephen and, after the order merged with the Cistercian monks in the middle of the 12th century, the monks of Furness Abbey began to use Piel Island as a warehouse and storage area.

Piel Castle, on the island, was a house fortified in the early part of the 14th century and at the time it was the largest of its kind in the northwest. Intended to be used as one of the abbey's warehouses and to offer protection from raiders, in later years the castle also proved to be a useful defence against the King's customs

men and a prosperous trade in smuggling began. The castle has, over many years, been allowed to fall into ruin and now presents a stark outline on the horizon.

WALNEY ISLAND
2 miles W of Barrow-in-Furness on the A590

This 10-mile-long island is joined to the Furness Peninsula by a bridge from Barrow docks and is home to two important nature reserves that are situated at either end of the island. **North Walney National Nature Reserve** covers some 350 acres within which are a great variety of habitats including sand dunes, heath, salt marsh, shingle, and scrub. As well as having several species of orchid and over 130 species of bird either living or visiting the reserve, there is also an area for the preservation of the Natterjack toad, Britain's rarest amphibian. Unique to the Reserve is the Walney Geranium, a plant that grows nowhere else in the world. North Walney also boasts a rich prehistoric past, with important archaeological sites from mesolithic, neolithic, Bronze, and Iron Age times.

Situated on the island's long foot, **South Walney Nature Reserve** is home to the largest nesting ground of herring gulls and lesser black-backed gulls in Europe. It is also the most southerly breeding ground of such species as the oystercatcher, tern, and ringed plover, and in all, over 250 bird species have been recorded. A stopover for many migratory birds, the reserve has considerable ecological interest with mudflats, sandy beaches, rough pasture, and fresh water. There are waymarked trails around the reserve, with a number of hides.

The island's southernmost tip, **Walney Point**, is dominated by a 70ft lighthouse which was built in 1790 and whose light was, originally, an oil lamp.

DALTON-IN-FURNESS

5 miles N of Barrow-in-Furness off the A590

Lying in a narrow valley on the part of Furness which extends deep into Morecambe Bay, it is difficult to imagine that this ancient place was once the leading town of Furness and an important centre for administration and justice. The 14th century pele tower, **Dalton Castle**, was built with walls six feet thick to provide a place of refuge for the monks of Furness Abbey against Scottish raiders and it still looks very formidable. It is now owned by the National Trust and houses a small museum with an interesting display of 16th and 17th century armour, along with exhibits about iron mining, the Civil War in Furness, and the life and work of George Romney, the 18th century portrait painter. He was best known in his day for his many portraits of Nelson's mistress, Lady Hamilton, with whom he formed a romantic attachment, in spite of having a wife in Kendal. He is buried in the graveyard of the red sandstone **Church of St Mary**, where his grave is marked with the inscription *'pictor celeberrimus'*.

Visitors to Dalton will find that it is time well spent looking around the many fascinating facades in and close to the market place, such as the unique, cast-iron shop front at No 51, **Market Street**. In the market place itself is an elegant **Victorian Drinking Fountain** with fluted columns supporting a dome of open iron work above the pedestal fountain. Nearby stands the market cross and the slabs of stone that were used for fish-drying in the 19th century.

From the mostly pedestrianised Tudor Square, visitors can board a bus to the award-winning **South Lakes Wild Animal Park**, which has been designated the Region's Official Top Attraction by the Cumbria Tourist Board. It's the only place in Britain where you can see rare Amur and Sumatran tigers (the world's biggest and smallest tigers). At feeding time (2.30pm each day) they climb a 20 foot vertical tree to 'catch' their food. Ring-tailed lemurs wander freely through the park, visitors can walk with emus and hand feed the largest collection of kangaroos in Europe. The 17 acres of natural parkland are also home to some of the rarest animals on earth, among them the red panda, maned wolves and tamarin monkeys as well as some 150 other species from around the world, including rhinos, giraffes, tapirs, coatis and the ever-popular meerkats. In 2005, pygmy hippos, mandrills and penguins were added to the menagerie. Other attractions include a safari railway, adventure play area, many picnic spots, a gift shop and café.

To the south of the town lies **Furness Abbey** (English Heritage), a magnificent ruin of eroded red sandstone set in fine parkland, the focal point of south Cumbria's monastic heritage. Furness Abbey stands in the **Vale of Deadly Nightshade**, a shallow valley of sandstone cliffs and rich pastureland. The abbey itself was established in 1123 at Tulketh, near Preston, by King Stephen. Four years later it was moved to its present site and, after 20 years, became absorbed into the Cistercian Order. Despite its remoteness, the abbey flourished, with the monks establishing themselves as guides across the treacherous sands of Morecambe Bay.

GRIZEBECK

15 miles N of Barrow-in-Furness on the A595/A5092

This small village on the edge of the Lake District National Park nestles against the flanks of the **Furness Fells**. Although it stands at the junction of roads leading to the Furness Peninsula and the South

Cumbria coast, the village and the area around is peaceful and unhurried, offering the visitor an inviting alternative to some of the busier and more crowded Lakeland towns.

BROUGHTON-IN-FURNESS

19 miles N of Barrow-in-Furness on the A595/A593

At the heart of this attractive, unspoilt little town is the **Market Square** with its tall Georgian houses, commemorative obelisk of 1810, village stocks, fish slabs and some venerable chestnut trees. The old Town Hall, occupying the whole of one side, dates back to 1766 and now houses the town's Tourist Information Centre and the Clocktower Gallery, which exhibits paintings, ceramics, mirrors and glassware. On August 1st each year, Broughton's Lord of the Manor comes to the Square to read out the market charter granted by Elizabeth I, while councillors dispense pennies to any children in the crowd.

One of the town's famous short-term residents was Branwell Brontë, who was employed here as a tutor at **Broughton House**, a splendid double-fronted, three-storey town house just off the Square. Branwell apparently found time to both enjoy the elegance of the town and to share in whatever revelries were in train.

Wordsworth often visited Broughton as a child. Throughout his life he loved this peaceful corner of Lakeland and celebrated its charms in some 150 poems; his 20th century poetical successor, Norman Nicholson, was similarly enchanted.

Some of the Lake District's finest scenery - the Duddon Valley, Furness Fells, Great Gable and Scafell are all within easy reach, and about three miles west of the town is **Swinside Circle**, a fine prehistoric stone circle, some 60 feet in diameter, containing 52 close-set

BROUGHTON CRAFT SHOP

Griffin Street, Broughton-in-Furness, Cumbria LA20 6HH
Tel: 01229 716413
e-mail: fletcher@ukf.net
website: www.lakeslate.co.uk

The **Broughton Craft Shop** provides the opportunity of discovering unique craftsman-made gifts in the heart of one of south Lakeland's most appealing market towns. Owner John Fletcher is a craftsman himself and only selects items with exceptional character, integrity and originality. He seeks out talented sculptors, potters and artists from all over the country – and adds his own range of beautiful handmade Lakeslate jewellery. "Think of the colours and textures of the Lake District," he says, "and one of its most enduring is that of slate – the beautiful grey-green rock which has been hewn for centuries."

Handworking different shades of slate from Elterwater, Kirkstone, Broughton and beyond, John creates the most delicate and beguiling jewellery. Some pieces remain elegantly simple and unadorned; others are decorated with delicate traceries of silver inlay which provide a bright contrast to the smooth darkness of the stone, and add a grace which brings true artistry to the extensive range of Lakeslate earrings, brooches and pendants. And if you have a special design in mind, John is happy to discuss individual commissions. The Craft Shop is open from 9.30am to 5.30pm, Tuesday to Saturday, but please phone if you are making a special journey.

stones and two outlying 'portal' or gateway stones.

About three miles north of the town, the peaceful hamlet of **Broughton Mills** will attract followers of the Coleridge Trail. During the course of his famous 'circumcursion' of Lakeland in August 1802, the poet stopped to refresh himself at the Blacksmith's Arms where he "Dined on Oatcake and Cheese, with a pint of Ale, and two glasses of Rum and water sweetened with preserved Gooseberries". The inn, built in 1748, is still there and barely changed since Coleridge's visit.

CONISTON AND SOUTHWEST CUMBRIA

Three distinct areas lie within the southwest quarter of Cumbria. The enchanting scenery around Coniston Water and its environs is very much on the tourist trail, and also has strong literary connections. John Ruskin, the 19th century author, artist, and critic made his home at Brantwood on the shore of Coniston and the lake is also the setting for many of the adventures recounted in *Swallows and Amazons* as told by Arthur Ransome. Wordsworth went to school in Hawkshead where the desk he defaced with his name can still be seen. But probably the most popular of Coniston's literary denizens is Beatrix Potter, who, after holidaying at Near Sawrey as a child, later bought a house at Hill Top as well as many acres of farms which she bequeathed to the National Trust. Further west is Cumbria's 'Empty Quarter', a vast terrain of magnificent mountains and desolate fells beloved of climbers and walkers. England's highest mountain, Scafell Pike, rises here; the country's deepest lake, Wast Water, sinks to a depth of some 200 feet and is

surrounded by sheer cliffs soaring up to 2,000 feet, and the village of Wasdale Head claims to have the smallest church in England.

Bordering this untamed landscape is the narrow coastal strip, stretching from Whitehaven down to Millom, which has its own identity as well as a quiet charm. The coastline is dominated by small 18th and 19th century iron mining communities set between the romantic outline of the Lakeland fells and the grey-blue waters of the Irish Sea.

CONISTON

Beatrix Potter, John Ruskin, Arthur Ransome, Sir Donald Campbell - all of them have strong connections with **Coniston Water**, the third largest and one of the most beautiful of the central Cumbrian lakes. Beatrix Potter lived at Sawrey near Lake Windermere but she also owned the vast **Monk Coniston** estate at the head of Coniston Water. On her death, she bequeathed it to the National Trust, a body she had helped to establish and to which she devoted much of her time and fortune.

Ruskin came to Coniston in 1872, moving into a house he had never seen. Brantwood, on the eastern side of the lake, is open to the public and enjoys superb views across the water to the great crumpled hill of the **Old Man of Coniston**, 800 metres high. From its summit there are even more extensive vistas over Scotland, the Isle of Man, and on a clear day as far as Snowdonia.

Arthur Ransome's *Swallows and Amazons* has delighted generations with its tales of children's adventures set in and around the Lake District. As a child he spent his summer holidays near Nibthwaite at the southern end of the lake and recalled that he was always "half-drowned in tears" when he had to leave. Later he bought a house overlooking Coniston Water and many locations in his books can be recognised today.

Coniston Water

Sir Donald Campbell's associations with the lake were both glorious and tragic. In 1955 he broke the world water speed record here; 12 years later, when he was attempting to beat his own record, his boat, **Bluebird**, struck a log while travelling at 320mph. In March 2001 his widow was present as the tailfin of the boat was at last hauled up to the surface. For 34 years the 15 feet rear section had lain on a bed of silt, 140 feet down and right in the middle of the lake. Plans are still under way for the boat to be restored and placed on display at the Ruskin Museum, but it could take some time. Sir Donald's body was later recovered and was buried on September 12th 2001 in the village cemetery - an event that was comparatively little covered by the media, who were obviously more concerned with the tragic events in New

York and Washington the day before.

Nowadays, boats on Coniston Water are restricted to a 10mph limit, which is an ideal speed if you're travelling in the wonderful old steamship, the **Gondola**. So called because of its high prow which enabled it to come in close to shore to pick up passengers, *Gondola* was commissioned by Sir James Ramsden, General Manager of the Furness Railway Company and first Mayor of Barrow, and was launched on Coniston Water in 1859. She retired in 1936, but found a new career as a houseboat in 1945. Abandoned after a

RUSKIN MUSEUM

Coniston, Cumbria LA21 8DU
Tel: 015394 41164   Fax: 015394 41132
website: www.ruskinmuseum.com

The Ruskin Museum tells the Story of Coniston. From the dynamic
geological history to 300 years of colourful but raw excavation in the
old coppermines. Guided walks are available on preset dates. From the
inspirational art work (including originals plus sketches on computer) and heart warming philosophies
of John Ruskin, to the dramatic, suspense-filled saga of Donald Campbell's record breaking attempts on
Coniston Water (poignant Powerpoint display of photos, including K7s recovery in 2001, plus video of
the fatal crash and memorabilia) the heritage of this unique area offers something for everyone.

storm in the 1960s, she was saved by a
group of National Trust enthusiasts and
restored and rebuilt by Vickers
Shipbuilding. She was relaunched in
1980. Up to 86 passengers can now
travel in opulent comfort on her
regular trips around the lake. Coniston
Launch also offers lake cruises in its
two timber launches, and at the
boating centre craft of every kind are
available to rent.

Coniston village was once an
important copper mining centre and it
was from the Old Man of Coniston and
some of the surrounding hills that
copper was extracted. Mined from the
days of the Romans, the industry's
heyday in Coniston was in the 18th and
19th centuries but, with the discovery of
more accessible deposits, the industry
went into decline and the village
returned to pre-boom peacefulness. At
2,631 feet, the Old Man of Coniston is a

considerable climb but many make the
effort and the summit can be bustling
with fell walkers enjoying the glorious
views.

Coniston's most famous inhabitant
was John Ruskin, the 19th century
author, artist, critic, social commentator
and one of the first conservationists. He
lies buried in Coniston churchyard and
the **Ruskin Museum** nearby contains
many of his studies, pictures, letters,
photographs and personal belongings, as
well as his collection of geological
specimens. Here, too, is his funeral pall
made of Ruskin lace embroidered with
wild flowers. The lace was so called
because Ruskin had encouraged the
revival of flax hand-spinning in the area.
Lace pieces made to his own designs and
based on the sumptuous ruffs worn by
sitters in portraits by Titian, Tintoretto
and Veronese were attached to plain
linen to make decorative cushions, table

BRANTWOOD

Coniston, Cumbria LA21 8AD
Tel: 015394 41396   Fax: 015394 41263
website: www.brantwood.org.uk

Brantwood is the most beautifully situated house in the Lake District
and enjoys the finest lake and mountain views in England. The home
of John Ruskin from 1872 until his death in 1900, Brantwood became
one of the greatest literary and artistic centres in Europe. Tolstoy, Mahatma Gandhi, Marcel Proust
and Frank Lloyd Wright can all be numbered amongst Ruskin's disciples. The house is filled with
Ruskin's drawings and watercolours, together with much of his original furniture, books and personal
items. There is also an extensive programme of events at Brantwood, including concerts and exhibitions.

POPPI RED

The Pamper Emporium in the Heart of the Lake District
Main Street, Hawkshead, Cumbria LA22 0NT
Tel: 015394 36434 website: www.poppi-red.6.uk

Wander gently into the picturesque Lakeland village of Hawkshead, on the quieter western shore of Lake Windermere, (and you can wander because the centre is blissfully traffic-free) and one of the first welcoming sights to greet you is Poppi Red – a fantastic display of pink and scarlet among the whitewashed cottages, slate roofs and cobbled streets of the village.

You are drawn in siren-like by the fantastic colours, seductive sounds of jazz swing and the enticing smell of freshly ground coffee. Poppi Red is a 'pamper emporium' of pottery, jewellery, scarves, knitwear, cushions, unusual books and cards... unique ideas to delight your friends, family, loved ones and of course, yourself. There is not just 'something' for everyone, there is an entire hamper full. *Cupcakes & Cartwheel* pottery from the States with its ornate shapes and acid drop hues that's gone down a wow in New York; from Italy, intricate silk purses and ruby red lamps with feather-trimmed shades and, from Paris, *Mathilde M*, a new range of toiletries, presented on an old rustic table rescued from the Hawkshead bonfire.

Often in the shop, you'll be met by Kim Merrick, proprietor, buyer, inspiration behind Poppi Red. Bright, bubbly, incredibly hospitable, with an engaging sense of fun and frivolity - if ever a business were created in its founder's image, this is it.

Poppi Red offers a wonderfully, old fashioned shopping experience, with cheery staff all from the village, service as it used to be and a beautifully laid out shop. To some it's a little bit of New England, to others it has a shabby chic Frenchness.

Everyone agrees that the displays are fabulous. You can meander around and see something different every time, meanwhile partners can relax in the café with a drink, and some of the scrumptious cakes and delicacies, which are baked at home in a local Lakeland farmhouse. The café is also fully licensed, so you can enjoy a warming cup of glühwein in winter and a refreshing Pimms in summer too.

Prices are as attractive as the gifts, which is why no one ever leaves empty handed. And every purchase is gift-wrapped, using bright red crepe paper and jet-black raffia.

Open all year 7 days per week 9am-6pm

covers and bedspreads - many of these are on display.

From the jetty at Coniston, a short ferry trip takes visitors to John Ruskin's home, **Brantwood** which occupies a beautiful setting on the eastern shores of Coniston Water. It was his home from 1872 until his death in 1900. When he arrived for the first time he described the house, which he had bought for £1,500 without ever seeing it, as "a mere shed". He spent the next 20 years extending the house, by adding another 12 rooms, and laying out the gardens. The view from the Turret Room he had built was, Ruskin declared, "the best in all England". Sadly, Ruskin's later years were blighted by mental illness: "He was," said a biographer, "at times quite mad".

Visitors today can wander around rooms filled with Ruskin's watercolours, paintings by Turner (who was one of his heroes), see his study which is lined with wallpaper he designed himself, and watch a 20-minute video which provides a useful introduction to his life and works. There's also a well-stocked bookshop, a craft shop, an excellent tea room, restaurant and 250 acres of grounds where there are well-marked nature trails and where a theatre season is held during the summer.

AROUND CONISTON

GRIZEDALE
3 miles SE of Coniston off the B5285

The village lies at the heart of the 9,000-acre **Grizedale Forest** which was acquired by the Forestry Commission in 1934 and is famous for its theatre and sculpture. The Commission's original intention of chiefly cultivating the forest for its timber met with much resistance and, over the years, many pathways have been opened and a variety of recreational activities have been encouraged. The Visitor Centre vividly illustrates the story of the forest as well as showing how the combination of wildlife, recreation, and commercial timbering can work together hand in hand. The forest, too, is famously the home of some 80 tree sculptures commissioned since 1977.

HAWKSHEAD
3 miles E of Coniston on the B5285

There are more Beatrix Potter connections in the enchanting little village of Hawkshead. Her solicitor husband, William Heelis, worked from an office in the Main Street here and this has now been transformed into **The Beatrix Potter Gallery**. The gallery features an exhibition of her original drawings and illustrations alongside details of the author's life.

Hawkshead has specific Wordsworth connections, too. **Hawkshead Grammar School** was founded in 1585 by Edwin Sandys, Archbishop of York, and between 1779 and 1787 the young William Wordsworth was a star pupil. The earliest of his surviving poems was written to celebrate the school's 200th year. The school is open from Easter to September and visitors can inspect the classrooms during the summer holidays, see the desk where William carved his name and have a look around the headmaster's study. Ann Tyson's Cottage, where Wordsworth lodged while he attended the school, has also survived. It stands in Wordsworth Street and is now a guest house.

Situated at the head of **Esthwaite Water**, enjoying glorious views of Coniston Old Man and Helvellyn, Hawkshead is a delightful village of narrow cobbled lanes with a pedestrianised main square dominated by the Market House, or Shambles, and another square linked to it by little

Hawkshead

Distance:	5.0 mile (8.0 kilometres)
Typical time:	180 mins
Height gain:	50 metres
Map:	Explorer OL 7
Walk:	ww.walkingworld.com ID:3277
Contributor:	Mark & Tracey Douglas

Access Information:

Hawkshead is 6 miles south west of Ambleside. Buses are either Stagecoach 505 Windermere-Coniston or the Cross Lakes Shuttle from Bowness, April-Oct. Tel: 015394 45161 for details. There is a large pay and display car park in the centre of Hawkshead.

Description:

Hawkshead is one of the most beautiful small villages in the Lakes. An ancient township that has flourished since Norse times and belonged to Furness Abbey until the 12th Century. Much loved by Beatrix Potter and William Wordsworth, and home to the Beatrix Potter Gallery, The Grammar School where Wordsworth was educated and home to the fashion label which bears the village name. Hawkshead is surrounded by beautiful scenery, much of which is owned by the National Trust. Cars are even banned from the village centre (cars park in the large car park where the walk starts)

This pleasant , undulating walk starts in the village centre and heads across pastureland, woodland and meadow, skirting Blelham Tarn to reach the National Trust Property of Wray Castle on the banks of Windermere and returning over open farmland.

Additional Information

There are numerous pubs, shops, tearooms etc in Hawkshead including the Hawkshead store home of the famous high street label. This store is opposite the car park at the start of the walk.Wray Castle is owned by the National Trust The grounds are open to the public, and are well worth visiting for the sake of the

specimen trees - wellingtonia, redwood, gingkoa, weeping lime and varieties of beech. There is a mulberry tree planted by William Wordsworth in 1845. Watbarrow Wood is the wooded bank between the castle and the lake, and has several pleasant paths leading through it to the water's edge. There are spectacular views across Windermere. The castle is not currently open to the public.

Features:

Hills or Fells, Mountains, Lake/Loch, Pub, Toilets, Museum, Church, Castle, National Trust/NTS, Wildlife, Birds, Flowers, Great Views, Butterflies, Cafe, Gift Shop, Food Shop, Good for Kids, Industrial Archaeology, Mostly Flat, Public Transport, Nature Trail, Restaurant, Tea Shop

Walk Directions:

1 From the carpark turn right out onto North Lonsdale Road, and then turn left, as the road bears left cross the road and turn right down a track, with a high wall on your right, turning right down a track to reach a small footbridge. Cross the footbridge and turn left following the stream and then almost immediately cut across the field to reach a kissing gate. Continue through the fields following the Footpath waymarks (taking the left hand path at a finger post) to reach a narrow lane. Turn left along the lane looking for a kissing gate on your right.

2 Go through the kissing gate and continue straight ahead up the field on a stony path with the fence on your right. Pass through a couple of gates/ stiles to reach a double gate at a metalled public road at Loanthwaite Farm.

3 Pass through the gate onto the metalled road and turn left. Continue through the farm buildings and after the house turn right into a narrow lane/ bridleway.

4 Look out for a stile almost immediately on your left and cross the field and pasture into woodland, heading by a tall marker/ gatepost. Keep ahead in the same direction to reach the gate at the rear of the Outgate Inn.

5 Pass through the gate and at the main road turn right past the front of the Inn and continue along the road for 300m ignoring the first footpath sign to reach a bridleway on your right.

6 Head down the bridleway, through woodland to reach Blelham Tarn within 1km. Keep straight ahead with the tarn on your right to eventually reach on old iron gate at a public road.

7 For safety, a permissive path has been created down the field to avoid the road. Turn right with the fence on your left to reach a gate, and then turn right down the road and keep straight ahead (ignoring the road to the left signpost Low Wray Campsite). The road will gently ascend and passes the main gate of Wray Castle (visit the gardens if open, and you have time). Keep ahead on the road past the lodge, church and the old vicarage and as the road descends look out for a gate on the right.

8 Go through the gate and follow the path with a hedge on your left down to cross a stone footbridge and through the trees into a field where the path follows a fenceline on your left. Rising gently the path becomes a clear farm track at a gate, follow the farm

track to reach Hole House. Pass through the houses and buildings and on reaching the road keep straight ahead ignoring the roads on your left and right. Look out for a turn off down to the right within 200m.

9 Heading right down the lane into High Tock How Farm/ B & B turning left before reaching the buildings and follow the fence and waymarkings to a gate on the hilltop. Pass through the gate and turn left (signposted Loanthwaite and Hawkshead) keeping in the same general direction before crossing the field diagonally down to a gate in the far corner. Passing through the gate heading straight ahead, before turning left across the field to a gate in front of a line of trees. Pass through the gate and straight ahead with the line of trees on your right through another two gates to reach the gate at the bridleway at Waymark 6.

10 Pass through the gate onto the road and turn left through the farm buildings at Loanthwaite and retrace your initial steps back to Hawkshead.

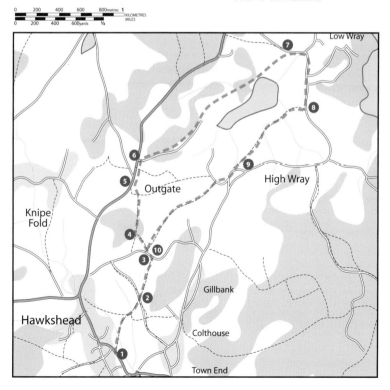

snickets and arched alleyways which invite exploration. The poet Norman Nicholson observed that, "The whole village could be fitted into the boundaries of a large agricultural show; yet it contains enough corners, angles, alleys and entries to keep the eye happy for hours."

The **Church of St Michael & All Angels**, with its massive 15ᵗʰ century tower, seems rather grand for the village but it too was built at a time when Hawkshead was a wealthy town. Inside, there are some remarkable wall paintings from the late 1600s and also look out for the "Buried in Woolen" affidavit near the vestry door. In 1666 the Government had decreed that corpses must not be buried in shrouds made from "flaxe, hempe, silke or hair, or other than what is made of sheeps wool onely". The idea was to help maintain the local woollen industry and this was one way of ensuring that even the dead got to help out. The church is the focal point of the annual Lake District Summer Music Festival and a popular venue for concerts and recitals. In the churchyard is a war memorial erected in 1919 and modelled on the ancient runic cross at Gosforth.

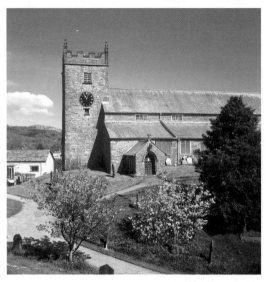

Hawkshead Church

Some lovely walks lead from Hawkshead to **Roger Ground** and Esthwaite Water, possibly the least frequented of the Lakes, and also to the nearby hamlet of **Colthouse** where there's an early Quaker Meeting House built around 1690. Esthwaite Water was much loved by Wordsworth, as he shows in *The Prelude*:

My morning walks were early; oft before the hours of school
I travelled round our little lake, five miles
Of pleasant wandering. Happy time!

THE OLD SCHOOL HOUSE

Hawkshead, Cumbria LA22 0NT
Tel: 015394 36403
e-mail: oldschoolhousehawkshead@fsmail.net

Dating back to around 1710, **The Old School House** stands in its own grounds in a quiet corner of beautiful Hawkshead, just 200 yards from the bustling village centre. It's run by local couple Eileen and Peter Johnston and their family who offer genuine Lakeland hospitality and a wealth of local knowledge as well as comfortable accommodation and delicious food. Both en suite and standard rooms are available, all of them spacious and well-appointed, and tastefully decorated in a style in character with the house. An important amenity in a village not built for the motor car is the ample off road private parking.

BORWICK LODGE

Outgate, Hawkshead, Ambleside,
Cumbria LA22 0PU
Tel: 015394 36332
e-mail: info@borwicklodge.com
website: www.borwicklodge.com

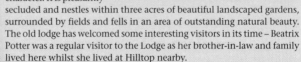

Set right in the heart of the Lake District, in a delightful and tranquil setting, **Borwick Lodge** is a rather special 17th century country residence of charm and

character. It is pleasantly secluded and nestles within three acres of beautiful landscaped gardens, surrounded by fields and fells in an area of outstanding natural beauty. The old lodge has welcomed some interesting visitors in its time – Beatrix Potter was a regular visitor to the Lodge as her brother-in-law and family lived here whilst she lived at Hilltop nearby.

Although extensively modernised, Borwick Lodge is furnished to the highest standard whilst retaining its 'olde worlde' friendly atmosphere. It has a four-Diamonds Silver Award from the English Tourism Council and the tastefully decorated en suite bedrooms have complimentary tea and coffee making facilities, colour TV, radio and hair dryer. There are also some beautifully appointed king-size four-poster rooms for special occasions. Breakfast is served in the elegant dining room with a choice of a full English or Continental breakfast based on fresh, home-made local produce. Please note that Borwick Lodge is a strictly non-smoking establishment.

WEST VALE COUNTRY HOUSE & RESTAURANT

Far Sawrey, Hawkshead, Ambleside, Cumbria LA22 0LQ
Tel: 015394 42817 Fax: 015394 45302
e-mail: enquiries@westvalecountryhouse.co.uk
website: www.westvalecountryhouse.co.uk

West Vale Country House & Restaurant commands a superb position in the heart of the Lake District National Park, on the edge of the village of Far Sawrey and overlooking Grizedale Forest and the Old Man of Coniston. This is a truly idyllic little retreat where you really can "escape from it all" and leave your

cares behind. On arrival, you will find a complimentary decanter of sherry awaiting you in your room, a courteous and welcoming gesture that is typical of this outstanding hotel. No wonder it has received a shower of awards, including five-Diamond ratings from the English Tourism Council, the RAC and the AA, and a five-Diamond Gold award from Visit Britain.

It has also been awarded two rosettes for its cuisine. This can be sampled in the elegant restaurant where a fine menu created with imagination and flair is served with style and courtesy. The accommodation at West Vale is equally impressive with all the en suite bedrooms tastefully and individually designed with guests' comfort in mind. West Vale is a great place to relax but if you are feeling active, there are facilities for riding, sailing, cruising, biking and climbing all within easy reach.

BUCKLE YEAT

Near Sawrey, Hawkshead, Ambleside, Cumbria LA22 0LF
Tel: 015394 36446
e-mail: info@buckle-yeat.co.uk
website: www.buckle-yeat.co.uk

The children's writer, Beatrix Potter's connections with the Lake District are well known and her former home, Hill Top Farm, is now open to visitors. It stands almost next door to **Buckle Yeat**, a charming 17th century Lakeland cottage which is now the home of Robert and Helen Kirby who welcome bed & breakfast guests to their delightful house. It has an oak-beamed lounge with a warming log fire, antique furniture and plenty of comfortable armchairs – a great place to relax after a long day's walking and to makes plans for the next day.

Breakfast is served in the spacious dining room and begins with fresh baked bread rolls and a selection of cereals, yoghurts, fresh fruit and oatmeal porridge. This is followed by a full English breakfast prepared to order – the Kirbys cater for all diets. During the day, the dining room doubles as a tea room serving traditional cream teas and home-made cakes. Accommodation at Buckle Yeat comprises double or twin-bedded rooms, all individually furnished and tastefully decorated. All are en suite and provided with colour TV, hairdryer and hospitality tray. Please note that Buckle Yeat is non-smoking.

NEAR SAWREY

4 miles E of Coniston on the B5285

After holidaying here in 1896, the authoress Beatrix Potter fell in love with the place and, with the royalties from her first book, *The Tale of Peter Rabbit*, she purchased **Hill Top** in 1905. After her marriage in 1913 to a local solicitor, she actually lived in another house in the village and used the charming 17th century cottage as her study.

Oddly, she wrote very little after the marriage, spending most of her time dealing with the management of the farms she had bought in the area.

Following Beatrix Potter's death in 1943, the house and the land she had bought on the surrounding fells became the property of the National Trust and, in accordance with her will, Hill Top has remained exactly as she would have known it. One of the most popular Lakeland attractions, Hill Top is full of Beatrix Potter memorabilia, including some of her original drawings. The house is very small, so it is best avoided at peak holiday times. **Tarn Hows**, part of the 4,000-acre Monk Coniston estate bought and sold on to the National Trust, was created to resemble a Swiss lake and is very rich in flora and fauna - it has been designated a Site of Special Scientific Interest.

GREAT LANGDALE

9 miles N of Coniston on the B5343

One of the most dramatic of the Lake District waterfalls is **Dungeon Ghyll**, which tumbles 60 feet down the fellside. The 'dungeon' is actually a natural cave. Nearby is the well-known Old Dungeon Ghyll Hotel, which makes an excellent starting point for walks in this spectacularly scenic area where the famous peaks of Crinkle Crags, Bowfell

WHEELWRIGHTS LAKE DISTRICT HOLIDAY COTTAGES

Elterwater, nr Ambleside,
Cumbria LA22 9HS
Tel: 015394 38306
Fax: 015394 37618
e-mail: enquiries@wheelwrights.com
website: www.wheelwrights.com

For more than a quarter of a century Wheelwrights has been letting some of the most sought after cottages in the heart of the beautiful Lake District National Park. From the comfort of one of their cottages set amidst stunning scenery, you will be able to take advantage of a whole host of activities such as walking, climbing, boating, fishing, horse riding, steam railways, theatres, cinemas, exhibitions, visitor centres, shopping...... not forgetting the wonderful range of

eating places to satisfy all appetites!

You may want a small cosy cottage or one large enough for a special family gathering, you may want a romantic hideaway or just a comfortable base in which to relax after an action packed day. Whatever your requirements, you will be able to find what you are looking for in Wheelwrights' portfolio of properties.

As a small company, they pride themselves on their personal service and the detailed knowledge their staff have of all their cottages, enabling them to give helpful advice in response to any special requirements as well as the ability to advise on the right cottage for all occasions.

If, after checking their website or brochure you would like more detailed information on any property, please do not hesitate to call and discuss individual requirements.

and the Langdale Pikes provide some serious challenges for hikers and ramblers.

SEATHWAITE
5 miles W of Coniston off the A593

A mere five miles or so from Coniston as the crow flies, by road Seathwaite is nearly three times as far. It stands in one of the Lake District's most tranquil and least known valleys, **Dunnerdale**. Little has changed here since the days when William Wordsworth, who knew the area as Duddon Valley, captured its natural beauty in a sequence of sonnets. In his poem *The Excursion*, he wrote about the Rev Robert Walker, the curate of Seathwaite. 'Wonderful Walker' as Wordsworth referred to him, served the church here for some 67 years though he also filled various other jobs such as farm labourer and nurse as well as spinning wool and making his own clothes. Fell walkers and hikers who prefer to escape the masses will delight not only in the solitude of this glorious valley but also in the wide variety of plant, animal, and birdlife that have made this haven their home.

HARDKNOTT PASS
5 miles W of Coniston off the A593

Surrounded by the fell of the same name, this pass is one of the most treacherous in the Lake District yet it was used by the Romans for the road between their forts at Ambleside (Galava) and Ravenglass (Glannaventa). Of the remains of Roman occupation, **Hardknott Fort** on a shoulder of the fell, overlooking the Esk Valley, is the most substantial and also provides some of the grandest views in the whole of the Lake District.

BOOT
8 miles W of Coniston off the A595

Lying at the eastern end of the **Ravenglass and Eskdale Railway**, this is a wonderful place to visit whether arriving by train or car. A gentle walk from the station at Eskdale brings you to this delightful village with its pub, post office, museum, waterfall and nearby St Catherine's Church in its lovely secluded riverside setting.

ESKDALE GREEN
10 miles W of Coniston off the A595

One of the few settlements in this beautiful and unspoiled valley, the village lies on the route of the Ravenglass and Eskdale Railway. Further up the valley lies a group of buildings that make up Eskdale Mill where cereals have been ground since 1578, when it is recorded that the brothers Henry and Robert Vicars were the tenants, paying an annual rent of eight shillings (40p). The original machinery for grinding oatmeal is in full working order and operated daily.

Hardknott Fort

RAVENGLASS

Lying as it does at the estuary of three rivers - the Esk, the Mite, and the Irt - as well as enjoying a sheltered position, it is not surprising that Ravenglass was an important port from prehistoric times. The Romans built a naval base here around AD78, which served as a supply point for the military zone around Hadrian's Wall. They also constructed a fort, **Glannaventra**, on the cliffs above the town, which was home to around 1,000 soldiers. Little remains of Glannaventra except for the impressively preserved walls of the Bath House. Almost 12 feet high, these walls are believed to be the highest Roman remains in the country.

One of the town's major attractions is the 15-inch narrow gauge **Ravenglass and Eskdale Railway** which runs for seven miles up the lovely Mite and Esk River valleys. Better known to locals as "La'al Ratty", it was built in 1875 to transport ore and quarried stone from the Eskdale Valley and opened the following year for passenger traffic. Since then the railway has survived several threats of extinction. The most serious occurred at the end of the 1950s when the closure of the Eskdale granite quarries wiped out the railway's freight traffic at a stroke. However, at the auction for the railway in 1960 a band of enthusiasts outbid the scrap dealers and formed a company to keep the little railway running.

Today, the company operates 12 locomotives, both steam and diesel, and 300,000 people a year come from all over the world to ride on what has been described as 'the most beautiful train journey in England'. There are several stops along the journey and at both termini there is a café and a souvenir shop. At Ravenglass Station there is also a museum which brings to life the history of this remarkable line and the important part it has played in the life of Eskdale.

A mile or so east of Ravenglass stands **Muncaster Castle** which has been in the ownership of the Pennington family since 1208. In 1464 the Penningtons gave shelter to King Henry VI after his defeat at the Battle of Hexham. On his departure Henry presented them with his enamelled glass drinking bowl, saying that as long as it remained unbroken the Penningtons would survive and thrive at

Ravenglass and Eskdale Railway

MUNCASTER CASTLE

Ravenglass, Cumbria CA18 1RQ
Tel: 01229 717614 Fax: 01229 717010
e-mail: info@muncaster.co.uk
website: www.muncaster.co.uk

Muncaster Castle is an impressive castellated mansion which has been owned by the Pennington family since 1208. Back in 1464 the Penningtons gave shelter to King Henry VI after his defeat at the Battle of Hexham. On his departure Henry presented them with his enamelled glass drinking bowl saying that as long as it remained unbroken the Penningtons would live and thrive at Muncaster. It remains intact and the Penningtons are indeed still here. A tour introduces visitors to the many Muncaster treasures (including tapestry, silver, and porcelain collections), the stunning Great Hall, Salvin's octagonal library and the barrel ceiling in the drawing room.

Muncaster is also famous for its gardens and, in particular, the rhododendrons, azaleas, and camellias which are best viewed between March and June. The woodland gardens themselves cover some 77 acres and, as well as the beauty of the vegetation, there are some splendid views over the Lakeland fells. These extensive grounds also contain a fascinating Owl Centre which is home to more than 180 birds of 50 different species. Other attractions include a very well-equipped children's play area with an aerial runway, scramble net and fireman's pole; a nature trail and orienteering course, plant centre, gift shop and licensed café. The gardens and owl centre are open daily throughout the year; the castle is open each afternoon from the end of March to the end of October (closed Saturday).

Muncaster. Apart from the many treasures, the stunning Great Hall, Salvin's octagonal library and the barrel ceiling in the drawing room, Muncaster is also famous for its gardens. The collection of rhododendrons is one of the finest in Europe, gathered primarily from plant-hunting expeditions to Nepal in the 1920s, and there are also fine azaleas, hydrangeas and camellias as well as many unusual trees. For many visitors the chief attraction is the **World Owl Centre**, where many endangered owl species are bred. Snowy owls have become great favourites on the back of the Harry Potter craze, and many visitors have enquired about keeping them as pets. The staff at the Centre have to point out that the snowy owl is a mighty predator with a five feet wingspan. Mighty as he is, he is not the mightiest of the owls at the Centre: that honour goes to the Eurasian eagle owl, whose

full splendour can be seen at the daily demonstrations. Muncaster's latest attraction is the Meadow Vole Maze (these little creatures are the staple diet of barn owls, and visitors can find out what it's like to be a vole on the run from a hungry owl).

Originally part of the Muncaster Castle Estate, **Muncaster Water Mill** can be traced back to 1455, though it is thought that this site may be Roman. The situation is certainly idyllic, with the mill race still turning the huge wooden water wheel and the Ravenglass and Eskdale Railway running alongside. In November 1996, Pam and Ernie Priestley came to the mill and Ernie put his years of engineering experience to use as the miller. The mill is open every day from Easter to the end of October, working just as it has done for hundreds of years. Visitors can see the machinery in action, and also enjoy some delicious refreshments in the 17th century byre tea rooms. Naturally, the organic flour ground here is used in all the cakes, breads, and scones, and the flour is also on sale.

AROUND RAVENGLASS

BOOTLE
7 miles S of Ravenglass on the A595

This ancient village is particularly picturesque and quaint. The river Annas flows beside the main road and then dives under the village on its way to the sea. High up on **Bootle Fell**, to the southeast of the village, lies one of the best stone circles in Cumbria. Over the years, many of the 51 stones that make up the **Swinside Stone Circle** have fallen over. When it was originally constructed and all the stones were upright, it is likely, as they were also close together, that the circle was used as an enclosure.

SILECROFT
10 miles S of Ravenglass off the A595

Perhaps of all the villages in this coastal region of the National Park, Silecroft is the perfect example. Just a short walk from the heart of the village is the beach, which extends as far as the eye can see. On the horizon lies the distant outline of the Isle of Man. There is also a Site of Special Scientific Interest close by, a tract of coastal scrubland which provides the perfect habitat for the rare Natterjack toad.

MILLOM
13 miles S of Ravenglass on the A5093

This small and peaceful town stands at the mouth of the River Duddon with the imposing **Black Combe Fell** providing a dramatic backdrop. Originally called Holborn Hill, the present day name was taken from nearby **Millom Castle** which is now a private, working farm. Like many neighbouring towns and villages in Furness, Millom was a small fishing village before it too grew with the development of the local iron industry. **Millom Folk Museum** tells the story of the town's growth and also has a permanent memorial to Norman Nicholson (1914-1987) who is generally regarded as the best writer on Lakeland life and customs since Wordsworth himself. Nicholson's book *Provincial Pleasures* records his affectionate memories of Millom, the town where he spent all his life. Other displays include a full-scale reproduction of a drift and cage from nearby Hodbarrow mine. South of Millom, at Haverigg, is the **RAF Millom Museum** situated in the former Officers Mess. Visitors to the site will find a fascinating collection of over 2,000 photographs of the wartime activities of the RAF in the area, various artefacts connected with the period and a number of items recovered from local crash sites. The museum also has a fine collection of aero engines including a Rolls Royce Merlin, a Westland Whirlwind helicopter, the cockpit section of a De Havilland Vampire jet trainer and an example of the HM14 or Flying Flea. The Duddon Estuary is an important site for wildlife, and the RSPB site at **Hodbarrow** is home not only to birds but to many kinds of flora and fauna. **Hodbarrow Beacon**, which still stands, was built in 1879 as a lighthouse to assist vessels taking iron ore from the mines to destinations in Europe.

DRIGG
2 miles N of Ravenglass on the B5343

The main attractions here are the sand dunes and the fine views across to the Lakeland mountains and fells. There is an important nature reserve, **Drigg Dunes**, on the salt marshes that border the River

CUMBRIAN LODGE

Gosforth Road, Seascale, Cumbria CA20 1JG
Tel: 019467 27309 Fax: 019467 27158
e-mail: cumbrianlodge@btconnect.com
website: www.cumbrianlodge.com

Offering the ultimate in luxury, the **Cumbrian Lodge** has had much thought put into its development. When international banker David Morgan decided to leave the world of corporate finance, he wanted to create an up-scale fine-dining restaurant with rooms. Having spent three nights a week in hotels in his former career, he had identified the features that he valued and, likewise, those aspects of hotels that were annoying.

David was attracted to Lakeland because of its natural beauty but also because from his late teens to mid-twenties, he would travel to Wasdale each weekend to climb. He still enjoys a pint in the area's excellent pubs but felt that the region lacked a high quality boutique-style hotel with a warm relaxed atmosphere, attentive service and good-value fine food and wines.

After buying Cumbrian Lodge (formerly known as Victoria Villa Hotel and Egloff's Eating House) David selected local firms to carry out a complete refurbishment and landscaping of the grounds. The hotel now has six guest bedrooms, all beautifully decorated in relaxing natural tones and with extravagant extras such as the flat screen TVs and the Siberian goose down duvets dressed in finest quality high threadcount Egyptian cotton. The bathrooms are provided with luxurious thick ultra-soft towels and fine complimentary toiletries from The White Company.

The hotel's bar has been skilfully crafted in maple, while the pale blue walls and original abstract art work continue the understated colour theme. Seating is divided between bespoke built-in benches covered in stylish faux suede and eye-catching Bombo tables and bar stools.

The restaurant mirrors the bar's fresh colour scheme and provides a perfect setting in which to enjoy Head Chef Richard Hickson's superb cuisine. Amongst his signature dishes, loved by locals and visitors alike, is geschetzeltes schweinefleisch – thinly sliced pork fillets sautéed in butter with onions, mushrooms, a pinch of paprika, a squeeze of lemon juice, a splash of white wine and fresh cream, served with rösti and fresh vegetables. To complement cuisine of this high order, David has carefully selected a range of wines representing good value for money, whether it be the easy-drinking house Chardonnay or Cabernet Sauvignon, or a fine Bordeaux.

Irt but - take note, adders are common here. The reserve is home to Europe's largest colony of black-headed gulls.

SEASCALE
4 miles N of Ravenglass on the B5343

One of the most popular seaside villages in Cumbria, Seascale enhanced its resort status in 2000 by restoring the **Victorian Wooden Jetty** to mark Millennium Year. Stretching out into the Irish Sea, it is the focal point for fishing, beach casting, wind surfing and water-skiing, and also provides the starting point for many walks, including the Cumbrian Coastal Way which passes along the foreshore. Two Victorian buildings stand out: the **Water Tower**, medieval in style and with a conical roof, and the old **Engine Shed** which is now a multi-purpose Sports Hall. A couple of miles north of the village is the **Sellafield Visitors Centre** where you can get switched on to the debate about electricity and nuclear power through a range of interesting exhibits, interactive features and presentations.

GOSFORTH
5 miles N of Ravenglass on the A595

On the edge of this picturesque village, in the graveyard of **St Mary's Church**, stands the tallest ancient cross in England. Fifteen feet high, the **Viking Cross** towers above the huddled gravestones in the peaceful churchyard. Carved from red sandstone and clearly influenced by both Christian and pagan traditions, the cross depicts the crucifixion, the deeds of Norse gods and Yggdrasil, the World Ash Tree that Norsemen believed supported the universe. The interior of the church also contains some interesting features. There's a **Chinese Bell**, finely decorated with Oriental imagery, which was captured in 1841 at Anunkry, a fort on the River Canton, some delightful carved faces on the chancel arch and a collection of ancient stones the most notable of which dates from Saxon times and depicts the Lamb of God trampling on the serpents of pagan faith.

A major attraction in this appealing village is **Gosforth Pottery**, where Dick and Barbara Wright produce beautifully crafted work and also give pottery lessons.

To the east of Gosforth runs Wasdale, the wildest of the Lake District valleys but easily accessible by road. The road leads to **Wast Water**, which is just three miles long but is the deepest lake in England. The southern shores are dominated by huge screes some 2,000 feet high that plunge abruptly into the lake and they provide an awesome backdrop to this tranquil stretch of water. A lake less like Windermere would be hard to find as there are no motorboats ploughing their way up and down the lake; this is very much the country of walkers and climbers and from here there are many footpaths up to some of the best fells in Cumbria.

Wasdale Head, just to the north of the lake, is a small, close-knit community with an inn that has provided a welcome refuge for walkers and climbers since the mid-1800s. **Wasdale Church** is claimed to be the smallest in England - although this title is hotly disputed by Culbone in Somerset and Dale Abbey in Derbyshire. The church was built in the 14th century and it is hidden away amidst a tiny copse of evergreen trees. Local legend suggests that the roof beams came from a Viking ship and it is certainly true that until late Victorian times the church had only an earth floor and few seats.

As well as the deepest lake and the

COUNTRY CUTS ORGANIC MEATS

Bridge End Farm, Santon Bridge, Holmrook,
Cumbria CA19 1UY
Tel/Fax: 019467 26256
website: www.country-cuts.co.uk

Country Cuts Organic Meats is based at Bridge End Farm, a fully organic farm with Organic Certification UK2. It nestles on the plateau between the Irish Sea and the stunning Wasdale Valley which is part of the beautiful Lake District National Park. It's a unique natural setting of clover enriched meadows through which the River Irt meanders, a landscape unchanged and unspoilt for hundreds of years.

The farm is run by the Phizacklea family who took the decision to follow an organic farming scheme in the light of the mistrust and uncertainties surrounding the production of meat. They wanted to hark back to a gentler and healthier way of life but with the advantage and convenience of modern technology. "Organic farming simply means that no chemicals are used in the production of meat," they say. The grass is fertilised using the animals' own waste products instead of chemical fertilisers. The abundance of clovers in pastureland and natural meadows provide the goodness the animals need to thrive.

The Phizackleas also participate in the Environmentally Sensitive Area Scheme and have recently replanted miles of hedges and re-built dykes so that in the fullness of time they will provide a natural habitat for some of England's unique wildlife and birds. Several ponds have already been created attracting wild fowl of all descriptions including water hens, water rails and even the occasional osprey. The whole combination encourages the return of wildlife of all forms.

The end result of all this is the top quality meat on display at the farm shop which aims to provide the best priced and excellent value organic matured beef, fell crossed lamb and mutton, rare breed pork, from which they make their own delicious sausages, air-dried bacon, hams, gammon and 'farma' ham, burgers and specialities. Or you could try their delicious, organic chicken and turkey, free range geese and ducks, wild venison and game.

The Phizackleas have recently extended the range of products on sale in the farm shop to include tea, coffee, fish, eggs, crisps, biscuits, bread, jams, chutneys, relish, sauces, pasta, rice, cheese, fruit and yoghurt drinks, vegetables and much more.

The Farm Shop and Attic Gift Shop are open daily from 10am-5pm. Nationwide mail order is available via phone/fax, e-mail or website

Wast Water

beautiful Anglican Cross, in excellent condition, that is certainly 1,000 years old. The Bridge Inn here plays host each November to the 'World's Biggest Liar' competition when contestants from all over the country vie in telling the most prodigious porkies.

CALDER BRIDGE
7 miles N of Ravenglass on the A595

From this small, grey, 19th century settlement there is an attractive footpath to **Calder Abbey**. It was founded by monks of Savigny in 1134 but amalgamated with the Cistercians of Furness Abbey after it was ransacked by the Scots a few years later. Following the Dissolution the monastery buildings lapsed slowly into the present-day romantic ruin. To the northeast of the village, the River Calder rises on Caw Fell. **Monk's Bridge**, the oldest packhorse bridge in Cumbria, was built across it for the monks of Calder Abbey.

smallest church, Wasdale also boasts the highest mountain, **Sca Fell Pike** (3,205ft) - and the world's biggest liars. This latter claim goes back to the mid-1800s when Will Ritson, "a reet good fibber", was the publican at the inn. Will enthralled his patrons with tall stories of how he had crossed foxes with eagles to produce flying foxes and had grown turnips so large he could hollow them out to make a comfortable residence. In the same spirit, the 'World's Biggest Liar' Competition takes place every November, usually at the Bridge Inn at Santon Bridge mentioned above.

SANTON BRIDGE
3 miles NE of Ravenglass off the A595

The churchyard of **Irton Church**, reached from Santon Bridge via an unclassified road, offers the visitor not only superb views of the Lakeland fells to the west but also the opportunity to see a

EGREMONT
12 miles N of Ravenglass on the A595

This pretty town is dominated by **Egremont Castle** with walls 20 feet high and an 80 foot tower. It stands high above the town, overlooking the lovely River Ehen to the south and the market place to the north. The castle was built between 1130 and 1140 by William de Meschines on the site of a former Danish fortification. The most complete part still standing is a Norman arch that once guarded the drawbridge entrance. Nearby is an unusual four-sided sundial and the stump of the old market cross dating from the early 13th century.

Egremont's prosperity was based on the good quality of its local red iron ore and jewellery made from it can be bought at the nearby **Florence Mine Heritage Centre**. Visitors to the mine, the last deep working iron ore mine in Europe, can join an underground tour (by prior arrangement) and discover why the miners became known as the Red Men of Cumbria. The museum here also tells the story of the mine, which was worked by the ancient Britons, and there is a re-creation of the conditions that the miners endured at the turn of the 20th century.

In September every year the town celebrates its **Crab Fair**. Held each year on the third Saturday in September, the Fair dates back more than seven centuries - to 1267 in fact, when Henry III granted a Royal Charter for a three-day fair to be held on "the even, the day and the morrow after the Nativity of St. Mary the Virgin". The celebrations include the Parade of the Apple Cart when a wagon loaded with apples is driven along Main Street with men on the back throwing fruit into the crowds. Originally, the throng was pelted with crab apples - hence the name Crab Fair - but these are considered too tart for modern taste so nowadays more palatable varieties are used. The

festivities also feature a greasy pole competition (with a pole 30 feet high), a pipe-smoking contest, wrestling and hound-trailing. The highlight, however, is the **World Gurning Championship** in which contestants place their heads through a braffin, or horse collar, and vie to produce the most grotesque expression. If you're toothless, you start with a great advantage!

Lowes Court Gallery, in a listed 18th century building, holds fine art exhibitions throughout the year. The premises also house the Tourist Information Centre.

WHITEHAVEN

The first impression is of a handsome Georgian town but Whitehaven was already well established in the 12th century as a harbour for use by the monks of nearby St Bees Priory. After the Reformation, the land was acquired and developed by the Lowther family in order to expand the coal industry. By the mid-1700s, Whitehaven had become the third largest port in Britain, its trade based on coal and other cargo business, including importing tobacco from Virginia, exporting coal to Ireland, and transporting emigrants to the New

---

THE BEACON

West Strand, Whitehaven, Cumbria, CA28 7LY
Tel: 01946 592302 Fax: 01946 598150
e-mail: thebeacon@copelandbc.gov.uk
website: www.copelandbc.gov.uk

Situated on Whitehaven's attractive harbourside, The Beacon is home to the town's museum collection. It traces the social, industrial and maritime heritage of the area, using local characters, audio-visual displays and fascinating museum pieces. The Met Office Weather Gallery, where you can monitor, forecast and broadcast the weather, offers panoramic views of the town and coast.

Also, don't miss the Harbour Gallery, which offers free entry to the changing exhibitions; the gift shop and café. Guided heritage walks are available through town and over the headland to Haig Colliery Mining Museum. Disabled access and facilities.

World. When the large iron-steamships arrived however, the harbour's shallow draught halted expansion and the port declined in favour of Liverpool and Southampton. For that reason much of the attractive harbour area - now full of pleasure craft and fishing smacks - and older parts of the town remain largely unchanged.

The harbour and its environs have been declared a Conservation Area and located here is **The Beacon** where, through a series of innovative displays, the history of the town and its harbour are brought to life.

Whitehaven Harbour

The displays reflect the many aspects of this harbour borough with a collection that includes paintings, locally made pottery, ship models, navigational instruments, miners' lamps, and surveying equipment. The Beilby 'Slavery' Goblet, part of the museum's collection, is one of the masterpieces of English glass-making and is probably the finest example of its kind in existence.

Also here are the **Harbour Gallery**, with an ongoing arts programme, and the **Met Office Gallery**, where visitors can monitor, forecast and broadcast the weather. They can also learn about the "American Connection" and John Paul Jones' attack on the town in 1778, or settle down in the cinema to watch vintage footage of Whitehaven in times past. John Paul Jones had been an apprentice seaman at Whitehaven before going to the New World, where he became well known in the War of Independence. In 1777 he became Captain of the privateer *The Ranger* and led a raid on Whitehaven with the intention of firing on the ships in the harbour. Thwarted by light winds, the party raided the fort and spiked the guns, then managed to damage only three ships before retreating under fire.

There's more history at **The Rum Story**, which tells the story of the town's connections with the Caribbean. The display is housed in the original 1785 shop, courtyards, cellars and bonded warehouses of the Jefferson family, the oldest surviving UK family of rum traders. Visitors can learn about the various processes involved in the making of rum, travel through realistic re-creations of far-off villages and experience the sights, sounds and smells of life on board the slave ships.

In Solway Road, Kells, the **Haig Colliery Mining Museum** features the world's only Bever Dorling Winding Engines, various displays about the mining industry and exhibits on mining disasters. Haig Colliery was the last deep coal mine worked in the West Cumberland coalfield. Sunk between 1914 and 1918, it closed in 1986 and was later sold for restoration.

As well as the elegant Georgian buildings that give Whitehaven its air of distinction, there are two fine parish churches that are worth a visit. Dating from 1753, **St James' Church** has Italian ceiling designs and a beautiful Memorial Chapel dedicated to those who lost their lives in the two World Wars and also the local people who were killed in mining accidents. The younger **St Begh's Church**, which was built in the 1860s by EW Pugin, is striking with its sandstone walls. In the graveyard of the parish church of **St Nicholas** is buried Mildred Gale, the grandmother of George Washington. In 1699, a widowed mother of three, Mildred married George Gale, a merchant who traded from Whitehaven to Maryland and Virginia. Her sons were born in Virginia but went to school in Appleby. When their mother died they returned to Virginia; one of them, Augustin, became the father of George Washington, first President of the United States of America.

In the Market Place are both the **Cumberland Toy & Model Museum** containing more than 100 years of toys with many visitor-operated displays, and **Percy House Gallery** which showcases contemporary art and design in the town's oldest house which dates back to 1598.

Whitehaven is interesting in other ways. The grid pattern of streets dating back to the 17th century gives substance to its claim to be the first planned town in Britain. Many of the fine Georgian buildings in the centre have been restored and **Lowther Street** is a particularly impressive thoroughfare.

Also of note is the **Harbour Pier** built by the canal engineer John Rennie, and considered to be one of the finest in Britain. There is a fascinating walk and a Nature Trail around **Tom Hurd Rock**, above the town.

AROUND WHITEHAVEN

ST BEES
3 miles S of Whitehaven on the B5343

St Bees Head, a red sandstone bluff, forms one of the most dramatic natural features along the entire coast of northwest England. Some four miles long and 300 feet high, these towering, precipitous cliffs are formed of St Bees sandstone, the red rock which is so characteristic of Cumbria. Far out to sea, on the horizon, can be seen the grey shadow of the Isle of Man and, on a clear day, the shimmering outline of the Irish coast. From St Bees the 190-mile **Coast to Coast Walk** starts on its long journey across the Pennines to Robin Hood's Bay in North Yorkshire.

Long before the first lighthouse was built here in 1822, there was a beacon on the headland to warn and guide passing ships away from the rocks. The present 99ft high lighthouse dates from 1866-7, built after an earlier one was destroyed by fire. St Bees Head is now an important Nature Reserve and the cliffs are crowded with guillemots, razorbills, kittiwakes, gulls, gannets, and skuas. Bird watchers are well-provided for with observation and information points all along the headland. There is a superb walk of about eight miles along the coastal footpath around the headland from St Bees to Whitehaven. The route passes Saltam Bay and Saltam Pit, which dates from 1729 and was the world's first undersea mineshaft. The original lamp house for the pit has been restored and is

Fleswick Bay, St Bees

now used by HM Coastguard.

St Bees itself is a delightful place to explore, with its main street winding up the hillside between old farms and cottages. The Priory at St Bees grew in size and importance until it was destroyed by the Danes in the 10th century: the Benedictines later re-established the priory in 1129. **The Priory Church of St Mary and St Bega** is all that is now left and although it has been substantially altered there is still a magnificent Norman arch and a pre-Conquest, carved Beowulf Stone on a lintel between the church and the vicarage, showing St Michael killing a dragon. The most stunning feature of all is much more modern, a sumptuous Art Nouveau metal work screen. In the south aisle is a small museum.

Close by the church are the charming

Abbey Cottages and **St Bees School** with its handsome clock-tower. The school was founded in 1583 by Edmund Grindal, Archbishop of Canterbury under Elizabeth I, and the son of a local farmer. The original red sandstone quadrangle bears his coat-of-arms and the bridge he gave to the village is still in use. Among the school's most famous alumni is the actor and comedian Rowan Atkinson, creator of the ineffable Mr Bean.

CLEATOR MOOR
3 miles SE of Whitehaven on the B5295

Cleator developed rapidly in the 19th century because of the insatiable demand during the Industrial Revolution for coal and iron ore. As the Cumbrian poet Norman Nicholson wrote:

> *From one shaft at Cleator Moor*
> *They mined for coal and iron ore.*
> *This harvest below ground could show*
> *Black and red currants on one tree.*

Cleator is surrounded by delightful countryside and little evidence of the town's industrial past is visible. But there is a thriving business nearby - the **Kangol Factory Shop** in Cleator village which stocks a huge range of hats, scarves, bags, caps and golf wear.

ENNERDALE BRIDGE
7 miles E of Whitehaven off the A5086

The bridge here crosses the River Ehen, which, a couple of miles upstream runs out from **Ennerdale Water**, one of the most secluded and inaccessible of all the Cumbrian lakes. The walks around this tranquil lake and through the quiet woodlands amply repay the slight effort of leaving the car at a distance. The Coast to Coast Walk runs the whole length of Ennerdale and this section is generally considered to be by far the most beautiful.

THE LINDEN TREE

65 Main Street, Cockermouth, West Cumbria CA13 9JS
Tel: 01900 828867
website: www.lindentree.co.uk

The interior of The Linden Tree is a feast for the eyes with its dazzling collection of colourful jewellery and gifts, all cleverly displayed to maximum effect. Owner, Gloria Bridle has developed a comprehensive range of beautiful jewellery, gifts and accessories over many years, sourcing work from abroad in

collections from Israel, USA , India, and Denmark. Recent additions include a stunning range of jewellery from the workshop of Shelia Fleet in Orkney. The Linden Tree is one of Cumbria's major stockists of PILGRIM Danish Jewellery a brand that is increasing in popularity on the fashion scene.

Designs are available in a variety of collections from fun and funky, delicate and romantic to bold and chunky. Choose from sterling silver to shell, precious stones, ceramic, wood or resin; or why not design your own piece from our growing stock of beads and findings.

Whether you are looking for a thoughtful and unusual gift for Christmas or birthday, or a special piece of jewellery for yourself to match your outfit then Gloria, Judith and their staff are always happy to help customers select from the vast range on offer. The shop is open from 9am to 5.15pm, Monday to Saturday; prices range from £5 to over £100 with gift vouchers also available. Mail order can be arranged.

ANNABELLES

80 Main Street, Cockermouth,
Cumbria CA13 9LP
Tel: 01900 825338

High fashion ladies clothes, shoes and accessories from leading designers can all be found at **Annabelles**, a stylish shop on Cockermouth's Main Street. It's owned and run by Anne Trafford who has gathered together a huge range of absolute 'must-have' items. There's cashmere knitwear from Magaschoni, Escada sportswear, Lejaby underwear and beautiful creations from Crea Concept, Michael Ambers, Marina Auraam, Frank Usher,

Betty Barclay, Mariella Rosati, Kapalua and Caractere. There's also a wide choice of accessories such as jewellery, scarves and belts.

Friendly and helpful staff add to the pleasure of shopping here. Annabelles is actually two shops with Anne's mother and father running David's Shoes where you'll find another amazing collection, this time of shoes from all around the world. There are shoes for fashionable occasions, shoes for comfort, shoes for the working day. Taken together, Annabelles and David's Shoes can kit you out completely!

COCKERMOUTH

A market town since 1226, Cockermouth has been fortunate in keeping unspoilt its broad main street, lined with trees and handsome Georgian houses, and dominated by a statue to the Earl of Mayo. The earl was Cockermouth's MP for ten years from 1858 before being appointed Viceroy of India. His brilliant career was brutally cut short when he was stabbed to death by a convict at a prison settlement he was inspecting on the Andaman Islands.

But Cockermouth boasts two far more famous sons. Did they ever meet, one wonders, those two young lads growing up in Cockermouth in the 1770s, both of them destined to become celebrated for very different reasons? The elder boy was Fletcher Christian, who would later lead the mutiny on the *Bounty;* the younger lad was William Wordsworth, born here in 1770 at Lowther House on Main Street, an imposing Georgian house now maintained by the National Trust. Now known as **Wordsworth House**, it was built in 1745 for the Sheriff of Cumberland and then purchased by the Earl of Lowther; he let it to his land agent, John Wordsworth, William's father. All five Wordsworth children were born here, William on 7th April 1770. Many of the building's original features survive, among them the staircase, fireplace, and fine plaster ceilings. A few of the poet's personal effects are still here; costumed actors provide insights into what life was like here; and the delightful walled garden by the River Cocker has been returned to its Georgian splendour. The garden is referred to in *The Prelude.*

Built in 1134 by the Earl of Dunbar,

THE neo: ART GALLERY, BOOKSHOP, COFFEE SHOP

25-31 Market Place, Cockermouth, Cumbria CA13 9NH
Tel: 01900 829900
e-mail: info@neo-gallery.co.uk website: www.neo-gallery.co.uk

The sheer diversity of arts and crafts concentrated within Cockermouth's Market Place helps to make the cultural scene within the town so exciting. **The neo** is a commercial gallery which is, nonetheless, artist-run by a small, friendly team. It is a bright, bold-looking modern space with, typically, several adventurous exhibitions per year: notably, Cumbrian landscape painter Derek Eland has held two very successful exhibitions here and a third, of all new work, is planned for summer 2006. Ben Gates and David Mellor (who also live in Cumbria) make highly idiosyncratic and often interactive sculptures, and have also enjoyed successful exhibitions. The neo represents artists from Scotland too: Edinburgh born Celia Washington will be exhibiting at the neo in 2006.

Alongside the exhibitions proper, there is always a selection of other artists' work within the space,

especially painting, printmaking and sculpture. Notwithstanding, the use of space is skilful and there is room enough to accommodate a diverse selection of art and design-related literature in the bookshop. This includes books for children, poetry and prose and an increasing selection of specialist 'artist's' books including collectables. The coffee shop is relaxed, regulars and visitors alike meet to read the papers and browse the art and books. All of the drinks and cakes here are Certified Organic and where applicable, Fairtrade. The neo is open throughout the year from 10am-5pm Mondays to Saturdays. Occasionally it is open on Sundays.

Cockermouth Castle saw plenty of action against Scottish raiders (Robert the Bruce himself gave it a mauling in 1315), and again during the Wars of the Roses; in the course of the Civil War it was occupied by both sides in turn. Mary, Queen of Scots, took refuge at the castle in 1568 after her defeat at the Battle of Langside. Her fortunes were so low that she was grateful for the gift of 16 ells (about 20 yards) of rich crimson velvet from a wealthy merchant. Part of the castle is still lived in by the Egremont family; the remainder is usually only open to the public during the Cockermouth Festival in July.

Opposite the castle entrance, **Castlegate House** is a fine Georgian house, built in 1739, which hosts a changing programme of monthly exhibitions of the work of Northern and Scottish artists - paintings, sculptures, ceramics and glass. To the rear of the house is a charming walled garden which is open from time to time during the summer.

Just around the corner from Castlegate House is the **Toy & Model Museum** which exhibits mainly British toys from around 1900 to the present. There are many visitor operated displays including 0 and 00 gauge vintage tinplate trains, Scalextric cars, Lego models and even a 1950s helicopter to fly. There are prams and dolls houses, and a working railway in a garden shed.

Almost next door, **Jennings Brewery** offers visitors a 90-minute tour which ends with the option of sampling some of their ales - Cumberland Ale, Cocker Hoop or the intriguingly named Sneck Lifter. The last independent brewing company in Cumbria, Jennings have been brewing traditional beers since the

PERCY HOUSE GALLERY

38-42 Market Place, Cockermouth, Cumbria CA13 9NG
Tel: 01900 829667
website: www.percyhouse.co.uk

Percy House Gallery occupies the oldest town house in Cockermouth, a charming building built in 1598 for Henry Percy, 9th Earl of Northumberland. Many of the original features still remain, including the flagged stone floor, bread oven, oak beams, fireplaces and a carved plaster ceiling. In this unique setting the gallery presents displays of jewellery, textiles, glassware, ceramics, metalware, paintings and photographs. There are sculptures produced locally and the upper area features a selection of textiles, painting and sculpture which complement the historical aspect of Percy House. Open from 10am-5pm, Monday to Saturday.

QUINCE & MEDLAR

13 Castlegate, Cockermouth, Cumbria CA13 9EU
Tel: 01900 823579   website: www.quinceandmedlar.co.uk

A listed Georgian property standing beside Cockermouth Castle, **Quince & Medlar** has been described as "vegetarian heaven" by *Food Illustrated Magazine*. This outstanding non-smoking, licensed vegetarian restaurant has three times been winner of the National Vegetarian Restaurant of the Year. Carefully prepared and creatively presented food is served in the friendly and intimate candlelit dining room. The restaurant is open from 7pm, Tuesday to Saturday – booking is strongly advisable. "Even carnivores say a visit here is a real treat!" said *The Observer*.

1820s and today there are more than 100 Jennings pubs across the north of England.

A short walk from the Brewery brings you to the **Kirkgate Centre**, which is housed in a converted Victorian primary school. Run by volunteers, the Centre offers a wide range of events and activities including live music, amateur and professional drama, films, dance, workshops, exhibitions of art and local history.

The **Printing House Museum** occupies a building dating back to the 16th century and follows the progress of printing from its invention by Johann Gutenberg in 1430 to the end of the letterpress era in the 1960s, when computers took over. On display is a wide range of historical presses and printing equipment, the earliest being a Cogger Press dated 1820. Visitors are offered the opportunity to gain hands-on experience by using some of the presses to produce cards or keepsakes.

Another ancient building is Percy House in the Market Place which was built in 1598 for Henry Percy, 9th Earl of Northumberland. Many of the original features still remain including the flagged stone floor, oak beams and fireplaces. The house is now home to the **Percy House Gallery** which has an interesting collection of arts and crafts on display. These include jewellery, textiles, glassware, ceramics, metalware, paintings and photographs.

Located just south of the town, the **Lakeland Sheep & Wool Centre** provides an introduction to life in the Cumbrian countryside with the help of a spectacular visual show, 19 different breeds of live sheep and a wide variety of exhibits. The Centre also hosts indoor sheepdog trials and sheep-shearing displays for which there is a small charge.

AROUND COCKERMOUTH

BRIGHAM
2 miles W of Cockermouth off the A66

St Bridget's Church, which was probably founded as part of a nunnery, contains many interesting features, including pre-Norman carved stones, a rare 'fish window' and a window dedicated to the Rev John Wordsworth, son of William and vicar of Brigham for 40 years. One of the tombs in the graveyard is that of Charles Christian, the father of Fletcher Christian, the *Bounty* mutineer. Fletcher himself was baptised in the church on the day of his birth, as it was thought unlikely that he would survive.

BRIDEKIRK
2 miles N of Cockermouth off the A595

The village **Church** contains one of the finest pieces of Norman sculpture in the country, a carved font with a runic inscription and a mass of detailed embellishments. It dates from the 12th century and the runic inscription states that: *Richard he me wrought / And to this beauty eagerly me brought.* Richard himself is shown on one side with a chisel and mallet. Not only is this a superb example of early English craftsmanship but it is exceedingly rare to find a signed work from this period. Ancient tombstones stand round the walls of this cruciform church and inside it has an unusual reredos of fleur-de-lys patterned tiles.

LINSKELDFIELD
6 miles NE of Cockermouth off the A595 or A591

Opened in 2005, **Linskeldfield Tarn Nature Reserve** is home to a great variety of birds including goldeneye, European widgeon, shovellers, pintail, little grebe, whooper swan and cormorant. With Skiddaw as a backdrop, the six-acre site of peat and wetland also shelters otters, red squirrels and carp. There's a custom-built 12-person birdwatching hide and free parking. The tarn is easily accessible from the nearby osprey watching centre at Dodd Wood.

HIGH & LOW LORTON

5 miles SE of Cockermouth on the B5289

There is a yew tree, pride of Lorton Vale... wrote Wordsworth in his poem *Yew Trees*, and astonishingly it's still there behind the village hall of High Lorton. It was in its shade that the Quaker George Fox preached to a large gathering under the watchful eye of Cromwell's soldiers. In its sister village, Low Lorton, set beside the River Cocker, is Lorton Hall (private) which is reputed to be home to the ghost of a woman who carries a lighted candle. Less spectral guests in the past have included King Malcolm III of Scotland, who stayed here with his queen while visiting the southern boundaries of his Kingdom of Strathclyde of which this area was a part.

EAGLESFIELD

2 miles SW of Cockermouth off the A5086

The most famous son of this small village is **John Dalton**, who was born here in 1766. The son of Quaker parents, Dalton was teaching at the village school by the time he was 12. Despite having had no formal education himself, he became one of the most brilliant scientists, naturalists, and mathematicians of his age and was the originator of the theory that all matter is composed of small indestructible particles called atoms. He was also the first to recognise the existence of colour blindness. He suffered from it himself and in medical circles it is known as Daltonism. A memorial to this remarkable man now marks the house where he lived in Eaglesfield.

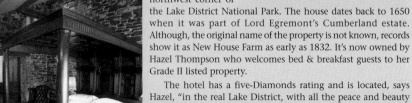

NEW HOUSE FARM

Lorton, Cockermouth, Cumbria CA13 9OU
Tel: 01900 85404 Fax: 01900 85478
e-mail: hazel@newhouse-farm.co.uk
website: www.newhouse-farm.co.uk

A winner of the Cumbrian Hotel of the Year Award by *Which? Hotel Guide*, New House Farm is situated in the beautiful Buttermere Valley in the northwest corner of

the Lake District National Park. The house dates back to 1650 when it was part of Lord Egremont's Cumberland estate. Although, the original name of the property is not known, records show it as New House Farm as early as 1832. It's now owned by Hazel Thompson who welcomes bed & breakfast guests to her Grade II listed property.

The hotel has a five-Diamonds rating and is located, says Hazel, "in the real Lake District, with all the peace and beauty without the crowds". Many guests stay on a bed, breakfast and dinner basis – the delicious evening meals offer dishes such as local Solway shrimps followed by Pheasant cooked in cider. Adjacent to New House Farm is The Barn Tearooms, a gorgeous stone building with many of its original features still intact. It serves an appetising selection of wholesome fare, all of it home-cooked on the premises.

WORKINGTON

The largest town on the Cumbrian coast, Workington stands at the mouth of the River Derwent and on the site of the Roman fort of Gabrosentum. Its prosperity was founded on the three great Cumbrian industries - coal, iron and shipping. In later years, Workington became famous for its fine quality steel, especially after Henry Bessemer developed his revolutionary steel making process here in 1850. The seat of the Curwen family for over 600 years, **Workington Hall** has an interesting history. Originally built around a 14th century pele tower, the hall was developed over the years with extensive alterations being made in the 18th century by the then lord of the manor, John Christian Curwen. Now a stabilised ruin, it has several commemorative plaques which give a taste of the hall's history. The most famous visitor was Mary, Queen of Scots who sought refuge here when she fled from Scotland in 1558. She stayed for a few days during which time she wrote the famous letter to her cousin Elizabeth I bemoaning her fate, "for I am in a pitiable condition....having nothing in the world but the clothes in which I escaped," and asking the queen "to have compassion on my great misfortunes". The letter is now in the British Museum. Workington's **Church of St John the Evangelist** is a very grand affair built at enormous expense in 1823 to give thanks for the defeat of Napoleon at Waterloo. It is a copy of St Paul's, Covent Garden, and its walls were built with stones from the local Schoose and Hunday quarries. The interior was splendidly restored by Sir Ninian Comper in 1931. St Michael's is the ancient parish church, restored after a fire in 1994.

The **Helena Thompson Museum** tells the story of Workington's coal mining, ship-building, and iron and steel industries for which the town became internationally renowned. The Georgian Room gives an insight into the variety of decorative styles which were popular between 1714 and 1830, with displays of beautiful cut-glass tableware, porcelain from China, and period pieces of furniture. Bequeathed to the town by the local philanthropist Miss Helena Thompson, the museum was opened in 1949 and contains some of her own family heirlooms. One particularly interesting exhibit is the Clifton Dish, a locally produced 18th century piece of slipware pottery, while further displays demonstrate the links between this local industry and the famous Staffordshire pottery families. Fashion fiends will be interested in the display of women's and children's dresses from the 1700s to the early 1900s, together with accessories and jewellery.

Workington is at the start of the C2C (Coast to Coast) cycle route that runs to Sunderland and Newcastle. A short distance south of town is **Harrington Reservoir Nature Reserve**, a haven for wildlife with a rich variety of wild flowers, insects, butterflies, birds and animals.

AROUND WORKINGTON

MARYPORT
6 miles NE of Workington on the A596

Dramatically located on the Solway Firth, Maryport is a charming Cumbrian coastal town rich in interest and maritime history. The old part is full of narrow streets and neoclassical, Georgian architecture which contrast with sudden, surprising views of the sea. Some of the first visitors to Maryport were the

MARYPORT MARITIME MUSEUM

Senhouse Street, Maryport, Cumbria CA13 6AB
Tel: 01900 813738 Fax: 01900 819496
e-mail: maryport.museum@allerdale.gov.uk

Did you know that Maryport has connections with the ill fated *Titanic*, or Fletcher Christian, of *Mutiny on the Bounty* fame? Visit **Maryport Maritime Museum** and discover the fascinating and proud maritime heritage of this delightful town. The building, formerly the Queens Head Public House, is built on one of the earliest plots of land developed by Humphrey Senhouse when the town was built. The Museum houses a wealth of objects, pictures, models and paintings that illustrate Maryport's proud maritime tradition; from a whale's tooth to a blunderbuss; from sailmakers' tools to telescopes;from a mutineer, Fletcher Christian, to a great shipowner, Thomas Henry Ismay of the great White Star Line, owners of the ill fated *Titanic*.

Romans, who built a clifftop fort here, **Alauna**, which is now part of the Hadrian's Wall World Heritage Site. The award-winning **Senhouse Roman Museum** tells the story of life in this outpost of the empire. Housed in the striking Naval Reserve Battery, built in the 1880s, the museum holds the largest collection of Roman altars from a single site in Britain. Modern Maryport dates from the 18th century when Humphrey Senhouse, a local landowner, developed the harbour at what was then called Ellenport to export coal from his mines, and named the new port after his wife, Mary. Over the next century it became a busy port as well as a ship-building centre; boats had to be launched broadside because of the narrowness of the harbour channel. The town declined, along with the mining industry, from the 1930s onwards. It nevertheless attracted the artist LS Lowry, who was a frequent visitor and loved painting the harbour. Today, Maryport is enjoying a well-earned revival, with newly restored Georgian quaysides, clifftop paths, sandy beaches and a harbour with fishing boats.

The town's extensive maritime history is preserved in the vast array of objects, pictures and models on display at the **Maritime Museum** overlooking the harbour. Housed in another of Maryport's more interesting and historic buildings, the former Queen's Head public house, the museum tells of the rise and fall of the harbour and docks. Other exhibits include a brass telescope from the *Cutty Sark* and the town's connections with the ill-fated liner, the *Titanic*, and with Fletcher Christian, instigator of the mutiny on the *Bounty*. The *Titanic* was part of the fleet of the White Star Line, which was founded by a Maryport man, Thomas Henry Ismay. Fletcher Christian was also more or less a local man, being born at nearby Cockermouth in 1764.

Close by is the **Lake District Coast Aquarium**, where a series of spectacular living habitat re-creations introduce visitors to the profusion of marine life found in the Solway Firth - thornback rays (which can be touched), some small sharks, spider crabs and the comically ugly tompot blenny among them.

ASPATRIA

14 miles NE of Workington on the A596

Lying above the shallow Ellen Valley, Aspatria's main interest for most visitors lies in the elaborate **Memorial Fountain**

THE MANOR HOUSE

Oughterside, Aspatria, Cumbria CA7 2PT
Tel/Fax: 016973 22420
e-mail: richardandjudy@themanorhouse.net
website: www.themanorhouse.net

Built in the 1700s as a gentleman farmer's residence, **The Manor House** retains many of its original features and more than eight acres of land on which sheep still graze. It's now the home of Judy and Richard Mortimer who welcome bed & breakfast guests to their dignified old house. It has spacious bedrooms with large en suite bathrooms, generously sized beds (singles are doubles; the doubles are kings), and comfortable mattresses. The rooms are provided with lots of thoughtful 'extras' to make your stay as comfortable as possible. Big English breakfasts are cooked on the AGA and usually served in the conservatory.

Guests are welcome to use the dining room or conservatory to relax, play games, pore over maps or whatever. Feel free to sit or stroll in the garden – garden seats are sited to catch the sun at any time of day. Beyond the house, the lane becomes a track which passes conservation areas rich in wildlife. Despite its rural setting, the Manor House is only half a mile from the A596, with easy access to the Lake District National Park. Set well away from the house is a certificated caravan site for five touring vans, with gravel pitches and electric hook-ups.

to 'Watery Wilfred', Sir Wilfred Lawson MP (1829-1906), a lifelong crusader for the Temperance Movement and International Peace. According to one writer, "No man in his day made more people laugh at Temperance meetings". Also worth a visit is the much restored **Norman Church** that is entered through a fine avenue of yew trees. Inside are several ancient relics including a 12th century font with intricate carvings, a Viking hogback tombstone, and a grave cover with a pagan swastika engraving.

ALLONBY

11 miles N of Workington on the B5300

This traditional Solway village is backed by the Lake District fells and looks out across the Solway Firth to the Scottish hills. Popular with wind-surfers, the village has an attractive shingle and sand beach which received a Seaside Award in

1998. The Allerdale Way and the Cumbrian Cycle Way both pass close by, and the village is also on the **Smuggler's Route** trail. Smuggling seems to have been a profitable occupation around here - a government enquiry into contraband trade reported in 1730 that "the Solway people were the first working-class folk to drink tea regularly in Britain".

In the early 1800s, Allonby was a popular sea-bathing resort and the former seawater baths, built in 1835 and now Grade II listed buildings, still stand in the old **Market Square**. In those days, the upper floor was in popular use as a ballroom for the local nobility. Allonby still keeps much of its Georgian and early Victorian charm with cobbled lanes, alleyways, and some interesting old houses. It was also an important centre for herring fishing and some of the old kippering houses can still be seen.

Holme St Cuthbert

14 miles N of Workington off the B5300

This inland hamlet is also known as Rowks because, in the Middle Ages, there was a chapel here dedicated to St Roche. Northeast of the hamlet, and enveloped among low hills, is a lovely 30-acre lake known as **Tarns Dub**, which is a haven for birdlife. A couple of miles to the southwest, the headland of **Dubmill Point** is popular with sea anglers. When the tide is high and driven by a fresh westerly wind, the sea covers the road with lashing waves.

Beckfoot

16 miles N of Workington on the B5300

At certain times and tides, the remains of a prehistoric forest can be seen on the sand beds here and, to the south of the village, is the site of a 2nd century Roman fort known as **Bibra**. According to an inscribed stone found here, it was once occupied by an Auxiliary Cohort of 500 Pannonians (Spaniards) and surrounded by a large civilian settlement. The small stream flowing into the sea was used in World War I as a fresh water supply by German U-boats.

A mile or so south of Beckfoot is the recently opened **Bank Mill** which promises a great day out for all the family. The site contains a Butterfly House, home to the largest species of butterfly and moth in the world; a lizard house with species from all around the world; and a Nature Reserve that provides a refuge for the endangered Natterjack toads. Foxes and badgers also can be seen and there's a hide for birdwatchers. Also on site is a coffee shop and plant nursery.

Silloth

18 miles N of Workington on the B5300

This charming old port and Victorian seaside resort is well worth exploring and its two-mile-long promenade provides wonderful views of the Solway Firth and the coast of Scotland. With the coming of the railways in the 1850s, Silloth developed as a port and railhead for Carlisle. The Railway Company helped to develop the town and had grey granite shipped over in its own vessels from Ireland to build the handsome church which is such a prominent landmark. The region's bracing air and low rainfall helped to make Silloth a popular seaside resort. Visitors today will appreciate the invigorating but mild climate, the leisurely atmosphere, and the glorious sunsets over the sea that inspired Turner to record them for posterity. The town remains a delightful place to stroll, to admire the sunken rose garden, the pinewoods, the two miles of promenades and the busy dock where local fishermen offload their catches of Solway shrimps.

Silloth's 18-hole golf course was the 'home course' where Miss Cecil Leitch

Christ Church, Silloth

(1891-1978), the most celebrated woman golfer of her day, used to play. Another keen woman golfer was the great contralto, Kathleen Ferrier, who stayed in the town for part of her tragically short life. One of the most popular attractions is the **Solway Coast Discovery Centre**, where Auld Michael the Monk and Oyk the Oystercatcher guide visitors through 10,000 years of Solway Coast history.

WIGTON

For centuries, Wigton has been the centre of the business and social life of the Solway coast and plain, its prosperity being based on the weaving of cotton and linen. It has enjoyed the benefits of a Royal Charter since 1262 and the market is still held on Tuesdays. Horse sales are held every April (riding horses and ponies) and October (Clydesdales,

heavy horses and ponies). Today, most of the old town is a Conservation Area and, particularly along the **Main Street**, the upper storeys of the houses have survived in an almost unaltered state. On street corners, metal guards to prevent heavy horse-drawn wagons damaging the walls can also still be seen.

One mile south of Wigton are the scant remains of the Roman fort of **Olenacum**; most of its stones were removed to rebuild Wigton in the 18th and 19th centuries.

AROUND WIGTON

ABBEYTOWN
5 miles W of Wigton on the B5302

As its name suggests, Abbeytown grew up around the 12th century **Abbey of Holm Cultram** on the River Waver and many of the town's buildings are

HUNNISETT REED ANTIQUES

The Barn, Burnfoot Grange, Burnfoot, Wigton CA79 9HL
Tel: 016973 49621 Fax: 016973 44584
e-mail: susan@hunnisett-reed.freeserve.co.uk

Hunnisett Reed Antiques is situated in the small market town of Wigton, which is 11 miles south of the border city of Carlisle and 30 minutes drive from Penrith and the M6. The proprietors, Suzi and Bill live on the premises and have the showrooms in one of

their barns. The property was originally a farm dating back to the 16th century. In 1662 it was converted into a merchant's house and is one of the oldest buildings remaining in Wigton.

Suzi and Bill stock a good and varied selection of hand-finished country oak and pine antique furniture, along with complimentary antiques. The furniture is restored and finished in their own workshop on the premises. They are open by appointment or by chance, but it is best to telephone first to avoid disappointment.

The town of Wigton has good Georgian architecture and a number of cafes and restaurants. It is within easy reach of the Solway coast and close to the Lake District.

constructed of stone taken from the abbey when it fell into ruins. The red sandstone **Church of St Mary** is still the parish church and was restored in 1883, a strange yet impressive building with the original nave shorn of its tower, transepts and chancel. The east and west walls are heavily buttressed and a porch with a new roof protects the original Norman arch of the west door. Within the church buildings is a room, opened by Princess Margaret in 1973, which contains the gravestones of Robert the Bruce's father and that of Mathias and Juliana De Keldsik, relations of Abbot Robert. Nearby, there are some lovely walks along the River Waver, which is especially rich in wildlife.

Skinburness
11 miles W of Wigton off the B5302

A lively market town, in the Middle Ages, Skinburness was used by Edward I in 1299 as a base for his navy when attacking the Scots. A few years later a terrible storm destroyed the town and what survived became a small fishing hamlet. From nearby **Grune Point**, the start of the **Allerdale Ramble**, there are some tremendous views over the Solway Firth and the beautiful, desolate expanse of marshland and sandbank. Grune Point, which was once the site of a Roman fort, now forms part of a designated Site of Special Scientific Interest notable for the variety of its birdlife and marsh plants.

Newton Arlosh
5 miles NW of Wigton on the B5307

Situated on the **Solway marshes**, the village was first established by the monks of Holm Cultram Abbey in 1307 after the old port at Skinburness had been destroyed by the sea. The village church is one of the most delightful

examples of a Cumbrian fortified **Church**. In the Middle Ages, there was no castle nearby to protect the local population from the border raids and so a pele tower was added to the church. As an additional defensive measure, the builders created what is believed to be the narrowest church doorway in the country, barely two feet seven inches across and a little over five feet high. The 12-inch arrow-slot east window is also the smallest in England. After the Reformation, the church became derelict but was finally restored in the 19th century. Inside, there is a particularly fine eagle lectern carved out of bog oak.

KESWICK AND THE NORTHERN LAKES

For many visitors this part of the county is classic Lakeland, the scenery dominated by the rounded, heather-clad slopes of the Skiddaw range to the north of Keswick, and the wild, craggy mountains of Borrowdale, to the south. Yet, despite this area's popularity, there are still many hidden places to discover and many opportunities to leave the beaten track.

The major town, Keswick, on the shores of Derwent Water, is a pleasant Lakeland town that has much to offer the visitor. The lake too, is interesting as, not only is it in a near perfect setting, but it is unusual in having some islands - in this case four. It was the view over the lake, from Friar's Crag, that formed one of John Ruskin's early childhood memories. The area is also rich in history, from prehistoric times through Roman occupation to the period of industrial growth.

The Lakeland Fells are home to Herdwick sheep, one of the country's hardiest breeds. Their coarse fleece cannot be dyed, but Herdwick sheep of various ages yield wool in a variety of subtle shades of grey and black which produces an unusual and very durable tweed-like weave.

KESWICK

For generations, visitors to Keswick have been impressed by the town's stunningly beautiful setting, surrounded by the great fells of Saddleback, Helvellyn and Grizedale Pike. Tourism, now the town's major industry, actually began in the mid-1700s and was given a huge boost by the Lakeland Poets in the early 1800s. The arrival of the railway in 1865 firmly established Keswick as the undisputed 'capital' of the Lake District with most of the area's notable attractions within easy reach.

The grandeur of the lakeland scenery is of course the greatest draw but, among the man-made features, one not to be missed is the well-preserved **Castlerigg Stone Circle**. About a mile to the east of the town, the 38 standing stones, some of them eight feet high, form a circle 100 feet in diameter. They are believed to have been put in place some 4,000 years ago and occupy a hauntingly beautiful position. Beautiful, but forbidding, as evoked by Keats in his poem *Hyperion*:

A dismal cirque of Druid stones, upon a
forlorn moor,
When the chill rain begins at shut of eve,
In dull November, and their chancel vault,
The Heaven itself, is blinded throughout
night.

Keswick old town developed along the banks of the broad River Greta, with a wide main street leading up to the attractive **Moot Hall** which now houses the town's and the National Park's tourist information centres. A little

LITTLEFIELD B&B

32 Eskin Street, Keswick, Cumbria
Tel: 017687 72949
e-mail: littlefield@keswick98.fsnet.co.uk website:www.keswick98.fsnet.co.uk

Just five minutes from the town centre, **Littlefield B&B** offers a warm welcome and a "home from home" atmosphere. Your hostess, Alison Maddock, is always prepared to go that extra mile for her guests, whether you would like packed lunches, a flask filled, a home-baked cake or have special dietary requirements. Littlefield has five guest bedrooms, ranging from a single to a superior en suite double, and a comfortable lounge where guests can browse through the extensive collection of guides. Other amenities include drying facilities, lockable storage for bicycles, and discount tickets for the Theatre by the Lake.

KESKADALE FARM

Newlands Valley, Keswick, Cumbria CA12 5TS
Tel: 017687 78544 Fax: 017687 78150
e-mail: keskadale.b.b:kencomp.net website: www.keskadalefarm.co.uk

Occupying a breathtaking position with magnificent views, **Keskadale Farm** offers the choice of self-catering or bed & breakfast accommodation in wonderfully peaceful surroundings. Bed & breakfast guests stay in the traditional Lakeland farmhouse which has been in Margaret Harryman's family for generations. A hearty farmhouse breakfast is included and there's a choice of two en suite bedrooms and one with private bathroom. Guests also have the use of a cosy lounge with real log fire, colour TV and plenty of books. Self-catering guests have the choice of an apartment sleeping six plus cot, or a luxury caravan for four situated in its own peaceful garden.

further south, in **St John's Street**, the church of that name was built in the very same year as the Moot Hall and its elegant spire provides a point of reference from all around the town. In the churchyard is the grave of Sir Hugh Walpole, whose once hugely popular series of novels, *The Herries Chronicle* (1930-3), is set in this part of the Lake District.

In the riverside Fitz Park is the town's **Museum & Art Gallery** which is well worth a visit not just to see original manuscripts by Wordsworth and other lakeland poets but also for the astonishing 'Rock, Bell and Steel Band' created by Joseph Richardson of Skiddaw in the 19th century. It's a kind of xylophone made of 60 stones (some a yard long), 60 steel bars and 40 bells. Four 'musicians' are required to play this extraordinary instrument.

Moot Hall, Keswick

Surrounded by a loop of the River Greta to the northwest of the town is a museum which must be pencilled in on any visit to Keswick. This is the **Cumberland Pencil Museum**, which boasts the six feet long 'Largest Pencil in the World'. The 'lead' used in pencils (not lead at all but actually an allotrope of carbon) was accidentally discovered by a Borrowdale shepherd in the 16th century and Keswick eventually became the world centre for the manufacture of lead pencils. The pencil mill here, established in 1832, is still operating although the wadd, or lead, is now imported.

Other attractions in the town centre include the **Cars of the Stars Museum**, home to such gems as Laurel and Hardy's Model T Ford, James Bond's Aston

Martin, Chitty Chitty Bang Bang, Batman's Batmobile, Lady Penelope's pink Rolls-Royce FAB 1, the Mad Max car, Mr Bean's Mini and Harry Potter's Ford Anglia. There are film set displays and vehicles from series such as *The Saint, Knightrider, Bergerac* and *Postman Pat*, and Del Boy's 3-wheel Reliant from *Only Fools and Horses* is there, too. **The Teapottery** makes and sells a bizarre range of practical teapots in the shape of anything from an upright piano to an Aga stove. Keswick's most recent visitor attraction to open is **The Puzzling Place**, an ingenious display of mind-bending illusions, including computer video clips, three-dimensional holograms and an anti-gravity room where everything you've learned about gravity will be turned on its head as you watch water flow uphill and other impossibilities. There's also a large selection of puzzles, brain-teasers and associated novelty goods on sale.

A short walk from the town centre,

along Lake Road, leads visitors to the popular **Theatre by the Lake**, which hosts a year-round programme of plays, concerts, exhibitions, readings and talks. Close by is the pier from which there are regular departures for cruises around Derwentwater and ferries across the lake to Nichol End where you can hire just about every kind of water craft, including your own private cruise boat. One trip is to the National Trust's **Derwent Island House**, an Italianate house of the 1840s on a wooded island.

Another short walk will bring the visitor to **Friar's Crag**. This famous view of Derwent Water and its islands, now National Trust property, formed one of John Ruskin's early childhood memories, inspiring in him "intense joy, mingled with awe". Inscribed on his memorial here are these words: "The first thing which I remember as an event in life was being taken by my nurse to the brow of

Friar's Crag on Derwentwater." The Crag is dedicated to the memory of Canon Rawnsley, the local vicar who was one of the founder members of the National Trust, which he helped to set up in 1895. Keswick is host to several annual festivals, covering films, Cumbrian literature, jazz and beer. And on the first Sunday in December a colourful Christmassy Fayre is held in the Market Place.

AROUND KESWICK

THRELKELD
3 miles E of Keswick off the A66

From Keswick there's a delightful walk along the track bed of the old railway line to the charming village of Threlkeld, set in a plain at the foot of mighty **Blencathra**. The village is the ideal starting point for a number of mountain

THRELKELD MINING MUSEUM

Threlkeld Quarry, Keswick, Cumbria CA12 4TT
Tel: 017687 79747

Entranced by the spectacular scenery of the Lake District, visitors are often unaware that in the past this was also a significant mining area. This industrial heritage is brought vividly to life at the **Threlkeld Quarry & Mining Museum** where visitors can browse through the collection of mining artefacts, wander through the locomotive shed and machine shop, or join the 40-minute tour through a recreated mine. At Threlkeld Quarry, men were employed from the 1870s until 1982 quarrying granite for railway ballast and road making, as well as producing granite setts and masonry stone. Several of the original buildings remain, including the locomotive shed which now houses various industrial diesel locomotives.

On display in the Museum is a fine collection of small mining and quarrying artefacts and more are now held at the new Mining Museum in Keswick. There's also an excellent mineral collection and in the Geology Room a fascinating table top relief map of the Lake District, enhanced by rock specimens. The Museum Shop stocks the largest selection of mining, geology and mineralogy books in the north of England, (including a second-hand section), beautiful minerals from around the world, along with gemstone jewellery and a complete range of mine exploration and caving gear.

THE MILL INN

Blencathra Business Centre, Threlkeld,
Keswick, Cumbria CA12 4TR
Tel: 017687 79994 Fax: 017687 79996
e-mail: info@piemill.co.uk
website: www.piemill.co.uk

Situated in the lea of the Blencathra fell range and the picturesque Mungrisdale Valley, **The Mill Inn** is an appealing 17th century coaching inn where landlords Jim and Margaret Hodge offer a warm welcome to all their visitors. This is a genuine traditional hostelry where you can enjoy a pint of real ale along with home-cooked food served in front of a roaring log fire. The food is freshly prepared on the premises and is based on Cumbrian ingredients such as locally

bred lamb and regionally caught fresh fish. The regular menu includes the inn's famous speciality pies and a traditional Sunday Roast is always on offer at the weekends. Full vegetarian alternatives are available and special diets can be catered for. If you visit during early November you can experience the inn's world-famous charity Pie-Fest and enjoy more than 14 different types of pie along with live music and real ales. The Mill Inn also offers quality accommodation in six spacious, non-smoking rooms. There are three double rooms, all with en suite facilities; and three twin rooms with either en suite facilities or private bathroom. All rooms have TVs.

THE PIE MILL

e-mail: info@piemill.co.uk
website: www.piemill.co.uk

"Fresh from the oven, straight to your door" is the promise made by **The Pie Mill**, the website for The Mill Inn *(see above)* where you can order these famous pies made with local ingredients to distinctive and unique recipes which embody the character of Cumbria. There are nine scrumptious varieties to choose from, all named after Cumbrian locations. They include 'Blencathra', an award-winning beef in ale pie made with Cumbrian Galloway beef in locally brewed Cumberland Ale; 'Old Man' containing tender

pieces of wild venison and cranberries combined in a port gravy; 'Carrock' – lamb with fresh mint and a hint of oregano and rosemary; and 'Souther' – local lamb cooked gently in spices with apricots. Then there's 'Skiddaw' which is made with Cumbrian Galloway beef and ox kidney to give a distinctively strong flavour; "Swindale', a delicious mixture of wild venison, pheasant and rabbit in a rich, red wine gravy, and 'Bowscale', chicken and mushroom cooked in a white wine and rich herb gravy. Vegetarians are not forgotten – 'Buttermere' is a tasty blend of roasted vegetables in a rich tomato, red wine and basil sauce.

walks, including an ascent of Blencathra, one of the most exciting of all the Lake District mountains. Threlkeld is famous for its annual sheepdog trials though its economy was built up on the several mines in the area and the granite quarry to the south. At **Threlkeld Quarry & Mining Museum** visitors can browse through the collection of vintage excavators, old quarry machinery and other mining artefacts, wander through the locomotive shed and machine shop, or join the 40-minute tour through a re-created mine. The museum has interpretive displays of Lakeland geology and quarrying and is used as a teaching facility by several university geology departments.

MATTERDALE END
8 miles E of Keswick on the A5091

This tiny hamlet lies at one end of Matterdale, a valley that an essential stop on any Wordsworth trail: it was here, on April 15th 1802, that he and his sister saw that immortal

Host of golden daffodils,
Beside the lake,
beneath the trees,
Fluttering and dancing in the breeze.

THIRLMERE
4 miles S of Keswick off the A591

This attractive, tree-lined lake, one of the few in the Lakes that can be driven around as well as walked around, was created in the 1890s by the Manchester Corporation. More than 100 miles of pipes and tunnels still supply the city with water from Thirlmere.

The creation of the huge **Thirlmere Reservoir**, five miles long, flooded the two hamlets of Armboth and Wythburn. All that remains of these places today is Wythburn chapel towards the southern end. Overlooking the narrow lake is

Helvellyn, Wordsworth's favourite mountain and one that is also very popular with walkers and climbers today. At 3,116 feet, it is one of the four Lakeland fells over 3,000 feet high and the walk to the summit should not be undertaken lightly - but those reaching the summit will be rewarded with some spectacular views. The eastern aspect of the mountain is markedly different from the western as it was here that the Ice Age glaciers were sheltered from the mild, west winds.

BORROWDALE
Runs South from Keswick via the B5289

"The Mountains of Borrowdale are perhaps as fine as anything we have seen," wrote John Keats in 1818. Six miles long, this brooding, mysterious valley, steep and narrow with towering crags and deep woods, is generally regarded as the most beautiful in the Lake District. Just to the south of Derwent Water are the **Lodore Falls**, where the Watendlath Beck drops some 120 feet before reaching the lake. Further along the dale, in woodland owned by the National Trust, lies the extraordinary **Bowder Stone** which provides an irresistible photo-opportunity for most visitors. A massive 50ft square and weighing almost 2,000 tons, it stands precariously on one corner apparently defying gravity. Just south of Rosthwaite the road turns westwards to the village of **Seatoller** where there's a National Park Information Centre and a minor road turns off to **Seathwaite**, which enjoys the unenviable reputation of being the wettest place in England with an average of 131 inches a year. From Seatoller, the B5289 slices through the spectacular **Honister Pass**, overlooked by dramatic 1,000 foot high Honister Crag. At the top of the pass, the 18th century **Honister Slate Mine** has been re-opened and is once again producing the beautiful green

ASHNESS FARM

Borrowdale, Keswick, Cumbria CA12 5UN
Tel: 017687 77361
e-mail: enquiries@ashnessfarm.co.uk
website: www.ashnessfarm.co.uk

Occupying a superb position in the beautiful Borrowdale valley overlooking Derwentwater, Ashness Farm belonging to the National Trust is a working Lakeland fell farm with its origins in the 16th century that also offers comfortable accommodation. The farm specialises in the rearing of some rare breeds, including its Swaledale and Herdwick sheep and belted Galloway cattle. Tenants Anne and Mark Cornthwaite also have Gloucester Old Spot pigs, Lakeland fell ponies, goats and even a couple of llamas. "We encourage our visitors," they say, "to come and appreciate Cumbrian family farm life from close up, and to share a little of what means so much to us."

Accommodation comprises five en suite double rooms, two can be offered as twin beds, all with

central heating and a magnificent view across Derwentwater. A traditional English farmhouse breakfast is served in the recently refurbished dining room, alternative breakfasts and special dietary needs can also be catered for, evening meals are available by arrangement using their own farm reared meat. You are invited to relax by the log fire in the lounge which has its original oak beams. Anne and Mark have produced a very helpful leaflet detailing various walks exploring the glorious scenery all around them.

slate that adorns so many Lakeland houses and is famous throughout the world. Buckingham Palace, The Ritz, New Scotland Yard and RAF Cranwell are among the prestigious buildings donned with this stone. Helmets and lights are provided for a guided tour through great caverns of the mine to show how a mixture of modern and traditional methods is still extracting the slate which was formed here some 400 million years ago.

BUTTERMERE

8 miles SW of Keswick on the B5289

Half the size of its neighbour, Crummock Water, Buttermere is a beautiful lake set in a dramatic landscape. To many connoisseurs of the Lake District landscape, this is the most splendid of them all. The walk around Buttermere gives superb views of the eastern towers of **Fleetwith Pike** and the great fell wall made up of High Crag, High Stile, and Red Pike.

Standing above the village is the small, picturesque **Church of St James**, where the special features of interest include an antique organ and a memorial to fellwalker and author Alfred Wainwright.

CRUMMOCK WATER

9 miles SW of Keswick on the B5289

Fed by both Buttermere and Loweswater, this is by far the largest of the three lakes. In this less frequented part of western Cumbria, where there are few roads, the attractions of Crummock Water can usually be enjoyed in solitude. Best seen from the top of Rannerdale Knotts, to the east, the lake has a footpath running around it though, in places, the going gets a little strenuous.

Crummock Water

BRAITHWAITE

3 miles W of Keswick on the B5292

This small village lies at the foot of the Whinlatter Pass, another of Cumbria's dramatic routes. The summit of this steep road, the B5292, is some 1,043 feet above sea level and, on the westerly descent, there are magnificent views over Bassenthwaite Lake. The road runs through the **Whinlatter Forest Park** one of the Forestry Commission's oldest woodlands, which has a Visitor Centre, trails and walks for all ages and abilities, an orienteering course, adventure playground, viewpoints, gift shop and a tearoom with a terrace overlooking the woodlands and valley. Many of the record numbers who visited the centre in 2002 came to see live footage of the Lake District ospreys beamed to a viewing facility or to see the birds through high-powered telescopes at the Dodd Wood viewing point. **The Lake District Osprey Project** is a partnership of the Forestry Commission, the Lake District National

---

LAKELAND PHOTOGRAPHIC HOLIDAYS

Fern Howe, Braithwaite, Keswick, Cumbria CA12 5SZ
Tel: 017687 78459
e-mail: info@lakelandphotohols.com
website: www.lakelandphotohols.com

With its glorious scenery and ever-changing moods, what better place for a photographic holiday than the Lake District? Based at Fern Howe, a Victorian house on a wooded fell-side in Braithwaite village, **Lakeland Photographic Holidays** offers full board accommodation (breakfast, packed lunch and evening meal) and instruction in the finer points of photography by John Gravett, a professional photographer and regular contributor to the photographic press. With a maximum of ten guests at any one time, John's aim is to help each participant develop his or her own style, using techniques in the field and nightly feedback sessions. They offer photographers, of all ages and all photographic abilities, both film and digital based, the ideal environment in which to pursue their hobby and relax with family and friends.

Amenities include a fully equipped darkroom, a digital 'darkroom' equipped with two computers, and an extensive photographic and general library. Gail Gravett is also a keen photographer and has completed a Certificate in Professional Cookery, specialising in vegetarian cooking. Meals are served in the dining room followed by coffee in the lounge, conservatory or, in good weather, on the patio. Accommodation, themed in line with the Lake District environment, comprises five en suite twin or double rooms; two en suite single rooms, and one single room with shared facilities.

LAKELAND COTTAGE HOLIDAYS

Melbecks, Bassenthwaite, Keswick CA12 4QX
Tel: 01768 776065 Fax: 01768 776869
e-mail: info@lakelandcottages.co.uk
website: www.lakelandcottages.co.uk

Established over 25 years ago, **Lakeland Cottage Holidays** offers a wide variety of properties located in the Northern Lake District. This family-run business aims to ensure that you have a worry free and enjoyable holiday in this beautiful and spectacular landscape.

The range of properties on offer provide accommodation from two people up to parties of 21 - sufficient in size to cater for that special family get together or celebration. A selection of properties have their own swimming pools, whilst many others provide complimentary week-long leisure club membership. Many of them accept pets by prior arrangement. The surrounding fells and valleys offer a wide variety of activities from sailing and windsurfing on the lakes, to climbing on the abundant crags, or paragliding. Or you may simply choose to wander the footpaths and quiet country lanes, taking tea in a local farmhouse.

The properties range in style from modern, well-equipped bungalows through traditional townhouses, country cottages to large family houses situated within their own grounds. Around half the properties are located in the charming market town of Keswick, with its open plan, pedestrianised market square, home to the well-known landmark Moot Hall. Other properties are located in the surrounding villages and hamlets, each with their own character and charm. You can gather around an open log fire after a bracing walk on the fells, or retire to one of the many hostelries and sample the delights of the local Jennings beer.

Short breaks are offered at any time throughout low season, and within two weeks of the holiday in the mid and high season weeks. The comprehensive, full colour brochure is available free by post, or you can visit the website which offers online availability and booking. You can also take a virtual 360 degree tour of some of the properties. All are independently inspected and rated annually by VisitBritain. The properties range in grade from a two-star Victorian former rectory situated in the slopes of Cat Bells overlooking the Borrowdale valley, to the luxuriously appointed five-star barn conversions nestling on the northern side of the Skiddaw. Whatever the size and style of accommodation you seek, Lakeland Cottage Holidays is sure to have a property that will meet your requirements.

Park Authority and the RSPB whose aim is to protect the nesting ospreys and to encourage others to settle and breed in other suitable locations.

LOWESWATER
10 miles W of Keswick off the B5289

Reached by narrow winding lanes, Loweswater is one of the smaller lakes, framed in an enchanting fellside and forest setting. Because it is so shallow, never more than 60 feet deep, Loweswater provides an ideal habitat for wildfowl, which also benefit from the fact that this is perhaps the least visited lake in the whole of Cumbria. To the east of the lake lies the small village of the same name, while to the north stretches one of the quietest and least known parts of the National Park, a landscape of low fells through which there are few roads or even paths.

BASSENTHWAITE LAKE
4 miles NW of Keswick on the A66

Here's one for the Pub Quiz: Which is the only lake in the Lake District? Answer: Bassenthwaite, because all the others are either Waters or Meres. Only 70 feet deep and with borders rich in vegetation, Bassenthwaite provides an ideal habitat for birds - more than 70 species have been recorded around the lake. Successful breeding is encouraged by the fact that no power boats are allowed on the lake and some areas are off limits to boats of any kind. Also, most of the shoreline is privately owned, with public access restricted mostly to the eastern shore where the Allerdale Ramble follows the lakeside for a couple of miles or so.

At the northern end of the lake, at Coalbeck Farm, **Trotters World of Animals** is home to many hundreds of animals - rare breeds, traditional farm favourites, endangered species, birds of prey and reptiles. In addition to the ring-tailed lemurs, wallabies, racoons and gibbons, 2002 saw the arrival of rough-coated lemurs, lechwe antelope, red, fallow and sika deer and guanaco. Visitors to the 25-acre site can bottle-feed baby animals, cuddle bunnies, meet Monty the python, take a tractor trailer ride, watch the birds of prey demonstrations, find a quiet picnic spot or sample the fare on offer in Trotters Tea Room. And for the smaller children there's an indoor soft play climbing centre.

Rising grandly above Bassenthwaite's eastern shore is **Skiddaw** which, ever since the Lake District was opened up to tourists by the arrival of the railway in the 19th century, has been one of the most popular peaks to climb. Although it rises to some 3,054 feet, the climb is both safe and manageable, if a little

LINK HOUSE

Bassenthwaite Lake, Cockermouth, Cumbria CA13 9YD
Tel/Fax: 017687 76291
e-mail: info@link-house.co.uk website: www.link-house.co.uk

Set in one of the quieter parts of the Lake District National Park and enjoying stunning views of the surrounding fells, **Link House** is a traditional Victorian country house complete with period features and private lakeside access. Owners Keith and Wendy Atkinson offer quality bed & breakfast accommodation in eight comfortable bedrooms, all equipped with colour TV, hair dryer, radio alarm and tea/coffee-making facilities. The full cooked breakfast uses fresh local produce and three-course evening meals are available by arrangement. There's sailing and fishing on nearby Bassenthwaite Lake, and gentle or strenuous walking all around. Cockermouth Golf Course is also just a mile away.

Dodd Wood

Distance:	2.5 mile (4.0 kilometres)
Typical time:	90 mins
Height gain:	80 metres
Map:	Explorer OL 4
Walk:	www.walkingworld.com ID:933
Contributor:	Craig Lannigan

Access Information:

There is a regular bus service, stopping at Mirehouse from Keswick. Parking is limited and costs approximatley £1.50 for the day.

Description:

You commence this walk from the car park at Mirehouse. There are toilet, tea and tourist facilities at the stone building at the far end of the car park. The walk takes you past many nature trail signposts and over a weir. A gently ascending path leads you to junctions with forest tracks and through Dodd Wood itself. The wood in places is imposing and can be eerie if you are a lone walker. Sounds are echoed and the path underfoot is soft with pine needles which crunch at every step.

As you continue to ascend gently you will notice the vegetation around becoming less dense and teases you with intermittent views over the lake. Very quickly, you emerge from the wood and onto the foothills of Ullock Pike. To your left is the striking Bassenthwaite Lake and to your right the summit of Skiddaw. Continuing onwards, the path begins to descend, ultimately to the A591. A short section of road-walking reveals another path, heading towards the shore of the lake through fields and over stiles. The route takes you back to another section of the A591 which is again crossed. A forest path now follows above the line of the main road and leads to a lay-by and a tarmacked track up to the car park building from whence you came.

Additional Information

Additional routes around Dodd Wood are well worth the effort, particularly as this route will take under two hours to complete. The nature trails are well marked out and enjoyable.

Features:

Hills or Fells, Mountains, Lake/Loch, Toilets, Great Views, Food Shop, Moor, Nature Trail, Woodland

Walk Directions:

1 Begin the walk from the car park at Mirehouse. Use the shop and / or toilet facilities available at the stone building at the far end of the car park. Looking to your right, you will see a series of available forest walks as depicted with a wooden bridge just behind. Walk past the advertised walks and across the bridge, following the footpath that gently rises ahead until you come to a junction with a forest track. At the junction turn left and begin walking downhill for approximately 40 metres.

2 The path now splits into a lower and higher path. Take the right-hand side path that is less defined and rises uphill. Follow this path for 1km through some lovely isolated pine-canopied aisles which rise gently, teasing you with intermittent views of Bassenthwaite Lake. Be very careful not to pass by the next change of direction. The path

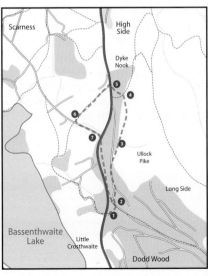

ahead takes you to a later waypoint but misses the spectacular views of the lake. Turn right at the pictured junction and follow the path that gently rises ahead.

3 Continue along the path for about 300 metres, again through tree-lined aisles which are blanketed with pine needles, making it unusually soft underfoot. The path ahead becomes less defined and greatly covered with vegetation. You will follow this for another 300 metres and every metre forward reveals a striking comprehensive view of Bassenthwaite Lake and the fells beyond. It is certainly worth dwelling on this section of the walk as it provides maximum views with minimum effort. To your right, if you can pull yourself away from the views left, you will see the summit of Skiddaw beyond Ullock Pike. This path comes to an end after a small descent and the path double backs on itself to the left. Contine along the gently descending gravel track for 200 metres. Bassenthwaite Lake is now on your right-hand side and begins to disappear behind the looming trees in the foreground of your view.

4 The path ends in another notable double back as pictured and this path is to be followed until you reach the main A591, which is only another 200 metres away. When you reach the road turn right towards the hotel, which stands back a little. Walk along the front of the hotel grounds until both entrances to the grounds have been passed.

5 Cross over the road and you will notice in front of you a bus stop next to a series of stone steps descending along a dry-stone wall. This is the onward route. Follow this path which bears to the right and cross the stile in front of you. You will be faced with an open field headed by a small wire fence. Head for the centre of the field and walk towards the centre of the fence, where you will see another stile. Go over the stile. Follow the path ahead which takes you towards a copse of trees. The path then bears to the left and takes you over another three stiles in quick succession. After the third stile you will find yourself once more on the road. Turn left and head towards the junction with the A591 again.

6 When the Keswick sign appears in front of you, turn right and cross over the road. The entrance to a path which runs alongside the main road for just over 1km will soon appear. This a lovely low-level forest section with lots to see.

7 The path ends at a small lay-by for cars and a path leading ahead towards a gate. Follow this rising path for 150 metres and you will come to the path junction that takes you down to the bridge you first walked over. Another 50 metres and you are in the car park once again.

unattractive lower down, and typically takes around two hours. From the summit, on a clear day, there are spectacular views to Scotland in the north, the Isle of Man in the west, the Pennines to the east, and to the south the greater part of the Lake District.

Also on the eastern shore is the secluded, originally Norman, **Church of St Bridget & St Bega** which Tennyson had in mind when, in his poem *Morte d'Arthur*, he describes Sir Bedivere carrying the dead King Arthur:

to a chapel in the fields,
A broken chancel with a broken cross,
That stood on a dark strait of barren land.

This then would make Bassenthwaite Lake the resting place of Excalibur but, as yet, no one has reported seeing a lady's arm, "clothed in white samite, mystic, wonderful", rising from the waters and holding aloft the legendary sword.

Set back from the lakeside, **Mirehouse** is a 17th century building which has been home to the Spedding family since 1688. Literary visitors to the house included Tennyson, Thomas Carlyle, and Edward Fitzgerald, the poet and translator of *The Rubaiyat of Omar Khayyam*. As well as some manuscripts by these family friends, the house also has a fine collection of furniture and visitors can wander around the wildflower meadow, the walled garden and the lakeside walk.

BROOKHOUSE COTTAGE HOLIDAYS

Brook House, Bassenthwaite Village,
Nr Keswick, English Lakeland CA12 4QP
Tel/Fax: 017687 76393
e-mail: a.m.trafford@amserve.net
website: www.holidaycottageslakedistrict.co.uk

The self-catering properties featured by **Brookhouse Cottage Holidays** occupy an idlyllic location beside a beautiful stream with ducks and a white wooden footbridge. A gentle stroll along the riverside takes you to the 17th century village inn where good food is served every day; Bassenthwaite Lake is a pleasant two miles walk away. The Brookhouse cottages have a homely atmosphere, are clean and well cared for and of various sizes.

The Nest is a small interesting stable conversion on ground level which sleeps two people. Brook House 1, which can sleep up to 10 guests, is a delightful beamed cottage overlooking the stream with its own private walled garden. Brook House 2 is a charming beamed cottage with an enclosed patio that can sleep eight, or up to 11 if you also rent the adjacent ground floor Studio. The Studio can also

be let separately. All properties are attractively furnished and decorated and equipped with colour TV. If you prefer bed & breakfast, owner Alison Trafford also welcomes guests at Bassenthwaite Hall Farm, a lovely 17th century farmhouse which has been fully modernised without losing its olde-worlde character.

THE OLD SMITHY CRAFTS, GIFTS AND TEAROOM

Caldbeck, Wigton, Cumbria
Tel: 016974 78246
website: www.rawsonpottery.co.uk or
www.caldbeckvillage.co.uk

Open all year round seven days a week from 9.30am-6pm, **The Old Smithy Crafts, Gifts and Tearoom** is a business run by Kathryn and Richard Rawson based on the Quaker ethos. The tearoom is the perfect place to enjoy a relaxing cup of tea or coffee. Superb home-made cakes, light meals or snacks are served all day and freshly prepared to order. As far as possible all ingredients are from supplies which are Fairtrade and ethically sourced and organic where available. In the fine weather you can enjoy your food outside on the grassy area by the beck.

Shop visitors can browse among the extensive range of both local and world arts and crafts including

ceramics by Rawson Pottery. Locally and ethically sourced and Fairtrade foods including pickles, sauces, honey, jams, sweets, confectionary and Kendal mint cake also feature in the shop. The Old Smithy also hosts regular events such as pottery painting workshops, crafts demonstrations and more. Everyone is welcome including walkers, cyclists, dog owners and the disabled. The Smithy will endeavour to provide access to all comers. Every Thursday, Kathryn and Richard have two stalls on Keswick Market where they display a selection of the many crafts and speciality foods available at The Old Smithy.

ULDALE

11 miles N of Keswick off the A591

To the northeast of Bassenthwaite Lake stretches the area known locally as the 'Land Back of Skidda', a crescent of fells and valleys constituting the most northerly part of the Lake District National Park. This peaceful region is well off the tourist track and offers visitors a delightful landscape of gently undulating bare-backed fells and valleys sheltering unspoilt villages such as Uldale. The village boasts a friendly traditional pub, The Snooty Fox, and a Victorian school which now houses the **Northern Fells Gallery** where a wide range of work by Cumbrian artists - watercolours, jewellery, copperwork, ceramics, knitwear and woodcarvings - can be seen, all available to buy. This tranquil village has one small claim to fame: it was the daughter of an Uldale farmer who eloped with and married the legendary huntsman John Peel (see Caldbeck).

CALDBECK

13 miles N of Keswick on the B5299

Caldbeck is perhaps the best-known village in the northern Lakes because of its associations with **John Peel**, the famous huntsman who died in 1854 after falling from his horse. His ornate tombstone in the churchyard is decorated with depictions of hunting horns and his favourite hound. Also buried here are John Peel's wife Mary and their four children. John Peel was Master of Hounds for over 50 years and was immortalised by his friend John Woodcutt Graves, who worked in a Caldbeck mill making the grey woollen cloth mentioned in the song, "D'ye ken John Peel with his coat so grey?" The tune itself is based on an old Cumbrian folk song adapted by William Metcalfe, a chorister and organist at Carlisle Cathedral.

A few paces from Peel's tomb lies 'The Fair Maid of Buttermere', mentioned earlier, whose grave bears her married name, Mary Harrison. With its picturesque church, village green, cricket pitch, pond and blacksmith's forge, Caldbeck has all the ingredients of a picture postcard village. Some 200 years ago Caldbeck was an industrial village, with corn mills, woollen mills, and a paper mill all powered by the fast-flowing 'cold stream' - the Caldbeck. **Priest's Mill**, built in 1702 by the Rector of Caldbeck, next to his church, was a stone grinding corn mill, powered by a waterwheel which has now been restored to working order. It is open to the public and has an accompanying Mining Museum and a collection of old rural implements. Also at the mill is **The Wool Clip**, the retail

outlet for a local co-operative of farmers and craft workers producing high quality items using wool from local sheep.

About a quarter of a mile outside the village is the limestone gorge known as **The Howk**, a popular beauty spot where the Caldbeck rushes past the restored ruins of one of the old bobbin mills.

HESKET NEWMARKET
13 miles N of Keswick off the B5305

Set around a well-kept village green, this pleasing little village used to have its own market, as the name suggests, and much earlier there was probably also a racecourse here since that is what Hesket meant in Old Scandinavian. It could well be the reason why the village's main street is so wide. Although the market is no longer held, Hesket hosts two important agricultural events each year: an Agricultural Show and Sheepdog Trials. There's also a vintage motor cycle rally in May. In a converted barn at the back of the Old Crown pub, **Hesket Newmarket Brewery** was set up in 1988, and beer sales, which were at first limited to the pub, soon spread across Cumbria. Many awards have come the way of Hesket Newmarket beers, which include Skiddaw Special Bitter, the nearly black Great Cockup Porter and the pale but potent Catbells Pale Ale.

IN AND AROUND PENRITH

Penrith is the most historic of Lakeland towns and was almost certainly settled long before the Romans arrived. They quickly appreciated its strategic position on the main west coast artery linking England and Scotland and built a fort nearby, although nothing visible remains today. Most of the town's oldest

buildings have also disappeared, victims of the incessant Border conflicts down the centuries. Penrith today is a busy place, its location close to the M6 and within easy reach not only of the Lakes but also the Border Country and the Yorkshire Dales making it a hub of this northwestern corner of England.

Only a few miles from the town, **Ullswater**, eight miles long and the second longest lake in Cumbria, is also one of its most beautiful. The area around Penrith has some interesting old buildings, notably Shap Abbey and Brougham Castle, as well as two outstanding stately homes, Hutton-in-the-Forest where the Inglewood family have lived since 1605, and Dalemain, a fine mixture of medieval, Tudor and Georgian architecture. Sadly, Greystoke Castle, which according to Edgar Rice Burroughs was the ancestral home of Tarzan, is not open to the public.

PENRITH

In Saxon times Penrith was the capital of the Kingdom of Cumbria but after the Normans arrived the town seems to have been rather neglected - it was sacked several times by the Scots before **Penrith Castle** was finally built in the 1390s. Richard, Duke of Gloucester (later Richard III) strengthened the castle's defences when he was Lord Warden of the Western Marches and was responsible for keeping the peace along the border with Scotland. By the time of the Civil War, however, the castle was in a state of ruin. The Cromwellian General Lambert demolished much of what was left and the townspeople helped themselves to the fallen stones to build their own houses. Nevertheless, the ruins remain impressive, standing high above a steep-sided moat.

A short walk from the castle leads to the centre of this lively town with its charming mixture of narrow streets and wide-open spaces.

Penrith has a splendid Georgian church in a very attractive churchyard, surrounded by a number of interesting buildings. The oldest part of **St Andrew's Church** dates from Norman times but the most recent part, the nave, was rebuilt between 1719 and 1772, possibly to a design by Nicholas Hawksmoor. Pevsner described it as "the stateliest church of its time in the county". Of particular interest is the three-sided gallery and the two chandeliers which were a gift from the Duke of Portland in 1745 - a reward for the town's loyalty during the Jacobite Rising. A tablet on the wall records the deaths of 2,260 citizens of Penrith in the plague of 1597.

The church's most interesting feature

MALEIKA

30 Devonshire Arcade, Penrith, Cumbria CA11 7SX
Tel: 01768 899470

Meryl Durdy and daughter Kate opened their gift shop, **Maleika**, in the Devonshire Arcade back in 1991. It was then quite small but such was the shop's success that it now occupies a huge space at the pillared entrance to the arcade. Outside, there's an extensive selection of baskets of every kind; inside is a complete A-Z of quality gifts and decorative items – from aromatherapy to woodcraft; candles to ornaments; jewellery oils and soaps, cushions and glassware, and much, much more. Meryl and Kate are proud of the fact that many of the items they sell are Fairtrade products.

THE GEM DEN

31 King Street, Penrith, Cumbria CA11 7AY
Tel: 01768 899989 Fax: 01768 862111
e-mail: sue@thegemden.co.uk
website: www.thegemden.co.uk

Ever thought of making a pet of a trilobite? As Sue Kane of **The Gem Den** points out "They're lovable and easy to care for!" At Sue's "treasure trove of gems" there are plenty of other striking and unusual items. She always stocks large crystal display pieces as well as small tumbled stones and collectors' specimens. Amongst the jewellery items are many pieces in sterling silver set

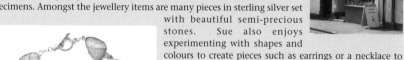

with beautiful semi-precious stones. Sue also enjoys experimenting with shapes and colours to create pieces such as earrings or a necklace to match your own clothes – some can even be made for you while you visit the town.

The Gem Den also has vast stocks of stones and beads and work in silver or gold, wind chimes, eggs, globes, wands, bowls, coasters, equipment and grits. Sue is happy to accept commissions such as creating a hallmarked silver pendant incorporating an ammonite. The Gem Den is located on King Street, the main road (A6) into Penrith and is open from 10am-5pm, Monday to Saturday, except for Bank Holidays. Penrith itself is just off the M6 at junction 40.

however, is to be found in the churchyard, in the curious group of gravestones known as **Giant's Grave** - two ancient cross-shafts, each 11 feet high, and four 10th century hogback tombstones which have arched tops and sharply sloping sides. According to a local legend the stones mark the burial place of a 5th century King of Cumbria, Owen Caesarius. Also buried somewhere in the churchyard is Wordsworth's mother, but her grave is not marked.

Overlooking the churchyard is a splendid Tudor house, bearing the date 1563, which is now a restaurant but was at one time Dame Birkett's School. The school's most illustrious pupils were William Wordsworth, his sister Dorothy, and his future wife, Mary Hutchinson. William is also commemorated by a plaque on the wall of the Robin Hood Inn stating that he was a guest there in 1794 and again in 1795.

About a mile west of Penrith, on the A66, **Rheged Discovery Centre** opened in Easter 2000 and dedicates itself to "a celebration of 2,000 years of Cumbria's history, mystery and magic - as never seen before". Named after Cumbria's Celtic Kingdom, this extraordinary grass-covered building is also home to Britain's only exhibition dedicated to mountains

and mountain adventure. It also has a giant cinema screen, speciality shops, pottery demonstrations, an artists' exhibition, restaurants and a children's play area.

Penrith is dominated by **Beacon Hill Pike**, which stands amidst wooded slopes high above the town. The tower was built in 1719 and marks the place where, from 1296, beacons were lit to warn the townsfolk of an impending attack. The beacon was last lit during the Napoleonic wars in 1804 and was seen by the author Sir Walter Scott who was visiting Cumberland at the time. Seeing it prompted Scott to hasten home to rejoin his local volunteer regiment. It is well worth the climb from the Beacon Edge, along the footpath to the summit, to enjoy a magnificent view of the Lakeland fells. It was on top of this hill, in 1767, that Thomas Nicholson, a murderer, was hanged. The gibbet was left on the summit and so was Nicholson's ghost, seen in the form of a skeleton hanging from the noose. The red sandstone from which many of Penrith's Victorian houses were built was quarried along the escarpments of Beacon Edge, and one of the old quarries, at **Cowraik**, is now a local nature reserve and is a Site of Special

Scientific Interest for the geological interest of the quarry faces.

AROUND PENRITH

ARMATHWAITE
10 miles N of Penrith off the A6

Set on the western bank of the River Eden, the village has a particularly fine sandstone bridge from which there is a lovely view of Armathwaite Castle (private), the home of the Skelton family, one of whose forebears was Poet Laureate to Henry VIII. Close by, visitors to the **Eden Valley Woollen Mill** can see traditional looms rattling away and browse through a huge range of knitwear produced from the finest wools and mohair. Also worth seeking out in **Coombs Wood** to the south is another of the Eden Benchmarks. Entitled *Vista* and

THE FOX & PHEASANT

Armathwaite, Carlisle, Cumbria CA4 9PY
Tel: 016974 72400

Standing close to the River Eden, **The Fox and Pheasant** was originally a 16th century coaching inn, later extended with the addition of a former shooting and fishing lodge. In converted stables is the delightful main bar with flagstones, wooden beams and inglenook fireplace, a great place to sample host Steven Thorpe's selection of between four and six quality real ales. The comfortable Eden Lounge has even more open fires and for more formal dining, there's the Victorian Restaurant which serves a good choice of quality food based on local produce. Accommodation is also available in individually furnished bedrooms.

HEATHER GLEN COUNTRY HOUSE HOTEL & RESTAURANT

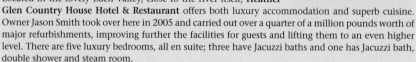

Ainstable, nr Carlisle, Cumbria CA4 9QQ
Tel: 01768 896219 Fax: 01768 896367
e-mail: heatherglen@btconnect.com
website: www.activehotels.co.uk

Located in the lovely Eden Valley, close to the river itself, **Heather Glen Country House Hotel & Restaurant** offers both luxury accommodation and superb cuisine. Owner Jason Smith took over here in 2005 and carried out over a quarter of a million pounds worth of major refurbishments, improving further the facilities for guests and lifting them to an even higher level. There are five luxury bedrooms, all en suite; three have Jacuzzi baths and one has Jacuzzi bath, double shower and steam room.

For gourmets, Heather Glen is a dream come true. Jason is a highly experienced chef who has worked with top culinary artists such as Gary Rhodes and many more throughout his career to date. He has cooked for a whole host of high class dignatries including Royal family members, MPs and TV stars. Jason uses all of his experience coupled with the produce that is on the Heather Glen's doorstep

from Penrith smoked salmon and chive blini's to local black pudding with smoked panccetta and leek cream. His main courses are in the same vein with local roe deer on haggis mash and Eden Valley lamb shank with redcurrant and mint reduction. He bases his menus around the finest ingredients sourced from local suppliers. The lunch and dinner menus focus on fresh game, fish and meats, all innovatively prepared and cooked to perfection. The hotel also offers a daily bar and lounge menu featuring typical country fare.

created by Graeme Mitchison, this remarkable sculpture seems to make the Lazenby Sandstone flow into liquid shapes.

EDENHALL
4 miles NE of Penrith off the A686

An old tradition asserts that in the 8th century the monks of Jarrow, fleeing from Viking invaders with the body of St Cuthbert, stopped here briefly. As a result the village church is dedicated to the saint. Part of the **Church of St Cuthbert** appears to be pre-Norman but most of the structure dates from the 1100s. Close to the church is the **Plague Cross** which stands where there was once a basin filled with vinegar. This acted as a disinfectant into which plague victims put their money to pay for food from the people of Penrith. A visitation of the plague in the 16th century killed a quarter of the village's inhabitants.

Edenhall is particularly famous for the story of the 'Luck of Eden Hall', a priceless glass cup which, according to legend, was stolen from some fairies dancing round the garden wall by a butler in the service of the Musgrave family back in the 15th century. Despite the fairies' entreaties, the butler refused to return the six-inch high glass to them. As he departed with the precious goblet, the fairies laid a curse upon it: "If ever this cup shall break or fall, Farewell the luck of Eden Hall". On inspection, the glass was identified as a 13th century chalice of enamelled and gilded glass that is thought to have come from Syria and may well have been brought back by a Crusader. It was a treasured heirloom of the Musgraves for many generations and is now in the Victoria & Albert Museum in London. The goblet is still intact but Eden Hall has long since disappeared.

CHURCH COURT COTTAGES

Gamblesby, Cumbria CA10 1HR
Tel: 01768 881682 Fax: 01768 889055
e-mail: markcowell@tiscali.co.uk website: www.gogamblesby.co.uk

Four red sandstone cottages surround a courtyard in tranquil, picturesque Gamblesby, a village hidden away beneath the fells of the North Pennines just one mile from the scenic A686 which links Penrith to Northumberland via Alston. From Melmerby, where you leave the main road to come to Gamblesby, the road climbs dramatically up the fell to Hartside viewpoint 1,903 feet above sea level with spectacular views over the Eden Valley to the mountains of the Lake District National Park and southwest Scotland.

Herdwick Cottage was once the farm's granary. It sleeps two in a double bedroom with en suite bathroom, whilst Hawthorn Cottage sleeps two in a double bedroom and also has a sofa bed. All the accommodation in Hawthorn Cottage is on the ground floor. The original barn was split into two cottages and The Barn sleeps four in one double and one twin room downstairs. Upstairs is a very large open plan living room/kitchen/diner with vaulted ceilings and original beams and views of the hills. The gable end of The Barn is in the original red sandstone. Next

door is Helm Cottage with a king sized bed in a bedroom/lounge with an en suite shower room upstairs. Down the spiral staircase is a large kitchen/diner. All guests have shared use of the garden and courtyard which have tables and benches. There are excellent walks to the neighbouring village of Melmerby with its famous organic Village Bakery, the Shepherd's Inn and the village shop and wine cellar. Dogs welcome at no extra charge. Short breaks starting either Friday or Monday are available all year round.

LANGWATHBY

5 miles NE of Penrith on the A686

Langwathby has a huge village green where maypole dancing takes place on the third Saturday in May. The green is medieval in origin and would once have been surrounded by wood and mud houses, perhaps to protect cattle but also for defence against border raids. After the Civil War and the growth in prosperity in the late 1600s, these wattle and daub cottages were replaced by stone buildings. West of the village, at Langwathby Hall Farm, **Eden Ostrich World** offers visitors the chance to see these splendid birds in a farm setting in the heart of the Eden Valley. The farm is also home to rare breed sheep, cattle and pigs, donkeys, deer, wallabies, alpacas and many other creatures from around the world.

LITTLE SALKELD

7 miles NE of Penrith off the A686

Little Salkeld boasts Cumbria's only fully operational **Watermill** producing stoneground organic flours by water power. Tours are available daily except on Wesnesday and Saturday and there's a mill shop selling a wide range of organic foods.

A lane from the village leads to **Long Meg and her Daughters**, a most impressive prehistoric site and second only to Stonehenge in size. Local legend claims that Long Meg was a witch who, with her daughters, was turned to stone for profaning the Sabbath, as they danced wildly on the moor. There are more than 60 stones in the Circle (actually an oval), which is approximately 300 feet across. The tallest, Long Meg, is a 15 feet column

THE HIGHLAND DROVE INN

Great Salkeld, Penrith, Cumbria CA11 9NA
Tel: 01768 898349
website: www.highland-drove.co.uk

Acclaimed by Les Routiers as the Northern Dining Pub of the Year, 2004, **The Highland Drove Inn** is the very epitome of a traditional country inn. Dating back many hundreds of years, it is set deep in the lovely Eden Valley, in the picturesque village of Great Salkeld which is well-known for its castle-like church, complete with dungeon. Since taking over the inn in 1998, the father and son team of Donald and Paul Newton have revived its fortunes as a social hub for Great Salkeld and the surrounding villages.

They have also established a deserved reputation for the high quality of the food served in Kyloes restaurant (named after the original Highland cattle). Traditional local dishes are featured and the specials are changed on a daily basis according to the freshness of the locally purchased meat, game and fish. Despite the excellence of its food, the Highland Drove is still essentially a pub where locals come to enjoy the wide range of cask conditioned real ales, a wide range of other beers and ciders, plus an impressive selection of wines. As befits a traditional country inn, accommodation is available with five modernised en suite rooms available for visitors.

of Penrith sandstone, the corners of which face the four points of the compass. Cup and ring symbols and spirals are carved on this stone which is over 3,500 years old. The circle is now known to belong to the Bronze Age but no one is certain of its purpose. It may have been used for rituals connected with the changing seasons since the midwinter sun sets in alignment with the centre of the circle and Long Meg herself. The brooding majesty of the site was perfectly evoked by Wordsworth:

A weight of awe, not easy to be borne,
Fell suddenly upon my spirit – cast
from the dread bosom of the unknown past,
When first I saw that family forlorn.

In 1725 an attempt was made by Colonel Samuel Lacy of Salkeld Hall to use the stones for mileposts. However, as work began, a great storm blew up and the workmen fled in terror believing that the Druids were angry at the desecration of their temple. It was the same Colonel Lacy who gave his name to the **Lacy Caves**, a mile or so downstream from Little Salkeld. The Colonel had the five chambers carved out of the soft red sandstone, possibly as a copy of St Constantine's Caves further down the river at Wetheral. At that time it was fashionable to have romantic ruins and grottoes on large estates and Colonel Lacy is said to have employed a man to live in his caves acting the part of a hermit.

KIRKOSWALD
8 miles NE of Penrith on the B6413

The village derives its name from the **Church of St Oswald**: Oswald was the King of Northumbria who, according to legend, toured the pagan north with St Aidan in the 7th century. The church is unusual in having a detached bell tower standing on top of a grassy hill some 200

yards from the main building (this is in a valley, so the bells could not be heard by the villagers).

This once thriving market town still retains its small cobbled market place and some very fine Georgian buildings. There's also a striking ruined 12th century **Castle**, formerly the home of the Featherstonehaugh family.

One of Kirkoswald's most splendid buildings is the **College**, its name recalling the days when St Oswald's was a collegiate church. The two-storey house with its sloping-ended roof was originally built as a pele tower and converted into the college for priests in the 1520s. The manor house opposite has a particularly attractive entrance front in sandstone, which was added in 1696.

Just to the northwest of Kirkoswald are the **Nunnery Walks** which start at a Georgian house built in 1715 on the site of a Benedictine Nunnery founded during the reign of William Rufus. Narrow footpaths have been cut into the sandstone cliffs along the deep gorge of **Croglin Beck** and they pass through beautiful woodland to reveal exciting waterfalls. The walks are open to the public during the summer months.

MELMERBY
9 miles NE of Penrith on the A686

Melmerby nestles at the foot of **Hartside Pass**, its spacious village green dissected by three becks. Even today, every householder in Melmerby has grazing rights on the green. Horses are grazed more commonly now, but in the past it would have been more usual to see flocks of geese - indeed, there was once a cottage industry here making pillows and mattresses from goose feathers. Overlooking the 13-acre village green is **Melmerby Hall**, a defensive tower that was extended in the 17th and 18th centuries. The village church, with its tower, is a Victorian building, but the first known rector of the church on the site came here in 1332.

A curious meteorological feature here is what is known as the **Helm Winds**, localised gusts which sweep through the valley with the force of a gale while the surrounding countryside is perfectly calm.

From Melmerby the main road climbs out of the Eden Valley to the east and the landscape changes suddenly. The road passes Fiend's Fell, close to the highest point in the Pennine Chain, the summit of Cross Fell. Early Christians erected a cross on the highest point of the fell to protect travellers from the demons who haunted the moors. Today, a cairn marks the spot where the cross once stood.

ALSTON

20 miles NE of Penrith on the A689/A686

England's highest market town sits 1,400ft up on the North Pennines, reached by the A686 which is acknowledged as one of the most scenic routes in the world. Alston has a cobbled main street and, from the picturesque **Market Cross**, narrow lanes radiating out with courtyards enclosing old houses. Many of the older buildings still have the outside staircase leading to the first floor - a relic from the days when animals were kept below while the family's living accommodation was upstairs. This ancient part of Alston is known as **The Butts**, a title acquired by the need of the townspeople to be proficient in archery during the times of the border raids.

Because the town centre has changed so little since the late 1700s, it proved to be an ideal location for ITV's 1999 reworking of Charles Dickens' *Oliver Twist* scripted by Alan Bleasdale. The town council has created an **Oliver Twist's Alton trail** with each of the 24 sites featured in the series marked by a picture of Mr Bumble.

An unusual feature of Alston was the number of watermills in and around the town and the mill race was once the central artery of the old town. The tall spire of **St Augustine's Church** is a well known local landmark and its churchyard contains a number of interesting epitaphs, as well as affording wonderful views of the South Tyne Valley.

Alston supports an astonishing diversity of shops and pubs and is home to a wide variety of craftspeople, ranging from blacksmiths to candlemakers, wood turners to potters. **Gossipgate Gallery**, housed in a converted congregational church built 200 years ago and with its

---

JUST GLASS

Cross House, Market Place, Alston, Cumbria CA9 3HU
Tel: 01434 381263

Occupying a quaint old building dating back to the 1600s, **Just Glass** is a treasure house of antique glass. Owner Margery Graham is an acknowledged expert in the field and always has a dazzling array of covetable items on display including a large stock of beautiful decanters. The pieces range from elegant 18th century objects to Victorian decorative glass such as cranberry, Mary Gregory, vaseline and North East pressed glass, along with items from specialist names such as Davison's pearline, Bristol blue and Gateshead yellow and blue. Just Glass is open Wednesday, Thursday, Saturday, Sunday or by appointment.

Alston

gallery shop a huge range of artefacts is for sale, including original watercolours and prints, jewellery, glass, ceramics, sculpture and striking turned wooden bowls made from native woods.

Alston is the southern terminus of the **South Tynedale Railway** and its restored Victorian station, complete with vintage signalbox, has featured in many television and film period productions. The station has a shop and refreshment room, and nearby in the original goods yard the Alston Model Railway Centre has a permanent exhibition of 6 layouts in different gauges. The narrow gauge (2ft) steam railway runs regular services during the summer months travelling through the beautiful South Tyne Valley. At the northern terminus of

original gas lights still intact, is the premier centre in the North Pennines for contemporary art and craft. A programme of exhibitions runs non-stop from February to December, and in the

North Pennines Heritage Trust

Nenthead House, Nenthead, Alston,
Cumbria CA9 3PD
Tel: 01434 382037
e-mail: info@npht.com

Welcome to **Nent Valley**. Visit the 200-acre centre at Nenthead, in the North Pennines, an Area of Outstanding Natural Beauty. It offers a unique insight into the lives of the miners who transformed these fells. Visitors have the chance to experience the underground world through guided trips in Carr's Mine, last commercially worked for lead in 1920. There is the huge "Power of Water" interactive area, where visitors can open sluice gates to operate water wheels and drive machinery. **Brewery Shaft** is an impressive 328-feet deep, with a viewing platform for visitors to gaze down into the depths and be amazed at the courage of anyone daring to descend.

Around the centre are various restored buildings, which contain exhibitions and interactive displays about the geology of the area, the local wildlife and social history of the area. The 200-acre site includes woodland walks, mountain streams and a waterfall, whilst the surrounding area is ideal for walkers of all ages and gives access to the spectacular scenery of the North Pennines. There is a café where you can rest your legs and take refreshments, and a well-stocked shop to purchase postcards, books and gifts.

the 2½-mile long track travellers can join a stretch of the Pennine Way that runs alongside the River South Tyne. In between Alston station and the A686 is **The Hub**, an exhibition of historic vehicles together with a wealth of local images and the stories that bring them alive.

To the south of the town is **Alston Moor**, 50 square miles of superb open landscape. The moor was once at the centre of an extremely important lead mining region, one of the richest in Britain. Lead and silver were probably mined on the moor by the Romans, but the industry reached its peak in the early 1800s when vast quantities of iron, silver, copper, and zinc were extracted by the London Lead Company. A Quaker company, it was a pioneer of industrial welfare and also built the model village of Nenthead to house the miners. Here, not only were the workers and their families provided with a home, but education was compulsory and there were some public baths. **Nenthead Mines Heritage Centre** is a 200-acre site high in the hills that tells the story of the lead and zinc mining industry. One of the main visitor attractions is 'The Power of Water', an impressive interactive area that looks at the technology used, including three working water wheels that drive model machinery. Another is the Brewery Shaft with its 328 feet drop and amazing virtual stone feature.

BROUGHAM
1 mile SE of Penrith off the A66

About a mile southeast of Penrith, the substantial and imposing remains of **Brougham Castle** (English Heritage) stand on the foundations of a Roman fort. The castle was inherited in the 1640s by the redoubtable and immensely rich Lady Anne Clifford, whose patrimony as Countess of Pembroke, Dorset and Montgomery also included another six northern castles. She spent a fortune restoring them all in medieval style and when told that Cromwell had threatened to destroy them replied, "As often as he destroys them I will rebuild them while he leaves me a shilling in my pocket". Brougham was her favourite castle and she died here in 1676 at the age of 86. From the castle there's a delightful riverside walk to **Eamont Bridge** and the circular **Mayburgh Earthwork**, which dates from prehistoric times. Close to the village, on the banks of the River Eamont, is **Giant's Cave**, the supposed lair of a man-eating giant called Isir. This local tale is linked with the legend of Tarquin, a giant knight who imprisoned 64 men in his cave and was eventually killed by Sir Lancelot. Some people also claim that Uther Pendragon, King Arthur's father, lived here and that

Brougham Castle

he too ate human flesh. A nearby prehistoric earthwork has been known as **King Arthur's Round Table** for many centuries. Lady Anne also rebuilt the chapel that stands on a hill above the castle, next to Brougham Hall. The old parish church of Brougham is the remotely located **St Ninian's**, also known as Ninekirks, which contains some family box pews that are screened so that they look almost like cages.

CLIFTON
3 miles S of Penrith on the A6

One of the last battles to be fought on English soil took place at nearby **Clifton Moor** in December 1745. Bonnie Prince Charlie was in retreat and his exhausted troops were easily routed by the English forces. Eleven soldiers were killed and are buried in Clifton churchyard, but some of the wounded Highlanders were hanged from the Rebels' Tree on the outskirts of the village. The tree is a sorry sight nowadays with its gaunt, dead branches, but it is still a place of pilgrimage for the Scots.

To the southeast of the village is **Wetheriggs Country Pottery**, which was founded in 1855. Visitors can try their hand at the often messy business of throwing a pot, paint a pot, paint on glass and make a candle, and also take a conducted tour of the steam-powered pottery, the only one of its kind in the UK. The pottery was scheduled as an Industrial Monument in 1973, and its steam engine was restored by none

other than Fred Dibnah, the famous steeplejack.

ASKHAM
3 miles S of Penrith off the A6

Askham is a pleasant village set around two greens. In the centre of the village is one of its most interesting shops, the **Toy Works** which combines a traditional toy shop with a toymaker's workshop. **Askham Fell**, which rises to the west, is dotted with prehistoric monuments including one known as the Copt (or Cop) Stone, which is said to mark the burial site of a Celtic chieftain.

LOWTHER
4 miles S of Penrith off the A6

Lowther Castle is now only a shell, most of it having been demolished in 1957, but it was clearly once a grand place; after one visit Queen Victoria is reputed to have said that she would not return to the castle as it was too grand for her. The ancestral owners of the castle were the illustrious Earls of Lonsdale, a family of statesmen and

Askham, with Lowther Castle Beyond

CUMBRIA & THE LAKE DISTRICT

sportsmen. The most famous is perhaps the 5th Earl (1857-1944), known as the Yellow Earl because of the colour of the livery used on his private carriage. He was the first President of the Automobile Association and permitted his family colours to be used by that organisation. The earl was also a patron of amateur boxing and the Lonsdale Belt emerged from his interest.

Within the castle park is the **Lakeland Bird of Prey Centre**, a sanctuary for a large collection of hawks, eagles, falcons and owls from around the world. There are daily flying demonstrations at 1pm and 3pm, weather permitting, and the site also has a tea room and gift shop.

Lowther village itself was built in the 1680s by Sir John Lowther, who moved his tenants here to improve the view from the new house he was building. He also built **St Michael's Church** where several generations of the Lowthers are buried in a series of magnificent tombs beginning with a medieval style alabaster monument to Sir Richard who died in 1608.

BAMPTON
8 miles S of Penrith off the A6

For several hundred years this small village was well known for its **Grammar School**, two of whose pupils rose swiftly in the church hierarchy. One was Hugh Curwen, who as a Protestant became Chaplain to Henry VIII, as a Catholic under Queen Mary was elevated to the Archbishopric of Dublin, and then prudently re-embraced Protestantism when Elizabeth succeeded to the throne. Another Bampton boy was less pliable: Edmund Gibson was baptised in the church here in 1669 and later became a fiery Bishop of London who repeatedly denounced the degenerate morals of the age - with little apparent effect.

A couple of miles south of Bampton, **Haweswater** is the most easterly of the lakes. It is actually a reservoir, created in the late 1930s to supply the growing needs of industrial Manchester. Beneath the water lies the village of **Mardale** and several dairy farms for which Haweswater Valley was once famous. By 1940, the lake had reached its present extent of four miles and Manchester Corporation set about planting its shores with conifers. Today the area is managed as a nature reserve. Walkers have a good chance of seeing woodpeckers and sparrowhawks, buzzards and peregrine falcons, and with luck may even catch sight of golden eagles gliding on the thermals rising above Riggindale. An observation is manned throughout the breeding season if the eagles are nesting.

Above Haweswater runs the **High Street**, actually a Roman road, which is now one of the most popular fell walks in the Lake District. It overlooks the remote and lovely Blea Tarn and the lonely valley of Martindale, a cul-de-sac valley to the south of Ullswater, where England's last remaining herd of wild red deer can often be seen.

SHAP
10 miles S of Penrith on the A6

This small village on the once congested A6 enjoys some grand views of the hills. In coaching days Shap was an important staging post for the coaches before they tackled the daunting climb up **Shap Fell** to its summit some 850 feet above sea level. Much earlier, in medieval times, the village was even more significant because of nearby **Shap Abbey**, constructed in the local Shap granite which has been used in many well-known buildings, St Pancras Station and the Albert Memorial in London among them.

The Abbey stands about a mile to the west of the village, just inside the National Park, and it's well worth seeking it out to see the imposing remains of the only abbey founded in Westmorland; the only one in the Lake District mountains; the last abbey to be consecrated in England (around 1199) and the last to be dissolved, in 1540.

ORTON

15 miles S of Penrith on the B6260

By far the best approach to Orton is along the B6260 from Appleby to Tebay. This scenic route climbs up onto the moors, passing **Thunder Stone**, some mighty limestone bluffs and the pavements of **Great Asby Scar**, the setting for BBC-TV's *The Tenant of Wildfell Hall*.

A pretty village now, for centuries Orton was a market town of some consequence with a charter granted in the 13th century by Edward I and a licence to hold fairs accorded by the puritan Oliver Cromwell. Today, the only market is a farmers market held on the second Saturday of every month. There are reminders of Orton's former importance in the noble church tower, completed in 1504; in the attractive proportions of **Petty Hall**, an Elizabethan house at the lower end of the village (a private residence, incidentally); and in the grandeur of **Orton Hall**, built in 1662 and now converted into holiday apartments. Orton's most famous visitor was Bonnie Prince Charlie, on his way northwards after the crushing defeat of his troops at Derby.

The village stands below **Orton Scar**, on which a beacon was lit to warn people to seek safety from advancing Scottish raiders. The village church, in common with many in the Eden Valley,

has a massive 16th century tower that was built for defensive purposes and, presumably, was one place where the villagers sought shelter. Its features include an ancient oak parish chest and a stained glass window by Beatrice Whistler, wife of the American artist James McNeill Whistler.

From the church there's a pleasant walk of well under a mile to **Keld**, a tiny village of just 17 houses. So quiet today, in medieval times Keld was a busy little place servicing the monks of Shap Abbey nearby. It was the monks of Shap Abbey who built the village's oldest building, the early-16th century **Keld Chapel** (National Trust).

DALEMAIN

3 miles SW of Penrith off the A592

Dalemain House is one of the area's most popular attractions - an impressive house with a medieval and Tudor core fronted by an imposing Georgian façade. The house has been home to the same family since 1679 and over the years they have accumulated fine collections of china, furniture and family portraits. The grand drawing rooms boast some very fine oak panelling and in the Chinese Room is some beautifully preserved 18th century Chinese wallpaper and a rococo chimneypiece by Nathaniel Hedges in Chinese Chippendale style; visitors also have access to the Nursery (furnished with toys from all ages) and Housekeeper's Room. The Norman pele tower houses the regimental collection of the Westmorland and Cumberland Yeomanry, a troop of mounted infantry which the family usually led, while the 16th century Great Barn contains an interesting assortment of agricultural bygones. The extensive grounds include a medieval herb garden, a Tudor-walled knot garden with a fine early Roman

DALEMAIN HISTORIC HOUSE

Penrith, Cumbria CA11 0HB
Tel: 017684 86450 Fax: 017684 86223
e-mail: admin@dalemain.com
website: www.dalemain.com

Dalemain has been a much loved family home since
1679 and is set against the grandeur and
picturesque splendour of the Lakeland Fells and
parkland.

Behind the impressive façade you will discover
the surprise of Dalemain- its sheer variety. In the Georgian part of the house, the grand public rooms
include the breathtaking Chinese Room with its original 18th century Chinese hand-painted wallpaper.
Much of the house dates from Tudor times and here you will find a glorious confusion of winding
passages, quaint stairways and unexpected rooms including the Fretwork Room with its magnificent
16th century plaster ceilings and oak panelling. The interior is full of fine furniture, family portraits,
ceramics, dolls' houses and old toys, as well as housing the Westmorland and Cumberland Yeomanry
Museum.

The gardens at Dalemain are a pure delight with a series of differing themes including a rose
garden, a Tudor knot garden and a wild garden. A glorious woodland walk takes you high above Dacre
Beck while other footpaths lead you by the walls of 14th century Dacre Castle or to Pooley Bridge.
Besides the house and gardens, you can pause for refreshments in the Mediaeval Hall, with its range of
home-made lunches and afternoon teas. A gift shop offers a selection of souvenirs and the Plant
Centre sells a choice of English plants including old fashioned roses. The Agricultural and Countryside
Collections can be found in the 16th century Great Barn. Open Sunday to Thursday March to October
10.30am-5pm, (House and Gardens open 11am-4pm).

fountain, a wild garden alongside Dacre
Beck, a deer park, and woodland and
riverside walks.

DACRE

4 miles SW of Penrith off the A66

There is much of historic interest in this
village. The **Church** occupies a site of a
former monastery which was mentioned
by the Venerable Bede in his accounts of
Cumberland in the 8th century. A later
reference shows that in 926 the Peace of
Dacre was signed between Athelstan of
England and Constantine of Scotland.
Fragments of masonry are reputed to
have come from the monastery and the
four weather-beaten carvings of bears in
the churchyard are probably of Anglo-
Viking origin. The bears are shown,
respectively, sleeping, being attacked by a
cat, shaking off the cat and eating the
cat. A 14th century pele tower, **Dacre**

Castle (private) is a typical example of
the fortified house or small castle that
was common in northern England
during the Middle Ages. This was the seat
of the Dacre family, Catholic Earls of
Cumberland, and its turrets and
battlements have walls that are eight feet
thick.

POOLEY BRIDGE

5 miles SW of Penrith on the B5320

In Wordsworth's opinion Ullswater
provides "the happiest combination of
beauty and grandeur, which any of the
Lakes affords", an opinion with which
most visitors concur. The poet also noted
the curious fact that the lake creates a
sextuple echo, a natural phenomenon
that the Duke of Portland exploited in
the mid-1700s by keeping a boat on the
lake equipped "with brass guns, for the
purpose of exciting echoes".

PARK FOOT HOLIDAY ACCOMMODATION

Howtown Road, Pooley Bridge, Penrith, Carlisle, Cumbria CA10 2NA
Tel: 017684 86309 e-mail: holiday@parkfootullswater.co.uk
Fax: 017684 86041 website: www.parkfootullswater.co.uk

Set beside Lake Ullswater and surrounded by magnificent scenery, **Park Foot Holiday Accommodation** offers a wide choice of holiday options ranging from stands for touring caravans, dormobiles and tents to comfortable self-catering accommodation for between two to eight people in cottages, log cabins or a converted stables in the centre of Pooley Bridge. All visitors have access to the Park's many amenities which include a licensed bar and restaurant, beer garden, video games room, large screen TV, two pool tables, table tennis, discos and other entertainment. The Park is open from Easter until November.

The charming village of Pooley Bridge stands at the northern tip of Ullswater, and there are regular cruise departures from here during the season, stopping at Glenridding and Howton. Rowing and powered boats are available for hire, and since Ullswater is in effect a public highway, private boats can also be launched. A speed limit of 10mph applies over the whole of the eight-mile-long serpentine lake. The oldest building in Pooley Bridge is part of **Holly House**, which dates back to 1691, while the Bridge of the village's name dates from 1763 when the elegant structure over the River Eamont was built at a cost of £400.

WATERMILLOCK

7 miles SW of Penrith on the A592

This small village, perfectly situated on the shores of Ullswater, is hidden amongst the woodland which occupies much of the lake's western shores. About four miles southwest of the village, there is a series of waterfalls which tumble down through a wooded gorge and then into Ullswater. The name of the largest fall is **Aira Force** (70 feet high) and the second largest is **High Force**. They

can easily be reached on foot through the woodlands of **Gowbarrow Estate**, which is owned by the National Trust.

GLENRIDDING

14 miles SW of Penrith on the A592

A popular base for walkers about to tackle the daunting challenge of **Helvellyn**, Glenridding is the largest and busiest of Ullswater's lakeside villages. Lake cruises depart from here, rowing boats are available for hire and there's plenty of room for waterside picnics.

Aira Force

PATTERDALE
15 miles SW of Penrith on the A592

It is this village's magnificent setting that makes it such a popular tourist destination. Close to the head of Ullswater and with a series of fells framing the views, the scenery is indeed splendid. On the north side of the village is **St Patrick's Well**, which was thought to have healing properties, and the medieval chapel dedicated to the saint was rebuilt in the 1850s.

STAINTON
2 miles W of Penrith off the A66 or A592

The Alpaca Centre was set up in 1997 and has become a focal point for the development and expanding knowledge of the alpaca. The Centre is a working farm, breeding, rearing and selling alpacas and welcomes visits at any time of the year. There's a shop selling an array of garments fashioned from the exceptionally fine alpaca fibre, many hand-made in Peru. Upstairs is the **Just Wood Gallery** displaying a superb collection of furniture and ornamental pieces, many crafted in the centre's own workshop by Garry Stevenson and his son Shaun. Also at the centre is G&S Timber Crafts which supplies hard woods for wood turners, carvers and furniture makers.

GREYSTOKE
5 miles W of Penrith on the B5288

According to Edgar Rice Burroughs, **Greystoke Castle** was the ancestral home of Tarzan, Lord of the Apes, a fiction which was perpetuated in the 1984 film *Greystoke*. Tarzan's aristocratic credentials would have come as something of a surprise to the dignified Barons of Greystoke whose effigies are

BECKSTONES ART GALLERY

Beckstones, Greystoke Ghyll, Nr Penrith, Cumbria CA11 0UQ
Tel: 01768 483601
website: www.beckstonesartgallery.co.uk

Beckstones Art Gallery, quietly tucked away down a Lakeland country lane, is a picturesque sandstone building nestling at the heart of the tiny village of Greystoke Ghyll, an idyllic location for a gallery dedicated to the highest standards of contemporary art. Seemingly well off the beaten track, the gallery is actually only two miles from the A66 and roughly five miles from Penrith, Ullswater and Junction 40 of the M6. In the 25 years since it opened, its resolute policy of pursuing excellence has given it a national reputation for exhibiting paintings of the highest quality. It is a family run business with a relaxed atmosphere, and visitors are made genuinely welcome by friendly, knowledgable staff.

The artists who exhibit at Beckstones are chosen as the best in their own particular categories and come from every part of the United Kingdom. Subject matter covers an impressive range, and oils, watercolours and other media are all featured. Around 40 artists exhibit on a regular basis, and between 300 and 500 pieces, all originals, are available at any one time.

Kirkby Stephen

Distance:	2.4 mile (3.8 kilometres)
Typical time:	60 mins
Height gain:	99 metres
Map:	Explorer OL 19
Walk:	www.walkingworld.com
	ID: 2598
Contributor:	David and Chris Stewart

Access Information:

Kirkby Stephenn is on the Settle to Carlisle railway line although the station is a good mile or more away from the village. The village (or small town) is well served with buses from all around. Parking is not usually a problem. If you can't park in the market square by the church, there are usually places along by the shops and there is a free public car park behind the main square.

Description:

Take this peaceful little walk around the back of Kirkby Stephen in the Upper Eden Valley. For the most part it follows the River Eden and for a while a disused railway to the bridge at Stenkrith where the river has made extraordinary carvings into the limestone river bed. Talking of interesting carvings - look out along the way for poetry written by Meg Peacocke and carved into large stones by Pip Hall.

Features:

River, Pub, Toilets, Birds, Flowers, Butterflies, Cafe, Gift Shop, Food Shop, Public Transport

Walk Directions:

1 From Kirkby Stephen market place, head down past the toilets, following the signs to Frank's Bridge. Follow a small lane down past some houses and turn left to go over the footbridge. After crossing the bridge turn right to follow the footpath along the river.

2 As you enter a wide field bear right to follow the edge of the river. Go past a barn to the edge of the field.

3 Take the small footbridge over the stream and follow the path through the woods. After a while you come to a bridge over the disused railway line. Continue over the bridge as the path bears to the right.

4 Go through this gate to drop down onto the track of the old railway. Turn left to follow the gravelled track to Stenkrith bridge.

5 Bear right over the new blue footbridge over the Eden at Stenkrith bridge. Take time to view the fascinating shapes bored out by the water as it flows through the rocks under the bridge.

6 Just before reaching the road turn sharp right onto this path following the river. Return this way towards Kirkby Stephen.

7 At this field keep to the right to continue following the edge of the river. Another nice place for a picnic.

8 This bridge is structurally unsound. For your safety please return to Kirkby Stephen by turning left here, (the footpath is quite overgrown) and then right to the B6259. Turn right to follow the road back into the village.)Once safely repaired, cross the bridge and follow the path up the deep gully on the other side. The path curves round to the right to join the path you originally took on the outward journey. Notice more of Meg Peacocke's poetry carved in stone by the letter-carver Pip Hall near the barn.

9 Turn left and follow your tracks back to Frank's Bridge.

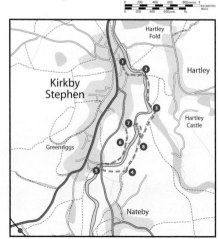

preserved in **St Andrew's Church**. As imposing and spacious as a cathedral, St Andrew's boasts a wonderful east window with much 13th century glass and, in the Lady Chapel, a figure of the Madonna and Child carved by a German prisoner-of-war. About 100 yards from the church stands the **Plague Stone** where, during medieval times, coins were left in vinegar in exchange for food for the plague victims. An ancient **Sanctuary Stone**, now concealed behind a grille, marks the point beyond which fugitives could claim sanctuary.

Greystoke village itself is a gem, its attractive houses grouped around a trimly maintained village green. Nearby are the stables where Sir Gordon Richards trained his two Grand National winners, Lucius and Hello Dandy.

HUTTON-IN-THE-FOREST

6 miles NW of Penrith on the B5305

The home of the Inglewood family since 1605, Hutton-in-the-Forest was originally a medieval stronghold and the **Pele Tower** still exists. The house has been added to and altered by successive generations, with the result that an unusual number of architectural and decorative styles can be seen. Among the notable features are the 17th century Gallery, the Hall dominated by a Cupid staircase, and a room decorated in the Arts and Crafts style. The splendid grounds include a beautiful walled garden built in the 1730s, topiary terraces that were originally laid out in the 17th century, fine specimen trees and a 17th century dovecote that form part of the Woodland Walk.

THE EDEN VALLEY AND EAST CUMBRIA

Carved through boulder clay and red

sandstone and sandwiched between the Lakeland fells and the northern Pennines, the Eden Valley is green and fertile - in every sense another Eden. This, too, is farming country and many of the ancient towns and villages have a market place. Appleby-in-Westmorland, the old county town of Westmorland, had an important market and also an annual horse fair which continues today and has gained a large following.

An attractive man-made feature of the valley is the collection of specially commissioned stone sculptures known as **Eden Benchmarks** dotted along its length. Each created by a different sculptor, they have been located beside public paths and, since they also function as seats, provide the perfect setting in which to enjoy the valley's unspoilt scenery.

KIRKBY STEPHEN

Surrounded by spectacular scenery, the old market town of Kirkby Stephen lies at the head of the beautiful Eden Valley. Although essentially part of the Valley, Kirkby Stephen has a strong Yorkshire Dales feel about it. Indeed, the church, with its long, elegant nave, has been called the Cathedral of the Dales.

Dating from Saxon times, rebuilt in 1220 and with a 16th century tower, **St Stephen's Church** is one of the finest in the eastern fells, dominating the northern end of the town from its elevated position. Until the last century the **Trupp Stone** in the churchyard received money from local people every Easter Monday in payment of church tithes. At eight o'clock, the curfew is still sounded by the **Taggy Bell**, once regarded by local children as a demon. Inside the church are a number of pre-Conquest stones, some of which show Norse influence. The most remarkable is

River Eden, Kirkby Stephen

sculpture is deceptively simple, suggesting perhaps the course of a river bed. There are also some pleasant strolls along the riverside to a fine waterfall where the River Eden cascades into Coop Karnel Hole. Look out for the unusual shapes of the weathered limestone rock. For more strenuous exercise, walkers could tackle a stretch of the **Coast to Coast** long distance footpath, which passes through the town.

AROUND KIRKBY STEPHEN

OUTHGILL
5 miles S of Kirkby Stephen on the B6259

This remote village has close links with the Clifford family of Skipton Castle, North Yorkshire. The village **Church of St Mary**, first built in 1311, was repaired by Lady Anne Clifford who, from 1643 when she finally obtained possession of the Clifford estates, devoted her life to restoring her many properties and lived in each of them for varying periods of time. Her estates included six castles - Skipton and Barden in Yorkshire; Appleby, Brough, Brougham and Pendragon in Westmorland. Lady Anne's zeal for restoration didn't stop at castles: she also repaired the Roman road between Wensleydale and the Eden Valley, a route she often travelled (along with a huge retinue) between her castles and her birthplace at Skipton. The route is now known as Lady Anne's Way but in times past it was aptly called the **High Way** since it was a regular place of employment for highwaymen such as Dick Turpin and William 'Swift' Nevison.

The landscape around Outhgill is remote and beautiful. To the south is

the 10th century **Loki Stone**, one of only two such carvings in Europe to have survived. Loki was a Norse God and presumably Viking settlers brought their belief in Loki to Kirkby Stephen.

Between the church and the market square stand the cloisters, which served for a long time as a butter market. The **Market Square** is surrounded by an ancient collar of cobblestones which marked out an area used for bull-baiting - a 'sport' that ceased here in 1820 after a disaster when a bull broke loose. There are many delightful walks from the town, to **Croglam Earthworks** for example, a prehistoric fort, or to nearby Stenkrith Park where the second of the **Eden Benchmarks** can be found. Created by Laura White in Ancaster limestone and titled *Passage*, the

Wild Boar Fell, a brooding, flat-topped peak where the last wild boar in England was reputedly killed, while tucked down in the valley are the romantic ruins of Lammerside and Pendragon Castles.

Pendragon Castle, about a mile north of the village, is shrouded in legend but there are claims that it was the fortress of Uther Pendragon, father of King Arthur. If so, nothing remains of that 6th century wooden castle. The present structure dates from the 1100s and was built by Hugh de Morville, one of the four knights who murdered Thomas à Becket, to guard the narrow pass of Mallerstang. Twice it was burned by the Scots and twice restored, on the latter occasion by the formidable Lady Anne Clifford in 1660. Another mile or so downstream, Lammerside Castle dates from the 12th century but only the remains of the keep survive. They can be found along a bridle path between Pendragon and Wharton Hall.

RAVENSTONEDALE
5 miles SW of Kirkby Stephen on the A685

Known locally as Rissendale, this pretty village of stone-built cottages clustered along the banks of Scandal Beck lies on the edge of the Howgill Fells. The parish Church of St Oswald is especially interesting: built in 1738, it is one of the few Georgian churches in Cumbria. The window at the east end commemorates the last woman in England to be put to death for her Protestant faith. Elizabeth Gaunt was sentenced in 1685 by the notorious Judge Jeffreys to be burnt at the stake for sheltering a fugitive rebel. She met her end at Tyburn in London.

CROSBY GARRETT
4 miles W of Kirkby Stephen off the A685

Local legend has it that the Devil, seeing all the stones lying ready to build Crosby Garrett Church, carried them in his leather apron to the top of a nearby hill. He reasoned that, as people grew old, they would be unable to climb the hill and attend church and thus would come to him rather than go to Heaven. Such tales apart, the church itself is said to be of Anglo-Saxon origin though the visible fabric is 12th century. Inside there are some superb carvings, particularly near the font. The church is also famous for its hagioscope, cut through the wall to allow people in the north aisle to see the altar. Near the church gates is a tithe barn, built in the 18th century to store farm produce given to the church as a religious tax. To the west of the village runs the Settle-Carlisle Railway whose splendid viaduct dominates Crosby Garrett.

WINTON
3 miles N of Kirkby Stephen off the A685

The oldest building in this quiet and picturesque hamlet is Winton Hall, built of stone and dated 1665, but looking older with its stone buttresses and mullion windows with iron bars. Those taking a walk on Winton Fell are likely to see red grouse lifting off from the large tracts of heather on the fellside. Indeed, the wildlife is much more prolific around this area where the limestone provides more plentiful food than on the fells around the lakes.

APPLEBY-IN-WESTMORLAND

The old county town of Westmorland, Appleby is one of the most delightful small towns in England. It was originally built by the Norman, Ranulph de Meschines, who set it within a broad loop of the River Eden which protects it on three sides. The fourth side is guarded by Castle Hill. The town's uniquely attractive main street, Boroughgate, has been described as the

TUFTON ARMS HOTEL

Market Square, Appleby, Cumbria CA16 6XA
Tel: 01768 351593 Fax: 01768 352761
e-mail: info@tuftonarmshotel.co.uk
website: www.tuftonarmshotel.co.uk

Located in the heart of the beautiful Eden Valley, in the medieval market town of Appleby in Westmorland, the **Tufton Arms Hotel** started life in the 16th century as a coaching inn. It's now a family run hotel with an inviting and friendly atmosphere and provides a relaxing and charming location for an enjoyable break. Guests are welcomed with a smile at reception and the staff express a genuine concern that your stay will be not just pleasant but memorable. It's quite likely you will immediately meet one of the owners, the Milsom family, who speak not of guests but of "friends who come to stay".

Good food is taken seriously here. Be prepared to spend some time sifting through the menus for a wide selection of tasty dishes. The award-winning team of chefs use fresh local produce, prepared with skill and flair to create delicious classic dishes with a modern twist. Dinner is served in the elegant Conservatory overlooking the cobbled mews courtyard and, to complement your meal the award winning wine list offers 200 wines expertly chosen for value and distinction.

Accommodation at the Tufton Arms maintains the high standards apparent throughout the hotel. Open the door to your bedroom or suite and enjoy the luxury. No two rooms are the same; all are individually furnished and decorated. You may find an antique in one corner which belonged at the Milsom farmhouse before they decided in 1989 to lovingly restore the hotel. Naturally, all rooms are en suite and provided with all the modern day comforts you would expect.

If you are planning a wedding or other function the hotel has three purposefully designed conference and function suites to choose from. Elegantly furnished in keeping with the hotel's character and ambience, the suites offer a luxurious backdrop to any occasion, and meet all modern business requirements.

There's plenty to see and do in the area. Country houses, castles and galleries are just a few of the places to visit, with fell walking, pony trekking and golfing providing more energetic pastimes. Fly fishing and shooting can be arranged – the Tufton Arms has access to some of the finest water on the River Eden, and its own driven and rough pheasant shoot.

finest in England. A broad, tree-lined avenue, it slopes down the hillside to the river, its sides lined with a pleasing variety of buildings, some dating back to the 17th century. At its foot stands the 16th century **Moot Hall** (still used for council meetings and also housing the Tourist Information Centre); at its head rises the great Norman Keep of **Appleby Castle** which is protected by one of the most impressive curtain walls in northern England. Attractions here include the dramatic view from the top of the five-storey keep and the attractive grounds which are home to a wide variety of animals and include a **Rare Breeds Survival Centre**.

Appleby-in-Westmorland

During the mid-1600s, Appleby Castle was the home of Lady Anne Clifford, the remarkable woman who has already been mentioned several times and to whom Appleby has good cause to be grateful. The last of the Clifford line, the

COURTYARD GALLERY

32 Boroughgate, Appleby, Cumbria CA16 6XG
Tel: 01768 351838
e-mail: courtyardgallery@btconnect.com
website: www.courtyardgallery.co.uk

Housed in a 17th century granary and reached by an outside stairway, **The Courtyard Gallery** has been established in the delightful little town of Appleby-in-Westmorland for more than 20 years. It provides a showcase for the work of more than 25 artists and craftspeople who have based themselves in the north of England. On display is a diverse selection of original watercolours and oils by artists such as Venus Griffiths, Rosemary Morrison, Pat Schaverien and Gareth Watson, along with mixed media and etchings by Roseanne Bellwood, Debbie Lucas and Piers Brown.

Other artists whose work is regularly on show include John Sibson, Chris Mouncey and Alan Stones. The gallery also displays a fine selection of glassware, jewellery (mostly silver), domestic and abstract sculpture, ceramic antiques, greetings cards and postcards. Whether you are looking for something to add distinction to your own home, or to find an inspired gift, you will almost certainly find it here. Another attraction at the gallery is its coffee shop which serves teas, coffees and some delicious home-made cakes.

diminutive Lady Anne (she was just four feet 10 inches tall) inherited vast wealth and estates, among them no fewer than six northern castles. She lavished her fortune on rebuilding or restoring them all. Churches and chapels in the area also benefited from her munificence and at Appleby, in 1651, she also founded the almshouses known as the Hospital of St Anne, for '12 sisters and a Mother'. Set around a cobbled square, the picturesque cottages and minuscule chapel still serve their original function, maintained by the trust endowed by Lady Anne.

Lady Anne died in 1676 in her 87th year and was buried with her mother, Margaret Countess of Cumberland, in **St Lawrence's Church**. The church is well worth visiting to see their magnificent tombs and also the historic organ, purchased from Carlisle Cathedral in 1684, which is said to be oldest still in use in Britain.

Just a few years after Lady Anne's death, James II granted the town the right to hold a Fair during the week leading to the second Wednesday in June. More than 300 years later, the **Gypsy Horse Fair** is still thriving with hundreds of gypsies flooding into the little town (population 1,800) with their caravans and horse-drawn carts. The trade, principally in horses, and the trotting races provide a picturesque and colourful spectacle.

AROUND APPLEBY-IN-WESTMORLAND

BRAMPTON
2 miles N of Appleby-in-Westmorland off the A66

This village, along with the surrounding area, was said to be haunted by the ghost of Elizabeth Sleddall, the wife of a 17th century owner of nearby Crackenthorpe Hall. Elizabeth died believing that she had been cheated out of her share of the estate, so to shame the false inheritors her spirit was seen being driven around the countryside in a coach drawn by four black horses. Her ghost became so troublesome that the local people exhumed her body and reburied the remains under a larger boulder. Her ghost, while no longer upsetting the local people, is said still to visit the hall.

DUFTON
3 miles N of Appleby-in-Westmorland off the A66

Behind this delightful hamlet lies **Dufton Gill**, a beautiful, secluded wooded valley through which runs a footpath. Also from Dufton there is a track carrying the Pennine Way up to High Cup Nick, a great horseshoe precipice at the edge of the northern Pennine escarpment that was formed by a glacial lake during the Ice Age.

GREAT ORMSIDE
2 miles SE of Appleby-in-Westmorland off the B6260

This was once an important fort guarded by a pele tower, and the ancient **Church of St James**, which dates from the 11th century, occupies a site on the steep-sided defence mound. Relics of pre-Christian burials have been found in the mound, as well as a Viking sword (now in the Tullie Museum in Carlisle). A silver gilt and enamel bowl from the 7th century has also been found and is regarded as one of the most important pieces of Anglo-Saxon metalware to survive. A particularly beautiful piece, richly decorated with vine scrolls, birds, and animals, it is now on permanent display in the Yorkshire Museum in York.

From the village a path leads across fields to the village of **Little Ormside**, with its large cedar tree said to have been brought back from Lebanon as a sapling by General Whitehead. On the voyage home he grew it in his hat and shared with it his daily ration of one pint of water.

WARCOP

5 miles SE of Appleby-in-Westmorland on the B6259

The largest village in this part of the Eden Valley, Warcop grew up as a crossing point of the river. The bridge, the oldest to cross the river, dates from the 16th century and the red sandstone buildings surrounding the village green, with its central maypole, make this a charming place to visit.

The **Church of St Columba** is built outside the village on the site of a Roman camp. An interesting building in its own right, it is particularly famous for the rush-bearing ceremony, which takes place in late June each year.

BROUGH

9 miles SE of Appleby-in-Westmorland on the A66/ A685

This small town, standing at the point where the **Stainmore Pass** opens into the Vale of Eden, is, in fact, two settlements: **Church Brough** and **Market Brough**. Church Brough is a group of neat houses and cottages clustered around a little market square in which a maypole stands on the site of the former market cross. **Brough Castle**, built within the ramparts of the Roman camp of Verterae, was constructed to protect the Roman road over Stainmore Pass. The building of this Norman castle was begun by William Rufus in 1095 but it was largely destroyed in 1174 by William the Lion of Scotland. Another fortification restored by the remarkable Lady Anne Clifford, the castle, with its

tall keep 60 feet high is well worth visiting, if only for the superb panorama of the surrounding fells seen from the battlements.

The distinctive low hills that lie to the west of Brough are drumlins - heaps of material deposited by Ice Age glaciers. In this area many drumlins are marked by broad, grassy ridges, remains of ancient lynchets or ploughing strips.

NORTH STAINMORE

11 miles SE of Appleby-in-Westmorland on the A66

The village lies on the Stainmore Pass which carries the old Roman road, now the A66, through a remote area of the North Pennines which David Bellamy described as "England's last wilderness". Near Stainmore summit are the foundations of **Maiden Castle**, a Roman fort built to guard the pass against marauders. A few yards over the Cumbrian border, into County Durham, is the stump of the ancient **Rey Cross** which was erected before AD 946 and which, until 1092, marked the boundary between England and Scotland. It is thought to be the site of the battle at which the last Viking King of York and North England, Eric Bloodaxe, was killed following his expulsion from the city.

GREAT ASBY

4 miles S of Appleby-in-Westmorland off the B6260

This pretty village is set in a wooded hollow, its houses separated by Hoff Beck. Alongside the beck is St Helen's Well which is said never to run dry or freeze. Nearby, are the splendid almshouses of St Helen's, built between 1811 and 1820. Across a footbridge is Asby Hall (private), built in 1670. It was once the home of the Musgrave family of Edenhall whose crest and coat of arms can still be seen above the door.

SCALEBECK HOLIDAY COTTAGES

Scalebeck, Great Asby, Appleby, Cumbria CA16 6TF
Tel: 01768 351006 Fax: 01768 353532
e-mail: mail@scalebeckholidaycottages.com
website: www.scalebeckholidaycottages.co.uk

Scalebeck Holiday Cottages enjoy a wonderfully peaceful
location in the picturesque Eden Valley, a perfect base for
exploring the Lake District, the Yorkshire Dales National Park,
Northumberland and the Scottish borders. This is also a great
walking area with an abundance of wildlife to be seen – deer, hares and red squirrels, for example,
while the woodpeckers, kingfishers, heron, buzzards and sparrow hawks provide a twitchers' delight.

There are three cottages in all: Witsend which sleeps up to five; Folly which sleeps up to five; and
Rum 'Un which also sleeps up to five. All the cottages have ground floor bedrooms and fully appointed
bathrooms with power shower over the bath. The open plan living rooms have stone-surround living

flame gas fires, beams and pleasant country views. Other
amenities include colour TV, video, DVD, CD player/radio
and microwave. There's also a laundry with coin-operated
washing machine, dryer, public telephone, cycle store and
games room with table tennis and pool. Within the 12
acres of grounds, shared with the owners, are separate large
grassed areas for outside games and dog walking; a
wildflower meadow; an unfenced stream and pond (young
children may need supervision), and a barbecue area. Please
note that all the properties are for non-smokers only.

TEMPLE SOWERBY

7 miles NW of Appleby-in-Westmorland on the A66

Temple Sowerby prides itself on the title
'Queen of Westmorland villages', an
accolade justified by its lovely setting in
the Eden valley, but somewhat qualified
by its position on the busy A66. (Here's a
bonus: the average rainfall here is half
that recorded in the Lake District
National Park to the west.) To the north,
the massive bulk of **Cross Fell**, the
highest point in the Pennines, swells
skywards to provide a spectacular
backdrop. The village itself, picturesquely
grouped around a sloping green and an
18th century red sandstone church, takes
its name from the medieval Knights
Templar who owned the manor of
Sowerby until their Order was suppressed
in 1308.

From Temple Sowerby there are
delightful walks through the Eden Valley

or, if you prefer a gentle stroll, it's only a
mile to the National Trust gardens at
Acorn Bank where Crowdundle Beck
splashes beneath an elegant 18th century
bridge. The 16th century manor house is
now a Sue Ryder Home and not open to
the public, but visitors are welcome to
explore the attractive gardens planted
with a collection of some 250 medicinal
and culinary herbs. A circular woodland
walk runs along the beck to a watermill
that was first mentioned on the site as
far back as the 14th century. At different
times it has been a saw mill, a corn mill
and a source of power for the local
gypsum mines; now restored, it is open
for visits.

CARLISLE

Carlisle is the largest settlement in
Cumbria, with a population of around
130,000, and is also its county town. The

city stands at the junction of three rivers, the Eden, the Caldew and the Petteril, and was already fortified in Celtic times when it was named Caer Lue, the 'hill fort'. It became a major Roman centre as the military base for the Petriana regiment, Luguvallum, guarding the western end of Hadrian's Wall, and also an important civilian settlement with fountains, mosaics, statues and centrally-heated homes.

Today, the squat outline of **Carlisle Castle** (English Heritage) dominates the skyline of this fascinating city. The original Norman castle was built of wood but, during the Scottish occupation in the 12th century, King David I laid out a new castle with stones taken from Hadrian's Wall. The 12th century keep can still be seen enclosed by massive inner and outer walls. Entry is through a great 14th century gatehouse, complete with portcullis, and with a maze of vaulted passages, chambers, staircases, towers, and dismal dungeons. Children, especially, enjoy the legendary 'licking stones' from which parched Jacobite prisoners tried to find enough moisture to stay alive. Archaeologists working outside the castle walls unearthed the remains of three Roman forts, and many of the finds are on display in a special exhibition at the castle. Carlisle Castle is everything a real castle should be and is still the headquarters of the King's Own Royal Border Regiment, whose **Regimental Museum** is located within the castle walls.

Carlisle Cathedral has many interesting features, including an exquisite 14th century east window that is considered to be one of the finest in Europe. Below the beautifully painted wooden ceiling of the choir, with its gold stars shimmering against a deep blue background, are the carved, canopied

THE LAIRD'S LARDER

16 Fisher Street, Carlisle, Cumbria CA3 8RN
Tel: 01228 537769
e-mail: info@thelairdslarder.co.uk
website: www.thelairdslarder.co.uk

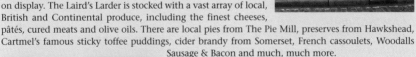

Fisher Street is one of the picturesque streets in Carlisle's charming old quarter and it's here that you'll find **The Laird's Larder** – a true gourmet's paradise. Run by Jodie and Lorraine Phillips, this independent delicatessen opened in 2004 and immediately attracted attention because of the astonishing range of produce on display. The Laird's Larder is stocked with a vast array of local, British and Continental produce, including the finest cheeses, pâtés, cured meats and olive oils. There are local pies from The Pie Mill, preserves from Hawkshead, Cartmel's famous sticky toffee puddings, cider brandy from Somerset, French cassoulets, Woodalls Sausage & Bacon and much, much more.

The Laird's Larder also stocks an extensive range of jams, chutneys and preserves, as well as a selection of wines, liqueurs, champagnes and ports. The staff will happily source products for your own particular requirements and, if you are thinking of buying a hamper as a present, they have themed ones on display or will make one up specially for you. The Laird's Larder also offers an extensive take-away menu including a wide selection of rolls and baguettes stuffed full with the Larder's own tasty foods.

Carlisle Castle

choir-stalls with their medieval misericords. These wonderful carved beasts and birds include two dragons joined by the ears, a fox killing a goose, pelicans feeding their young, and a mermaid with a looking glass. In St Wilfrid's Chapel is the superb 16th century Flemish Brougham Triptych which was originally in Cologne Cathedral.

It was at Carlisle Cathedral that Edward I solemnly used bell, book, and candle to excommunicate Robert the Bruce, and here, too, the bells were rung to welcome Bonnie Prince Charlie in 1745.

Although an appointment is usually necessary, a visit to the nearby **Prior's Tower** is a must. On the first floor of this 15th century pele tower is a wonderful panelled ceiling incorporating the popinjay crest and arms of the Prior

Senhouse. The 16th century Prior's gatehouse leads to a narrow lane called Paternoster which is named after the monks reciting their offices.

Like many great medieval cities, Carlisle was surrounded by walls. Guided walks and tours are available and the best view is to be found in a little street called **West Walls** at the bottom of Sally Port Steps, near the Tithe Barn. The walls date from around the 11th century and they remained virtually intact until the 1800s.

Close by is **St Cuthbert's Church**, the official city church of Carlisle and where the Lord Mayor's pew can be found. Although the present building dates from 1778, there has been a church on this site since the 7th century and the dedication is obvious, since St Cuthbert was Bishop of Carlisle in AD680. It is a charming Georgian building with several interesting features including a moveable pulpit on rails.

The award-winning **Tullie House Museum & Art Gallery**, in the centre of the city close to the Cathedral, is certainly another place not to be missed. Through skilful and interpretive techniques the fascinating, and often dark, history of the Debatable Lands, as this border region was called, is told. The museum's centrepiece is its story of the Border Reivers who occupied the lands from the 14th to the 17th century. The horrific stories of the Reivers have been passed down through the generations in the Border Ballads, and many of the Reivers family names are still known - the museum even offers a genealogy service, so that visitors find out if their ancestry goes back to these people. The city of Carlisle dates back far beyond those desperate days and Tullie House also has an extensive collection of Roman remains from both the city and the Cumbrian section of Hadrian's Wall. The Art Gallery features contemporary arts and crafts, and the spectacular underground Millennium Gallery has a stunning collection of local minerals, archaeological finds of wood and leather, artist-made glass and interactive exhibits. Old Tullie House showcases paintings and drawings by renowned Pre-Raphaelite artists, as well as other artworks and a selection of fine English porcelain. A short walk from the Museum leads to the **Linton Visitor Centre** in Shaddongate which provides an insight into the city's industrial heritage.

The **Guildhall Museum**, housed in an unspoiled medieval building constructed by Richard of Redeness in 1407, provides an ideal setting for illustrating the history of both the Guilds and the City. Not far from the Guildhall is the **Citadel**,

LOU LOU

Lowder Street, Carlisle, Cumbria
Tel: 01226 593595

Although Debby Waite only opened her shop **Lou Lou** in 2004, it has quickly established itself as *the* place in Carlisle to find the most interesting giftware, jewellery and fashion items. There's a wonderful range of fragrances and body products from L'Or, Ash shoes and clothing for women, Pupa make-up and body products, Pure handbags and other stylish items from Lolita Lempicka, E. Coudray and Eclat d'Arpege. Lou Lou is also the exclusive retailer for the Agent Provocateur range of perfumes.

Then there's the range of co-ordinates for children that

includes some very stylish footwear; classic patent shoes; a wide selection of jewellery, including Cavendish French silver jewellery; elegant handbags from leading designers; beautiful hand-made greeting cards; and a superb choice of candles, including Yankee Candles and accessories. So, whether you are looking to brighten up your own wardrobe; pamper yourself with quality body products and perfumes; or find a striking gift for someone, you'll almost certainly find just the right thing at Lou Lou.

WOODSTYLE JOINERY

Wood Bank Farm, Brisco, Carlisle CA4 0QP
Tel/Fax: 01228 512303
e-mail: joiners@woodstylejoinery.co.uk
website: www.woodstylejoinery.co.uk

At **Woodstyle Joinery** Alan Dickinson and his team of dedicated craftsmen have been using their cabinet making skills to produce superior garden furniture since 1988. The wood they use – either western red cedar or redwood – comes from ecologically managed sources and all their garden products are tanalised to ensure that they will endure for a lifetime whether you treat them or allow them to weather naturally.

One of their most popular lines is the garden summerhouse which represent the height of outdoor refinement. They include the eight-sided Grasmere summerhouse

which can be mounted on a rotating turntable so you can always keep your face to the sun. Other models range from the six-sided Langdale, through the five-sided Borrowdale to the four-sided Keswick. All are handcrafted from treated timbers and are available with a choice of Georgian paned, toughened glass windows and doors. There are a variety of colours and finishes to choose from and all the summerhouses can be specified to include additional features for a longer seasonal use – roof, wall and floor insulation, for example, glazed windows or internal cladding on wall and roof sections.

Other garden products include gazebos and arbours, rose arches, benches, picnic tables, swing seats, planters, gates, doors and fencing and screening system. Woodstyle also make Pergolas both using a housing jointed system or traditionally drawer pin morticed and tenaned jointed using either Green Oak or Pine.

Woodstyle also builds garages and workshops, mostly to the customer's specifications and offer

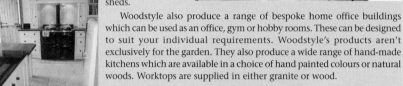

a range of extra features to go with them such as log stores, car ports and sheds.

Woodstyle also produce a range of bespoke home office buildings which can be used as an office, gym or hobby rooms. These can be designed to suit your individual requirements. Woodstyle's products aren't exclusively for the garden. They also produce a wide range of hand-made kitchens which are available in a choice of hand painted colours or natural woods. Worktops are supplied in either granite or wood.

Many examples of Woodstyle's garden and domestic furniture can be seen at their workshop and showroom which is open from 8am to 5pm, Monday to Friday; from 8am until noon on Saturday, and at other times by appointment.

which is often mistaken for the castle. In fact, this intimidating fortress with its well-preserved circular tower was built in 1543 on the orders of Henry VIII to strengthen the city's defences. Much of it was demolished in the early 1800s to improve access to the city centre but what remains is mightily impressive.

Across the road from the Citadel is the railway station. The first railway to Carlisle opened in July 1836 and Citadel Station, which opened in 1850, was built to serve seven different railway companies whose coats of arms are still displayed on the facade. So elegant was its interior - and much of it remains - that Carlisle was known as the 'top hat' station. Today it is still an important centre of communications; InterCity trains from Glasgow and London now link with lines to Dumfries, Tyneside, West Cumbria, and Yorkshire, and it is, of course, the northern terminus of the famous **Settle-Carlisle Railway** line.

One of the last great mainline railways to be built in Britain - it was completed in 1876 - the Settle to Carlisle line takes in some of the most dramatic scenery that the north of England has to offer. Scenic it may be but the terrain caused the Victorian engineers many problems and it is thanks to their ingenuity and skill that the line was ever finished. During the course of its 72 miles, the line crosses 20 viaducts and passes through 12 tunnels, each of which was constructed by an army of navvies who had little in the way of resources besides their strength and some dynamite to remove the rock.

Located on the northwestern edge of the city, **Kingmoor Nature Reserve** occupies an area of moorland given to the city in 1352 by Edward III. Citizens enjoyed the right to graze sheep on the moors and to cut peat for fuel. Later, Carlisle's first racecourse was established here with annual Guild races being held up until 1850. Then in 1913, Kingmoor became one of the first bird sanctuaries in England and today provides a peaceful retreat away from the bustle of the city. A half-mile circular path wanders through the woodland with gentle gradients of 1 in 20 making it fully accessible to wheelchairs and pushchairs, and with seats every 100 yards or so providing plenty of resting places. Another path links the reserve to **Kingmoor Sidings**, which since the old railway sheds closed has been colonised by a wide variety of wildlife.

AROUND CARLISLE

WREAY

5 miles S of Carlisle off the A6

This little village is known for its extraordinary **Church of St Mary**,

No 1 Guest House

1 Etterby Street, Stanwix, Carlisle CA3 9JB
Tel: 01228 547285

Just three quarters of a mile from the city centre, the **No 1 Guest House** stands on the line of Hadrian's Wall. Sheila Nixon has been offering outstanding bed & breakfast accommodation here since 1997 and such is No 1's reputation for hospitality and comfort that it's essential to book ahead. There are three excellent guest bedrooms, (one twin, one doulbe, one single), all with a four-Diamonds rating, en suite facilities and extras such as complimentary toiletries. Sheila serves a generous breakfast with plenty of choices – including a delicious scrambled egg and smoked salmon.

HIGH HEAD SCULPTURE VALLEY

High Head Farm, Ivegill, Carlisle, Cumbria CA4 0PJ
Tel/Fax: 016974 73552
e-mail: hhcfarm@pentalk.org
website: www.highheadsculpturevalley.co.uk

High Head Sculpture Valley really does provide a feast for all the
senses. Visitors can see magnificent life-size sculptures
imaginatively displayed in a natural wooded valley; listen to the
sound of birdsong; feel gentle summer breezes as they stroll
through beautiful rolling countryside; and taste and smell freshly
prepared Cumbrian food in the traditional farmhouse tearoom. This unique tourist attraction is the
creation of sculptor Jonathan Stamper who, together with his wife Bernadette, sons Daniel and Simon,
and daughter Eleanor, has made this one of the must-visit places in Cumbria.

Jonathan's sculptures, influenced by Barbara Hepworth and the late Josefina de Vasconcellas, are
inspired by the natural world, but he also specialises in
religious sculpture and figurative pieces. Visitors can watch
Jonathan and other artists at work, learn about their
techniques, inspirations and future projects, and perhaps
commission a unique sculpture for garden or home. As well
as the outdoor sculptures, there's a gallery showcasing a
changing exhibition of traditional and contemporary
sculptures, paintings, photography and ceramics. Families
are welcome here – children can take part in pond dipping,
hide & seek, birdwatching and enjoy themselves in the
outdoor play area.

designed by a local woman, Sarah Losh,
in memory of her sister and her parents.
It was built in 1835 and incorporates
many Italian Romanesque features. The
church is full of beautiful touches,
including the carvings, mostly by Sarah
herself, on the font.

BURGH BY SANDS

5 miles W of Carlisle off the B5307

On 7th July 1307, the body of King
Edward I was laid out in the village
church: he was already a dying man when
he left Carlisle to march against his old
enemy, Robert the Bruce. A monument to
Edward was erected on the marshes and a
later monument still marks the spot. At
the time of the king's death, the **Church
of St Michael** was already well over a
century old and is possibly the earliest
surviving example of a fortified church.
Dating from 1181 and constructed
entirely of stones from a fort on the

Roman wall, the church was designed for
protection against Border raids, which is
why its tower has walls seven feet thick.

BOWNESS-ON-SOLWAY

14 miles W of Carlisle off the B5307

Hadrian's Wall continues along the
Solway coast to Bowness and many of the
sandstone cottages around here contain
stones from the wall. Some of these
stones can easily be identified, such as the
small inscribed altar let into a barn near
the King's Arms. The Roman fort of **Maia**
once covered a seven-acre site, but today
there is only a plaque explaining where it
used to be. Bowness is sometimes said to
be the end of the Wall but in fact it just
turned a corner here and continued south
along the coast for another 40 miles.

Two miles south of the village lies
Glasson Moss National Nature Reserve,
a lowland raised mire extending to 93
hectares. Many species of sphagnum

moss are to be found here, and the birdlife includes red grouse, curlew, sparrowhawk and snipe.

LONGTOWN
9 miles N of Carlisle on the A7

Situated on the north side of Hadrian's Wall, only a couple of miles from the Scottish border, this is the last town in England. Its position on the River Esk so close to the border has influenced its history from earliest times. The Romans occupied this land and they were followed by other conquerors. The legendary King Arthur attempted to organise the Northern Britons against the pagan hordes who tried to settle and control this territory. In AD573 the mighty battle of Ardderyd was fought here and, according to legend, 80,000 men were slain.

On the outskirts of Longtown is **Arthuret Church**. The earliest records of the church date from 1150 and it was originally served by the monks of Jedburgh. But it is thought that the earliest church here may have been founded by St Kentigern in the 6th century; recent research has led some to believe that King Arthur was actually interred here after his last battle, Camboglanna, was fought a few miles east of Longtown at Gilsland. The present church, dedicated to **St Michael and All Angels**, was built in 1609, financed by a general collection throughout the realm which James I ordered after a report that the people of Arthuret Church were without faith or religion. The people that he referred to, of course, were the infamous Reivers, ungoverned by either English or Scottish laws. Archie Armstrong, favourite Court Jester to James I and later to Charles I, is buried in the churchyard.

CROSBY-ON-EDEN
4 miles NE of Carlisle off the A689

The tiny hamlet of **High Crosby** stands on the hillside overlooking the River Eden; the small village of **Low Crosby** sits beside the river, clustered around a Victorian sandstone church. Inside the church there's a modern square pulpit, intricately carved with pomegranates, wheat and vines. Apparently, it was carved from one half of a tree felled nearby; the other half was used to create a second pulpit, which was installed in the newly-built Liverpool Cathedral.

A couple of miles east of Crosby, The **Solway Aviation Museum** is one of only a few museums located on a 'live' airfield, in this case Carlisle Airport. Opened in 1997, the museum is home to several British jet aircraft of the 1950s and 1960s, among them the mighty Vulcan and the Canberra. Other exhibits include a wartime air raid shelter where a video presentation explains the story behind the museum, displays of the Blue Streak rocket programme, testing for which took place only a few miles from here, and a very impressive engine room which houses one of Frank Whittle's first development jet engines.

BEWCASTLE
14 miles NE of Carlisle off the B6318

Roman legionaries assigned to the fort at what is now Bewcastle must certainly have felt that they had drawn the short straw. The fort stood all on its own, about nine miles north of Hadrian's Wall, guarding a crossing over the Kirk Beck. The site covered around six acres and most of it is now occupied by the ruins of a **Norman Castle**. Most of the south wall is still standing but little else remains and the castle is best admired for its setting rather than its architecture.

A much more impressive survival dominates the village churchyard. Here stands the **Bewcastle Cross**, erected around AD670 and one of the oldest and finest stone crosses in Europe. Standing over 13 feet in height, its intricate Celtic carvings have survived the centuries of weathering and much of the runic inscription can still be made out in the yellow sandstone. One of the carvings, a semicircle with 13 radiating lines, three of which have crossbars, is believed to be a sophisticated sundial which not only indicated the 12 hours of the Roman clock but also the three 'tides' of the Saxon day - morning, noon and eventide.

WETHERAL

4 miles E of Carlisle off the A69

Wetheral stands above the River Eden, over which runs an impressive railway viaduct, carrying the **Tyne Valley Line**, which was built by Francis Giles in 1830. Wetheral **Parish Church** lies below the village beside the river and contains a poignant sculpture by Joseph Nollekens of the dying Lady Mary Howard clasping her dead baby. Nearby, occupying a lovely riverside setting, is one of the **Eden Benchmarks**, a sculptured bench in St Bee's sandstone by Tim Shutter, entitled *Flight of Fancy*.

St Constantine was the local patron and the church is dedicated to the Holy Trinity, St Constantine and St Mary. Constantine is said to have lived in caves in what are now National Trust woodlands alongside the river, a location known as **Constantine's Caves**. Constantine died as a martyr in AD657 and a life-sized statue of him can be seen in the grounds of **Corby Castle** to the south of the village. The castle, with its impressive 13th century keep and terraced gardens overlooking the Eden, is usually open during the summer months.

During the reign of William Rufus, one of his barons, Ranulph Meschin, founded a priory for Benedictine monks at Wetheral above a red-rock gorge of the River Eden. All that remains now is the imposing three-storey gatehouse.

BRAMPTON

Nestling in the heart of the lovely Irthing Valley, Brampton is a delightful little town where the Wednesday market has been held since 1252, authorised by a charter granted by Henry III. Overlooking the Market Place is the town's most striking building, the octagonal **Moot Hall** topped by a handsome clock tower.

Just around the corner, in **High Cross Street**, is the house (now a shop) which once witnessed one of the high points in Bonnie Prince Charles' rebellion of 1745. It was here that the Prince stayed during the siege of Carlisle and it was here, on November 17th, 1745 that the Mayor and Aldermen presented him with the keys to the city. A few months later, following the Prince's defeat, six of his supporters were hanged on the Capon Tree on the south side of the town and in sight of the Scottish hills. The tree survived until the last century and in its place there now stands a monument commemorating the doleful event.

Just off the Market Place is **St Martin's Church**, which was built anew in 1874 and contains one of the undiscovered secrets of the area - some magnificent stained glass windows designed by one of the founder members of the pre-Raphaelite brotherhood, Edward Burne-Jones. It was his fellow-member of the brotherhood, Philip Webb, William Morris's associate, who designed the church and insisted that contemporary stained glass should be installed.

Brampton Market

South of Brampton are **Gelt Woods**, lying in a deep sandstone ravine carved by the fast-flowing River Gelt. By the river is an inscribed rock called **Written Rock** which is thought to have been carved by a Roman standard bearer in AD207.

The area around Brampton had good reason to be grateful to the Dacres of Naworth, who as Wardens of the Northern Marches protected it against marauding Scots. However, the townspeople of Brampton in Victorian times must have had mixed feelings about a later descendant, Rosalind, wife of the 9th Earl of Carlisle. An enthusiastic supporter of total abstinence, she contrived to get most of the small town's 40 public houses and drinking rooms closed.

AROUND BRAMPTON

TALKIN
2 miles S of Brampton off the B6413

Talkin Tarn, now the focus of a 120-acre country park, has been a popular place for watersports for over 100 years. Glacial in origin, the Tarn was formed some 10,000 years ago and is continually replenished by underground springs. Modern day visitors can sail, windsurf, canoe or hire one of the original wooden

HULLERBANK

Talkin, Brampton, Cumbria CA8 1LB
Tel/Fax: 016977 46668
e-mail: info@hullerbank.freeserveco.uk
website: www.smoothhound.co.uk/hotels/huller.html

Hullerbank is a handsome Georgian farmhouse standing in its own grounds, set back some 50 yards from the road. It's the home of Brian and Sheila Stobbart who welcome bed & breakfast guests to their 'peaceful retreat'. There's a comfortable lounge with colour TV, a separate dining room where traditional breakfasts are served, and three guest bedrooms, two with en suite facilities, the third with a private bathroom. All rooms are equipped with colour TV, electric under-blankets and hospitality tray. Hadrian's Wall is nearby and the Lake District is an hour's drive away.

THE WEARY AT CASTLE CARROCK

Castle Carrock, Brampton, Cumbria CA8 9LU
Tel: 01228 670230 Fax: 01228 670089
e-mail: relax@theweary.com
website: www.theweary.com

The Weary really is something quite unique and special. Ian and Gill Boyd arrived here in 2001 and have transformed a pleasant 300-year-old Cumbrian stone house into an outstanding restaurant with rooms that provides the ultimate in luxury and comfort – one guest considered the standards equivalent to a five-star city hotel. Each of the five en suite bedrooms has

been individually designed in contemporary style and each is comprehensively equipped with flat screen TV, DVD, CD, Tivoli radio alarm, Bang and Olufsen telephone, comfortable Lloyd Loom chairs and, for ultimate privacy, blackout blinds.

The spacious bathrooms are fitted with superb power showers, large baths, glass basins and 17-inch TV linked to the DVD players. The food too is equally impressive and was recently granted the prestigious Michelin Award, as well as the Herdies restaurant of the year 2004. The award-winning chefs, Ian Wightman and Martin Allison, prepare everything to order using fresh produce at all times and local produce whenever possible. In addition to the restaurant, there's a bar and a walled garden area suitable for alfresco dining, early evening drinks or cocktails.

THE DROVE INN

Roweltown, Carlisle CA6 6LB
Tel: 016977 48202 Fax: 016977 48054
website: www.cumbriaholidays.co.uk

The Drove Inn offers the perfect combination of a friendly, traditional inn and, close by, quality self-catering accommodation. The inn dates back to the late 1800s and derives its name from the days when stock was driven to auction on foot.

The original longhouse is still evident but the inn has grown considerably over the years and has been tastefully

modernised to suit today's clientele. Kenneth Hope and his family have been here since 1974 and have built up an excellent reputation for the food on offer – with steaks a speciality. They offer a full menu with wine list, or just a snack, every evening of the week. Self-catering guests stay at Drove Cottage which sleeps up to nine people. On the ground floor there's an en suite twin room; on the first floor are two twin rooms and one double.

There's a lounge with colour TV and video; a fully equipped kitchen with microwave and fridge, bathroom and separate shower room. The Hope family farm 65 acres of land where guests are welcome to roam along with the hardy Swaledale sheep. Within the grounds is a beautiful stretch of the River Lyne where anglers can try their luck!

rowing boats. Talkin Tarn Rowing Club has been rowing on the tarn for 130 years and holds its annual regatta in July. Fishing licences are available, and there's a nature trail and an orienteering course, a play area for children under 8, a tea room and a gift shop; guided walks with a warden are also available for organised groups.

Low Row

3 miles E of Brampton off the A69

Within easy reach of the town is Hadrian's Wall, just three miles to the north. If you've ever wondered where the Wall's missing masonry went to, look no further than the fabric of **Lanercost Priory** (English Heritage). An impressive red sandstone ruin set in secluded woodland, the priory was founded in 1166 by Robert de Vaux. Lanercost is well preserved and its scale is a reminder that it was a grand complex in its heyday. However, the priory suffered greatly in the border raids of the 13th and 14th centuries. One such raid is known to have been led by William Wallace, an early campaigner for Scottish independence from English rule. When the Priory was closed in 1536, the sandstone blocks were recycled once again for houses in the town. But much of the Priory's great north aisle remains intact, set in a romantic and hauntingly beautiful position in the valley of the River Irthing. The Priory is well signposted and lies only three miles off the A69 (leave at Brampton).

Also most impressive is **Naworth Castle**, built around 1335 in its present form by Lord Dacre as an important border stronghold. The castle's supreme glory is the Great Hall, hung with French tapestries and guarded by four unique heraldic beasts holding aloft their family pennants. The Long Gallery extends for 116 feet and was used as a guardroom.

Gilsland

7 miles E of Brampton on the B6318

Hadrians wall was built between AD 122 and 128 as a great military barrier across the narrowest part of Britain, from the mouth of the River Tyne, in the east, to Bowness-on-Solway, in the west. The wall was finally abandoned in the late 4th century, and in later centuries many of the stones were used for local buildings and field walls. There are many ways of exploring the Wall (including the bus number AD122!), and for those with the energy to walk from end to end the newly opened Hadrian's Wall National Trail passes some of the country's greatest archaeological monuments.

Located in one of the most picturesque settings along the whole length of Hadrian's Wall and overlooking the River Irthing, **Birdoswald Roman Fort** is one of the best preserved mile-castles along the Wall and unique in that all the components of the Roman frontier system can be found here. Set high on a plateau with magnificent views over the surrounding countryside, the early turf wall, built in AD122, can be seen along with the fort. Originally, this fort would have covered five acres and it may have been the base for up to 500 cavalry and 1,000 foot soldiers. Gilsland village is also known for its sulphur spring and there was once a convalescent home for miners and shipyard workers here. It is now owned by the Co-operative Society and people still drink the waters as a cure for arthritis and rheumatism. Near the spring is the **Popping Stone**, traditionally the place where a man 'popped the question' to his lover. It was here that Sir Walter Scott successfully popped the question to Charlotte Carpenter.

LOCATOR MAP

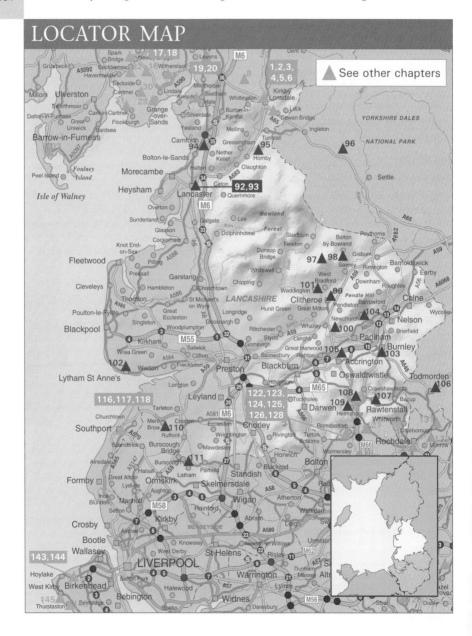

LANCASHIRE 2

As the well-known Lancashire comedian, Les Dawson, commented in his book on the county, it is "many things to many people" with "vast smoky grey blocks of heavy industry" but also a countryside of "lakes and woods and rolling hills". It is also a place of great history: the Wars of the Roses; the old Catholic families and their support of Charles I during the Civil War; the trials of the Pendle Witches; and the innovators who started the Industrial Revolution in the textile industry.

The county of Lancashire, perhaps more than any other area in the country, has suffered from cliched images of its landscape and people: the harsh life of the mill towns and the brashness of Blackpool. Before the reorganisation of the county boundaries in 1974, this large area also included Liverpool and Manchester in the south and the Furness Peninsula to the north. Though each, with their own distinctive character, are no longer in Lancashire, the Red Rose county, which has put many a king on the throne of England, has much still to offer.

ADVERTISERS AND PLACES OF INTEREST

The ancient county town of Lancaster, in the north, is an excellent place to start any journey of discovery. With a variety of museums and a wealth of interesting buildings, the life of Lancastrians through the ages is mapped out for any visitor to explore.

Looking Towards Morecambe Bay

Small and compact, it has the added advantage of having been off the general tourist routes which can make York, its larger, White Rose equivalent, somewhat hard going in the height of the season.

To the northeast lies Leck Fell, just south of Kirkby Lonsdale and Cumbria. It is easy for the visitor to mistake this for the Yorkshire Dales as there is a typical craggy limestone gorge along the little valley of Leck Beck, as well as one of the most extensive cave systems in the British Isles for the experienced potholer to explore. A natural route from Kirkby Lonsdale back to the county town is marked by the River Lune. For those who enjoy walking, the best way to enjoy this wonderful green and hilly area of Lancashire is to follow the Lune Valley Ramble which travels the valley's intimate pastoral setting, through woodland, meadows, and along the riverside itself.

To the west lies Morecambe Bay, a treacherous place where, over the centuries, many walkers have lost their lives in an attempt to make the journey to the Furness Peninsula in Cumbria considerably shorter. Walks across the sands, at low tide, should only be undertaken with the aid of one of the highly knowledgeable and experienced guides. However, despite its grim history, the bay offers superb views, including glorious sunsets, as well as being an important habitat for a wide variety of birds.

Extending across much of the north of the county is the Forest of Bowland, an ancient royal hunting ground that is dotted with small, isolated villages. With no major roads passing through the area, it has remained little changed and, with so many splendid walks and fine countryside, it is also relatively quiet even during the busiest summer weeks.

LANCASTER

An architecturally pleasing city, Lancaster is one of the most appealing of English county capitals. Most of the county's administrative offices are now based in Preston so Lancaster enjoys all the prestige of being the capital without the burden of housing the accompanying bureaucrats. (The city also takes pride in the fact that the Duke of Lancaster is the only duke in the kingdom who is a woman – no less a personage than HM the Queen for whom the dukedom is one of many subsidiary titles.)

Lancaster's story begins some 2,000 years ago when the Romans built a fort on a hill overlooking a sweep of the River Lune, a site now occupied by the unspoiled 15th century **Priory Church of St Mary**. Right up until the Industrial Revolution, Lancashire was one of the poorest counties in England, lacking the wealth to endow glorious cathedrals or magnificent parish churches. St Mary's is a notable exception, the finest medieval church in the county. It stands on the site of Lancashire's first monastery which was closed not, like most others, by Henry VIII, but by Henry V in 1413. Henry was at war with France, the monastery's mother abbey was at Sées in Normandy, so the 'alien priory' in Lancaster had to be dissolved. The present church contains treasures rescued from the closed priory such as the sumptuously carved wooden choir stalls from around 1345.

Each stall is covered by a superb canopy, lavishly carved with around a hundred small heads and faces surrounded by abundant foliage. Also of note are the fragments of Anglo-Saxon

LANCASTER CASTLE

Shire Hall, Castle Parade, Lancaster LA1 1YJ
Tel: 01524 64998 Fax: 01524 847914
website: www.lancashire.gov.uk

Lancaster Castle is owned by Her Majesty the Queen in right of her Duchy of Lancaster. For most of its history the castle has been the centre of law and order for the county, and this magnificent building is still in use as a prison and a crown court.

The castle has dominated the town for almost 1,000 years, ever since it was first established in 1093. But the hill on which it stands has a history which goes back 1,000 years further, almost to the birth of Christ. The Romans built the first of at least three military forts on the site in AD79. Little is known about Lancaster until 1093 when the Norman baron, Roger of Poitou, built a small motte and bailey castle which was replaced 50 years later by a large stone keep which still stands today as the oldest part of the castle. Throughout its long history it has witnessed many trials, including that of the Lancashire Witches of 1612, which resulted in the execution of 10 people.

Although still a working building, guided tours of the castle include the room where the witches were condemned to die; the beautiful Gillow furniture in the Grand Jury Room; the dungeons and 'Drop Room' from where the condemned went to their deaths; the Crown Court from where thousands were transported to Australia; Hanging Corner, the site of public hangings and the magnificent Shire Hall with its display of heraldic shields.

Criminals and convicts, monarchs and majesty, dungeons and death, treason and transportation, witches and martyrs, all have their place in the history of this most fascinating building.

crosses and some very fine needlework. The **Priory Tower**, also on the hilltop, was rebuilt in 1759 as a landmark for ships navigating their way into the River Lune. Nearby is one of Lancaster's links with its Roman past – the remains of a bath house which also served soldiers as an inn.

Close by is **Lancaster Castle**, one of the best-preserved Norman fortresses in the country. Dating back to 1200 and with a massive gatehouse flanked by sturdy twin towers, the castle dominates the centre of the city. For centuries, the castle served as a prison, only relinquishing that function as recently as 1996. At the back of the castle, the **Shire Hall** is still in use as a Crown Court and one of its more macabre attractions is the Drop Room where prisoners were prepared for the gallows. The Court's long history has been blemished by two shocking major miscarriages of justice. The first was in 1612 when the Pendle "witches" (see Chapter 4) were convicted of sorcery and executed; the second in 1975 when the "Birmingham Six" were found guilty of an IRA bombing and spent 15 years in prison before their names were cleared.

A short walk from the castle leads into the largely pedestrianised city centre, full of shops, the market, and much besides. The **City Museum** in the Market Place occupies the Old Town Hall, built between 1781-3 by Major Jarrett and Thomas Harrison. As well as the city's art collection and an area of changing exhibitions, there are displays and collections of material illustrating aspects of the city's industrial and social history. Also here is the **Museum of the King's Own Royal Regiment**, a regiment which was based in Lancaster from 1880 onwards.

Lancaster Castle

Lancaster grew up along the banks of the River Lune which is navigable as far as Skerton Bridge so there has always been a strong association between the town and its watery highway. Documents from 1297 make reference to the town's small-scale maritime trade, but it was not until the late 1600s and early 1700s that Lancaster's character as a port fully emerged. The splendid buildings of the 18th century Golden Age were born out of the port wealth, and the layout and appearance of the town was much altered by this building bonanza. Lancaster's importance as a port steadily declined throughout the 19th century so that many buildings originally intended for maritime purposes were taken over for other uses.

Lancaster enjoyed its era of greatest

prosperity during the 18th century when its quays were busy servicing a thriving trade with the West Indies in rum, sugar, cotton – and slaves. The city's rich maritime history is celebrated at **St George's Quay** which, with its great stone warehouses and superb **Custom House**, is now an award-winning **Maritime Museum**. Visitors today are given a vivid insight into the life of the mariners and quayside workers with opportunities for knot-tying and the practising of other maritime skills. Every year, over the four days of the Easter weekend, St George's Quay is home to the Lancaster Maritime Festival with a programme that involves boisterous "smugglers", sea songs, and shanties.

Fire destroyed most of Tudor and Jacobean Lancaster, but one notable survivor is the **Judge's Lodging** in Church Street, a charming Jacobean house built in the 1620s and now a museum: two museums in fact. There's the **Museum of Childhood** which includes the Barry Elder Doll collection, and the **Gillow and Town House Museum** containing many examples of the fine workmanship produced by the famous Lancaster cabinet-makers, Gillows. It was a scion of this family, Richard Gillow, who designed the city's Maritime Museum.

Close by is the **Cottage Museum** in a house, built in 1739, that was divided into two dwellings in the 19th century. Furnished in the style of an artisan's house of the early to mid-19th century, the museum is open from Easter to the end of September. Just around a corner or two, in Sun Street, is the **Music Room**, an exquisite early Georgian building originally designed as a pavilion in the long vanished garden of Oliver Marton. It is notable for some superb decorative plasterwork.

Lancaster's most prominent landmark, visible for miles around, is the extravagant, temple-like Ashton Memorial – "the grandest monument in England" according to Nikolaus Pevsner. Erected in 1907 as a memorial to his wife by the local MP and millionaire lino-manufacturer Lord Ashton, it stands on the highest point in Lancaster, set within a beautifully landscaped park and enjoying sweeping views of the Cumbrian hills and across Morecambe Bay. The building now houses exhibitions and multi-screen presentations about the life and times of Lord Ashton and the Edwardian period.

Williamson Park was Lord Ashton's own personal project as a means of providing work for local people during the cotton famine crisis in the textile industry during the American Civil War in the 1860s. Constructed on the site of old quarries, which gives the park its undulating contours, the park was

---

LANCASTER MARITIME MUSEUM

Custom House, St George's Quay, Lancaster LA1 1RB
Tel: 01524 64637 Fax: 01524 841692

The **Lancaster Maritime Museum** was opened in 1985 and occupies the former Custom House of 1764 by Richard Gillow and an adjacent warehouse.

Using sound, smells, reconstructions and audio visuals it tells the story of the port of Lancaster, the Lancaster Canal, fishing and the ecology of Morecambe Bay. A number of exhibitions can be seen and there is an education programme for children. Facilities include a shop, café, car parking and disabled access.

opened in 1896. As well
as the magnificent
Ashton Memorial there
is also a delightful
Butterfly House in the
now restored Edwardian
Palm House and a
Conservation Garden
and Wildlife Pool, which
opened in 1991.

Another place the
whole family can enjoy
is **Lancaster Leisure
Park** on Wyresdale
Road. Set in 42 acres of
landscaped parkland,
the site includes a mini-
marina, a Wild West
adventure playground, a
miniature railway, a rare breeds unit, a
children's farmyard, pony rides, a gift
shop, a tea garden, and a pottery shop.

Williamson Park, Lancaster

NORTH OF LANCASTER

HALTON

3 miles NE of Lancaster off the A683

The high mound, **Castle Hill**, which rises
above this ancient village on the River
Lune was firstly the site of a Roman camp
and later a Saxon castle. The village's
parish **Church of St Wilfrid** was founded
in the 7th century and although nothing
survives of that original foundation there
are some stone crosses, both inside the
building and out, that date from the 9th
century. One of them, unusually, bears
both pagan and Christian symbols.
Roman remains, in the form of a votive
altar (where offerings were made before a
military operation began), were found on
the site in the late 18th century. Around
the same time, a labourer tilling his
allotment on Halton Moor unearthed
more than 1,000 coins from the reign of
King Cnut (1017-35) and a gold necklace.

This treasure trove is now in the British
Museum.

NETHER KELLET

4 miles N of Lancaster off the B6254

This farming village has a traditional
village green which as well as being the
central focus of the community also
features several old wells and pumps.
This is appropriate since the Old Norse
word *chellet*, now Kellet, means "a
spring". Local brewers of home ale still
use the spring water because of its purity
and absence of chemicals. Quarrying has
taken place here for many centuries and
lime burning has been an important
local industry. Its remains, in the form of
lime kilns, can still be seen around the
village and the local pub is named the
Lime Burners Arms.

The village also has its own cave,
Dunold Mill, through which flows a
large stream that dives underground to
appear two miles further north at
Carnforth. During the mid-1800s the
cave was occupied by a hermit who lived
there until his death at the age of 100.
His descendants still live in the village.

THE LONGLANDS HOTEL

Tewitfield, Carnforth, Lancashire LA6 1JH
Tel: 01524 781256   Fax: 01524 781004
e-mail: info@thelonglandshotel.co.uk
website: www.thelonglandshotel.co.uk

The Longlands Hotel is traditionally an olde worlde coaching house, next to Tewitfield Locks on the Lancaster canal. Situated less than a mile from Junction 35 of the M6 motorway, it is within easy reach of the Lake District and the Yorkshire Dales, the seaside resort of Morecambe and the historic city of Lancaster. Golf and fishing are in abundance, with Tewitfield Fisheries being just one of the local fish farms, along with approximately 10 golf courses within a 30 mile radius.

Bar meals are served each lunchtime and evening, as well as an extensive a la carte menu, mixing the best of English and continental cuisine, served in the restaurant. To accompany your meal, wines can be chosen from the extensive wine list which features classic and New World wines. There are 12 en-suite bedrooms available, six having been purpose built. Facilities include showers, tea and coffee making facilites, full central heating and TVs. The acclaimed 'Longlands breakfast' is included in the tariff.

The Longlands is a lively, popular place and hosts live entertainment every Monday and a disco on Thursday and Saturday.

CARNFORTH

5 miles N of Lancaster on the A6

The town lies around what was once a major crossroads on the A6 but it is, perhaps, its former fame as a busy railway junction town - whose station was used as the setting for the 1940s film classic *Brief Encounter* - by which most people know Carnforth. The station has since declined in importance and is now just an unstaffed halt.

Bookworms will know Carnforth as home to one of the best second-hand bookshops in the country.

YEALAND

8 miles N of Lancaster off the A6

To the south of the village lies **Leighton Hall** – a fine early 19th century house which is open to the public. During the Middle Ages the land on which it stands, together with much of the surrounding area, was owned by the d'Avranches family. Over the centuries, the house and the land passed through many hands before becoming the property of the Gillows family of Lancaster. Now in the hands of the Reynolds family, a branch of the Gillows, the fine furniture seen in the hall reflects the trade that made the family fortune.

As with many estates in Lancashire, Leighton Hall was a Catholic house and one owner, Sir George Middleton, was fined heavily by Cromwell after the Civil War for his loyalty to Charles I and to his religion. Later, another owner of the hall, Albert Hodgson, suffered for his loyalty to Catholicism and the Stuart claim on the throne of England. Taking part in the Jacobite rebellion of 1715, Hodgson was captured at Preston and the Government troops inflicted such damage on the hall that little remained of the Tudor structure.

The hall, today, dates from 1800 when it was built out of pale, local sandstone to the Gothic designs of Harrison, a Chester architect. One of the finest houses in the county, the views from the extensive grounds are magnificent and take in the nearby Leighton Moss Bird Reserve.

SILVERDALE

8 miles N of Lancaster off the A6

The village lies at the northwesternmost corner of the county and has the Lakeland hills as a backdrop as

Approaching Silverdale Station

well as superb views over Morecambe Bay. The latter half of the 19th century saw Silverdale develop as a quiet seaside resort where those so inclined could take medicinal baths of fresh sea water in one of the many small villas situated along the coast. One frequent visitor was Elizabeth Gaskell who is said to have written some of her books whilst holidaying here.

However, Silverdale's history goes back well beyond the days of a genteel Victorian resort. Its name comes from a Viking family which settled here and which signifies that this was Sigward's or Soevers' valley. Fishing, naturally, was the key provider of local income but in the 18th century a copper smelting works was built here. All, however, that remains of the foundry is the chimney near **Jenny Brown's Point**, said to be named after an old woman who lived here in the 1700s.

Essentially, now a small residential

village, Silverdale is well worth visiting for the network of footpaths from here that pass through the limestone woodlands that are such a joy for the botanist, being rich in wild flowers in spring – primroses, violets, orchids, bird's eye primroses, rockroses, and eglantines abound.

Leighton Moss near Silverdale is a nationally known RSPB bird sanctuary. The reed beds are the most important part of the reserve because they have become a northern stronghold of the rare Bearded Tit and are also the major British breeding centre for the Bittern.

THE LUNE VALLEY

CATON

3 miles NE of Lancaster on the A683

Caton climbs up the hillside from the leafy glades of the Crook o'Lune, subject of one of Turner's paintings, to heather moorlands commanding a panoramic view of Morecambe Bay. A popular commuter town nowadays, in the 19th century Caton was a busy place with no fewer than eight cotton and wood-turning bobbin mills. Just to the south of the village, tucked away among the hills on the northern edges of the Forest of Bowland, is **Littledale**, one of Lancashire's most hidden gems. Chiefly wooded, a walk through the dale alongside Artle Beck to Littledale Hall is well worthwhile and provides a view of Lancashire that is not normally seen.

CLAUGHTON
6 miles NE of Lancaster on the A683

The Old Toll House Garage on the road into this village (which is pronounced Clafton), is famous for a rather curious reason. In the 1920s the garage owner painted the first white lines on the road at the nearby corner because of the many accidents that had occurred there. After much debate their value was recognised by the government of the day and from then onwards the use of white lines became accepted as a means of road marking, eventually spreading world-wide.

HORNBY
9 miles NE of Lancaster on the A683

Immortalised in paint by J.M.W. Turner, the ruins of Hornby Castle (private) were incorporated into a picturesque mock-medieval Hall in the 19th century. Perched atop a hill, the castle dominates the attractive village of Hornby. Sadly, it isn't open to the public but it's visible for miles around and there's a particularly photogenic view of it from the bridge over the River Wemming at the southern edge of the village.

The situation of this attractive village, by a bluff overlooking the valley of the River Lune, not only gives Hornby panoramic views of the surrounding countryside but also makes this a strategic position that has been utilised over the centuries. Just to the north of the village is the attractive stone-built **Loyn Bridge**, which takes the road over

Hornby Castle

the River Lune and on to Gressington. Constructed in 1684, it replaced a ford. Beside the bridge is **Castle Stede**, the best example of a Norman motte and bailey castle in Lancashire.

The graceful **Church of St Margaret of Antioch** dates from around 1300 when it was built as a chapel of ease to the parish church at Melling. Its unusual and impressive octagonal tower was ordered by Sir Edward Stanley, Lord Mounteagle, who made a vow before the Battle of Flodden Field in 1513 that if he returned victorious he would construct the tower in honour of his patron saint, St Margaret.

TUNSTALL

11 miles NE of Lancaster on the A683

The village is famous for its fine 15th century **Church of St John the Baptist**, that was known to the Brontë sisters and which is referred to in *Jane Eyre* as "Brocklebridge church". When the sisters were attending the Clergy Daughters' School at Cowan Bridge they walked the six-mile round trip to the church each morning. After attending service, they had their midday meal in the room above the church porch.

COWAN BRIDGE

13 miles NE of Lancaster on the A65

In 1823, the Rev. William Carus Wilson, vicar of neighbouring Tunstall, opened his Clergy Daughters' School at Cowan Bridge. Amongst his early pupils were four daughters of the Rev Patrick Brontë of Howarth – Maria, Elizabeth, Charlotte and Emily. Charlotte immortalised the school and its austere regime in *Jane Eyre* where it appears as "Lowood". It can still be seen though it is now part of a row of terraced cottages just north of the bridge

THE BRIDGE INN

Lower Tatham, Lancaster LA2 8NL
Tel: 015242 21326

Two linked buildings, one dating from 1642, the other from 1744, make up the Bridge Inn, a grand old hostelry which in coaching days was known as the Bridge End. The white-painted, slate-roofed exterior promises a wealth of character within, and that's exactly what the visitor will find in the bar, the snug, the non-smoking main restaurant, and the upstairs dining room. There's also a spacious beer garden looking out across peaceful, unspoilt countryside.

The pub is run with notable flair and style by Peter and Bernadette Williams who took over here in March 2005. They serve excellent food with a menu ranging from freshly-made sandwiches and

appetisers such as crispy chicken dippers, through salads and vegetarian dishes, to hearty main courses such as The Bridge game pie, local gammon steak and home-made lasagne. Wine is available by the bottle or glass. The inn has its own off-road parking and also a caravan park with space for five vehicles with electric hook-up, a disposal area and running water – caravanners can use the inn's toilet facilities. Lower Tatham itself is notable for its ancient stone bridge, the 13th century church of St Mary of Antioch and Hornby Castle which was famously painted by JMW Turner.

on the A65. The school moved to Casterton in 1833.

LECK

13 miles NE of Lancaster off the A65

Over the A65 from Cowan Bridge lies the small village of Leck. To the northeast of this village lies **Green Hill**, surrounded by moorland and the highest point, at 2,060 feet, in the county. At just over three feet higher than the top of the neighbouring fell, Gragarth, it was only a recent, more accurate survey, that distinguished Green Hill as the higher. This is the most northerly part of Lancashire and from the summit there are superb views of both Cumbria and North Yorkshire, as well, of course, as Lancashire.

WHITTINGTON

12 miles NE of Lancaster on the B6254

This delightful village, in the green and sheltered valley of the River Lune, is well worth a visit. It was Wordsworth, in his *Guide to the Lakes*, who recommended that Kendal be approached via the Vale of Lune and it remains a popular place today.

WEST OF LANCASTER

MORECAMBE

3 miles NW of Lancaster on the A589

Featuring prominently on the Lancashire coastline, Morecambe has long been one of the most successful and popular seaside resorts in the North, and it can truly be said to enjoy one of the finest views from its promenade of any resort in England – a magnificent sweep of coastline and bay, looking across to the Lakeland mountains.

Morecambe Bay, a vast wide, flat tidal plain situated between Lancashire and Cumbria, is the home of many forms of marine life as well as being a very popular and important habitat for birds. The Rivers Lune, Kent, Keer, Leven, and Crayke create the gulleys, mud, and sandbanks that make this not only one of the most important ornithological sites in Europe but also a great source of mussels and shrimps.

The largest estuary in Britain, Morecambe Bay is noted for its rich marine and bird life, for its vast expanse of sands and mudflats – and for their treacherous nature. Over the years, many have lost their lives in the Bay's ever-shifting quicksands while attempting to make the apparently straightforward crossing from Morecambe to Grange-over-Sands on the Cumbrian coast. In medieval times, this perilous track formed part of the main west coast route from Scotland to England and at one time the monks of the Furness peninsula acted as guides to those wishing to make their way to Cumbria without taking the long overland route. Today, you can join one of the **Cross Bay Walks** led by the Queen's Guide to the Sands, Cedric Robinson who has been guiding walkers across the Bay since 1963. Cedric is the 25th appointed guide to the sands since the original appointment in 1536. More details and times of walks can be obtained from the Tourist Information Centre.

Modern Morecambe is a relatively recent town that grew up as a direct result of the expansion of the railways to the north Lancashire coast. There were originally three villages, Bare, Poulton, and Torrisholme that were quiet fishing communities. In 1848 all this changed as the railways brought visitors from the textile towns of Lancashire and, especially, Yorkshire to what was jokingly called "Bradford-by-the-Sea". Hotels and boarding houses were built as well as the usual seaside amenities such as parks and promenades and soon the villages were absorbed into one thriving resort.

A lively resort, well-provided with every kind of traditional and modern holiday amusement, Morecambe has always vied with its much larger competitor to the south, Blackpool, in offering varied entertainment for its visitors. During the late 1800s, the town spent lavishly, building two grand piers, an elegant **Winter Garden**, sumptuous theatres and hotels, but the town's attempt to build a tower to rival Blackpool's was not a success. However, Morecambe did manage to introduce its Autumn Illuminations several years before Blackpool caught on to the idea.

Morecambe Parade

Of the many buildings dating from Morecambe's heyday as a holiday destination, one in particular, the **Midland Hotel** stands out. Situated on the seafront, at the southern end of the promenade, the hotel, which was built in the early 1930s to designs by Oliver Hill, is concave towards the sea and convex facing inland. The elegant, sweeping balconies of the luxurious rooms remain a superb feature of the hotel and, whilst filming *Brief Encounter* at nearby Carnforth both Celia Johnson and Trevor Howard made their home here along with others working on the film.

Like other resorts, Morecambe has changed with the times and major new attractions include the multi-million pound Bubbles Leisure Park and Superdome, as well as a Wild West

Theme Park. WOMAD, Morecambe's annual world music festival, attracts visitors from around the globe. There are also popular seafront illuminations in late summer, together with all the usual lively shops and variety of entertainment associated with a busy seaside resort.

But perhaps the town's most popular attraction is the **Eric Morecambe Statue** near the Stone Jetty. Few can resist the opportunity of posing in suitably one-legged fashion beside sculptor Graham Ibbeson's life-size statue. Lyrics from Eric's best-known song, *Bring Me Sunshine*, are carved into the granite steps leading up to the statue which is surrounded by flower beds and flashing lights that bring this "stage" to life even after dark.

In 1990 Morecambe was given substantial government funding for programmes of coastal protection and clearance of derelict land. The concept of the **Tern Project** was born. A team of engineers, landscape architects, planners, artists, sculptors and RSPB education officers joined forces to celebrate the bird life of the bay. Among the eye-catching results are steel cormorants and gannets on quarried rock on Central Drive, and flocks of metal birds on the perimeter fencing. At the heart of the project was the rebuilding and extending of the Stone Jetty, all that remains of the 1853 harbour. The designers also created a series of circular pavement features that include a huge stainless steel compass set in granite, a maze and a word search containing the names of more than 70 birds.

HEYSHAM

5 miles W of Lancaster on the A683

Southwards along the coast, Morecambe merges imperceptibly into Heysham, an ancient settlement with a quaint old main street that winds down to the shore. The town is notable for the tiny **St Patrick's Chapel** which is reckoned to be the oldest religious building in Lancashire. According to tradition, St Patrick himself built the now-ruined chapel as a thank-offering to God after surviving a shipwreck on the rocks below. Historians aren't too sure about the veracity of that legend, but there's no doubting the interest of the chapel graveyard. Hewn out of the rock are six body-shaped coffins with an incised space above them in the shape of a cross. These 8th or 9th century coffins were originally covered by a similarly shaped slab of stone and would have been created as the final resting-place for Saxon notables.

The little **Church of St Peter** on the headland below the chapel is equally interesting. It dates back to Saxon and Norman times, with an Anglo-Saxon cross on which the Madonna and other figures have been crudely carved by 9th century masons and there is a rare Viking hog-back gravestone. It is one of the oldest churches in western Europe to have been in continuous use.

Alongside these antiquities is the modern port of Heysham with regular car-ferry sailings to the Isle of Man and to Northern Ireland and, of course, the two modern nuclear power stations, Heysham A and Heysham B.

SUNDERLAND

6 miles SW of Lancaster off the A683

This is, unbelievably, an old port and seaside resort which flourished until larger-berthed ships, silting channels, and the growth in the 19th century of rail-served Morecambe caused it to decline. A little wharf, quiet cottages, some with faded and evocative elegance, a sandy shore where sea thrift flourishes among the pebbles, are all that remains. The River Lune estuary is now a Site of Special Scientific Interest because of its wildlife value – visitors are likely to see such birds as redshank feeding on the rich supplies of worms, shellfish, and shrimps on the salt marshes, while a variety of wildfowl such as shell duck, widgeon, and mallard, are to be seen in autumn.

A particularly sad story acts as a reminder of Sunderland's time as a port. Sambo was a sea captain's servant at the time of the slave trade into Lancaster. Sambo fell ill of a fever just before the captain was setting off to the West Indies and was left in the care of an innkeeper. Sambo, believing himself abandoned, willed himself to die. Because he was not a baptised Christian, Sambo was not allowed to be buried in consecrated ground. In later years, his death and grave, marked by a simple cross and stone, became a potent local symbol of the anti-slavery cause.

His grave can be still seen, in a field at

the west side of Sunderland Point. It can be reached by walking along The Lane from the village foreshore, past Upsteps Cottage, where Sambo died, and turning left at the shore then over a stile on the left which gives access to the simple gravestone. Fresh flowers are usually to be seen here, anonymously placed on the grave.

GLASSON
4 miles SW of Lancaster on the B5290

A few miles south of Heysham, the river Lune pours into Morecambe Bay. On its south bank lies **Glasson Dock**, once an important commercial port for larger boats unable to negotiate the tricky river as far upstream as Lancaster. The dock was built in 1791 and the tiny lighthouse erected at the same time is still in place. The dock could accommodate 25 sea-going ships and traded extensively in slaves, rum, tobacco, sugar, and cotton. Glasson Dock today is a busy, colourful

marina, serving both sea-going craft and boats arriving at the western terminus of the Lancaster Canal. Constructed in 1797, the Lancaster Canal is one of the earliest engineering marvels of the Industrial Age. "The Lanky", as it's known, is a favourite with canal travellers since there's not a single lock in the whole of its 41 mile length, thanks to the ingenuity of the canal's designer, John Rennie. He accomplished his engineering tour de force by linking the level stretches with six elegant aqueducts, the most impressive of them the five-arched **Lune Aqueduct** near Lancaster which has attracted a stream of admiring visitors ever since it was first opened in 1797.

The canal was supplemented by the arrival of a railway line in 1883. This railway, long dismantled, is now the footpath and cycle-way to Lancaster's St George's Quay.

From Glasson there is a footpath along the coast to Plover Scar, where a lighthouse guards the River Lune estuary, and further along lie the ruins of **Cockersand Abbey**. The abbey was founded in 1190 by the Premonstratensian Order on the site of a hospital that had been the home of a hermit, Hugh Garth, before becoming a colony for lepers and the infirm. The 13th century Chapter House of the abbey remains since it was a burial chapel for the Dalton family of nearby Thurnham, descendants of Sir Thomas More.

THURNHAM
5 miles S of Lancaster on the A588

Just outside the village and at

Glasson Dock

the end of a sweeping drive lies **Thurnham Hall**, which has been built, over the years, around a 14th century pele tower. The home of the Dalton family for 400 years, they were responsible for the Elizabethan extensions and a fine Jacobean staircase. Still in private hands and not open to the public, although the hall has been divided up into flats, much of its original character has been retained.

GALGATE

4 miles S of Lancaster on the A6

The village of Galgate was originally located on the banks of the River Conder, which now forms part of the Lancaster Canal for about half a mile at this point. The village still contains some of its original mills, though they have now been put to other uses. One of them, a silk mill, was reputed to be the oldest working mill in the country, dating back to 1760 and closed down in the 1960s. Galgate has a craft centre, a marina for around 100 boats and there's a well-maintained pathway that leads from the village through locks to Glasson Dock.

DOLPHINHOLME

6 miles S of Lancaster off the A6

This small village of around 600 souls sits in the foothills of the Pennines at the edge of the Forest of Bowland. Dolphinholme was one of the first villages with a main street lit by gas. This was around 1806 and remains of the old gas holder can still be seen. A single street lamp has survived and is now fuelled by bottle gas.

COCKERHAM

6 miles S of Lancaster on the A588

This sleepy little village lies on the shore of Morecambe Bay between the estuaries of the Lune and the Wyre. Cockerham once boasted a windmill but it was in such an exposed position that a gale in 1802 sent the sails spinning and the friction set fire to the mill. Cockerham Hall, (private) is a fine and rare example of a medieval timber-framed building that dates from the late 15th century. It is now a farmhouse.

QUERNMORE

3 miles E of Lancaster off the A683

Lying at the head of the Conder Valley, this peaceful farming village had a pottery industry as well as slate quarrying in the 17th century. The word "quern" refers to a particularly ancient form of hand-mill that was hewn from the rocks found on the nearby moorside and, indeed, corn milling continued here until World War II.

To the east of the village lies **Clougha Pike**, on the western edges of the Forest of Bowland Area of Outstanding Natural Beauty and one of the few places in the area that is accessible to walkers. Although it is not the highest peak in the forest – it rises to just over 1,300 feet – the walk up Clougha Pike is very pleasant and offers splendid views from the summit, not only of the Lakeland Fells but also of Morecambe Bay and, on a clear day, Blackpool Tower.

LEE

7 miles SE of Lancaster off the A6

To the northwest of this typical Bowland village soars the highest summit in the forest, **Ward's Stone**. Dotted with outcrops of gritstone boulders, the top of the fell is marked by two triangulation pillars: one of which is just over three feet higher than the other though, on first inspection, they look the same height. The panoramic views from this point are magnificent and, to the north

DALESBRED

The Smithy, Austwick, via Lancaster LA2 8BA
Tel: 015242 51798
e-mail: simon@dalesbred.co.uk
website: www.dalesbred.co.uk

Occupying a former blacksmith's shop on the village green
at Austwick, **Dalesbred** was established in 1993 by Simon
and Sally Robinson to create beautiful original furniture
for the 21st century and beyond. Their furniture is made
primarily of oak with the option of using burr oak as inlays
and panels, although any hardwood is available. Each
item is numbered, dated, and inlaid with the Dalesbred Rams Head. Furniture restoration and polishing
is also undertaken. They also specialise in bespoke new upholstery made to measure as well as re-
upholstery of every kind.

and east, the Three Peaks of Yorkshire can be seen whilst the Lakeland fells roll away to the northwest.

FOREST OF BOWLAND

Designated an Area of Outstanding Natural Beauty in February 1964, this large scenic area is a veritable paradise for walkers and country lovers and is dotted with picturesque villages. The 11th largest of such designated areas, the Forest of Bowland is something of a misnomer. The term 'forest' is derived from the Latin 'foris' which was formerly used to denote a royal hunting ground, an unenclosed tract of land, rather than a distinct wooded area. In fact, even this description is not entirely correct. Throughout the 11th century the area was a "chase" – a private rather than a royal hunting ground. Before 1066, the broad acres of Bowland were the personal property of Earl Tostig of Northumbria, a brother of King Harold. Banished from his earldom, Tostig, with the help of the King of Norway, attempted to regain his lands and both he and the Norwegian king were killed at Stamford Bridge, just weeks before the fateful Battle of Hastings.

Following the Norman Conquest, Bowland became part of the Honour of Clitheroe and the vast estates that belonged to the de Lacy family. In time, by marriage, they came into the hands of the Earls of Lancaster and in 1399, when the then Duke of Lancaster ascended the throne as Henry IV, Bowland finally became one of nearly 100 royal hunting forests.

The remains of a Roman road can be clearly seen traversing the land and many of the village's names in this area date back to the Saxon period. Perhaps the most celebrated of the many routes across Bowland is the minor road from Lancaster to Clitheroe which crosses **Abbeydale Moor** and the **Trough of Bowland** before descending into the lovely Hodder Valley around Dunsop Bridge. This is a popular route in the summer months, with most lay-bys and parking places filled as people pause to take in the breathtaking moorland views.

SLAIDBURN
15 miles SE of Lancaster on the B6478

This pretty village of stone cottages and cobbled pavements lies in the heart of the Forest of Bowland. The village's focal point is the 13th century public house

Hark to Bounty. The inn was originally named The Dog but one day in 1875 the local Hunt gathered here. A visiting Squire, listening to the hounds giving voice outside, clearly distinguished the tones of his own favourite hound rising above the others. His exclamation of delight, "Hark to Bounty!" was so whole-hearted that the landlord changed the name of his pub on the spot.

The inn also contains an old courtroom, with its original oak furnishings, where from around 1250 the Chief Court of Bowland, or Halmote, was held. The only courtroom between York and Lancaster, it was used by visiting justices from the 14th century onwards, is said to have also been used by Oliver Cromwell when he was in the area, and continued in use right up until 1937.

From the village, a network of beautiful, little used lanes radiate westwards up into the fell country with some of the best walking that Lancashire has to offer. One walk in particular that offers solitude as well as excellent views of the Bowland landscape, leads to the lonely valley of the River Whitendale, northwest of the village. To the northeast of Slaidburn lies Stocks Reservoir, another popular walker's destination. Beneath its waters lie the remains of 20-odd dwellings that made up the hamlet of Stocks-in-Bolland. They were submerged in 1925 but in very dry summers the remains of the old Chapel bridge can be seen where it crosses the original Hodder river, along with the foundations of houses.

NEWTON
15 miles SE of Lancaster on the B6478

Little more than a hamlet, Newton lies on the main route between Clitheroe and Lancaster and so, in their time, both John Paslew, the last abbot of Whalley,

and the Pendle witches passed through on their way to trial in Lancaster. Here also is a **Quaker Meeting House** that was founded in 1767: the associated Quaker school, where the 19th century reformer John Bright was a pupil, has long since gone. Regarded with great suspicion by the Church of England, and by other nonconformists, because of their unorthodox views and their informality, the Quakers sought to settle in out of the way villages. Newton is typical of the places where they built their meeting houses and successfully lived according to their beliefs.

BOLTON BY BOWLAND
21 miles SE of Lancaster off the A59

Lying alongside a "bow", or bend, in the River Ribble this tranquil village with its two ancient green, stone cross and old stocks, lies on the southern edge of the forest area. Part of the Bolton Hall estate, the village has been protected from insensitive development – the most recent dwelling to be built is already more than 100 years old. The 15th century village **Church of St Peter & St Paul** is home to the famous **Pudsey Tomb** with its engraved figure of Sir Ralph Pudsey in full armour alongside figures of his three wives and their 25 children. In the folds of each lady's gown is inscribed with a Roman numeral indicating how many children she bore – respectively six, two and 17.

DUNSOP BRIDGE
14 miles SE of Lancaster off the B6478

Often known as the Gateway to the Trough of Bowland and located in a designated Area of Natural Beauty, Dunsop Bridge is, despite its remote location, the centre of the British Isles. The actual centre point, worked out by the Ordnance Survey, lies near

HOLDEN CLOUGH NURSERY

Holden, Bolton-by-Bowland, Clitheroe, Lancashire BB7 4PF
Tel: 01200 447615 Fax: 01200 447197
website: www.holdencloughnursery.co.uk
e-mail: enquiries@holdencloughnursery.co.uk

In the scenic Forest of Bowland, with distant views of majestic Pendle Hill, you will find **Holden Clough Nursery** nestling in the small village of Holden. Established as a working nursery in 1927, it is owned and run by Peter Foley, a plantsman all his working life and a well known lecturer and broadcaster. In addition to an ever-growing range of Alpine plants including Auriculas, Saxifrages and Sempervivum the nursery grows many herbaceous perennials, choice shrubs and climbers, dwarf conifers, heathers and hardy ferns, as well as ornamental grasses. Peter is now ably assisted by his son John who has an impressive collection of South African Crocosmia (*Montbretia*) that was recently featured on BBC2 *Gardener's World* and in the *The Garden* magazine of the Royal Horticultural Society.

Much of the stock is propagated on site in this Pennine location ensuring hardiness. Throughout the year popular Nursery Event Days are run in collaboration with local businesses and in addition to a presentation and question time session there is a demonstration, nursery walk and a chance to view other areas of the nursery not generally open. Booking on these events is essential. The nursery opens Monday to Friday (March to October) and Saturdays throughout the year 9am to 5pm, with other times and group visits by appointment. A worldwide mail order service is available.

SPRINGHEAD FARM HOLIDAY COTTAGES

Bolton by Bowland, Nr Clitheroe, Lancashire BB7 4LU
Tel: 01200 447245

In a serene setting in the beautiful Ribble Valley, **Springhead Farm Holiday Cottages** are ideally placed as a base for touring a particularly attractive part of the county. Susan and Richard Lund's cottages provide very comfortable self-catering accommodation in three properties sleeping four (Woodpecker), six (Kingfisher) or eight (Mallard). All are tastefully decorated and full of character, with all the amenities needed for a relaxing, go-as-you-please stay. Equipment includes TV, video, fridge, dishwasher, full-size cooker, microwave and washing machine, and all linen and towels are provided.

Each has central heating and two of the three also have open fires. One of Mallard's bedrooms is on the ground floor, which is fully accessible to wheelchair users. Children are very welcome, and cots and high chairs can be made available on request. This is excellent walking country, with the Forest of Bowland on the doorstep, but the farm itself also has plenty of interest, with cattle, calves and horses to see, a pleasant garden and a play area to keep the children occupied. A barbecue comes into its own on summer evenings. The village shop is a 10-minute walk away.

Whitendale Hanging Stones and, to confirm the claim, the explorer Sir Ranolph Fiennes unveiled a commemorative plaque here. British Telecom also offered the village a unique honour by putting their 100,000th phone box here.

St Hubert's Roman Catholic Church on Lancaster Road has an unusual provenance. It was built by the Towneley family when their racehorse Kettledrum won the 1861 Derby. The family spent a further £1,000 on the huge white angel that stands in the graveyard and commemorates Richard Henry Towneley.

WHITEWELL
15 miles SE of Lancaster off the B6478

Little more than a hamlet in the heart of the Forest of Bowland, Whitewell consists of a small church, built in the early 19th century on the site of a medieval chapel, and an inn, built on the site of the old manor house.

Just to the southeast lies **Browsholme Hall**, a Tudor mansion dating from 1507 that has the rare distinction of being occupied by the same family ever since. From the 16th century onwards, the owners, the Parker family, were also bowbearers, or warders, of the Forest of Bowland – the king's agent and upholders of the law in the forest. Though much of the original Tudor house can still be seen, there have been many additions over the centuries but it remains a homely building perhaps due to the continuous occupation by the same family and as a result of its remote location. The house is not open to the public.

CHIPPING
15 miles SE of Lancaster off the B6243

This picturesque village overlooking the River Loud is now a conservation area

Near Whitewell, Forest of Bowland

Chipping

Distance:	5.0 mile (8.0 kilometres)
Typical time:	180 mins
Height gain:	200 metres
Map:	Explorer OL 41
Walk:	www.walkingworld.com ID:3336
Contributor:	Jim Grindle

Access Information:

Chipping can be reached by buses from Clitheroe and Preston. It is on a minor road and is signposted from Longridge, on the B6342, or from Whalley, just off the A59. There is a large free car park near the church.

Description:

Despite its short length this walk will take you quite high and to the very fringe of Bowland - at Waymark 12 there is a sign for the new access land next to the footpath. Consequently for most of the time there are good views (Bowland, Pendle, Longridge Fell, even a glimpse of Beacon Fell) with a very gradual climb and no steep descents. Chipping with its pubs and tea room makes a very pleasant base for the day.

Additional Information

The chair factory which is passed at the start of the walk will almost certainly have the raw material in the shape of huge tree trunks, stacked outside. The factory makes much more than just chairs and produces the well-known Priory range of furniture.

Features:

Hills or Fells, Toilets, Play Area, Church, Wildlife, Birds, Flowers, Great Views, Good for Wheelchairs, Butterflies, Cafe, Food Shop, Public Transport, Tea Shop, Woodland

Walk Directions:

1 From the car park take the path leading past the toilets. Turn left on the road by the wall around the church and pass the red telephone box. Just after the last houses the road forks.

2 Take the right fork, going downhill and past the chair factory. Continue until you come to the lodge (the pond feeding the mill.) On the right you will find a stile next to a house.

3 Cross it, go uphill to a fence, turn left and follow it to the second stile. Now cross the field, roughly in the direction of the telegraph pole. The route stays high above a stream on an embankment and passes to the right of a deep hollow before you come to a stile at the end of a stone wall. From here aim for the left of the group of buildings. The path crosses two muddy patches over streams and brings you to a gate with a stile to its right.

4 Turn left on a farm track which leads to Windy Hill farm and a barn just before it on the right.

5 Turn right on a path uphill following the field boundary on your right until a gate and stile lead to an open area. Keep ahead untll just before the low hill in front; then go left, making for a plank footbridge and a stile on the far side of the field. Now go half right to a stile in the field corner.

6 Turn right on the track which leads uphill to Burnslack where the footpath is well signposted by a ladder stile before you reach the farm. There is a diversion here which may not be on your map, but it is very well marked and an enclosed path now takes you around to the back of the buildings.

7 Just in front of you is a signpost for the new access area. Turn left and follow the wall which makes a sharp turn left just before a group of derelict barns. On the bend is a stile which you cross to continue by the wall so passing the barns. The wall is intermittent after this, sometimes full height, sometimes low and sometimes replaced with fencing, but the way is clear enough and after 1km brings you to Saddle End. Turn left in front of a gate and notice board to pass between the farm buildings.

8 After you have gone through the farm, watch out for a power line post on the right - there is a stile up on an embankment here which is not too obvious from the direction in which you are walking. When you have crossed the stile, turn left and go to the end of a small wood which contains a flock of geese. Leave by the stile at the far end and then drop to a gate which you will see just below you on the left.

9 This field is very big and there is no obvious path. Just walk at right angles to the fence and soon you will see a small barn ahead of you. Make for the left of this.

10 To the right of the telegraph pole is a gate and a lane. Turn right on the lane and in 150m you will find the entrance to Peacock Hey Farm on the left.

11 Don't take the footpath signposted up the farm track but cross the stile, behind which the path is now enclosed at first and brings you to the back of Nan King's Farm. Turn left to go around the building and then ahead looking out for a signpost beneath a tree. Go straight across the field to the far side where you will find a stile on the left of a small copse. Cross it, turn right and go through the copse to a stile on the other side. Go to the far right corner of the field, crossing a gravelled drive, to a stile. Go over this and follow the right hand edge of the field to a ladder stile under a tree.

12 An enclosed path between newly planted trees brings you to a lane.

13 A left turn here will bring you back to Waymark 3 should you

wish to cut the walk short. To continue, though, cross the lane and the stile on the other side and then go over a footbridge. A little spur here leads up to the left hand telegraph pole where an arrow directs you left to follow a fence. You will find yourself at the back of the cottages at Old Hive.

14 Cross the stile in front and follow the path between the houses to a lane where you turn left. 100m down the lane you will find a stone track going up to the right. Turn up here and where the track turns left to enter a garden you will find a stile on the right. Turn left and follow the field edge to a lane.

15 Turn left to a T-junction.

16 Turn left once more on this lane which leads back into Chipping.

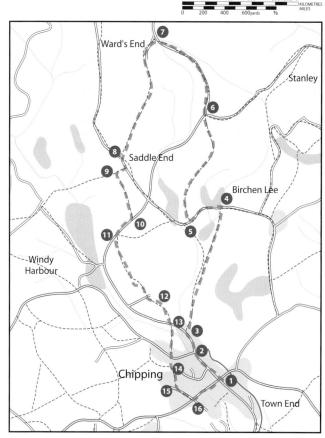

and it is also home to a post office, built in 1668, which claims to be Britain's oldest shop. Very much at the heart of the local agricultural communities, the annual village show is one of the best in Lancashire and its very name comes from the old English word for a market place - *chepyn*. In medieval times there were no fewer than five watermills along the banks of Chipping Beck and, later, one of the mills, Tweedies Mill, made ships' portholes which were used on the clipper ships bringing tea back from the east.

There are a number of attractive inns here and one of them, the Sun Inn, is associated with a melancholy tale. The story of Lizzie Dean whose ghost is said to haunt the inn is poignant, sad – and true. In 1835, Lizzie was 18 years old and a serving wench at the inn. She had fallen in love with a local man and a date had been set for their wedding at the church just across the road from the inn. Lizzie lodged at the inn and on the morning of her wedding she heard the church bells ringing. Looking out of her window she saw her intended bridegroom leaving the church with another maiden on his arm.

Humiliated and distraught, Lizzie crept up into the inn's attic and hanged herself. She left a note requesting that she should be buried beneath the path leading to the church porch so that her faithless lover would have to step across her body every Sunday on his way to divine service.

THE RIBBLE VALLEY

"A dramatic contrast of stark fellsides flecked with woolly sheep, and valleys green with woodland and lush pastures grazed by obviously contented sheep." It's not the conventional image of Lancashire as half-Blackpool, half wall-to-wall grimy chimneys. That's because the Ribble Valley is the county's best-kept secret – 150 square miles of peaceful countryside, almost two-thirds of it designated as Areas of Outstanding Natural Beauty.

The best overview of this beautiful area can be enjoyed by walking or driving along **Longridge Fell**. Within the space of a few miles, huge vistas unfold, not just of the Ribble Valley from Pendle Hill to Preston but also of the Fylde Plain, the Loud and Hodder valleys, and the Forest of Bowland. This is captivating countryside so it's no wonder that, according to one of her biographers, the Queen herself has divulged that she would like to retire to this region of rural Lancashire.

Flowing between the Forest of Bowland to the north and the hill country of Pendle to the south, the River Ribble cuts a pleasant and green course along a narrow valley. The **Ribble Way** middle-distance footpath follows the full 70 miles of the river, from its source at Ribblehead in North Yorkshire to the flat, tidal marshes of its estuary west of Preston.

A beautiful, unspoilt yet small area, the Ribble Valley has long been a favourite with the people of Lancashire. Not only is it easily accessible but there are numerous gentle walks in the sheltered valley and a wealth of wildlife is supported by the lush countryside. It is also a place of pretty villages which, even in the 21st century, remain almost unscathed.

The central point of the valley is Clitheroe, a typical ancient Lancashire market town that clusters around one of the smallest Norman castles in the country. The Normans were not the only invaders to build a fortification in the valley: further down stream lies

Ribchester and the Roman fort of Bremetannacum. Up river from Clitheroe lies Sawley and another interesting ruin. The Cistercian monks of Fountains Abbey founded a religious house here in the 13th century and their influence in the area of agriculture can still be seen in the surrounding fields.

The valley is also home to two great houses. The first, Stonyhurst, was originally the home of the Shireburn family and is now the world famous Roman Catholic public school. The second, on the outskirts of Preston, is Salmesbury Hall, a wonderful 14th century house that is also a major attraction for antiques collectors.

Finally, at the mouth of the river lies Preston, the county's administrative centre and a town with more to offer than first appearances would suggest. Best known to some as the home of the UK Snooker and World Indoor Bowls Championships, this ancient town also saw one of the key battles of the Civil War and it still continues the tradition of the Guild Celebrations. Dating back to medieval times and occurring once every 20 years, this week-long festival is well worth seeing. Our exploration of the Ribble Valley begins at its estuary near Preston and travels upstream through a fertile and versatile valley to the river's remote source in the bleak Pennine Hills.

PRESTON

"Proud Preston" is the largest town in the county and its administrative centre. It's 'Proud' because it was the first town in the county to receive a borough charter, (in 1179), the first borough in which every male over 21 had a vote in parliamentary elections (1798), the first town outside London to light its streets with gas lamps (1816), and in 1958 the

Preston bypass was the first stretch of motorway to be built in Britain. Civic pride was fostered even more by Preston's elevation in 2002 to the status of a city, one of only six in the UK so honoured to mark the Queen's Diamond Jubilee. Around the same time, multi-million pound plans were announced to redevelop the City Centre.

During the 19th century, Preston became a 'town of spires' as the evenly-split Protestant and Roman Catholic communities vied to build the most splendid churches. The palm is usually awarded to the Catholic St Walburge's Church whose slender 300ft steeple is the third tallest in England.

In Victorian times, Preston was a major cotton-weaving centre. The mill-owners' ruthless exploitation of the cotton workers provoked a major strike in 1854 and the bitter confrontation attracted the attention of Charles Dickens. He had already started to write a novel highlighting the degrading conditions and pitiful wages imposed on industrial workers by outrageously wealthy mill-owners. He came to Preston, staying at the Bull and Royal Hotel in Church Street, and his first-hand observations of the unacceptable face of Victorian capitalism displayed in that conflict were embodied in the grimmest novel he ever wrote, *Hard Times*. Many of Preston's old red-brick mills still stand, although now converted to a variety of imaginative uses.

Lancaster may enjoy the distinction of being the elegant county town, but Preston revels in its macho role as Lancashire's administrative centre – always busy, enterprising, forward-looking but still proud of a historical legacy that stretches back to Roman times. The port activity may have declined but the dockland area, now called **Riversway**, has become an area of regeneration with a marina catering for pleasure craft, yachts, and windsurfers. The complex forms part of the recently opened **Millennium Ribble Link** which forms a three-mile-long linear waterpark providing opportunities for walking, angling, cycling and boating as well as a newly commissioned sculpture trail. Also in Riversway is the new **Ribble Steam Railway,** opened in 2005, which boasts the largest single collection of standard gauge industrial locomotives in the country with more than 40 on site. Steam train rides are available on open weekdends and the site also contains a museum, shop and buffet.

The Miller Shopping Arcade, Preston

Though the town has both a Roman and a medieval past nothing of this is visible today. However, the lasting legacy of those days is reflected in the famous **Guilds Celebrations** which have been taking place every 20 years since 1500. The last Guild Celebration took place in 1992 and, already, preparations are being made for the next in 2012.

A popular annual event is the **Easter Egg Rolling** event held in **Avenham Park**, one of the city's two splendid Victorian parks: the other is the adjacent **Miller Park**, noted for its impressive floral displays and an elaborately designed fountain.

Preston featured in the *Domesday Book*

although at that time it was known as Priest-town and, in the 1260s, the Greyfriars settled here. The Catholic traditions of Preston continued, as they did elsewhere in the county, and this has, along with the associated loyalty to the crown, had a great part to play in the town's history. During the Civil War it was the Battle of Preston in 1648 which confirmed the eventual defeat of the supporters of Charles I. Later, at the time of the 1745 Jacobite rebellion, Preston played host to Prince Charles Edward, Bonnie Prince Charlie.

The many public buildings of Preston all reflect the prosperity of the town during the Victorian age. This wealth was built upon the textile industry helped by the general location of the town: midway between London and Glasgow, on a major railway route, and with extensive docks. Though the town's prosperity was built on cotton, textiles were not new to Preston as linen had been produced here from as far back as Tudor times. Preston was also the place where, in 1768, the single most important machine of the textile industry was invented: Richard

Arkwright's water-frame cotton spinning machine. Almost overnight, the cottage industries of spinning and handloom weaving were moved from the workers' homes into factories and the entrepreneurs of Preston were quicker than most to catch on. One gentleman in particular, John Horrocks, saw the potential of combining the spinning and weaving operations under the same roof and so he was able to take raw cotton in and produce the finished article on delivery. His firm became the largest of its kind in the world, further adding to the town's prosperity, but it did not do Horrocks himself much good as, by the age of 36, he was dead.

Although the great days of the textile industry are long gone in Preston, as elsewhere in Britain, the cotton workers of the town are remembered in a statue which stands outside the old **Corn Exchange.**

Looking at the town now it is hard to imagine those hectic days and maybe even harder to believe that, when the docks were completed here in 1892, Preston was the second largest container handling port in Britain. In 1900, 1,285 vessels carrying nearly half a million tons of cargo entered and left the port. Unfortunately, the battle of keeping the channel open and free of silt became too expensive, particularly as trade was lost to other, non-tidal ports, and the docks eventually closed.

One of the best places to start any exploration of the town is the **Harris Museum and Art Gallery**. Housed in a magnificent neoclassical building which dominates the Market Square, the museum and art gallery were opened in 1893. Funded by a successful local businessman and reminiscent of the British Museum, as well as the fine collection of paintings and watercolours by major 19th century British artists,

there is an excellent exhibition of the story of Preston. A varied programme of events and exhibitions continues throughout the year.

There are two other major museums in the town. Housed in the former county court building, and with limited opening times, the **Museum of Lancashire** helps visitors experience aspects of the county's fascinating past. The Fulwood Barracks, which were built in 1848 of Longridge stone, are home to the **Queen's Lancashire Regiment Museum**. With a rich history that covers many campaigns, the exhibits here are numerous and include the famous silver mounted Maida Tortoise, items connected with General Wolfe, souvenirs from the Crimea War, and artefacts from the Defence of Kimberley, the diamond town in South Africa which the 1st Battalion the Loyals defended without assistance from any other troops.

Preston's **Guild Hall**, built in 1972 to celebrate that year's Guild, is known, or at least its interior is, to many snooker and bowls fans since it is the venue for the UK Snooker and the World Indoor Bowls Championships.

As might be expected for a town on the banks of a river, there are many bridges but two crossings are particularly worthy of note. **Penwortham Old Bridge** is perhaps the most attractive in Lancashire; slightly hump-backed and built of a mixture of stone. Constructed chiefly of buff gritstone and pink sandstone in 1756, it replaced a bridge that had collapsed. By 1912 traffic had increased to such an extent that its use by motor cars and heavy carts was prohibited. For over 150 years, the bridge was the lowest crossing of the River Ribble. By contrast, the **Ribble Viaduct** is a completely different structure. One of the oldest works of railway engineering in the area and a construction of great elegance and dignity, it was built in 1838 and brought the railway from Wigan to the centre of Preston.

Located on the northern outskirts of the city is one of Preston's most popular visitor attractions, **The National Football Museum**. Containing the world's most significant football collections, including the official FIFA collection, the museum offers more than 1,000 objects, photographs, more than 90 minutes of film and a number of lively interactive displays, including one that gives the visitor access to every League ground in England.

AROUND PRESTON

SALMESBURY
4 miles E of Preston on the A59

To the east of the village, close to the busy A59, lies **Salmesbury Hall**, built by the Southworth family. The hall seen today, an attractive black and white timbered manor house, is actually the second house they built since their original hall was burned to the ground by Robert the Bruce in the early 1300s. Thinking that the original position, close to a crossing of the River Ribble was too vulnerable to attack, the family built their subsequent home in what was then an isolated location.

More peaceful times followed and the hall, surrounded by a moat and with a drawbridge, was a

reflection of the family's wealth. A staunchly Catholic family, their 15th century chapel contains a mullioned Gothic window that was rescued from Whalley Abbey after the Dissolution in the 1530s. However, it was the loyalty to their faith that finally saw the demise of the Southworth family. Their continued practice of Catholicism saw Sir John Southworth imprisoned in Manchester in the late 16th century and, by the time of his death a few years later, the family, having kept their faith, had seen their fortune dwindle away.

The hall was sold to the Braddyll family who, having a house near Ulverston, simply stripped Salmesbury Hall of its assets. Somehow the hall survived but by the 1870s it was in a shocking state of repair. First, Joseph Harrison stepped in and began a successful restoration programme, to the point where he was able to entertain the likes of Charles Dickens. However, the building work took all his money and, facing ruin, Harrison committed suicide. By 1925, the hall was once again in a dilapidated condition and was only saved from demolition by a timber

Salmesbury Hall

merchant by the efforts of the Salmesbury Hall Trust, a group that is still managing the property today. The hall's unusual history is only equalled by the unconventional manner in which it, quite literally, earns its keep. With no assets left, after being stripped by the Braddylls, the hall is once again full of antiques but these are all for sale. As salerooms go, this has to be one of the most atmospheric.

CLITHEROE

Perhaps the most appealing little market town in Lancashire, Clitheroe nestles around its miniature Norman castle. The town has a reputation for high quality specialist shops acclaimed for their individuality, some of which have gained international recognition: establishments such as Cowman's Sausage Shop in Castle Street which offers 58 different varieties of sausage, amongst them Welsh pork & leek, venison and wild boar. Fifty-nine varieties if you count the special Christmas sausage, only available during the festive season and containing exotic ingredients such as port, juniper berries and ground almonds. As with the French, traditional Lancashire meat cuisine wastes no part of the animal. Black pudding, tripe and onions, chitterlings, lamb's fry and sweetbreads are still popular dishes here although rarely seen in southern England. Interestingly, there's an annual competition between French and Lancashire butchers to see who makes the best black pudding.

In King Street there's Byrne's Wine Merchants which stocks more than 1550 wines and 100 malt whiskies. *Which? Wine Guide* judged the shop to be the best wine merchant in the country. Also

CHEESIE TCHAIKOVSKY

38 York Street, Clitheroe, Lancashire BB7 2DL
Tel: 01200 428366 Fax: 01200 428315
e-mail: jankcurtis@yahoo.co.uk

Located just out of the centre of the delightful town of Clitheroe, Cheesie Tchaikovsky is a haven for any foodlover.

Although small, the friendly delicatessen & specialist cheese shop is crammed with delicious foods and aromas. There is a wide range of cheeses from British artisan makers as well as Continental classics such as the deliciously ripe Epoisses de Bourgogne. Jan makes all the cakes and sandwich fillings daily as well as a variety of handmade breads, using stoneground organic flour on Thursday, Friday & Saturday.

Discover the perfect gift from handmade ceramics to pewter cheeseknives or have a bespoke hamper or speciality cake made to order. Nothing is too much trouble for this team of knowledgeable and enthusiastic staff.

well worth visiting is the **Platform Gallery**, housed in a refurbished railway station of 1870. The gallery presents a regularly-changing programme of visual art exhibitions – paintings and prints, textiles, glassware, ceramics, jewellery, papier maché and baskets, with the majority of the work on show produced by regionally based artists.

Clitheroe also has a **sculpture trail** leading from Brungerley Bridge to Crosshill Quarry. The trail was started in 1993 by Thompson Dagnall who worked on this commission in the Ribble Valley for seven months. His main sculpture, *Saving Sheep*, portrays a shepherd rescuing a sheep from the swelling river's current. It stands on the site of Victorian bathing huts.

Clitheroe is Lancashire's second oldest borough, after Wigan, receiving its first charter in 1147 and since then the town has served the surrounding villages of the Ribble Valley as their market town. Like Lancaster, it too is dominated by an 800-year-old **Castle** standing on a 100ft high limestone crag high above the town. Today only the keep remains, the second smallest in England and one of the oldest stone structures in Lancashire. According to local legend, the large hole in the keep's east wall was the work of the Devil who threw a large boulder from the summit of nearby Pendle Hill. Boring historians say it was Oliver Cromwell's troops who inflicted the damage. Modern day visitors can stand within the keep as hidden voices recount the castle's history, complete with appropriate sound effects.

Standing on another prominent limestone mound, close to the castle, is **Clitheroe Castle Museum**, home to many exhibits and displays reflecting the history and geology of the Ribble Valley

Clitheroe Main Street

area. Archaeological finds illustrate life in the valley from the earliest days and in this section too can be seen the famous Hacking ferryboat now restored to its former glory. Closer to the present day is the recreation of an Edwardian kitchen, complete with its unique sound system that brings this turn of the century room to life.

As well as the local history displays the museum also has a fine collection relating to the geology of the area. Here, the appearance of the valley is explained in a series of unusual and interesting formats whilst the history of Salthill quarry is also explained. Now a nature reserve and place of Special Scientific Interest, the quarry is famous for the fossils which have been found there.

THE FREEMASONS ARMS

8 Vicarage Fold, Wiswell, Clitheroe, Lancashire BB7 9DF
Tel: 01254 822218
website: www.sugarvine.com

Serious lovers of good food and wine will find that it's well worth the effort of seeking out the tiny Lancashire village of Wiswell about four miles south of Clitheroe, off the A59. Here you will find **The Freemasons Arms**, a gourmet and wine-lover's idea of heaven. Chef-proprietor Ian Martin was already loaded with awards from his previous role as head chef at leading country house hotels when he took over here in November 2004. Already new awards are rolling in, including one from Les Routiers as Northern Wine Pub of the Year, 2006.

The wine list is indeed prodigious, some 15 pages listing more than 500 bins ranging from classic premier crus to wines from California, Australia and New Zealand. What's more, they are priced with minimal mark-ups. Such fine wines demand equally outstanding food and Ian's menu offers his trademark modern British cuisine based wherever possible on local produce – pork and beef from Bowland, Goosnargh poultry, Lune wild salmon, asparagus from Formby and cheeses such as Kirkham's Lancashire. Bread and chips are made daily on the premises. This outstanding pub/restaurant is open from noon until 2pm, and from 6pm to 9.30pm, Wednesday to Saturday; and from noon until 8pm, Sundays.

A short walk from the Castle Museum stands the parish **Church of St Mary Magdalen** which, though it was rebuilt by the Victorians, was founded in the 13th century. At that time the town also had a school; however, the present **Royal Grammar School** was not established until 1554. The school's official charter, granted by Mary Tudor but lost for many years, was eventually found in the vaults of a local solicitor's office in 1990.

The town's narrow, winding streets are full of character and charm and amidst the ancient buildings is the rather incongruous **Civic Hall Cinema**. Built in the 1920s, this unspoilt monument to the golden days of the silver screen is still lined with plush velvet, has retained its grand piano that was used to accompany the silent films, and remains the town's cinema.

Just outside the town can be found **Edisford Picnic Area**, a popular place for family outings that stands on the site of a battle ground where the Scots fought the Normans. Also near Clitheroe, at **Brungerley**, are a set of stepping stones across the river that are said to be haunted. Apparently the evil spirit living in the water drags a traveller to his watery death every seven years.

There are few grand houses in the Ribble Valley open to the public, but **Browsholme Hall** near Clitheroe is open at certain times in the summer. Dating back to the early 1500s, the Hall has been the family home of the Parkers for 600 years and there's a special pleasure in being shown around the house by a member of the family. The Parkers took their name from the family's hereditary role in medieval times as keepers of the deer park in the royal hunting ground of the Forest of Bowland.

AROUND CLITHEROE

WEST BRADFORD

1 mile N of Clitheroe off the B6478

This tucked away village, just south of the Forest of Bowland, was mentioned in the Domesday Book and there are records of some villagers paying the first poll tax levied by Richard II in 1379. The old part of the village is set around a green bordering the River Ribble. It's a pleasant spot with a stream running alongside the road through the bottom half of the village and access to the houses bordering the beck is made by crossing a quaint stone bridge.

WORSTON

1 mile NE of Clitheroe off the A59

Hidden away down a lane off the main road, Worston has remained unchanged over the years and can certainly be described as unspoilt. Keen-eyed film fans may even recognize the surrounding countryside since this was one of the locations used during the filming of *Whistle Down the Wind*. Behind the village inn, where the amusing and bizarre ritual of the village's Mock Corporation was revived in 1989, can still be seen the bull ring. Set into a stone, this was where the beast was tethered and baited with specially trained dogs in the belief that the 'sport' tenderised the meat.

DOWNHAM

3 miles NE of Clitheroe off the A59

Some 40-odd villages are sprinkled along the banks of the Ribble Valley, all of them built in the appealing local stone. One of the prettiest is Downham, renowned as the setting for the cinema classic *Whistle Down the Wind*. The village also provides location scenes for BBC-TV's period drama series *Born &*

Bred. Thanks for Downham's unspoilt appearance must go to the Clitheroe family which has owned the whole village since 1558 – the same year in which they acquired Whalley Abbey. It was the present Lord Clitheroe's grandfather who paid for the electricity supply cables to be laid underground back in the 1930s and the present squire, Lord Clitheroe of Downham, still refuses to permit the skyline to be spoilt by TV aerials, satellite dishes, and even dormer windows. The village phone box has also come under the influence of the family and is not painted a distinctive pillar box red but grey, to tone in with the surroundings.

SAWLEY

4 miles N of Clitheroe off the A59

At the centre of this historic village, easily missed as the main road by-passes it, are the slight remains of **Sawley Abbey**, founded in the 13th century by the Cistercian monks of Fountains Abbey. As well as building their religious house, the monks had great influence over the whole of the surrounding area. Clearing their immediate surroundings, the monks cultivated the land and their ridge and furrow patterns can still be made out in the fields.

Although during the reigns of Edward I and II the abbots of Sawley were called to the House of Lords, none of the abbots were men of note except, perhaps, William Trafford, the last head of the community. With his colleague and neighbour, the last Abbot of Whalley, Trafford took part in the Pilgrimage of Grace in 1536 and, for his part in the failed uprising, was taken prisoner. Tried for treason at Lancaster in 1537, Trafford, with others like him, was found guilty and executed.

Although little of the abbey remains – much of the stone was cannibalised for village buildings – the site is wonderfully quiet and peaceful.

RIMINGTON

5 miles NE of Clitheroe off the A59

This small hillside village has twice won Lancashire's Best Kept Village competition. Its name means "farmstead on the boundary" and as the Lancashire/ Yorkshire boundary has changed over the years the village has been transferred from one county to the other. The most recent transfer was made in 1974 when people who had been Yorkshire born and bred suddenly found themselves Lancastrians.

This pleasant rural village was the home of Francis Duckworth, the famous composer of hymn tunes. These included one he named *Rimington*. His parents ran the village post office and shop next door to the Methodist chapel and a plaque on the chapel, now a private house, commemorates him.

GISBURN

7 miles NE of Clitheroe on the A59

Like Rimington, this village was also once in Yorkshire and, as many locals would like to believe, still is! One of the Ribble Valley's most pleasant and picturesque villages, Gisburn's history is dominated by the Lister family who, from humble beginnings rose to become the Lords of Ribblesdale. Their house, built in the early 17th century in Gisburne Park, is still standing though it is now a private hospital. Over the years, many

people were given shelter by the family and, in 1648, Cromwell is said to have rested at the house whilst on his way to fight at Preston.

PAYTHORNE

10 miles NE of Clitheroe off the A682

Although the source of the River Ribble lies to the north in Yorkshire, near the famous Three Peaks of Whernside, Ingleborough, and Pen-y-ghent, this village is the first on its banks on this side of the county boundary. It also marks the end of the river's journey through the rugged limestone scenery of moorlands and the start of its picturesque course through a lush green valley.

BARNOLDSWICK

10 miles NE of Clitheroe on the B6251

If you approach this former cotton town from the south, off the A56, you may wonder why the road is so straight. The answer is that it was specially constructed in the 1930s to service the new Rolls-Royce factory in the town. The 'B' in the names of jet engines such as the RB211 stands for Barnoldswick.

Canal Boat at Barnoldswick

MELT AT BACK RIDGE

Lilac Barn, Back Ridge Farm, Twitter Lane,
Waddington, Near Clitheroe BB7 3LQ
Tel: 01200 443377
Fax: 01200 443996
e-mail: info@themeltco.com
website: www.themeltco.com

Unusually, Melt is not to be found on a high street but down a narrow, winding country lane, in the heart of the beautiful Ribble Valley. They started life as a small, exclusive company who specialise in completely hand-made, fine-fragrance candles. The last few years have seen them move from the kitchen....to the garage, to a basement unit, and when the stairs eventually proved a little too much, they came to roost in an old, converted barn, at a working

farm, on the edge of the Forest of Bowland.

All Melt candles are completely handmade using only the highest quality materials – and as each candle takes up to 36 hours to produce, availability is exclusive to selected suppliers. All the candles carry a high percentage of blended & pure essential oils, and meet three very important criteria – that they look good, that they burn slowly using as much wax as possible, and thirdly that they smell even better when lit.

Demand for the products - and interest in the site – has meant that

Melt have recently opened a retail outlet, where visitors enjoy the stunning range of carefully selected skin-care, perfumes & accessories.

You may also visit their neighbours on site, including fine furniture makers, interior design, beauty therapy and remedial physiotherapy – to name but a few. Less than a mile away, you can visit an organic farm shop for fabulous cakes and coffee – that's if they haven't offered you one first! Please come along for a visit, they would be delighted to see you!

At the western end of the town is **Bancroft Mill Engine Museum**. The mill was the last weaving shed to be built in Lancashire, in 1922. The mill closed in 1978 but the grand 600hp cross-compound steam engine was preserved and there are regular demonstrations of it in action. The museum also displays tools and documents connected with the weaving industry.

WADDINGTON
2 miles NW of Clitheroe on the B6478

This is one of the area's best known villages – its attractive Coronation Gardens have appeared on many postcards and even on biscuit tin lids. King Henry VI spent a whole year here in 1464/5, not because he particularly appreciated its charms but because he was hiding at Waddington Hall from the Yorkists who had defeated him at the Battle of Hexham. When his hiding place was discovered he escaped by a secret tunnel that led from the Hall's dining room. He was quickly captured at Brungerley Bridge, down river near Clitheroe, then imprisoned in the Tower of London where he died in 1471.

Waddington has several times won first prize in Lancashire's Best Kept Village competition and it's easy to see why. Waddington Brook splashes the length of the village and 18th century almshouses cluster around the green.

About ten years ago Waddington's villagers enjoyed a certain amount of fame when, for the sake of a TV series, they agreed to renounce their TVs for a whole month. This cold turkey treatment proved too much for some and they had to be resuscitated by having their sets returned.

GREAT MITTON
3 miles SW of Clitheroe on the B6246

Standing opposite the Three Fishes Hotel, which takes its name from the three fishes on the Whalley Abbey coat of arms, is the attractive **All Hallows' Church**. Housing some of the finest relics to be seen in any British church, this is most certainly worth a visit. Built in around 1270, though undoubtedly there was a wooden Saxon structure hereabouts, little has been done to the building since although a tower was added in 1438 and the pews are Jacobean. However, it is the **Shireburn Chapel** that draws most visitors to the church. It was added in 1440 by the Shireburn family of Stonyhurst who claimed to be the direct descendants of the first rector, Ralph the Red of Mytton. The family tombs here are regarded as the best in the county. One of the earliest is the fine alabaster tomb of Sir Richard Shireburn (who died in 1594) and his wife Maude who is dressed in capacious petticoats. The latest is of another Richard who died in 1702 at the age of nine after eating poisonous berries. Following the fashion of the time the monument displays copious macabre items – a skull, hour glass, sickle, more bones than seem necessary and, emerging from the ground, two skeletal hands.

Confirmation that a settlement existed here before the days of the land ownership by the abbey comes with the name of the village itself. Mitton is derived from the Saxon word 'mythe' which means a farm at the junction of two rivers – perfectly describing the location as, close by, the River Hodder feeds into the River Ribble.

HURST GREEN
5 miles SW of Clitheroe on the B6243

This pretty village of stone-built cottages nestling in the Ribble Valley is best known for its nearby public school. **Stonyhurst College**, the world famous Roman Catholic school, began life as the residence of the local lords of the manor. The present building, begun in around 1523, was the work of Hugh Shireburn although additions were made in 1592 by Sir Richard Shireburn. The core of this imposing building set beside a lake is late-Elizabethan but there have been major additions almost every century, all of them blending remarkably well with their predecessors.

Sir Richard Shireburn was an ambitious man who served the Tudor monarchy well. As well as being the Chief Forester of Bowland, he was also one of Henry VIII's commissioners studying the state of the monasteries. He was an eager participant in the suppression of Whalley Abbey. Though the family publicly adopted the new Protestant religion under Elizabeth I, it was with little enthusiasm and in a short time the Shireburn family, like many other Lancashire families, returned to their Catholic faith. It seems strange then that Cromwell, on his way to and from the Battle of Preston, should take shelter at Stonyhurst although rumour has it that the ardent Puritan slept with a pistol at his side and his guards around him.

In 1794, after the house had been left for some considerable time and had fallen into a state of disrepair, the owner, Thomas Weld, offered the property to the Jesuits who had set up an English Catholic School in Flanders. Unwelcome in France following the revolution, the Jesuits gladly accepted and after restoring the original building they extended it during the 19th century. Their finest addition must be the replica of King's College in Cambridge: **St Peter's Church** was built in 1835 and contains many treasures including a 7th century copy of St John's Gospel and a cape of Henry II that was used by Henry VIII at the battle of the Field of the Cloth of Gold.

One of Stonyhurst College's most famous sons was Sir Arthur Conan Doyle, the creator of Sherlock Holmes. The Conan Doyle desk (into which he carved his name) is one of the many artifacts on show when the college is occasionally open to the public during the summer holidays. The exterior of the college can always be seen from the minor road that runs through its grounds.

STYDD

7 miles SW of Clitheroe off the B6245

Just to the north of Ribchester lies the small hamlet of Stydd. All that remains of the monastery founded here by the Knights Hospitallers of St John of Jerusalem is the Norman **Chapel**, standing alone surrounded by meadows. It contains effigies of some of the knights. A crusading and military order established in 1113, the Knights Hospitallers provided help and assistance to pilgrims travelling to the Holy Land. Their commandery, as their religious houses were called, at Stydd was dissolved by the mid-14th century and, although at one time there were over 50 of their small monasteries in the country, only 15 survived to the 1530s.

RIBCHESTER

8 miles SW of Clitheroe on the B5269

Situated on the banks of the River Ribble the village is famous for its **Roman Fort**, Bremetannacum, on the northern bank. It was the Roman governor Gnaeus Julius Agricola who in 79AD first established a fort here at the crossroads of two important roads, one linking Manchester and Carlisle; the other running from York to the west coast. It also guarded a ford over the River Ribble. Although little of the fort's walls remain, the granary or storehouse with its hypocaust

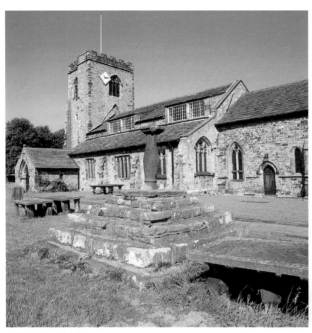

Ribchester Church

After Clitheroe, bustling Longridge is the only other town of any size in the area. Like Clitheroe it offers a good selection of independently owned shops along with a range of antique galleries, and is widely known for its Lancashire Cheese Dairies.

The village lies at the foot of **Longridge Fell** from whose 1,150ft elevation, especially at Jeffrey Hill or Kemple End, there are superb views northwards over the Loud Valley to Chipping: to the south the land drops away towards the River Ribble. For many years this area was an important source of building stone and several of Preston's civic buildings, including the Harris Library and Museum, and the docks at Liverpool were constructed with Longridge stone.

In the 1790s the stone was also used to build a row of 20 terraced cottages in Longridge – numbers 4 to 44 Higher Road, which now have listed building status. They were erected by a group of quarrymen who formed a club into which each member paid a fixed weekly sum. The money was used to pay the cost of materials, £138.3s.6d (£138.17p), for building each cottage. When a cottage was completed, the members drew lots as to who should occupy it. Known as **Club Row**, these mutually-funded cottages are the earliest known example of properties

(underfloor heating) has been excavated and has revealed some interesting coins, pottery, sculptures and inscriptions.

The fort's **Roman Museum** is designed to transport visitors back to the days of the Roman occupation and offers an excellent insight into those times. Sadly, the finest artefact unearthed here, an ornate bronze parade helmet recovered in 1795, is not on display here (though they do have a replica). The original can be seen at the British Museum in London.

In the village itself, the discovery of some pre-Norman crosses in and around **St Wilfrid's Church** suggest that this 13th century building occupies the site of a Saxon church. The church is named after the first Bishop of Ripon who in the 7th century played a prominent part in the Synod of Whitby.

built on the principles of a Building Society and have earned themselves an entry in the *Guinness Book of Records*.

GOOSNARGH
12 miles SW of Clitheroe on the B5269

Just to the west of the village lies **Chingle Hall**, a small moated manor house that was built in 1260 by Adam de Singleton. A Catholic family, the Singletons are said to have a chapel with three priest hides and, so the story goes, Cromwell once climbed down one of the hall's chimneys to spy on the Royalists below. As well as being the birthplace of St John Wall, one of the last priests to die for his faith, in 1620, it enjoys the reputation of being one of the most haunted houses in Britain and, as such, the hall has featured in countless TV and radio programmes.

GRIMSARGH
11 miles W of Clitheroe on the B6243

As well as having one of the largest village greens in Lancashire, covering some 12 acres, Grimsargh is also home to **Tun Brook Wood**. Following the line of the brook until it meets the River Ribble, this is one of the largest areas of deciduous woodland in the country.

THE FYLDE

The Fylde derives its name from the Anglo-Saxon word *gefilde* meaning level, green fields, an apt description of this low-lying area that extends from Fleetwood in the north to Lytham St Anne's in the south. It was once known as "Windmill Land" but nowadays windmills are few and far between. A notable exception is the striking example on the waterfront at Lytham. It was built in 1805, worked until 1929, and now houses a small museum.

This historic area of coastal Lancashire is known to most because of Blackpool: the brash, seaside resort that has been entertaining holidaymakers for generations. To the south lies another resort, Lytham St Anne's, which is not only somewhat more genteel but also the home of one of the country's best known golf courses and host to the British Open Championships. Both places grew up as a result of the expansion of the railway system in the Victorian age, when they were popular destinations for the mill workers of Lancashire and Yorkshire.

However, the Fylde is also an ancient region that was known to both the Saxons and the Romans. To the north of this region, around the Wyre estuary, the salt marshes have been exploited for over 2,000 years and the process continues at the large ICI plant. Fishing and shipping too have been important sources of revenue here. Fleetwood is still a port though smaller than it was whilst, surprisingly though it might seem today, Lytham was also an important port along the Ribble Estuary.

Inland, the fertile, flat plain has been farmed for many centuries and, with few major roads, the quiet rural communities lie undisturbed and little changed by the 21st century. A haven for wildlife, and particularly birds and plants, the two estuaries, of the Ribble and the Wyre, provide habitats that abound with rare and endangered species of plants and birds. A relatively undiscovered region, the Fylde has much more to offer than a white knuckle ride and candy floss and is well worth taking the time to explore.

BLACKPOOL

Blackpool is as unique to England as Las Vegas is to the United States. Everyone is familiar with Blackpool's brash, warm-hearted attractions but did you know that this single town has more beds available for the 16 million people who visit each year than the whole of Portugal has for its visitors?

Today, Blackpool is the largest town in the present county of Lancashire. Little more than a fishing village among the sand dunes of the Fylde coast 150 years ago, Blackpool's huge expansion followed the arrival of the railway. Up until then, travel to and from the village involved considerable discomfort, taking a day from Manchester and two days from York. The great Victorian railway companies put Blackpool well and truly on the map by laying the railway lines right to the coast and building the grand stations – the town had three. Local developers enthusiastically began creating new attractions for their visitors. The first pier was constructed in 1863, followed by two more over the next 20 years. A glass-domed Winter Gardens opened in 1875, and 10 years later the town's electric tram system began operating, the first in Britain and today the only one. The Pleasure Beach with its permanent fairground rides and amusements arrived in 1890 with the aim of providing "an American-style amusement park where adults could feel like children again".

But the developers' real master-stroke was the construction of the world-famous Blackpool Tower. Modelled on the Eiffel Tower and completed in 1894, the tower stands some 518 feet high, incorporates a Ballroom and Grand Theatre, both of which are decorated in a wonderfully over-the-top rococo style. The Tower Ballroom is a much loved institution where tea dances are still a regular feature. It was, for many years from the 1960s to the 1980s, the venue for BBC-TV's enormously popular Come

Dancing series. The tower's centenary celebrations in 1994 were numerous and extravagant and included painting the tower gold.

The introduction of the Blackpool Illuminations helped extend the summer season into autumn, and the late 20th century saw yet more visitor attractions added to the mix. The Pleasure Beach now boasts the tallest, fastest and, it is claimed, the most thrilling roller-coaster ride in the world; The Sandcastle is an all-weather indoor complex where visitors can enjoy waterslides, wave pools and water flumes in sub-tropical temperatures; and The Sea Life Centre provides close-up views of a wide range of marine creatures, including deadly sea snakes.

The North Pier, designed by Eugenius Birch, was opened at the beginning of the 1863 season. It soon became the place to promenade and is now a listed building. Eugenius Birch (1818-1884) was the most famous of all the pier engineers; he was also a talented artist and mechanic. His Blackpool pier was one of many – others included Margate, Aberystwyth, Brighton West, Eastbourne, Hastings, Lytham and Plymouth – the last opened in the year of his death.

One of the town's less well known attractions is the Grundy Art Gallery in Queen Street which has an interesting collection of Victorian oils and watercolours, contemporary prints, modern British paintings and a fascinating exhibit on Old Blackpool.

Despite its reputation as a brash and lively resort, Blackpool also has its quiet, secluded corners where visitors can escape the hustle of the crowds. There are seven miles of sea front, from the North Shore down as far as Squire's Gate and Lytham, where the pace of life is gentler and the beaches are quieter.

Central Pier, Blackpool

splendid end to the season.

A couple of miles inland from The Pleasure Beach, **Martin Mere** is a Wildlife Trust bird reserve where more than 160 species have been recorded. The 10-acre lake is the year round home for hundreds of geese, swans, ducks and even flamingos, and a temporary resting-place for thousands more. Nearby, **Stanley Park** is spacious, well-maintained and peaceful, and noted for its Italian garden

Blackpool Tramways have provided a most enjoyable way of exploring these less busy sides of the town and its environs for many years. And it should also be remembered that the world's first electric street tram system opened here in 1885. The route was extended along the Lytham road in 1895 and later connected with other routes in nearby Lytham St Anne's. Still a popular means of transport here today, many of the tramcars date from the 1930s or 1950s and the managing company has a special selection of vintage cars which they run on special occasions. One of these occasions is the now annual **Illuminations** which, following a ceremonial lighting much like that of the Christmas lights in London, is a

and pleasure lake. Adjacent to the park, **Blackpool Zoo** is home to more than 400 animals from all around the world, including lions, tigers, elephants, gorillas, lemurs, exotic birds and creepy-crawlies. A popular attraction is the Dinosaur Safari which takes visitors back through time to the world of dinosaurs, experiencing erupting volcanoes, spouting geysers and terrifying reptiles along the way.

AROUND BLACKPOOL

A short drive out of Blackpool, at Peel just off the A583, is **Penny Farm**, a recovery and rehabilitation center run by the International League for the Protection of Horses. The site has stabling for up to 28 horses, open-fronted barns where visitors can make friends with the horses, an exercise area and a visitor centre with a coffee shop and gift shop.

THORNTON

5 miles N of Blackpool on the B5268

Situated in the west bank of the Wyre estuary, this small town is dominated by **Marsh Mill**, which stands over 100 feet high and was constructed in 1794. The grinding of corn ceased here soon after World War I but the building has been restored and it is now a tourist attraction.

At this point the Wyre estuary is wide and provides shelter for shipping, an advantage that was utilised by both the Romans and the Scandinavians. They both took advantage of the salt deposits here and, today, the large ICI plant is still extracting salt. The **Wyre Estuary Country Park**, taking the whole estuary from Fleetwood up river as far as Shard Bridge, is an excellent place from which to discover the area. An initial stop at the **Wyreside Ecology Centre**, which provides all manner of information about the estuary, is a sensible starting point. From here a number of footpaths take in many of the places along the river as well as leading visitors through important areas of salt marsh which contain a wide range of plants, insects, and birds.

CLEVELEYS

5 miles N of Blackpool on the A584

This popular seaside resort is less boisterous than its neighbour, Blackpool, to the south and it is altogether more attractive architecturally. This is hardly surprising as the town began to grow after an architectural competition, organised in 1906, in which Sir Edwin Lutyens, the designer of modern Whitehall, London, was involved.

FLEETWOOD

8 miles N of Blackpool on the A587

Cleveleys in turn links up with Fleetwood which until 1836 was just a small fishing village. Local landowner Sir Peter Hesketh-Fleetwood decided to develop the area as a seaside resort and employed the leading architect, Decimus Burton, who had designed London's Regent Street as well as large parts of St Leonards-on-Sea and Hove.

The opening of the railway extension from Preston to Fleetwood was a key player in the town's development and the impressive North Euston Hotel, which opened in 1842, reflects those railway links. Queen Victoria used Fleetwood as she travelled to Scotland for her annual holiday. However, this was all before the railway companies managed to lay a railway over Shap Fell in Cumbria in 1847 and thus provide a direct rail link to Scotland. Sir Peter was bankrupted but the town itself continued to flourish as a port and seaside resort.

The town's **Museum**, overlooking the River Wyre, illustrates the town's links with the fishing industry which suffered greatly from the Icelandic cod wars of the 1970s.

The town's most famous product is known around the world. In 1865, a local chemist named James Lofthouse created a compound of liquorice, capsicum, eucalyptus and methanol designed to relieve the sore throats and bronchial troubles endured by fishermen at sea. He called the mixture **Fisherman's Friend** and it was remarkably successful. The only problem was that the bottles in which it was sold frequently shattered in the rough Atlantic seas. So Lofthouse transformed the liquid into a lozenge which is still produced by his descendants and has enormous sales world-wide.

Rossall Point
7 miles N of Blackpool off the A587

Situated at the northern tip of the Fylde coast, this was where the Hesketh-Fleetwood family, the force behind the creation of Fleetwood, had their home. Their impressive mansion is still standing and is now part of Rossall School.

Preesall
8 miles N of Blackpool on the B5270

The village's original name, Pressoude, as it was mentioned in the *Domesday Book*, is thought to mean a salt farm near the sea and certainly in 1872 rock salt deposits were discovered beneath the village. From then on, for around 30 years, Preesall became a centre for salt mining and in 1883 the Fleetwood Salt Company was established to develop the field. The bulk of the salt was extracted in the form of brine and by the end of 1891 there was a reliable pipeline pumping the salt under the River Wyre to Fleetwood. However, as much of the salt was extracted from underneath the expanding village, subsidence soon became a problem. In 1923 this led to the opening up of a huge pit, known locally as "Bottomless" to the west of the village.

Knott End-on-Sea
8 miles N of Blackpool on the B5270

This small coastal resort on the River Wyre estuary grew into a substantial fishing settlement in the 17th and 18th centuries. It was also a pilot base for the upstream ports of Wardleys and Skippool, and later developed into a ferry port. Today its broad flat sands and bracing sea air, along with the decline in the fishing industry, have turned the town into a small, quiet holiday resort that is also favoured by those who have retired.

Looking out to sea, at low tide, a rocky outcrop can be seen which, some historians have suggested, is the remains of the masonry of a Roman harbour. Whether this is the port that in the 2nd century Ptolemy marked on a map as Portus Setantiorum is certainly in doubt but it is undeniable that such a building existed as the Romans were planning an invasion of Ireland from this stretch of coast.

Pilling
10 miles N of Blackpool off the A588

This quiet scattered village, on the edge of rich, fertile marshland, was for many years linked to the market town of Garstang by a little, winding, single-track railway known affectionately as the "Pilling Pig" because the train's whistle sounded like a pig having its throat cut. The last passengers were carried in 1930; the last goods train ran in 1950.

Said to be the second largest village in Britain, Pilling boasts no fewer than five churches. One of them, **Old St John's** is notable as a "time-warp" church, virtually unchanged since its completion in 1717. Flagged floors, pews and box-pews of unvarnished oak, and a three-decker pulpit have all survived unscathed thanks to the building of a new church in the village in 1887.

There has been a watermill at Pilling since 1242. The present windmill dates back to 1808 and was built on a raft of brushwood. It is now a private residence.

Another building of interest is The Olde Ship Inn, built in 1782 by George Dickson, a slave trader. Now a listed building, the inn is reputed to be haunted by a lady dressed in Georgian

School Lane, Pilling

of a grassy knoll, are the remains of **Greenhalgh Castle**, built in 1490 by Thomas Stanley, the first Earl of Derby. Severely damaged during a siege by Cromwell's troops in 1645-46, the castle was one of the last strongholds in Lancashire to have held out and only surrendered when its Governor died.

Nearby Gubberford Bridge is reputedly haunted. It was during the Civil War siege that a Roundhead soldier named Peter Broughton was standing on the bridge one winter evening when he was approached by a beautiful woman dressed all in white. To his amazement, he recognised the wife who had left him for another man some five years earlier.

She was advancing towards him, smiling and with her arms outstretched, when a Royalist captain, Robert Rowton, burst onto the bridge. In the altercation that followed it emerged that she had bigamously married the captain. Enraged, Rowton stabbed her in the breast and she died within minutes. The two soldiers from opposing sides then joined forces to bury beside the bridge the body of the woman they had both known as wife. It was only a death-bed confession by Peter Broughton many years later that brought the deed to light. By then Rowton was dead but the unquiet soul of the White Lady has found no rest and on misty winter evenings she paces silently up and down the bridge.

attire wandering around with a pale and worried look on her face.

GARSTANG

12 miles N of Blackpool on the A6

This is an ancient, picturesque town whose market dates back to the time of Edward II and is still held every Thursday in the central square with its handsome former Town Hall of 1755. A bell is rung at 10am to signify the opening of trading. Another long-standing institution is the Garstang Agricultural Show which was founded in 1809 and is held on the first Saturday in August.

The town is also home to an excellent **Discovery Centre** which deals with a variety of aspects of the region, including the history of the nearby Forest of Bowland and the natural history of the surrounding countryside.

Just to the east of the town, on the top

A little to the north of Garstang, on the B6430, are the remains of a stone-built **Toll House** which probably dates from the 1820s when parts of the turnpike from Garstang to Lancaster were realigned. Although a ruin, the toll house is more than usually interesting as the posts for the toll gates can still be seen on either side of the road. This stretch of road ialso features some of the finest **Turnpike Milestones** in the county. To the south of Garstang they are round-faced stones with cursive lettering dating from the 1750s but to the north the stones are triangular, with Roman lettering, and date from the time of the turnpike's realignment in the early 19th century.

HAMBLETON
6 miles NE of Blackpool on the A588

A centre for ship building in medieval times, Hambleton is now a quiet village set around a bend of the River Wyre. A network of narrow lanes radiate from the village and wind through the charming north Fylde countryside.

The village stands on one of the narrowest parts of the river and there was certainly a ford in Roman times, as relics have been found here. However, it is probable that the ford goes back even further, to the Iron Age around 500 BC. On the site of the ford now stands the 325-yard **Shard Bridge**, built in 1864 and still operating as a toll bridge.

POULTON-LE-FYLDE
4 miles E of Blackpool on the A586

This is one of the oldest towns in the ancient area known as 'Amounderness'. The Romans were known to have been in the area and it was probably their handiwork that constructed the **Danes Pad**, an ancient trackway. The town developed as a commercial centre for the surrounding agricultural communities and its Market Place remains its focal point. In 1732, a great fire, started by sparks from the torches of a funeral procession, destroyed most of the thatched cottages that surrounded the market square in those days and a nationwide appeal was launched to help meet the rebuilding costs. Consequently, little of old Poulton can be seen in the centre of the town.

The present **Church of St Chad** dates from the early 17th century, though the

Poulton-le-Fylde

majority of the building is Georgian, and it stands on the site of the original Norman church. Inside there's a splendid Georgian nave from which a magnificent staircase leads to typically Georgian galleries running around three sides. As Poulton was a key town in the area for centuries, it is not surprising that there are several magnificent memorials to the local Fleetwood-Hesketh family also to be found here.

Fire seems to have played an important role in the life of the town and one ancient custom still kept is **Teanlay Night**, which involves the lighting of bonfires on Hallowe'en. Each bonfire is encircled with white-coloured stones which are then thrown into the flames by the onlookers and left until the next day. The successful retrieval of one's own stone is considered a good omen for future prosperity.

Strolling around Poulton-le-Fylde now, it is hard to imagine that the town was once a seaport. But, until relatively recently ships sailed up the River Wyre to **Skippool Creek**. Today, the creek is home to the Blackpool and Fleetwood Yacht Club and from here the ocean-going yachts compete in major races around Britain.

The town had a rail link long before Blackpool and it was here that the early holidaymakers alighted from their trains to take a horse and trap the remaining few miles. Fortunately for Poulton, in 1846, the railway reached Blackpool and the town could, once again, return to a more peaceful existence. It is this quiet and charm, as well as sensitive approaches to planning, that have led it to become, in recent years, a much sought after residential area for businessmen now able to travel the M55 to Manchester and Liverpool.

Incidentally, Poulton's "le-Fylde" tag

was added to distinguish the town from Poulton-le-Sands – nowadays better known as Morecambe.

SINGLETON
5 miles E of Blackpool on the B5260

Singleton's most famous son is Robert Gillow who lived here in the first half of the 18th century. He left to become an apprentice joiner at Lancaster and later founded the cabinet making business that became Waring & Gillow of Lancaster.

The village Gillow knew was completely demolished in 1853 after it was bought for £70,000 by Alderman Thomas Miller, a cotton manufacturer from Preston. He then rebuilt it as a model village complete with a church, school, public house – The Millers Arms, naturally, and an ornate black-and-white shed for the village fire engine which still stands although it is now an electricity sub-station.

The parish church of this quiet little Fylde village, **St Anne's Church**, was built as part of Miller's model village in 1860. In the sanctuary is a black oak chair which bears the inscription "John Milton, author of *Paradise Lost* and *Paradise Regained* 1671" but no-one seems to know where the chair came from and whether the great author did indeed use it.

GREAT ECCLESTON
8 miles NE of Blackpool off the A586

This quiet traditional agricultural community on the banks of the River Wyre was, during the 17th and 18th centuries, known locally as Little London because it was the social centre for the surrounding area. This was probably directly linked to the generous number of public houses and inns in the village at that time.

Every Wednesday, a bustling open air market is held in the charming village square. However, unlike most markets Great Eccleston's first took place in 1974 following a campaign started by the parish council a few years previously. The wide variety of stalls attract visitors from not only the immediate surroundings but also coaches from outside the rural area.

ST MICHAEL'S ON WYRE

10 miles NE of Blackpool on the A586

The River Wyre at this point is still tidal and for centuries the inhabitants of St Michael's and other villages in the area have suffered the threat of flooding. An old flood bank has been constructed from the village bridge and below, beyond the overgrown banks, are the fertile fields of the flood plain.

Mentioned in the *Domesday Book* as Michelscherche, is it likely that the first church in the village was founded in the 7th century. As well as many memorials to the Butler family the church also contains a splendid 14th century mural that was only discovered in 1956 when repair work was being undertaken in the sanctuary.

The Butler family, whose home – Rawcliffe Hall – lies a few miles down river, are known to have been in this area for 800 years and their house is built on the site of a Saxon dwelling. Another of the staunchly Catholic Lancashire families, the Butlers finally lost their house and the influence that they had in the area. The house is now part of a private country club.

CHURCHTOWN

12 miles NE of Blackpool on the A586

This delightful village has many buildings of both architectural and historic interest and none more so than the **Church of St Helen** which dates

back to the days of the Norman Conquest. Featuring architectural styles from almost every period since the 11th century, this church is well worth exploring. The oldest parts of the building are the circular pillars near the nave which date from around 1200. The roof is the original Tudor structure. Built on the site of a Saxon church, St Helen's is dedicated to the mother of Emperor Constantine and the circular churchyard is typical of the Saxon period.

Known as the "Cathedral of the Fylde", the church has been subjected to flooding by the River Wyre and in 1746 such was the damage caused by the rising waters that the rebuilding of the church looked necessary. However, the builder brought in to survey the scene, suggested that moving the river would be a cheaper option and this method of preserving the church was undertaken. The original course of the river can be seen by taking the footpath from the churchyard in the direction of the new river course.

WOODPLUMPTON

12 miles E of Blackpool off the B5269

This charming little village, centred around its church still has its well preserved village stocks behind which is a mounting block that is now designated as a historic monument. **St Anne's Church** is also a building of historic note and the keen-eyed will be quick to spot the octagonal cupola shape of tower that is reminiscent of the architecture of Christopher Wren. Completed in 1748, the tower was built to house a new timepiece, a clock, which replaced the sundial that for many years adorned the old tower. Bearing the date 1637, this can now be found in the churchyard.

Many small towns and villages in Lancashire have their own tale of witches to tell and Woodplumpton is no exception. In St Anne's churchyard a huge boulder marks the grave of Margaret Hilton, better known in her day as "Meg the Witch". It's said that one day the local squire made a wager with her that she could not turn herself into a hare and outrun their pack of dogs. (This transformation into a hare was apparently a standard feature of any self-respecting witch's repertoire). Meg accepted the bet, stipulating only that one particular black dog should be excluded.

The race duly took place but the squire cheated, letting slip the black dog which managed to nip the hare's back legs just before it vanished into thin air. From that day, Meg suffered from a severe limp – and a nasty temper. Every kind of rural mishap was attributed to her black arts. She was eventually found dead in her cottage, crushed between a water barrel and a well, and her body was buried in the churchyard by torchlight on May 2nd, 1705. But her body kept rising to the surface so a massive boulder was rolled over her grave. (Similar measures were taken at Samlesbury, to the east of Preston. In the churchyard there's a witch's grave through which iron spikes have been driven to prevent her from returning to plague her neighbours.)

CLIFTON AND SALWICK
11 miles SE of Blackpool off the A583

Both Salwick and its neighbour, Clifton, were formed from part of the old Clifton estate. As well as the pleasant walks along the banks of the canal, visitors can also enjoy the delights of The Windmill pub which is, unlike most pubs of that name, housed in a converted windmill.

KIRKHAM
8 miles SE of Blackpool off the A583

Mentioned in the *Domesday Book*, there was a settlement here in Saxon times,

known as Ciric-ham, and before that the Romans had a fort though it is now lost under a modern housing estate. Kirkham was first granted a charter to hold a weekly market in 1287 and since then it has been serving the needs of the surrounding farming communities. Some fine Georgian inns and houses reflect the town's importance in stagecoach days and the steep main street contains a number of old-fashioned family-run shops. In the cobbled market square, used for markets and fairs since 1296, The Fishstones are still to be seen – flat stone slabs set on stone uprights to form a broken circle. These were the counters from which fish was sold.

FRECKLETON
9 miles SE of Blackpool on the A584

This is the largest village in the Fylde with a population of more than 7,000. The name is derived from the Anglo-Saxon *Frecheltun* meaning 'an enclosed area' and this is how it featured in the Domesday Book. Situated on the northern banks of the River Ribble, the long straggling village was, until the river was canalised, surrounded by marshland.

During World War II the village suffered an appalling tragedy. On a sweltering, thundery day in August 1944 an American Liberator plane took off from nearby Warton aerodrome but because of the adverse weather, the pilot decided to turn back. As it descended over Freckleton, the plane clipped some trees and crashed into the village school. Thirty-six children and 36 adults perished. A disaster fund was set up but villagers bitterly disagreed about how it should be spent. It wasn't until 33 years later that the money was used to build the village's Memorial Hall.

LYTHAM ST ANNE'S

4 miles E of Blackpool on the A584

Located on the northern bank of the Ribble Estuary, Lytham St Anne's is based on a much older community, already well-established by the time of the Norman Conquest. It has a short pier, a gracious Victorian Promenade, and an attractive grassy expanse called the Beach. Here stands a handsome white-washed windmill, one of very few to have survived from the days when the flat plain of the Fylde was dotted with hundreds of them.

There are actually two towns here: Lytham, which is mentioned in the *Domesday Book*, and St Anne's, which was largely developed in the 1870s as a rather upmarket resort. Before the development of the resort, in the Victorian age, Lytham was an important port on the Ribble estuary and was home to the first

fishing company on this stretch of the northwest coast. Shipbuilding also continued here until the 1950s when the last vessel constructed in the shipyards was the Windermere Car Ferry. During the 1940s, parts of the famous Mulberry harbour were constructed in secret here in preparation for the invasion of Normandy in 1944.

The arrival of the railway linking Lytham with Preston prompted a group of Lancashire businessmen to plan the construction of a health resort between the old established port and the rapidly expanding town of Blackpool to the north. There was scarcely a cottage on their chosen site when the work began in 1875 but the growth of the carefully planned town was spectacular. In just 30 years the population increased from 1,000 to 17,000 inhabitants.

The **Promenade**, running the full length of the seafront from St Anne's to

SIDES ARTS & FRAMES

1 Tudor Buildings, South Westby Street,
Lytham St Annes, Lancashire FY8 5JE
Tel: 01253 737409
e-mail: sides@btconnect.com

"Art and frames without boundaries" says the sign outside Dave Seidel's **Sides Arts & Frames** shop. Inside, you'll find an extensive collection of original paintings, limited edition prints, canvases, bronze art and a regularly changing display of sculptures. The work of international artist Jurgen Gorg is often on show here, along with pieces by British painters Steve Johnston, Sue Howells, George Mitchell, and local artist Les Darlow. The shop also stocks a selection of art cards, some of them hand-made, and art posters.

A line that is becoming increasingly popular is 'glass art'. A sheet of glass is covered with abstract designs in various metals, another sheet of glass is placed on top and then they are fired in a furnace. Very colourful and striking, they would certainly provide an eye-catching talking point for any room. Dave's own speciality is contemporary picture framing and you can watch him at work in his open studio at the back of the shop. Sides Art & Frames is located in the centre of the town, conveniently close to the Pleasant Street car park.

Lytham was constructed in 1875 and on the landward side there are several fine examples of Victorian and Edwardian seaside villas. Beyond the attractive Promenade Gardens, laid out by a local character, Henry Gregson, is **St Anne's Pier**. Opened in 1885, the elegant pier was built in a mock Tudor style and up until 1897 fishing smacks and pleasure boats were able to tie up at the end of the jetty. Lytham also had a pier, built in 1865, but during a gale in 1903 two sand barges dragged their anchors and sliced the structure in two. Undeterred, and with the Pavilion still standing at the far end, the pier was rebuilt only to be almost entirely destroyed by fire in 1928.

In fact, the town has had its fair share of disasters associated with the sea. By far the worst of these occurred in 1886 and it is still Britain's greatest lifeboat disaster. The crew of the St Anne's lifeboat, with the help of the Southport lifeboat, set out to answer a distress signal put up by a German ship, the *Mexico*. The sea was so rough that 15 members of the lifeboat crew were lost. The tragedy led to the improvement of lifeboat design. In the **Alpine Garden** on the Promenade is a monument which pays tribute to the men who lost their lives. The statue features the stone figure of a coxswain looking out to sea with a rope in one hand and a lifebelt in the other.

As well as being an elegant place full of

fine Victorian and Edwardian architecture, Lytham St Anne's also contains some reminders to the more distant past. **Lytham Hall**, now privately owned by a large insurance company, started life as a farming cell of the Durham cathedral in 1190. After the Reformation, the estate changed hands several times, until in 1606 it became the property of Sir Cuthbert Clifton, the first squire of Lytham. The fine Georgian hall standing today was the building that John Carr of York built for Thomas Clifton between 1757 and 1764. The extensive grounds, once part of the estate, are now **Lytham Hall Country Park**, where visitors can follow several nature trails to discover the birds and wildlife living here which includes three species of woodpecker, the Lesser Whitethroat, and the Hawfinch.

There has been a **Windmill** at Lytham

Lytham Windmill

for more than 800 years though the present structure dates from 1805. A well known landmark along the coast, the building has a solid white tower with a cap that looks rather like an upturned boat. In 1929 the wind set the four sails turning the wrong way, ruining the machinery and firing the mill, which has never worked since. Now renovated, the windmill is home to a permanent exhibition on the building's history and on the process of breadmaking. Adjacent to the windmill, and the original home of the Lytham lifeboat, Old Lifeboat House is home to the **Lifeboat Museum**. Both buildings have limited opening times. Two other museums worthy of a visit are the **Lytham Motive Power Museum**, with its large model railway layout and an outdoor display of rolling stock, and the **Toy and Teddy Museum**, housed in the Porrit Victorian building with a varied collection of childhood memorabilia.

For those interested in discovering more about the abundant wildlife of the dune system here, a visit to **Lytham St Anne's Nature Reserve** is a must. Established in 1968, the reserve is an important scientific site as well as being just a small part of what was once a very extensive sand dune system. As well as the rich plant life, the dunes are home to several rare species of migrating birds including osprey, black redstart, and Lapland buntings.

No description of Lytham St Anne's is complete without a mention of the **Royal Lytham and St Anne's Golf Course**. The club originated after a meeting held in 1886 when a group of 19 keen golfers sought to furnish themselves with suitable facilities. The course opened in 1898 and it is still considered by many to be one of the finest golf links in the country and is a regular host of the British Open.

THE FORESTS OF PENDLE AND ROSSENDALE

The Pennine Hills, the 'backbone of England', are such a well-known geographical feature that it comes as something of a surprise to find that the name was created as recently as 1750 by a fraudulent professor. Charles Bertram claimed to have discovered a medieval chronicle describing Britain as it was in Roman times. In this non-existent tome, he said, the Romans had named this range of hills 'Alps Penina' because they resembled the Apennine Hills of central Italy. The professor's fake chronicle was soon discredited but his spurious name, the 'Pennines', has been universally adopted.

In the 1720s, Daniel Defoe jogged on horse-back through the area and wrote it off as 'a howling wilderness....the English Andes'. A century later the wild, poverty-stricken area Defoe had travelled through was throbbing with the sound of churning mill wheels, its sky murky with the smoke of thousands of coal-fuelled factories. That sooty, industrial image lingers on despite the fact that this area of Lancashire has re-invented itself in the past few decades. The waste from coal-pits has been transformed into smoothly-landscaped country parks and energetic local councils are also striving to make the most of the region's natural attractions: swooping hills, stark moorlands and contrasting wooded valleys.

But the area still takes pride in its industrial past, now recognised by its designation as an official Heritage Area. Bacup, for example, as well as being the highest town in Lancashire at 827ft above sea level, is also acknowledged by English Heritage as the best preserved cotton town in Britain. And the Queen Street Mill at Haile Syke near Burnley is the only surviving steam-powered cotton mill in the country. Here, more than 300 deafening Lancashire looms clatter away in the imposing weaving shed where hundreds of metres of cotton cloth are produced weekly. In Burnley itself, the Weavers Triangle is one of the finest examples of a Victorian industrial townscape still in existence.

South-east Lancashire also possesses some grand buildings from an earlier era. Gawthorpe Hall at Padiham is a Jacobean gem; Towneley Hall, dating back to the 1400s, houses Burnley's excellent Museum & Art Gallery, and Turton Tower, north of Bolton, is a lovely old building which began as a medieval pele.

Despite its industrial history, the southern border of Lancashire boasts some attractive villages. Withnell Fold, five miles southwest of Blackburn, is an idyllic model village entirely built by the Parke family in the mid-1800s to house the workforce employed at their paper mill. Rivington, near Chorley, is a captivating small village set around a village green and alongside a huge reservoir beneath whose waters half of the old village lies submerged.

BURNLEY

This cotton town is rich in history as well as being the largest town in this area of East Lancashire. Incorporating some 50 square miles, the town offers visitors a wealth of contrasts, from some of the best preserved industrial landscapes in Britain to the magnificent, untouched moorlands just to the east. First established at the beginning of the 9th century, the town nestles in a basin between the River Calder and the River Brun, from which it takes its name.

With the Industrial Revolution and the building of the Leeds and Liverpool Canal, Burnley not only expanded but grew in stature until, by the end of the 19th century, it was the world's leading producer of cotton cloth. Burnley's fine Victorian **Town Hall** of 1888, is one of many monumental public buildings in the area erected during that period of unparalleled English prosperity.

A walk along the towpath of the canal, through an area known as the **Weavers' Triangle** is like taking a step back in time. This is an area of spinning mills and weaving sheds; foundries where steam engines and looms were made; canal-side warehouses; domestic buildings, including a unique row of workers' cottages; and a Victorian school house. The Weavers' Triangle Visitors Centre is housed in the former wharfmaster's house and canal toll office. The centre is open to the public on several afternoons a week during the summer months and on most bank holidays. A short walk from the Visitors' Centre is **Oak Mount Mill** engine house. The splendid old steam engine, originally installed in 1887, has recently been restored and is now operated by electric motor. Opening times are variable.

Even more impressive is the **Queen Street Mill** which is the only surviving steam-powered cotton mill in Britain. A visit here provides a unique insight into Victorian factory life as the 300 deafening looms are powered by the magnificent steam engine, Peace. The mill was recently designated by the government as a museum with an outstanding collection – one of only 53 in the country to receive the award.

The history of Burnley can also be explored by boat along the Leeds and Liverpool Canal. This famous waterway leaves the Weavers' Triangle via a huge embankment which carries the canal across the town. Known as the 'straight mile', it is in fact less than that but no less exciting and, at 60 feet above the ground, is one of the most impressive features of the canal's length.

Situated on the Todmorden Road on the outskirts of Burnley, is the **Towneley Hall Art Gallery and Museum**. The home of the Towneley family since the 14th century, right up until 1902, parts of the present building date from the 15th century. Visitors can not only view the art collections, the Whalley Abbey Vestments, and the museum of local crafts and industries, but also take in a tour of the house. The kitchens, with their open fires, the servants' hall, a priest's hole and the fascinating family rooms are all on display. The grounds too are open to visitors and contain a traditional Victorian flower garden, woodland nature trails, and a fascinating series of sculptures hewn from the trees around. Subjects include a giant magpie, a crocodile emerging from the water, and a huge cricket. The grounds also include a

Bowling in Queen's Park, Burnley

natural history centre, a **Museum of Local Crafts and Industries** and facilities for golf, tennis, bowls, and other outdoor pursuits.

Two other interesting places to visit whilst in Burnley are the **Burnley Heritage Centre**, where memorabilia on

TOWNELEY HALL ART GALLERY & MUSEUMS

Burnley, Lancashire BB11 3RQ
Tel: 01282 424213
website: www.towneleyhall.org.uk

Towneley Hall offers the perfect day out for all the family - a country house, a museum and an art gallery all in one. Towneley Hall was the home of the Towneley family from the 14th century until 1902. Charles (1737-1805) was one of the 18th century's best known collectors of antique sculpture and gems. His portrait can be seen in the gallery. Today visitors can still catch a glimpse of how the family lived. Original period rooms include the Elizabethan long gallery and the Regency rooms. See how they compare with life below stairs in the Victorian kitchen and the servants dining room.

The museum's collections surround you - glass, ceramics and 17th century Lancashire oak furniture. Pictures by many favourite Victorian artists can be seen in the art galleries, including works by Sir Edward Coley Burne-Jones, John William Waterhouse and Sir Edwin Landseer. The Whalley Abbey vestments are another highlight. Embroidered in silk and silver thread on cloth of gold, they were brought to Towneley in the 16th century and are now extremely rare. A programme of temporary exhibitions ensures something new to see on every visit. Open daily except Fridays - check for times.

display from the town's past include old photographs, a Lancashire loom, and a replica 1930s kitchen and living room. **The Stables Museum**, at Shores Hey Farm in Brierley, is run by the Horses and Ponies Protection Association. A must for horse lovers, the exhibitions include information about the rescue and care of neglected horses, ponies, and donkeys as well as a display of the life of the canal horse.

Lovers of ghost stories will want to visit the **Rosehill Hotel** which has a resident ghost. She's called Rose and she was an employee at the hotel. In 1860, Rose had an affair with a relative of the hotel proprietor and became pregnant. This was an era when Victorian sexual morality was at its most rigid (and hypocritical). If Rose's illicit pregnancy became known, the hotel's reputation would suffer disastrously. Rose disappeared, completely. The hotel owner said she had been dismissed and left the town but those who knew of her condition suspected murder. Beneath the hotel there were cellars which were later filled with tons of rubble and it's believed that poor Rose was buried there, emerging from time to time when her successors as chambermaids were cleaning the rooms. She has been heard talking to herself about the daily chores to be done but otherwise has never troubled either the maids or the guests.

NORTH OF BURNLEY

BRIERFIELD
2 miles N of Burnley on the A682

This industrial town has magnificent views of Pendle Hill as it lies on a steep slope at the bottom of which is an attractive **Quaker Bridge** over Pendle Water. At the beginning of the 19th century, coal was discovered in the area.

Within a few years three pits had opened, thus sealing Brierfield's fate as a place of industry. The laying of turnpike roads, followed by the opening of the Leeds and Liverpool Canal, gave the growing village a further boost and by 1833 a handloom weaving business was also flourishing here. The humid climate and expanding transport system made Brierfield an ideal place for the burgeoning cotton industry, which had become the main source of employment here by the end of the 19th century.

NELSON
3 miles N of Burnley on the A56

Nelson is now inseparable from its neighbours Colne and Burnley and shares the same valley running along the length of Colne Water. Nelson is a modern textile town which takes its

24 Faced Sundial, Marsden Park, Nelson

name from the hotel, The Lord Nelson, which stands by the railway line running along the valley bottom. Although the town itself might have been the product of the industrial age, two of its suburbs, Little and Great Marsden, have a history that stretches back for centuries. Here lies **Marsden Park**, and once Marsden Hall, the home of the de Walton family until their line died out in 1912. The hall was acquired by the local authority which demolished most of it but developed the parkland.

COLNE
5 miles N of Burnley on the A56

Before the Industrial Revolution turned this area into a valley devoted to the production of cotton cloth, Colne was a small market town that specialised in wool. Unfortunately, there are few reminders of the days before industrialisation but **St Batholomew's Church**, founded in 1122, is still here and contains some interesting interior decorations and furnishings. In the centre of the town, next to the War Memorial is another memorial. The statue is of Lawrence Hartley, the bandmaster on the ill-fated *Titanic* who, heroically, stayed at his post with his musicians and played *Nearer my God to Thee* as the liner sank beneath the waves of the icy Atlantic in 1912.

Colne is also the unlikely home of the **British in India Museum**, where exhibits covering many aspects of the British rule over the subcontinent, from the 17th century until

1947 can be seen. The collection includes coins, medals, uniforms, model soldiers and a working model of the railway from Kalka to Simla.

Collectors of curiosities will enjoy the unique form of punishment devised for minor malefactors in Colne and preserved in the **Town Museum**. Stocks and pillories enjoyed a long history as a way of humiliating offenders and providing innocent amusement for bystanders. But many of Colne's busy citizens could not spare the time to leave their work and make their way to wherever the stocks were fixed. So a movable cart was constructed, capable of seating three offenders side by side, and the Town Beadle would wheel it around the town so that everyone could join in the fun.

WYCOLLER
6 miles NE of Burnley off the B6250

This hamlet lies amidst the moorlands that rise to the east of the textile towns of the Colne valley and up to the bleak summits of the Pennines. Now almost deserted, this was once a thriving place as an important centre for the wool trade and as a handloom weavers' settlement

Wycoller Beck

but it lost most of its inhabitants to the new factories in the west.

Fortunately, the place has been saved by the creation of a **Wycoller Country Park**, surrounding the village, and many of the buildings have been restored. There is also a delightful old hump-backed packhorse bridge crossing a stream and, above the village, a single slab gritstone bridge, **Clam Bridge**, that is thought to date from the Iron Age. Now a ruin, **Wycoller Hall** was the inspiration for Ferndean Manor in Charlotte Brontë's *Jane Eyre*: Wycoller was one of the villages to which the sisters walked from their house at Haworth.

Pendle Hill

EARBY

10 miles NE of Burnley on the A56

The town lies almost on the county border with Yorkshire and here can be found the **Earby Mines Museum** housed in the old Grammar School building. With the largest collection of lead mining tools and equipment used in the Yorkshire Dales on display, there is much to see, including examples of the minerals extracted, a lead crushing mill, and other working models.

PENDLE HILL

5 miles N of Burnley off the A6068

Dominating the landscape here is the great whale-backed mass of Pendle Hill, rising to 1920ft. above sea-level. The hill became notorious in the early 1600s as the location where the **Pendle Witches** supposedly practised their black arts. It also has a more uplifting association, though, since it was from the summit of Pendle Hill in 1625 that George Fox saw a vision which inspired him to found the Society of Friends, or Quakers.

Pendle Hill lies at the heart of Lancashire's 'Witch Country', so called because of the events of 1612. On the 18th March of that year, a Halifax pedlar named John Law refused to give some pins to a beggar, Alison Device. She spat out the usual beggar's curse on him. He died almost immediately of a heart attack. The effect of a curse or just a co-incidence? The early 1600s were the years of the great witch-hunts so the authorities had little difficulty in attributing John Law's sudden death to Alison Device's supernatural powers.

Alison was arrested. Under torture, she incriminated eight other 'witches'. All of them were then charged with communing with the Devil and committing a total of 16 murders. They were tried, found guilty and hanged at Lancaster Castle on August 20th, 1612. All except one: Old Mother Demdike, 80 years old and half-blind, escaped the gallows by dying in gaol. During their trial, the 'Pendle Witches' seem to have taken pride in implicating each other. In effect, they hanged themselves by their fanciful tales of spells, potions, and the coven's naked caperings, fuelling the popular imagination that there really were witches who could affect the lives of other people. The infamous witches were, in the main, old women who dabbled with plants and herbs, knowing which could heal and which, when ingested, would spell certain death.

The Victorian novelist W.H. Ainsworth was inspired to write a colourful melodrama based on the trial, *The Lancashire Witches – A Romance of Pendle Forest*, and although it's doubtful that 'witchcraft' was any more prevalent around Pendle Hill than anywhere else in the country at that time, the legend has proved very durable. Every year now, on the evening of October 31st, Halloween, Pendle Hill is flecked with the dark figures of masked, black-cloaked figures making their way to its summit.

The story of the Pendle Witches is known to everyone with an interest in the occult, but there has always been something of a mystery about why one of them, Alice Nutter, was involved. Unlike the others who were either very poor or even beggars, Alice was a lady of substance. She lived at Roughlee Old Hall, a captivating Elizabethan manor house of 1576 which still stands (but is not open to the public). A recent theory is that she was a Roman Catholic and on her way to a clandestine service when she was caught up with the witches. To avoid betraying her co-religionists, she kept silent about her real motives for being on Pendle Hill on the crucial night.

Something of this old, dark tragedy still broods over Pendle and many memories and places which hark back to those grim days remain. Those interested in finding out more about the trials should visit the **Pendle Heritage Centre** in Barrowford, about three miles southeast of the Hill. The centre is housed in a sturdy 17th century farmhouse built by the Bannister family, one of whose descendants was Roger Bannister, the first man to run a mile in less than four minutes. The centre also houses an art gallery, a cruck barn with animals, an 18th century walled garden and a pleasant woodland walk.

To the west of the hill's summit lies **Apronfull Hill**, a Bronze Age burial site, that is said to be the place from which the Devil threw stones at Clitheroe Castle, creating what is known as the Devil's Window.

NEWCHURCH

4 miles N of Burnley off the A6068

This charming Pendle village was named following the consecration of a new church in 1544 by John Bird, Bishop of Chester. Earlier, during the Middle Ages, Newchurch was a cow and deer rearing centre, as well as part of the old hunting forest of Pendle but by the reign of Elizabeth I the area was becoming deforested and farming was beginning to take over as the primary source of income.

Newchurch did not escape from stories of witchcraft that surrounded the notorious Pendle witches trial in the 17th century, and many ghostly tales and shadowy traditions are said to be associated with the village. By the 18th century, however, the witch hunts were over and the village grew rapidly as part of the expanding textile industry, first with handloom weavers and then with the construction of a factory for washing and dyeing wool.

An old tradition continues here – the **Annual Rushbearing** when dry rushes are scattered on the church floor and in the pews. Originally this was to keep parishioners warm and although the advent of central heating makes it no longer necessary the villagers still process through the village carrying rushes and singing hymns accompanied by a brass band. A Rushbearing Queen is crowned and after a short service in the church everyone repairs to the school for a grand tea.

PADIHAM
2 miles W of Burnley on the A646

This charming small town of narrow winding lanes and cobbled alleyways still retains characteristics typical of the early days of the Industrial Revolution. However, there was a settlement here long before the Norman Conquest and

Padiham was also the market town for the western slopes of Pendle. A market is still held here every Wednesday and Friday.

One of Lancashire's most impressive stately homes is **Gawthorpe Hall** (National Trust) which stands on the bank of the River Calder, surrounded by gardens and woodland. The Shuttleworth family have lived at Gawthorpe since the early 1400s but the present house is a gracious 17th century mansion, restored and extended in the 1850s by Sir Charles Barry. This was the era of High Victorian extravagance and no expense was spared on the opulent decorations and furnishings. The Hall has many pictures on loan from the National Portrait Gallery which add extra lustre to the already notable collection. Open to the public between Easter and October, the house has beautiful period furnishings, ornately

WITCHES GALORE

Newchurch-in-Pendle, nr Burnley, Lancashire BB12 9JR
Tel: 01282 613111
website: www.witchesgalore.co.uk

The only shop in a pretty hillside village, **Witches Galore** rightly calls itself 'a little shop with a big reputation' where a coven of witches sits outside the shop, proffering an invitation to 'Drop in for a Spell'. Owner Maureen Stopford, here for almost a quarter of a century, stocks a vast range of 'monstrous merchandise'. There are hundreds of souvenirs of the famous Pendle Witches, including puppet witches, china figures, T-shirts, books, postcards, posters and, of course, broomsticks, all representing the lighter, less spooky side of witchcraft. You can also pick up a gruesome gargoyle or some fiendish Hallowe'en outfits. It's all great fun and a must-visit location on the trail of the Pendle Witches.

The shop is open every day (including Saturday and Sunday) from 11am to 5pm, except for Wednesday when it doesn't open until 1.30pm because Maureen, the 'Witch of Pendle' "needs a lie-in after a heavy Tuesday night of casting spells"! If you want to pay a visit outside these witching hours, just contact Maureen because, as she says "We do sincerily want to please you!"

decorated ceilings and the original wood panelled walls and is also home the nationally important Kay-Shuttleworth collection of fine needlework and lace.

READ

5 miles W of Burnley on the A671

Situated on the banks of the River Calder it was during a skirmish near **Read Old Bridge** in April 1643 that the Royalist cause in Lancashire was lost.

Read Hall (private) was the home of one of Lancashire's most famous families, the Nowells. It was Roger Nowell who, in 1612, committed the Pendle witches to trial. The Nowells left the hall in 1772 and in 1799 the house was completely rebuilt in the Georgian style seen today.

WHALLEY

7 miles W of Burnley on the B6246

One of Lancashire's most attractive villages, Whalley grew up around a

crossing of the River Calder, between Pendle Hill and the Nab. There are old cottages and Tudor houses, Georgian houses in the main street and three out of the four inns at the crossroads date from the 1700s. Soaring above the village is the **Whalley Viaduct**, an impressive 48-arched structure built in 1850 to carry the Blackburn to Clitheroe railway line across the broad valley of the Calder. Rather touchingly, where the viaduct crosses the lane leading to **Whalley Abbey** the arches have added Gothic details that harmonise with the nearby 14th century gatehouse to the abbey.

The abbey was the last to be built in Lancashire, started in the early 1300s, but for the Cistercian monks whose work it was, Whalley was not their first choice. They had already established a religious house at Stanlow, on the banks of the River Mersey and now under a huge oil refinery, in 1172.

Seeking somewhere less harsh and more fertile land, the monks moved to Whalley in 1296 but their attempts to build were hampered as Sawley Abbey felt threatened by the competition for the donations of land and goods expected from the local population. Building finally began in 1310 and by 1400 the imposing and impressive abbey had taken shape. The demise of the abbey came, as it did to all religious houses, under Henry VIII but Whalley's abbot, joining forces with the abbot of Sawley, took part in the Pilgrimage of Grace in an attempt to save their houses. This failed and the abbots were both executed.

Now owned and cared for by the Diocese of Blackburn,

Whalley Abbey

Whalley Abbey is one of the best preserved such places in the country and its future secure as it also acts as a conference centre.

Whalley's **Parish Church** is almost a century older than the abbey, its oldest parts dating back to 1206. Built on the site of an even older place of worship, the churchyard is home to three ancient crosses and the church itself contains a set of the some of the finest choir stalls anywhere. They were brought here from the abbey after the Dissolution and though they are not elaborate there are some intriguing carvings on the lower portions. Even more intriguing though are the puzzling tombstones in the churchyard, each one inscribed with impossible dates such as April 31st 1752 and February 30th 1839.

PENDLETON
6 miles NW of Burnley off the A59

Recorded in the *Domesday Book* when the village was part of the vast parish of Whalley, this small settlement of cottages and working farms has retained much of its traditional air – only seven new houses have been built here in the last 100 years. A beck runs through the middle of the village which was designated a Conservation Area in 1968. The discovery of a Bronze Age burial urn in the village in 1969 would indicate that there were settlers here as long ago as 1600BC.

From the village there is a steep road, to the southeast, that climbs up to the **Nick of Pendle** from where there are magnificent views.

RISHTON
7 miles W of Burnley on the A678

Originally a Saxon settlement, the name means the fortified village or dwelling place amid the rushes, and, during the Middle Ages, the village grew in

importance as an early textile centre with the operation of its fulling mill. By the 17th century, Rishton had gained a name for the manufacture of linen cloth and, in 1766, it became the first village to weave calico. As the Industrial Revolution advanced, the industry moved from the weavers' homes into newly built mills.

The manor of Rishton, once owned by the Petre family, was part of the larger estate of Clayton-le-Moors and the manor house, Dunkenhalgh Hall, is said to have been named after a Scottish raider called Duncan who made his home here. Elizabethan in origin, the hall is now a private hotel.

OSWALDTWISTLE
7 miles W of Burnley on the A679

This typical Lancashire textile town has produced many miles of cotton cloth over the years. You can still hear the deafening clatter of looms at **Oswaldtwistle Mills** in Collier Street, one of the last working cotton mills in the country. Cotton has been woven here for more than 200 years under the watchful eyes of just two owners – the Walmsleys and the Tattersall/Hargreaves family. The town can justifiably be considered the heart of the industry since it was whilst staying here, at what is now Stanhill Post Office, that James Hargreaves invented his famous 'Spinning Jenny' in 1764. Although he was forced to leave the area after sometimes violent opposition to his machine from local hand spinners, the town's prosperity is largely due to textiles and, in particular, calico printing. However, Oswaldtwistle is a much older settlement than its rows of Victorian terraced houses would suggest as the name means the boundary of the kingdom of Oswald, who was a 7th century Northumbrian king.

GREAT HARWOOD

6 miles W of Burnley on the B6535

Before the Industrial Revolution, this was a quiet village of farms and cottages nestling between two streams. Famous for its fine woollen cloth, at the beginning of the 19th century cotton handloom weaving and then, by the 1850s, the introduction of the factory system and the cotton mills took over. Today only one mill remains but at the industry's height the town supported 22 mills. Not surprisingly, Great Harwood's most famous son was very much linked with cotton. In 1850, John Mercer, an industrial chemist, developed the technique of processing cotton to give it a sheen and the technique, mercerisation, is still used today. The free-standing clock tower in the Town Square was erected in 1903 to commemorate Mercer's contribution to the life of his home town.

ACCRINGTON

5 miles SW of Burnley on the A680

This attractive Victorian market town, as is typical in this area, expanded as a result of the boom in the textile industry of the 18th and 19th centuries. Of all Lancashire's indoor markets, Accrington enjoys the grandest surroundings, housed in a magnificent **Market Hall** built in 1868. Accrington is also the place to visit for a real flavour of the old Lancashire: in April it hosts the **Lancashire Food Festival**, followed in May by the annual **Clog Dancing Festival**. The town is the home of the **Haworth Art Gallery**, one of the most appealing galleries in the country – a charming Jacobean-style house built in 1909 and set in beautiful parkland. The gallery owns the largest collection of Tiffany glass – there are 130 pieces – in Europe. The collection was presented to the town by Joseph Briggs, an

NURSERY END GARDEN CENTRE

Harrington Street, Clayton-le-Moors, Accrington, Lancashire BB5 4DF
Tel: 01254 389611 Fax: 01254 872660
website: www.nurseryend.co.uk

Nursery End Garden Centre has been established since the late 1980s but in March 2005 it changed hands and became a family run concern. Extensive changes and improvements have been made to make this one of the best garden centres in the area, catering for the garden enthusiast and amateur alike.

Here you will find everything you would expect in a top quality garden centre, including a wide range of trees, shrubs, herbaceous perennials and herbs, as well as seasonal bedding, composts, decorative stone, pots and all manner of gardening sundries.

Accrington man, who emigrated to New York and worked with Louis Tiffany for nearly 40 years. Briggs joined the studio in 1890 and rose through the company ranks to become the manager of the Mosaic department before finally becoming Tiffany's personal assistant.

After the First World War, the fashion for Tiffany glassware waned and during the economic depression of the 1920s Briggs was given the sad job of selling off the remainder of the Tiffany stock. Returning to his native Accrington in 1933 with his collection of glass, Briggs gave half to the town and distributed the remainder amongst his family.

To the west of the town centre, the **Accrington Railway Viaduct** is another magnificent monument to Victorian builders. Erected for the former East Lancashire Railway it sweeps across the River Hyndburn in a graceful curve of 19 arches 60 feet high. Also worth a visit are the imposing **Town Hall** with its Corinthian portico and the elegant glass-roofed **Arcade** of 1880.

BACUP
7 miles S of Burnley on the A671

At 827ft the highest town in Lancashire, Bacup was built in the 19th century for the sole purpose of cotton manufacture. It remains one of the best examples of a textile town in England even though the town suffered more than most when the mills began to close. A stroll through the town centre will reveal carefully restored shops and houses, with the grander homes of the mill owners and the elegant civic buildings acting as a reminder of the town's more prosperous times. Also, look out for what is claimed to be the shortest street in the world – Elgin Street off the Market Place which is just 17ft long.

An excellent time to visit the town is

MAKEPIECE

2 Dale Street, Todmorden, Lancashire OL14 5PX
Tel: 01706 815888
e-mail: info@makepiece.co.uk
website: www.makepiece.co.uk

Opened in the autumn of 2004, **Makepiece** was the brainchild of knitwear designer Nicola Sherlock and her business partner Beate Kubitz, both of whom wanted to establish a business based on an ethical and aesthetic response to our landscape and the desire for design with principles. These principles include: "Buy as locally as possible – we even keep our own sheep"; pay people properly; look after animals; and create real fashion, not passing fads. "We all desire beautiful designs and lovely things," says Nicola, "but don't really want to pay in environmental damage, exploitation or pollution." She uses luxury yarns from Makepiece's own flocks and from farms where she can be sure that the land is sustained and people and animals are treated fairly.

Each garment is meticulously finished by hand to ensure it is perfect to wear and enjoy. As Beate puts it: "Makepiece is both an ethic and an aesthetic. We make clothes that are not just for the body, they're for the soul." Nicola and Beate's enterprise received a major accolade when it was selected by the Crafts Council to exhibit at the prestigious New Designers showcase exhibition in London in June 2005.

Coconut Dancers, Bacup

century. The introduction of the cotton industry to the town happened at around the same time. Lower Mill, now a ruin, was opened in 1840 by the Whitehead brothers who were some of the area's first manufacturing pioneers. The **Weaver's Cottage**, purpose-built for a home weaver, is one of the last buildings remaining of its kind and is open to visitors at weekends during the summer.

during the Easter weekend when the town's famous troop of Morris dancers take to the streets. Known as the **Coconut Dancers**, their costume is unique and involves wearing halved coconut husks strapped to their knees and blackening their faces. The dancers maintain that the correct name is Moorish, not Morris, Dancers, and that the tradition goes back to the times of the Crusades.

Also in the town, and housed in a former Victorian mill owner's house called Oakhill, is the **Rossendale Museum**. Naturally, the area's industrial heritage is given a prominent position but collections of the region's natural history, fine art and furniture, and ceramics are on display too.

At one end of the town stands a new railway station which marks the end of a very old railway line – the **East Lancashire Railway**. Opened in 1846 and run commercially until 1980, when the last coal train drew into Rawtenstall, the line is now in the hands of the East Lancashire Railway Preservation Society. Running a passenger service (at weekends with additional summer services), the steam trains offer an enthralling 17-mile round trip along the

RAWTENSTALL

7 miles S of Burnley on the A682

The town first developed as a centre of the woollen cloth trade with the work being undertaken by hand workers in their own homes before steam-powered mills were introduced in the early 19th

ROSSENDALE MUSEUM

Whitaker Park, Haslingden Road, Rawtenstall,
Rossendale, Lancashire BB4 6RE
Tel: 01706 217777/244682
Fax: 01706 250037

Rossendale Museum is a former 19th century mill owner's house set in Whitaker Park. Displays include a Victorian drawing room, fine and decorative art, local and natural history, and costume. Temporary exhibitions are held throughout the year. There is disabled access to ground floor and audio and large print guides are available. Admission is free and a gift shop and cafe round off your visit.

Rawtenstall Station

River Irwell between Rawtenstall and Bury, via Ramsbottom. The railway also operates regular Red Rose Diner trains with Pullman style dining cars offering travellers a gourmet meal and an evening of pure nostalgia.

Rawtenstall itself is noted for having the only remaining temperance bar in Britain – Herbal Health on Bank Street which serves traditional non-alcoholic drinks such as sarsaparilla or dandelion & burdock.

At Rawtenstall, you can join the **Irwell Sculpture Trail**, the largest public art scheme in the United Kingdom. New sculptures are appearing all the time and more than 50 regional, national and international artists are being commissioned to produce sculptures with an environmental theme. The Trail follows a well-established 30-mile footpath stretching from Salford Quays through Bury into Rossendale and on up to the Pennine Moors.

HASLINGDEN

7 miles S of Burnley on the A56

The market in this town, which serves much of the Rossendale Valley, dates

CLIFTON HOUSE PERIOD INTERIORS

198 Blackburn Road, Haslingden, Rossendale,
Lancashire BB4 5HW
Tel: 01706 831625 Fax: 01706 231635
e-mail: cliftonhouse62@hotmail.com
website: www.cliftonhouseperiodinteriors.com

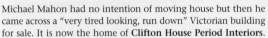

Michael Mahon had no intention of moving house but then he came across a "very tired looking, run down" Victorian building for sale. It is now the home of **Clifton House Period Interiors**. Michael still doesn't know quite what prompted him to buy the dilapidated building. The place had been sadly neglected over the years but many of its original features were still in place – fireplaces, a cast iron range, a stained glass window, carved oak panelling and ornate plasterwork on the ceilings in the drawing and dining rooms. "I realised," says Michael "that my future was going to be in the past."

After painstaking restoration, he opened part of the house as a private Victorian Dining Rooms which proved to be immensely successful. Many customers pleaded with him to sell some of the furnishings which he occasionally did. "I enjoyed so much replacing them and realised there was a gap in the market here." So he closed the restaurant and together with three lifelong friends converted the house into a vast emporium of 15 magnificent rooms stocked with beautiful reproduction period furniture, fabrics, pictures, mirrors, fixtures, fittings and accessories. Clifton House also offers a design service, sourcing and delivering the best furnishings available.

back to 1676, when the charter was granted by Charles II. Tuesdays and Fridays, market days, still bring the town alive as people flock to the numerous stalls. In Victorian times a familiar figure at the market was Miles Lonsdale, better known as the Haslingden Miser. To avoid spending money on food he would gather up discarded fish-heads from the fishmonger's and fry them up for an unpalatable, if inexpensive, meal. After his death in 1889 it was discovered that Miles owned stocks and shares worth more than £16,000 - about £1.2m in today's money.

HELMSHORE

8 miles S of Burnley on the B6214

This small town still retains much evidence of the early Lancashire cotton industry. Housed in an 18th century water-powered fulling mill and a Victorian cotton spinning mill, is the **Helmshore Textile Museum**. The older building dates from 1789 and was one of the first fulling mills to be built in the Rossendale area. The two working mills are packed with national textile treasures and in the 'Revolution' gallery visitors can have fun with fibres and fabrics, follow the lives of the Weaver family, trace the history of Lancashire's textile industry and meet

the great Lancashire inventors Arkwright, Kay, Hargreaves and Crompton.

GOODSHAW

5 miles S of Burnley on the A682

Just to the north of Crawshawbooth in the small village of Goodshaw and set high above the main road lies **Goodshaw Chapel**, a recently restored Baptist house of worship that dates from 1760.

BLACKBURN

The largest town in East Lancashire, Blackburn is notable for its modern shopping malls, its celebrated three day market, its modern cathedral, and Thwaites Brewery, one of the biggest independent brewers of real ale in the north of England. Hard though it may be to imagine today, at the height of the textile industry, Blackburn was the biggest weaving town in the world. At that time there were 120 mills in operation, their multiple chimneys belching out soot and smoke.

In 1931, the town received arguably its most influential visitor when Mahatma Gandhi toured the area on a study trip of Lancashire's textile manufacture. Examples of the early machines,

---

HELMSHORE MILLS TEXTILE MUSEUM

Holcombe Road, Helmshore, Rossendale, Lancashire BB4 4NP
Tel: 01706 226459

An 18th century water powered fulling mill and a Victorian cotton spinning mill, both in working order on one site. Newly designated as a museum with a Collection of Outstanding National Importance, this museum has developed an interactive gallery for families on the history of the Lancashire cotton industry. Spinning mules, water wheel, an original Arkwright's water frame and other machinery dating from the Industrial Revolution can also be seen. Easily reached from Junction 5 of M65 (Haslingden) or from end of M66. Open from Easter to October every afternoon. There is some disabled access and an induction loop. Free parking makes visiting easy and refreshments are available in the cafe. A gift shop sells a range of souvenirs.

Blackburn Cathedral

recognised in 1926 when the Diocese of Blackburn was created and the Gothic-style St Mary's Church, built in 1826, became the **Cathedral** of the See of Blackburn. The church was expanded to the east but the advent of World War II curtailed the original grand design. Inside there are two notable modern features – a spiky metalwork crown over the high altar and, above the west door, a modern metalwork sculpture of the figure of Christ, his hands raised in benediction.

The town's old manor house, Witton House, has long since been demolished but the grounds have been turned into an excellent local amenity. The 480 acres of **Witton Country Park** contain nature trails through woodlands up on to heather covered hill tops. Closer to the town centre, the 60-acre **Corporation Park** is one of the county's most attractive urban parks.

including James Hargreaves' Spinning Jenny and his carding machine, invented in 1760, can be seen at the **Lewis Textile Museum**, which is dedicated to the industry. The town's **Museum and Art Gallery** has, amongst its treasures, several paintings by Turner, the Hart collection of medieval manuscripts, and the finest collection of Eastern European icons in Britain.

Mentioned in the Domesday Book, the town was originally an agricultural community before the production of first woollen and then cotton cloth took over. Much of the town seen today was built on the prosperity brought by the cotton trade, a fact symbolized on the dome of **St John's Church** (1789) where there's a weathervane in the shape of a weaving shuttle.

Blackburn's importance as a centre for the surrounding community was

AROUND BLACKBURN

HOGHTON

4 miles W of Blackburn on the A675

Originally a collection of hamlets with handloom weavers' cottages, the village was, during the 17th century, a place where Roman Catholics still practiced their faith in defiance of the law. It was at **Arrowsmith House** that Edmund Arrowsmith said his last mass before being captured and sentenced to death for being a Catholic priest and a Jesuit.

It is however, today, best known as the home of Lancashire's only true baronial residence **Hoghton Tower** which dates from 1565. The de Hoghton family have owned the land in this area since the time of the Norman Conquest and the house was built in a style in keeping with their social position and importance. The famous banqueting hall, on the ground floor, is where James I is said to have knighted the Sir Loin of Beef in 1617. The name of the house is today rather misleading since the tower was blown up by Cromwell's troops in 1643 when they overran the Royalist garrison stationed here. Another famous visitor, who caused less disruption, was William Shakespeare who came to perform with William Hoghton's troupe of players. As well as the famous banqueting hall, other rooms open to the public include the beautifully preserved ballroom, the King's bedchamber, and the audience chamber. The grounds, too, are well worth a visit and are as perfectly preserved as the house.

BRINDLE
5 miles SW of Blackburn on the B6256

An ancient village itself, Brindle's **St James' Church** celebrated its 800 year anniversary in 1990. The church was originally dedicated to St Helen, the patron saint of wells. 'Bryn' is the Old English word for a spring and there are still numerous springs in the village.

WITHNELL FOLD
5 miles SW of Blackburn off the A674

A short walk from Brindle that crosses the Leeds and Liverpool Canal leads to the village of Withnell Fold whose name comes from 'withy knool' – a wooded hill. It was developed as a model village in the 1840s with 35 terraced cottages each with its own garden. The whole village was owned by the Parke family who also owned the cotton mills and paper mill for whose workers the houses were provided. The mills have long since closed but the old mill chimney still towers above the village. Withnell Fold does have a small claim to fame. The

paper mill, built in 1844 overlooking the canal, was once the world's biggest exporter of high-quality bank note paper.

TOCKHOLES
3 miles SW of Blackburn off the A666

This interesting, textile village was once an isolated centre of nonconformism. Standing next to a row of cottages is the **United Reformed Chapel**, founded in 1662, though it has been rebuilt twice, in 1710 and in 1880. The **Parish Church** also has some unusual features. As well as the unique lance-shaped windows, there is an outdoor pulpit dating from the days when the whole congregation could not fit inside the building. Close to the pulpit is the grave of John Osbaldeston, the inventor of the weft fork, a gadget that allowed power looms to weave intricate patterns.

Just to the south of the village lies **Roddlesworth Nature Trail**, a path that follows the line of an old coach drive. Along the trail, for which details can be obtained at the information centre, can be found the ruins of **Hollinshead Hall**. Built in the 18th century and once very grand, the ruins were tidied up in the early 1990s but, fortunately, the wishing well has withstood the ravages of time and neglect. Reminiscent of a small Georgian chapel, the well inside dates back to medieval times when its waters were thought to cure eye complaints.

DARWEN
3 miles S of Blackburn on the A666

Visitors to the town may be forgiven for thinking they have been here before as Darwen will be familiar to all viewers of the BBC series *Hetty Wainthropp Investigates*, which stars Patricia Routledge. Dominating the town from the west and situated high on Darwen Moor, is **Darwen Tower**, built to commemorate the Diamond Jubilee of

India Mill, Darwen

Queen Victoria in 1897. The view from the top of the tower, which is always open, is enhanced by the height of the hill on which it stands (1,225 feet) and with the help of the plaques at the top much of the Lancashire landscape, and beyond, can be identified.

A striking landmark, very visible from the tower, and standing in the heart of Darwen is the chimney of the **India Mill**. Constructed out of hand-made bricks, it was built to resemble the campanile in St Mark's Square, Venice.

To the west of Darwen lies **Sunnyhurst Wood** and visitor centre in the valley of a gentle brook that originates on Darwen Moor to the south. Acquired by public subscription in 1902 to commemorate the coronation of Edward VII this area of woodland, covering some 85 acres, is

rich in both bird and plant life. The visitor centre, housed in an old keeper's cottage, has an ever changing exhibition and there is also the Olde England Kiosk, built in 1912, which serves all manner of refreshments.

WEST LANCASHIRE

This area of Lancashire, with its sandy coastline and flat fertile farmland, is home to some elegant seaside resorts and ancient market towns. Following the reorganisation of the county boundaries in the 1970s and the creation of Merseyside, much of the coast and the southwestern area of Lancashire became part of the new county, and the towns of Southport, Crosby and Formby and their neighbours and hinterlands will be considered in the Merseyside chapter.

Behind the coast, the flat lands of the West Lancashire plain were once under water. Now with an extensive network of ditches, drainage has provided the old towns and quaint villages with rich fertile land that now produces a wealth of produce all year round and roadside farm shops are very much a feature of the area.

Although there are several rivers flowing across the land, the chief waterway, which is hard to miss, is the Leeds to Liverpool Canal. Linking the port of Liverpool with industrial Leeds and the many textile villages and towns in between, this major navigation changed the lives of many of the people living along its length. The section through West Lancashire, passing rural villages, is perhaps one of the more pleasant stretches. There are plenty of charming canal side pubs in the area and walks along the towpath, through the unspoilt countryside, have been popular for many years.

CHORLEY

A bustling and friendly place, Chorley is a charming town that is locally famous for its market that dates back to 1498. Today, there are two markets – the covered market and the open, 'flat iron' market. This peculiar and intriguing name stems from the ancient practice of trading by displaying goods on the grounds without the use of stalls.

Dating back to 1360 and standing on the site of a Saxon chapel, the **Church of St Lawrence** is the town's oldest building. The church is said to contain the remains of St Lawrence, brought back from Normandy by Sir Richard Standish, and whether they are his relics or not, during the Middle Ages the saint's shrine certainly brought pilgrims to the parish.

The Civil War also brought visitors to the town, albeit less welcome ones. Following defeat at the nearby Battle of Preston, Royalist troops were twice engaged in battle here by Cromwell's victorious forces. Though not a happy time for both the Royalists and the town, the skirmishes did place Chorley on the historical map of England.

Chorley was the birthplace, in 1819, of Henry Tate. The son of a Unitarian minister, Henry was apprenticed in 1832 to the grocery trade in Liverpool and by 1855 he had not only set up his own business but also opened a chain of six shops. Selling the shops, Henry entered into the world of the competitive sugar trade and founded the world famous business of **Tate and Lyle**. Opening a new sugar refinery equipped with the latest machinery from France, Henry cornered the refining business in Britain and amassed a huge fortune. A great benefactor, Henry not only gave away vast sums of money to worthy causes but also to the London art gallery, which now bears his name.

The jewel in Chorley's crown is undoubtedly **Astley Hall**. Built in the late 16th century and set within some beautiful parkland, the hall is a fine example of an Elizabethan mansion. A notable feature is its south wing – described as "more glass than wall". Inside, the moulded ceilings of the main hall and the drawing room are quite remarkable, as are the painted panels dating from the 1620s and representing a range of heroes that include Elizabeth I, Philip II of Spain and the Islamic warrior Tamerlane.

Extended in 1666, and again in 1825, this is truly a house of history and the rooms, which reflect the passing of the centuries, contain superb items of furniture from 1600 to the Edwardian period. Whether or not Cromwell stayed at the hall following the Battle of Preston is open to debate but his boots are here on display.

The hall was given to the borough in 1922 by Reginald Tatton and it was he who insisted that the

Astley Hall, Chorley

building should incorporate a memorial to those who had died in World War I. As a result, a small room has been devoted to the local men who fought and died for their country. Along with the display of photographs, there is a Book of Remembrance.

AROUND CHORLEY

LEYLAND
4 miles NW of Chorley on the B5253

The town is probably best known for its associations with the manufacture of cars and lorries, and the **British Commercial Vehicle Museum**, the largest such museum in Europe, is well worth a visit. It stands on the site of the former Leyland South Works, where commercial vehicles were produced for many years. On display are many restored vans, fire engines and lorries along with exhibits ranging from the horsedrawn era, through steam-powered wagons right up to present day vans and lorries. Perhaps the most famous vehicle here is the one used by the Pope and popularly known as the Popemobile.

Leyland is, however, an ancient settlement and documentary evidence has been found which suggests that the town was a Crown possession in Saxon times, owned by Edward the Confessor. The village cross marks the centre of the old settlement around which the town expanded and it is in this area of Leyland that the older buildings can be seen. Founded in the 11th century, much of the present **St Andrew's Church** dates from 1220 although there was some restoration work undertaken in the 1400s. The Eagle and Child Inn is almost as old, said to date from around 1230, and it served the needs
of travellers journeying along the ancient highway which passed through the town.

The 16th century Grammar School is today home to the town's **Heritage Museum**, a fascinating place that describes, through interesting displays and exhibits, the history of this ancient market town.

TARLETON
8 miles W of Chorley off the A59

This pleasant rural village, now by-passed by the main road to Preston, is home to **St Mary's Church**, one of the finest buildings in Lancashire. Built in 1719, it is constructed from brick except for the cut-stone belfry. No longer the village church (it was replaced in the late 19th century by a larger building), it is still maintained and its churchyard has remained in use.

CROSTON
6 miles W of Chorley on the A581

This historic village in the heart of rural West Lancashire has been a centre for local farmers since it was granted a weekly market charter in 1283. Set beside the banks of the River Yarrow, a tributary of the River Douglas, much of the village, including the 17th century almshouses and the lovely 15th century church, is a designated conservation area. Church Street is a fine example of an 18th century Lancashire street, some of the houses bearing the date 1704; even older is the charming packhorse bridge dated 1682. The strong links with agriculture are still apparent in this area and the open farmland actually extends right into the village centre.

On **Coffee Day** the village turns out with decorated farm horses and carts to take part in a procession led by a band and morris dancers. The name is derived from the former 'Feoffing Day' when tenants paid their fees, or rents, to the squire.

ORMSKIRK

In the days when Liverpool was just a small fishing village, the main town in this area was Ormskirk, founded around 840AD by a Viking leader called Orme. Surrounded by rich agricultural land, the town has always been an important market centre with the locally-grown potatoes, 'Ormskirks', a firm favourite right across the north-west. The market is still flourishing, held every day except Wednesday and Sunday. In late Victorian times one of the traders in Ormskirk market was a certain Joseph Beecham who did a roaring trade selling his medicinal 'Little Liver Pills'. Joseph became a millionaire through the sales of his little pills; his son, the conductor Sir Thomas, went on to become the most popular and flamboyant figure of English musical life during the first half of the 20th century.

The town received its first market charter from Edward I in 1286 and today the market is still a key event in the region. The partial drainage of Martin Mere in the late 18th century, to provide more rich, fertile agricultural land, as well as the growth of nearby Liverpool, increased the prosperity of the town. Ormskirk was also touched by the Industrial Revolution and, while the traditional farming activities continued, cotton spinning and silk weaving also became important sources of local income. Today, the town has reverted to its traditional past.

The **Church of St Peter and St Paul**, in the centre of the town, unusually has both a steeple and a tower. The tower, added in the 16th century, was constructed to take the bells of Burscough Priory after the religious community had been disbanded by Henry VIII. However, the oldest feature found in the church is a stone carving on the outer face of the chancel's east wall that was probably the work of Saxon craftsmen.

A couple of miles southwest of Ormskirk, the recently opened **Farmer Ted's Farm Park** is designed for families with children up to 12 years old. Resident animals include llamas, pigs, sheep and goats; tractor rides and pedal tractors are available, and other facilities include a large fun barn, sand pit, farm shop and refreshment area.

NORTH OF ORMSKIRK

BURSCOUGH
2 miles NE of Ormskirk on the A59

Situated on the banks of the Leeds and Liverpool Canal, the village's Parish Church was one of the Million, or Waterloo, churches built as a thanks to God after the final defeat of Napoleon in 1815. A later addition to the church is the Memorial Window to those of the parish who died for their country during the First World War.

Little remains of **Burscough Priory**, founded in the early 1100s by the Black Canons. Receiving lavish endowments from the local inhabitants, the priory was at one time one of the most influential religious houses in Lancashire.

To the north of the village, **Windmill Animal Farm** offers visitors the chance to experience the everyday running of an actual working farm and the chance to watch, fee, touch and play with the animals. There are various indoor and outdoor play areas, pedal tractors, train rides to the lake, picnic areas, coffee shop and an attractive craft and gift shop.

RUFFORD

5 miles NE of Ormskirk on the B5246

This attractive village of pretty houses is notable for its church and its beautiful old hall. Built in 1869, the church is a splendid example of the Gothic revival period and its tall spire dominates the skyline.

Rufford Old Hall (National Trust) is an enchanting building. Its medieval part is constructed of richly decorated black-and-white timbering enclosing a glorious Great Hall where angels bearing colourful heraldic shields float from massive hammer-beam trusses. The Hall's 17th century additions are less spectacular but still very attractive and contain displays of historic costumes as well as an interesting local folk museum.

Rufford Old Hall

Generally regarded as one of the finest timber-framed halls in the country, the hall was the ancestral home of the Hesketh family, who lived at this site from the 1200s until Baron Hesketh gave the hall to the National Trust in 1936. From the superb, intricately carved movable wooden screen to the solid oak chests and long refectory table, the atmosphere here is definitely one of wealth and position.

Later additions to the house were made in the 1660s and again in 1821. Parts of these are now devoted to the **Philip Ashcroft Museum of Rural Life** with its unique collection of items illustrating village life in pre-industrial Lancashire. Another attraction here is the spacious garden alongside the canal.

MERE BROW

7 miles N of Ormskirk on the B5246

Just to the south of the village lies the Wildfowl and Wetlands Trust at **Martin Mere**, more than 350 acres of reclaimed marshland which was established in 1976 as a refuge for thousands of wintering wildfowl. Until Martin Mere was drained in the 1600s to provide rich, fertile farmland, the lake was one of the largest in England. Many devotees of the Arthurian legends believe that the pool into which the dying king's sword Excalibur was thrown (to be received by a woman's arm rising from the water *'clothed in white samite, mystic, wonderful'*), was actually Martin Mere.

Today, the stretches of water, mudbanks and grassland provide homes for many species of birds and, with a

Mere Sands

Distance:	4.3 mile (6.9 kilometres)
Typical time:	120 mins
Height gain:	0 metres
Map:	Explorer 285
Walk:	ww.walkingworld.com ID:1305
Contributor:	Jim Grindle

Access Information:

The Reserve is signposted off the A59 near Rufford Old Hall, itself signposted for miles around. The walk may be started from Rufford Station which is near Waymark 10 (trains on the Preston / Liverpool line). There is also a birdwatchers' bus service at weekends which does the rounds of the many superb sites in this area. It begins from Ormskirk Station. (For details ring Ormskirk County Information Centre on 01695-579062).

Description:

The route is centred on Mere Sands Wood Nature Reserve and follows a stream and a canal towpath near Rufford Old Hall, before taking to a bridleway around the edge of Rufford New Hall (still marked on OS maps as a hospital but now very exclusive apartments).

Additional Information

Mere Sands Wood was originally planted by Lord Hesketh who lived in the New Hall. The name indicates both that it stood on the edge of a lake (Martin Mere, formerly one of the largest in England, although shallow) and of course that the soil was sandy. This valuable mineral was extracted between 1974 and 1982 with a planning agreement that it would become a reserve when the sand was exhausted. The belt of trees on the edge of the site was left untouched during the sand-winning, while the quarried areas were landscaped to create lagoons with shallow edges. When you have finished your walk it would be worthwhile taking the path on the left of the car park and visiting the many hides. The Trust asks for a donation for

parking and you will find toilets inside the Visitor Centre.

Rufford Old Hall belongs to the National Trust and when it is open (Easter to October roughly) the walk may be started there by following the canal along the towpath away from the hall, until the swing-bridge between Waymarks 10 and 11 is reached. The hall is amongst Lancashire's finest Tudor buildings and was in the hands of the Hesketh family in Shakespeare's time. There is strong evidence that Shakespeare spent some of his so-called missing years as an actor here, before turning up in London. The Great Hall with its wooden screen and hammerbeam roof are superb and in contrast to the Victorian life portrayed in the rest of the house. (The cafe, shop and toilets at the hall are accessible without paying for entry to the hall, if you come on foot from the towpath).

Features:

Pub, Toilets, Church, Stately Home, National Trust/NTS, Wildlife, Birds, Food Shop, Woodland

Walk Directions:

1 This is the visitor centre at Mere Sands Nature Reserve. With your back to this building return across the car park, towards the entrance to the reserve. On the right several nature trails are signposted. Turn right along this gravel track around the edge of the reserve. Pass the entrance to a hide and continue until you come to a drainage ditch, on the far side of which are some houses. On the left is a gate.

2 Go through the gate with the stream on your right and pass along the edge of the village cricket-field. You reach a gate and a lane. Cross to the signpost on the far side and walk with the stream now on your left. You come to another lane, with a chapel on the far side.

3 Cross the bridge and continue by the stream which is again on your right. You come to yet another lane. Cross the bridge and again walk by the stream, this time on your left. You will pass an industrial site with lots of JCBs and scrap vehicles (but also quite a few new Beamers and Mercs parked among the grot). The path goes into a field where there is a large road-bridge over the A59.

4 The OS maps are not quite right here. The path turns right when you reach the bridge and about 50m along, a few steps lead up to the main road. You need to cross this but you will have a better view of the traffic if you turn right and walk about 100m along the road, until you are opposite a swing-bridge over the canal.

5 The white metal gates are usually open. Cross the A59 and then the canal to the towpath on the far side.

6 Turn left and follow the towpath (the OS maps suggest that there is no towpath a little further on, but there is). You come to a bridge when Rufford Church is in sight, just past some locks.

7 As you approach the bridge it seems as if you will have to cross the road, but at the last moment the towpath dips and goes under the bridge. There is a pub just along the road to the right at this point. Continue past Rufford Old Hall on the opposite side of the canal and

past a swing-bridge. If you wish to visit the hall halfway round the walk, this bridge gives access to the grounds. Otherwise stay on the towpath until you reach the next road-bridge.

8 Go under the bridge to find the steps up, for this is where you leave the towpath. Turn right and when you have crossed the canal you will see a lane on the far side of the road. Go along this short lane to its junction with the A59 by the Rufford Arms Hotel.

9 A nice spot for a drink. Cross to the newly surfaced lane opposite. This leads up to the gates of the renovated Home Farm where a gravelled track has been laid on the right to go round the gardens. Follow the track and rejoin the tarmac at gates on the opposite side of the house. This leads to a road.

10 Turn right - there is a pavement. In a few moments you will see the entrance to the Reserve on the far side of the road, although the Cattery sign is perhaps more obvious.

11 Go down the entrance drive past Waymark 2 to the car park and the Visitor Centre.

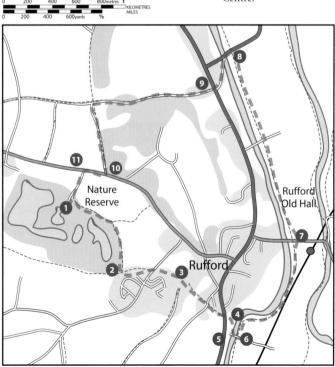

WWT MARTIN MERE

Nr Rufford, Lancashire

WWT Martin Mere is one of nine Wildfowl & Wetlands Centres run by the Wildfowl & Wetlands Trust (WWT), a UK registered charity. Visit WWT Martin Mere and come in close contact with wetlands and their wildlife. You can feed some of the birds straight from your hand. Special events and exhibitions help to give an insight into the wonder of wetlands and the vital need for their conservation.

People of all ages and abilities will enjoy exploring the carefully planned pathways. You can go on a journey around the world, from the Australian Riverway, through the South American Lake, to the Oriental Pen with its Japanese gateway, observing a multitude of exotic ducks, geese, swans and flamingos along the way. In winter, WWT Martin Mere plays host to

thousands of Pink-footed Geese, Whooper and Bewick's Swans and much more. Visitors can see swans under floodlight most winter evenings. Covering 150 hectares, the reserve (one of Britain's most important wetland sites) is designated a Ramsar Site and SSSI for its wealth of rare wetland plants.

The Wildfowl & Wetlands Trust is the largest international wetland conservation charity in the UK. WWT's mission is to conserve wetlands and their biodiversity. These are vitally important for the quality and maintenance of all life. WWT operates nine visitor centres in the UK, bringing people closer to wildlife and providing a fun day out for all the family.

network of hides, visitors can observe shy birds such as the Ruff, Black-tailed Godwit and Little Ringed Plover in their natural habitats. There are also a series of pens, near to the visitors centre, where many other birds can be seen all year round at closer quarters. The mere is particularly famous for the vast numbers of Pink-Footed geese that winter here, their number often approaching 20,000. Although winter is a busy time at Martin Mere, a visit in any season is sure to be rewarded. The visitor centre caters for everyone and, as well as the shop and café, there is a theatre and a wealth of information regarding the birds found here and the work of the Trust.

SCARISBRICK

3 miles NW of Ormskirk on the A570

Scarisbrick, which is part of the largest parish in Lancashire, lies in the heart of rich agricultural land that is intensively cultivated for vegetables, including carrots, brussel sprouts, cabbages, and early potatoes. A feature of this area is the large number of farm shops by the side of the road selling the produce fresh from the fields.

The first **Scarisbrick Hall** was built in the reign of King Stephen but in the middle of the 19th century the hall, which is screened from the road by thick woodland, was extensively remodelled by the Victorian architect Augustus Welby Pugin for Charles Scarisbrick.

HALSALL

4 miles W of Ormskirk on the A5147

This is a charming unspoilt village lying in the heart of fertile West Lancashire and close to the Leeds and Liverpool Canal – the longest canal in Britain with a mainline of 127.25 miles and 92 locks.

St Cuthbert's Church, which dates from the middle of the 13th century, is one of the oldest churches in the diocese of Liverpool and it remains one of the prettiest in the county. The distinctive spire, which was added around 1400, rises from a tower that has octagonal upper stages.

SOUTH AND EAST OF ORMSKIRK

GREAT ALTCAR
6 miles SW of Ormskirk on the B5195

Standing on the banks of the River Alt, this old farming village is famous as the venue for the Liverpool Cup, an annual hare coursing event. In the churchyard of the present church, erected by the Earl of Sefton in 1879, are a pedestal font and a stoup which came from the earlier churches that occupied this site.

AUGHTON
3 miles SW of Ormskirk off the A59

This picturesque village, surrounded by agricultural land, is dominated by the spire of St Michael's Church. An ancient place, it was mentioned in the *Domesday Book*; the register of church rectors goes back to 1246 and much of the building's medieval framework remains though it was restored in 1914.

Close by is Aughton Old Hall (private) which stands on a site that has been occupied since Saxon times. The ruins of a 15th century pele tower are visible in the garden and the house is reputed to have been Cromwell's base while he was active in the area.

LATHOM
3 miles NE of Ormskirk off the A5209

The stretch of the famous Leeds and Liverpool Canal which passes through

RAILWAY TAVERN

Hoscar Moss Road, Lathom, Lancashire L40 4BQ
Tel: 01704 892369

The Railway Tavern was originally built in the 1850s to provide food and lodging for the 'navvies' constructing the railway line from Wigan to Southport. The line is still operating but the inn has been totally refurbished in traditional style by owner Tricia Redford and now offers a welcoming atmosphere with open fires, carpets and air conditioning. Tricia has more than 40 years experience in the hospitality business, having trained with Trust House Forte, and since her arrival here in 2002 has made this a lively and popular venue.

A major attraction is the home-cooked food prepared by award-winning chef Steve Prescott who

bases his menu on local fresh produce, freshly prepared and cooked – even the chips come from local potatoes and there's definitely not a microwave in sight. Food is served in a separate non-smoking dining room and to accompany your meal, there's a good choice of real ales, (the inn boasts a CAMRA award), an excellent wine list that even features Dom Perignon champagne and, for the truly strong-headed, a premium cider called Old Rosie Cloudy Scrumpy. If the weather's kind, you can enjoy your refreshments in the beer garden and patio at the rear which enjoy grand views looking across to the Parbold Hills.

this village is well worth a visit and it includes the **Top Locks** area, a particularly interesting part of this major canal route.

To the south of the village, in Lathom Park, is Lathom House (private), formerly home of Lord Stanley, Earl of Derby, a Royalist who was executed during the Civil War. Only one wing of the original house remains but within the grounds are the ancient **Chapel of St John the Divine**, consecrated in 1509, and 10 adjoining almshouses built for the chapel bedesmen. It's a charming cluster of buildings in an attractive setting and visitors are welcome at the services held in the chapel every Sunday.

Parbold

5 miles NE of Ormskirk off the A5209

This is a charming village of pretty stone cottages as well as grand, late-Victorian houses built by wealthy Manchester cotton brokers. The village houses extend up the slopes of **Parbold Hill**, one of the highest points for miles around and from which there are superb views of the West Lancashire plain. At the summit stands a rough hewn monument, erected to commemorate the Reform Act of 1832, that is known locally, due to its shape, as Parbold Bottle.

Ashurst Beacon, another local landmark, was re-erected on Ashurst Hill by Lord Skelmersdale in 1798 when the threat of a French invasion was thought to be imminent.

Mawdesley

6 miles NE of Ormskirk off the B5246

A past winner of the Best Kept Village of Lancashire award, Mawdesley lies in rich farming country and was once associated with a thriving basket making industry. The village has a surprising number of old buildings. Mawdesley Hall (private),

originally built in the 1500s and altered in the late 18th century, was for many generations the home of the Mawdesley family.

At the other end of the village is Lane Ends House, built in 1590, which was occupied by a Catholic family and has a chapel in one of its attics. Other venerable buildings include Ambrose House (1577), Barret House Farm (1695), Back House Farm (1690) and Jay Bank Cottage (1692). By contrast, the oldest of the village's three churches dates back only to 1840.

Wrightington

8 miles NE of Ormskirk on the B5250

Bypassed by most people as they travel up and down the nearby M6 and overshadowed by the delights of the **Camelot Theme Park** at nearby Charnock Richard, this is another pleasant, rural Lancashire village.

Rivington

13 miles E of Ormskirk off the A673

One of the county's prettiest villages, Rivington is surrounded by moorland of outstanding natural beauty that forms the western border of the Forest of Rossendale. Overlooking the village and with splendid views over West Lancashire, **Rivington Pike**, at 1,191 feet, is one of the area's high spots. It was once a site of one of the country's chain of signal beacons.

Just to the south of the village, on the lower slopes of Rivington Moor, lies **Lever Park**, which was made over to the public in 1902 by William Hesketh Lever, who later became Lord Leverhulme. The park comprises an awe-inspiring pot pourri of ornamental, landscaped gardens, tree-lined avenues, ancient cruck-framed barns, a Georgian hall, and a treasure trove of natural history within

Rivington

its 400 acres. The park's moorland setting, elevated position, and adjoining reservoirs provide scenery on a memorably grand scale.

STANDISH

9 miles E of Ormskirk on the A49

This historic old market town has several reminders of its past, not least of which is the splendid **St Wilfrid's Church.** Built in a size and style that befitted the importance of the town in the late 1500s, the building stands on the site of a church that was certainly here at the beginning of the 13th century. A look around the interior of the church will provide a potted history of the area: there are tombs and memorials to all the important local families including the Wrightingtons, Shevingtons, and the Standish family themselves.

LOCATOR MAP

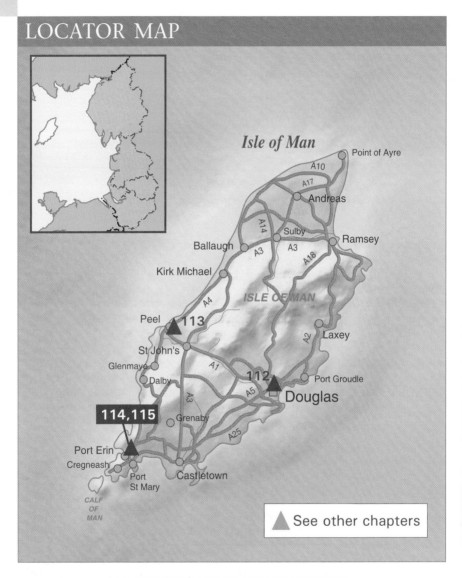

Isle of Man

Point of Ayre

A10

A17

Andreas

A14

Sulby

Ballaugh   A3   A3   Ramsey

A18

Kirk Michael

A4

ISLE OF MAN

Peel   113

A2   Laxey

St John's

Glenmaye   A1

Dalby   112   Port Groudle

A5   Douglas

A3

114,115   Grenaby

A25

Port Erin

Cregneash

Port   Castletown

St Mary

CALF OF MAN

▲ See other chapters

ADVERTISERS AND PLACES OF INTEREST

Although only 33 miles long and 13 miles wide, the Isle of Man contains a rich diversity of scenery and heritage and, perhaps best of all, exudes a sense of peacefulness epitomised by the Manx Gaelic saying: *traa-dy-liooar* – "Time enough".

Most British mainlanders are surprised to discover that the island is not part of the United Kingdom but a Crown Protectorate with the Queen as Lord of Mann represented in the island by the Lieutenant Governor. Its Parliament, the Tynwald, dates back more than 1,000 years – the oldest continuous parliament in the world. The island issues its own coins and notes with the currency having an equivalent value to that of the UK. Recently issued coins include Harry Potter crowns (2001) and another crown marking the Chinese Year of the Horse, 2002.

This island is perhaps best known for its annual TT motorcycle races, its tailless cat, Manx kippers, and as a tax haven for the wealthy. However, there is much more to this beautiful island which, set in the heart of the Irish Sea, is truly a world apart. With around 100 miles of coastline and several resorts, each with its own individual style and character, although the Isle of Man is by no means large, there is plenty to interest the visitor.

This magical place became an island around 10,000 years ago when the melt water of the Ice Age raised the sea level. Soon afterwards, the first settlers arrived, working and developing the island into the landscape seen today. The distinctive influences of the various cultures who have lived here still remain, leaving a land with a unique and colourful heritage.

Among the first arrivals were the Vikings and evidence of their era, from the early chieftains to the last Norse King, abounds throughout the Isle of Man. Against the skyline on the seaward side of road between Ballaugh and Bride are some ancient hilltop Viking burial mounds and, at the ancient castle in Peel, an archaeological dig revealed many hidden Viking treasures which are now on display at the Manx Museum in Douglas.

Despite their reputation for plunder, rape and pillage, the Vikings also made some positive contributions to life on the island, not least of which was the establishment of the Manx governmental

Douglas Bay

system, known as Tynwald. The Manx name for Tynwald Hill is 'Cronk Keeill Eoin', the hill of St John's Church. Although there is no evidence to confirm the story that it contains earth from all of the 17 parish churches here, it is not unlikely that token portions of soil were added to the mound in accordance with Norse tradition.

The Tynwald ceremony continues today with an annual meeting of the island's governors on Midsummer's Day at the ancient parliament field at St John's, where Manx citizens can also petition parliament.

The island's famous three-legged symbol seems to have been adopted in the 13th century as the armorial bearings of the native Kings of the Isle of Man, whose dominion also included the Hebrides. After 1266, when the native dynasty ended and control of the island passed briefly to the Crown of Scotland and then permanently to the Crown of England, the emblem was retained, and among the earliest surviving representations are those on the Manx Sword of State, thought to have been made in 1300. The Three Legs also appeared on Manx coinage from the 17th to the 19th century, and are still seen in everyday use in the form of the official Manx flag.

Why the Three Legs were adopted as the Royal Arms of the Manx Kingdom is unknown. Many heraldic emblems have no meaning and are simply chosen because they are distinctive. This may be the case with the Three Legs, though the emblem as such - something between a cross and a swastika - has a long history reaching far back into pagan times and was originally a symbol of the sun, the seat of power and light.

MANX ELECTRIC RAILWAY

Douglas, Isle of Man
Tel: 01624 663366

An ideal way to discover what the island has to offer is by train. Supported by a good bus network, you can be somewhere different each day exploring the sights and the scenery. From Douglas, the **Manx Electric Railway** takes you along the east coast to Laxey. Here you can climb to the top of the Great Laxey Wheel and go underground on the Mines Trail. Laxey is also the starting point for the Snaefell Mountain Railway which climbs the Island's highest peak. At the top you're rewarded with breathtaking views and refreshments in the Summit Hotel Café.

Further on from Laxey is the largest town in the north, Ramsey. In the town, there are plenty of shops to see, cafés to enjoy and pubs to visit. Nearby is Mooragh Park and boating lake. A short bus ride away is The Gibbs of the Grove. This Victorian period house was formerly the summer retreat of a Liverpool shipping merchant and his family. Inside the house you will find original furnishings, fittings and costumes. Outside in the spacious grounds and gardens are displays of vintage vehicles and agricultural equipment. The trains run daily between April and October and there are various themed events during the year.

DOUGLAS

The island's capital, Douglas is also a lively resort with a sweeping sandy beach and a two-mile long promenade, the focus of the island's nightlife. There's excellent shopping around Strand Street, a fine park, Noble's Park, on the edge of town with facilities for tennis, bowls, putting, crazy golf and a children's play area. Other attractions include the magnificently restored Victorian Gaiety Theatre, the Manx Superbowl, a casino, the Summerland sport and leisure centre which hosts live entertainment during the summer, a cinema complex, an Aquadrome and the Villa Marina entertainment complex.

(Douglas once had a traditional Victorian pier, designed and built by the noted railway builder John Dixon in 1869, the year Douglas became the island's capital. A thousand feet in length, it was dismantled in 1896 and reconstructed at Rhos-on-Sea, near Colwyn Bay in North Wales.)

From dawn to dusk, visitors can take a leisurely ride along the wonderful promenade aboard the **Douglas Bay Horse Tramway**, a remarkable and beautiful reminder of a bygone era. It was the brainchild of a civil engineer, Thomas Lightfoot, who retired to the island and, seeing the need for a public transport system along this elegant promenade, designed in 1876 the system still in use today. That the Douglas Tramway has

survived into the 21st century is remarkable especially since, in the early 1900s, attempts were made to electrify the line and extend the Manx electric railway along the promenade.

There is a story often told about the horses that pull the trams, which concerns a parrot that lived in a cage at a hotel close to one of the tram's stops. The bird learnt to mimic the sound of the tram's starting bell and used to practise this skill constantly. The tram horses would stop when they heard the bell and start off again immediately before the passengers could alight as the bird joined in the fun.

The Manx Electric Railway, completed in 1899, is the longest narrow-gauge vintage line in the British Isles and operates the oldest working tramcars in the world. The 18-mile journey departs from the northern end of Douglas promenade, stops at Laxey, terminus of the Snaefell Mountain Railway, and then continues to Ramsey.

Another delightful means of travel is the narrow-gauge Victorian **Steam Railway** that runs between Douglas and

Horse Drawn Tram, Douglas

The Promenade, Douglas

Port Erin. Following the line of the cliff tops, the memorable journey also travels through bluebell woods and through steep-sided rocky cuttings. This section of line is all that remains of a railway that once served the whole of the island. Many miles of the old railway network have been developed as footpaths. From Quarterbridge in Douglas **The Heritage Trail** is a 10.5-mile former railway route that cuts across the island to Peel on the west coast. It's a scenic but undemanding trail that passes close to historic Tynwald Hill. Picnic sites and useful information boards are situated along the way.

The Isle of Man's most famous export is probably the Manx cat, notable for having no tail. There are several stories of how the cat lost its tail but one, in particular, is delightful. At the time that Noah was building the Ark there were two Manx cats, complete with tails. Noah sent for all the animals to come to the Ark, two by two, but the Manx cats replied that there was plenty of time and continued to play outside. Finally, when the cats did decide to board the Ark, Noah was just slamming the door and the cats lost their tails. A variation on

this tale is that one of the cats reached the Ark safely, the other had its tail chopped off by the closing doors. The tailless cat went on to become the Manx cat and the one who managed to keep its tail became the ever grinning Cheshire cat.

No trip to the island is complete without a visit to the **Manx Museum** where the award-winning *Story of Mann* audio-visual presentation uncovers 10,000 years of the island's history. The Manx Museum complex also contains the superb National Art Gallery, the National Library & Archives, a Natural History Gallery as well as exhibits portraying many other aspects of life on the island, including the famous TT races.

One of the Isle of Man's most famous landmarks, the **Tower of Refuge**, looks out over Douglas Bay. Sir William Hilary, founder of the Royal National Lifeboat Institution, lived in a mansion overlooking the bay and, following a near disaster in 1830 when the Royal Mail Steam Packet *St George* was driven on to rocks in high seas, Hilary launched the Douglas lifeboat. Miraculously, all the crew of the *St George* were saved without the loss of one lifeboat man despite the extremely treacherous conditions. It was following this incident that Hilary decided that a form of refuge should be built for shipwrecked mariners to shelter in and so, with Hilary laying the foundation stone in 1832, the Tower of Refuge was built on Conister Rock out in the bay.

Noble's Park leads to the Grandstand that is the control centre for the **TT races**, rightly billed as the greatest motorcycle show on earth in the road racing capital of the world. Road racing started on the island as a practice for a race to be run in France for the Gordon Bennett Cup, presented by James Gordon Bennett, owner of the *New York Herald*. An Act of Parliament outlawed racing on public highways in Britain, but at a special session of the Tynwald in 1904 a bill entitled The Highways (Light Locomotive) Act gave permission for limited racing on the roads of the island on a few days a year. Interest in racing, both cars and motorcycles, swiftly grew, and in 1907 the first TT race was run over a short course based on St John's. Twenty five machines started, ten finished, and the winner was CR (Charlie) Collier, who achieved an average speed of 38mph on his single-cylinder Matchless. In 1911 the mountain course was adopted and has remained more or less unchanged since.

Perched on a headland overlooking Douglas Bay is a camera obscura known as the **Great Union Camera Obscura**. The camera was originally situated on the old iron pier, but when this was demolished in the 1870s the camera was resited on Douglas Head. In the camera, the natural daylight is focused on to a white panel through a simple system of lenses and angled mirrors and so provides a living image of the scene outside. At first apparently still, as with a photograph, viewers soon become fascinated as the 'picture' begins to move.

The Isle of Man was ruled for several centuries by the Stanley family, one of whom became Earl Derby. This notable gentleman organised the first Derby horserace, predating the Epsom Derby by many years. The main point of starting horse-racing on the island was to encourage the breeding of good horses. Fifty horses and donkeys who have retired or fallen on hard times are kept at the **Home of Rest for Old Horses**, set in 92 acres of open countryside just outside Douglas, on the A5 Castletown road.

NORTH OF DOUGLAS

ONCHAN
2 miles NE of Douglas on the A2

Virtually a suburb of Douglas, Onchan is the location of the Lieutenant-Governor's residence. An entry in the Onchan parish register records the marriage in 1781 of William Bligh RN to Miss Elizabeth (Betty) Betham, the daughter of the island's customs officer. In 1787 Captain Bligh took command of HMS *Bounty*, later the scene of the famous mutiny. The island has another connection with the *Bounty*. Peter Heywood, son of a deemster, was born on the island in 1773 and was 14 at the time of the mutiny. Though not on Bligh's ship at the time, he was put on trial in Tahiti and condemned to death. His sister Nessie travelled halfway across the world to beg for his life to be spared; her pleadings were successful, and Peter Heywood resumed his career in the Navy and rose to the rank of captain.

PORT GROUDLE
3 miles NE of Douglas on the A11

Close to Port Groudle lies Groundle Glen, a deep and in places rocky valley with a bubbling stream running through its length. Excellent specimens of beech grow in the upper sections of the glen whilst, lower down, pines and larches are abundant. There is also a small waterwheel in the lower half of the glen. Railway enthusiasts will be delighted to learn that on certain days in the summer the Groudle Glen Railway operates. Running on a track just 2ft wide for three-quarters of a mile along the cliffs, the railway's lovingly restored carriages are pulled by Sea Lion, the original 1896 steam engine.

LAXEY
5 miles N of Douglas on the A2

Set in a deep, wooded valley, this village is one of interesting contrasts. Tracing the river up from its mouth at the small tidal harbour leads the walker into **Laxey Glen**, one of the island's 17 National Glens that are preserved and maintained by the Forestry Department of the government.

Further up the glen is one of the island's most famous sights, the **Great Laxey Wheel** that marks the site of a once thriving mining community. Known as the Lady Isabella Wheel, with a circumference of 228 feet, a diameter of 72 feet, and a top platform some 72 feet off the ground, it is the largest working waterwheel in the world.

It was Robert Casement, an engineer at the mines, who constructed this

mechanical wonder and designed it to pump 250 gallons of water a minute from a depth of 200 fathoms. Officially opened in 1854, it was named the *Lady Isabella* after the wife of the then Lieutenant Governor of the Isle of Man. After considerable repair and reconstruction work, the wheel now operates just as it did when it first opened and it stands as a monument to Victorian engineering as well as the island's industrial heritage.

Also working in traditional style are the machines at **Laxey Woollen Mills** where genuine Manx tweed is woven on double-width and power looms: the finished products are on sale in the shop.

Situated above Laxey, in a beautiful natural glen, are the magnificent **Ballalheanagh Gardens**. The valley, of steep sides with winding paths and a crystal clear stream running through the bottom, is packed with rhododendrons, shrubs, bulbs, and ferns and is certainly a gardeners' paradise well worth seeking out.

From Laxey station, the **Snaefell Mountain Railway** carries visitors to the top of the island's only mountain. Built in 1895, the six original tram cars still climb the steep gradients to **Snaefell**'s 2,036 feet summit and this is certainly the way to travel for those unwilling to walk. Those reaching the top are rewarded with outstanding views of the whole

Lady Isabella Water Wheel, Laxey

island and out over the sea to Ireland, Scotland, and England. There is also a café at the summit offering welcome refreshments. Snaefell is the location of **Murray's Motorcycle Museum**, where more than 120 machines are on display, including Mike Hailwood's 1961 TT-winning Honda.

Manx Electric Railway

RAMSEY

12 miles N of Douglas on the A18

The second largest town in the island, Ramsey occupies a scenic location at the foot of North Barrule. This northernmost resort on the island has a busy working harbour, a long stretch of beach and a wide promenade. A popular amenity is **Mooragh Park**, a 40-acre expanse of gardens and recreational facilities with a 12-acre boating lake and lakeside café. During the summer months there's live musical entertainment in the park and around the 3rd week of July each year the park is one of several venues hosting events during **Yn Chruinnaght**, an inter-Celtic festival of music, dance and literature.

Other major crowd-pullers are the Round the Island Yacht Race, held each summer and starting and finishing in Ramsey, and the Ramsey Motorcycle Sprint, part of the TT festival, when bikers show off their skills along Mooragh Promenade.

In the mid-1800s the town assumed the title of "Royal Ramsey" following an unscheduled visit by Queen Victoria and Prince Albert in 1847. The royal yacht anchored in Ramsey Bay following a stormy crossing from Scotland so that the seasick Queen could recover. While Her Majesty recuperated on board, Prince Albert walked to the top of Lhergy Frissel and was much impressed by the view. A few years later the Albert Tower was erected to commemorate the Prince Consort's visit.

Just to the north of the town, lies the **Grove Rural Life Museum**, housed in a pleasantly proportioned Victorian house. Built as the summer retreat of Duncan Gibb, a wealthy Victorian shipping merchant from Liverpool, and his family, the rooms within the house have all been restored to their Victorian splendour and stepping into the museum is just like taking a step back in time. The outbuildings have not been neglected and they contain an interesting collection of vehicles and agricultural instruments that were seen on Manx farms in the late 19th century.

Ramsey is the northern terminus of the Manx Electric Railway, built in 1899. The **Manx Electric Railway Museum** tells the fascinating story of this world-famous Victorian transport system. From Ramsey the railway follows a scenic route southwards to Douglas, accompanied most of the way by the equally delightful coastal road, the A15/A2.

For serious walkers, there's the **Millennium Way** which starts about a mile from Parliament Square in Ramsey. Established in 1979 to mark the millennium year of the Tynwald parliament, the 28-mile long path passes through some magnificent countryside, picturesque towns and villages, before ending at the island's former capital, Castletown.

POINT OF AYRE

18 miles N of Douglas on the A16

This is the northernmost tip of the island and, not surprisingly, there is a lighthouse situated here. The area around the point is known as **The Ayres** and, at the Ayres Visitor Centre, a whole wealth of information can be found about this fascinating part of the island. Amongst the inland heath moorland, a variety of species of birds can be found nesting whilst, on the pebbled beaches, can be seen terns. The offshore sandbanks provide a plentiful supply of food for both the diving gannets and the basking grey seals.

ANDREAS

5 miles N of Ramsey on the A17

Andreas was originally a Viking settlement and the village church contains intricately carved crosses dating back to the days of these early occupants. The church tower's mutilated spire goes back to the 1940s when part of it was removed in case it proved to be dangerous to aircraft from the nearby wartime airfields.

SULBY

11 miles N of Douglas on the A3

Situated in the heart of the island, the village lies on the famous TT course, a circular route on the island's roads that takes in Douglas, Ramsey, Kirk Michael, and St John's. There are several scenic and picturesque walks from the village which taken in **Sulby Glen** and **Tholt-y-Will Glen**, both of which are renowned beauty spots, and to the south, over moorland, to Sulby reservoir. Bird watchers particularly will enjoy the walks over the higher ground as it provides the opportunity to see hen harriers, kestrels, peregrines, and curlews.

BALLAUGH

7 miles W of Ramsey on the A3

The village, which also lies on the TT race course, is close to the island's most extensive area of marshland, the perfect habitat for a range of birds, including woodcock and grasshopper warbler, as well as being the largest roost for hen harriers in Western Europe.

Situated on the edge of the Ballaugh Curraghs, **Curraghs Wildlife Park** is home to a wide variety of wetland wildlife that come from all over the world. Curraghs is the Manx word for the wet, boggy, willow woodland that is typical of this part of the island and the site, which was opened in 1965, gives visitors the opportunity to see the animals in their natural environments. This world-renowned wildlife park has been divided into several different habitats, including The Pampas, The Swamp, The Marsh, and the Flooded Forest, and here endangered animals from around the world, such as Canadian otters, spider monkeys, rhea, and Muntjac deer, live as they would in the wild.

The Curraghs Wildlife Park also has an enviable breeding record and, as many of the species are becoming rare in the wild, this is a very important aspect of the park's work. Not only have they successfully bred bald ibis, one of the most endangered birds in the world, but tapirs, lechwe antelope and many others also flourish in this environment. Not all the animals and birds are exotic – there are a great number of native species to be seen here too.

Visitors to the park are able to wander around the various habitats, following a well laid out path, and, aided by the illustrated brochure the whole family will find this an interesting and informative trail. There is also an adventure play area for young children and, during the summer, a miniature railway runs around the park. The lakeside café is open during the day for refreshments and, during the main summer season when the park is open until 9pm, barbecues are held here.

KIRK MICHAEL

10 miles N of Douglas on the A3

Close to the village lies **Glen Wyllin**, another of the island's 17 National Glens, and one that certainly deserves exploration. The varied woodland contains elm, ash, sycamore, alder,

beech, lime, holm oak and chestnut and in spring the woodland floor is carpeted with bluebell, primrose, wood anemone and wild garlic. Kirk Michael also lies on a 16-mile footpath that follows the route of an old railway line from Peel to Ramsey. After following the coast, and part of the Raad ny Foillan, the footpath branches off through pastoral countryside before reaching the port of Ramsey on the other side of the island.

A few miles south of Kirk Michael, in the oddly named village of Cronk y Voddy, the **Moaney Moor Open Farm** provides the opportunity for children to enjoy farm animals and small pets. There's a farm walk, and picnic and play areas.

WEST OF DOUGLAS

PEEL

12 miles W of Douglas on the A1

Located on the western side of the island, Peel is renowned for its stunning sunsets and the town is generally regarded as best typifying the unique character and atmosphere of the Isle of Man. Traditionally the centre of the Manx fishing industry, including delicious oak smoked kippers and fresh shellfish, Peel has managed to avoid any large scale developments. Its narrow winding streets exude history and draw the visitor unfailingly down to the busy harbour, sweeping sandy

Peel Castle and Beach

beach, and magnificent castle of local red sandstone.

Peel Castle, one of Isle of Man's principal historic monuments, occupies the important site of **St Patrick's Isle**. The imposing curtain wall encircles many ruined buildings, including St Patrick's Church, the 11th century Round Tower and the 13th century Cathedral of St Germans – the cathedral of Sodor and Mann and the very first diocese established in the British Isles, pre-dating even Canterbury. The great curtain wall also encloses the later apartments of the Lords of Mann. In the 11th century the castle became the ruling seat of the Norse Kingdom of Man and the Isles, first united by Godred Crovan – the King Orry of Manx folklore. Today, the castle provides a dramatic backdrop for a variety of plays and musical events during the summer.

Recent archaeological excavations have discovered exciting new evidence relating to the long history of the site. One of the most dramatic finds was the Norse grave of a lady of high social status buried in pagan splendour. The jewellery and effects buried with her can be seen on display, with other excavation finds, at the Manx Museum. The castle is also said to be haunted by the Black Dog, or Mauthe Dhoo. On dark windy nights, it can be heard howling in the castle's dungeons.

Connoisseurs of kippers speak highly of the tasty Manx kipper. At **Moore's Traditional Museum** you can watch a kipper curing process that remains unchanged since the late 1700s. Another

THE CREEK INN

Station Place, Peel, Isle of Man IM5 1AT
Tel: 01624 842216 Fax: 01624 843359
e-mail: jeanmcaleer@manx.net
website: www.creekinn.co.im

Occupying a prime position on the Quayside at Peel, **The Creek Inn** has been owned and run by the Turner family for some 30 years. This popular inn is well known locally for the quality of the food on offer with a menu that has something for everyone. Particularly popular are the dishes based on locally caught fish – Manx kippers, fresh crab salad, locally smoked cod or haddock, or the Seafarer's Lunch of home-made Manx kipper pâté served with a baguette, pickles and salad. Other choices include jacket potatoes, granary baguettes and tortilla wraps, while the daily specials might include a delicious shoulder of lamb in redcurrant sauce, home-made steak & kidney pie, or a cheese & broccoli bake. And on Sundays the inn lays on a superb roast dinner, compete with all the trimmings.

To accompany your meal there's a selection of between three and six real ales, and a choice of wines from around the world. Open from 11am every day, the Creek Inn hosts live music every Friday and Saturday evening. If you are planning to stay in this delightful corner of the island, the inn has four self-catering apartments to let, each of which sleeps two people.

major museum is **The House of Manannan**, a state of the art heritage attraction which was voted British Isles Museum of the Year in 1998. And for those researching their family history, **The Leece Museum** has an archive of documents and photographs of the town along with a varied display of artifacts connected with the life of a busy fishing port.

Peel gave its name to the only production car ever made on the island. The three-wheel Peel, produced between 1962 and 1966, was one of the tiniest cars ever made – the first model was only 4½ feet long and was powered by a 49cc DKW engine. The claim that it could carry a driver and a shopping bag was disputed by some who thought that it was a question of one or the other!

St John's

3 miles E of Peel on the A1

Roads from all over the island converge at the village of St John's because this is the site of the ancient **Tynwald Day Ceremony**, held on July 5th which is a public holiday throughout the island. This grand open-air event takes place on Tynwald Hill just north of the village. Here the Tynwald Court – a parliament that can trace its origins to the 9th century – assembles and the new laws of the land are proclaimed in both Manx and English. The serious business over, the rest of the day is devoted to various celebrations and activities culminating in a firework display.

Adjoining Tynwald Hill, the 25-acre **Tynwald Arboretum** was established in 1979 to mark the millennium of the island's parliament.

Glenmaye

3 miles S of Peel on the A27

A spectacular bridged gorge and waterfall dominate this glen which is one of the most picturesque on the island. Comprising over 11 acres, its beautiful sheltered woodland includes some relics of the ancient forests that once covered much of the Isle of Man. Another feature of this glen is the Mona Erin, one of the many waterwheels which once produced power for the Manx lead mines.

Dalby

4 miles S of Peel on the A27

Just south-west of Dalby village, **Niarbyl Bay** takes its name from the Manx Gaelic, Yn Arbyl, meaning "the tail", so named because of the long reef that curves out from the shoreline. There are stunning views to the north and south, and the grandeur of the south-western coast is seen at its best from this typically Manx setting. The beach here is an ideal place for picnics, relaxing and enjoying the tranquillity of the setting.

Port Erin

16 miles S of Peel on the A5

Situated between magnificent headlands, Port Erin's beach is certainly a safe haven. It is also a place of soft sands cleaned daily by the tide with rock pools to one side and a quay to the other. A long promenade above the sheltered sandy beach has a number of cafés and other amenities include bowls, tennis, putting, nearby Rowany golf course and some superb walks along coastal paths out to Bradda Head. Port Erin is also the terminus for the Steam Railway which runs from here to Douglas.

The town has its own Erin Arts Centre which since 1975 has hosted the annual **Mananan International Festival of Music and the Arts**, now recognised as one the island's most prestigious cultural events. The two-week long festival takes place from mid- to late-June and the eclectic programme ranges through classical music, opera and ballet, jazz and

FALCON'S NEST HOTEL

Station Road, Port Erin, Isle of Man IM9 6AF
Tel: 01624 834077 Fax: 01624 835370
e-mail: falconsnest@enterprise.net
website: www.falconsnesthotel.co.uk

Overlooking a beautiful sheltered sandy harbour beach, the **Falcon's Nest Hotel** is ideal for families, walking groups, golfers, railway enthusiasts and for the business traveller – it is only 10 minutes from the airport and 30 minutes from Douglas. A family-run concern, the hotel provides comfort and a relaxing atmosphere with superb quality service and cuisine to suit the most discerning visitor. The à la carte restaurant, which enjoys a magnificent sea view, provides the best of traditional English cuisine, including many local seafood delicacies such as Manx queenies, scallops, lobster and crab.

The former ballroom of the hotel has been converted to an elegant Victorian-style dining room where the hotel's renowned Sunday Carvery can be enjoyed. To accompany your meal, there's a

large selection of fine wines, offered at sensible prices. Three function rooms are available to suit parties of various sizes. Meals and snacks are also served in both bars during lunchtime and early evening – real ales and an extensive range of whiskeys are available. The Ophidian's Lair saloon bar with its pool table and jukebox provides a lively and convivial atmosphere, especially when live sports via satellite are being broadcast. In the residents lounge bar, which is also open to non-residents, guests can relax in front of an open fire and enjoy the magnificent views across the bay and headland.

The hotel has 37 en-suite bedrooms and sea views are available. All rooms are designed with guests' comfort in mind and offer many facilities, including

en-suite bathrooms, direct dial telephone, colour TV, hair dryer and hospitality tray. A room service menu is available. No single room supplements apply; there are special rates for children; and pets are welcome.

The hotel's other amenities include laundry facilities; photocopying, fax and e-mail – and the hotel can arrange competitive travel rates with ATOL/ABTA companies.

Port Erin Royal Hotel

The Promenade, Port Erin Isle of Man IM9 6LH
Tel: 01624 833116 Fax:01624 835402
e-mail: clg@porterinhotels.com
website: www.porterinhotels.com

Take a relaxing break on the Isle of Man and choose Port Erin in the southwest of the Island - long regarded as the leading Manx resort for the more discerning visitor. Here you will find a blue lagoon-like bay with heavenly sunsets, a beautiful sandy beach and plenty of coastal footpaths.
Port Erin makes a wonderful base for an Island holiday or short break. It is just two minutes from the glorious Manx countryside and 20 minutes from the bright lights of Douglas, the Island's capital.

The friendly and informal 80-bedroom three-star Royal Hotel stands on the upper promenade in Port Erin and overlooks the full expanse of the beautiful bay. Here you can enjoy full Manx cooked breakfasts and optional five course evening meals. Free airport transfers, free sporting extras and a regular free evening entertainment programme are all provided. The comfortable en suite bedrooms are equipped with TV, radio, direct-dial telephone, hospitality tray, hairdryer, iron and ironing board.

Just one call is needed and the in-house tour operator, Goldstar Travel Services (ATOL 3366) will do the rest. Travel by air or sea, car hire, local transport explorer tickets and holiday insurance can all be included as part of your package.

theatre, to films, Indian music and art exhibitions as well as special events for children.

Calf of Man

18 miles S of Peel

This small island, situated just off the southwestern tip of the island, is now a bird sanctuary owned by the National Trust. The puffins should be grateful – one of the previous owners, the Dukes of Athol, requested that his tenants living on the Calf pickled the nesting puffins! In 1777, a stone was found on the isle in the garden of Jane's Cottage, though in those days it was called The Mansion. Known as the Calf Crucifixion Cross, the stone is believed to date from the 8th century and it is one of the earliest Christian finds in Europe. The cross can be seen in the Manx Museum in Douglas.

In 2002, a new **Visitor Centre** was opened at the southernmost tip of the island. The scenic four-acre site also has a shop, café and car park and provides grand views of Spanish Head, the Calf of Man and the Irish Mountains of Mourne.

Calf Sound, the stretch of water between the island and the Isle of Man has seen many ships pass through and it was here that the largest armada of Viking longships ever assembled in the British Isles congregated before setting off to invade Ireland. Centuries later, men from nearby Port St Mary were granted a gallantry medal by Napoleon, thought to be the only such medal he presented to British subjects, when they came to the rescue of the crew of the *St Charles* schooner from France which had foundered in the sound.

Cregneash

19 miles S of Peel off the A31

Perched close to the southwestern tip of the island this village is now a living museum, **Cregneash Village Folk Museum**, which offers a unique experience of Manx traditional life within a 19th century crofting community. Its isolated position led the village to become one of the last strongholds of the island's ancient skills and customs and all this is beautifully preserved today.

Thatched Cottage, Cregneash

By combining small scale farming with other occupations, a small settlement of Manx men and women have successfully prospered here since the mid-1600s. In the carefully restored buildings, visitors can see the conditions in which they lived and managed to sustain life in this rugged landscape. The centrepiece of Cregneash is without doubt **Harry Kelly's Cottage**. Kelly, who died in 1934, was a renowned Cregneash crofter and a fluent speaker of the Manx language. Opened to the public in 1938, his cottage, still filled with his furniture, is an excellent starting point to any tour of the village. There are various other buildings of interest, including Turner's Shed, a smithy, and the Karran Farm.

The village is also one of the few remaining places where visitors get a chance to view the unusual Manx Loaghtan four-horned sheep, a breed which, thanks to Manx National Heritage and other interest groups, now has a secure future.

Port St Mary

13 miles SW of Douglas off the A31

This delightful little working port has both an inner and outer harbour, two piers, and excellent anchorage for visiting yachts. The beach, along a scenic walkway from the harbour, is no more than two miles from the beach at Port Erin but it faces in almost the opposite direction and lies in the most sheltered part of the island.

One of the finest walks on the Isle of Man is the cliff-top route from Port St Mary to Port Erin along the **Raad ny Foillan** - the road of the gull - a long distance footpath that follows the coastline right around the island. From Port St Mary, the first part of the walk takes in **The Chasms**, gigantic vertical rifts that, in some places, descend the full 400 feet of the cliffs.

Castletown

9 miles SW of Douglas on the A7

The original capital of the island, Castletown is full of character and charm, especially around the harbour area. Here, in August, is held the **World Tin Bath Championship**, one of the sporting world's more unusual contests, as well as snake racing and many other aquatic events.

The harbour lies beneath the imposing battlements of the finely preserved **Castle Rushen**, once home to the Kings and Lords of Mann. The present building was mostly constructed between 1340 and 1350 and has recently been restored to provide today's visitors with a vivid impression of what life was like in the fortress many years ago by presenting in authentic detail the sights, sounds, and smells of its heyday. Among the various points of interest is a unique one-fingered clock that was presented to the castle by Elizabeth I in 1597 and which still keeps perfect time.

The castle is also still used as a courthouse, for the swearing-in of new governors, and for registry office weddings. During the summer months there are regular spectacular displays re-enacting scenes from the castle's history, especially the events of 1651 when Royalists were forced to surrender Castle Rushen to Cromwell's parliamentary troops.

Like Peel Castle, Rushen too is said to the haunted, by a ghost known as the White Lady. Believed to be the ghost of Lady Jane Gray who travelled to the island from Scotland with her family, the spectre has been seen walking the battlements at night and occasionally passing straight through the castle's closed main gate during the day.

Also recently restored to its 19th century state of grace is the **Old House of the Keys**, the seat of the Manx parliament until it removed to Douglas in 1874. In the rather cosy former debating chamber visitors can vote on various issues which the parliament faced in the past, and some they may face in the future.

Castletown is also home to the island's **Nautical Museum**, where the displays centre around the 1791 armed yacht *Peggy* which sits in her own contemporary boathouse. Part of the original building is constructed as a cabin room from the time of the Battle of Trafalgar and there are many other artefacts on display, all with a maritime theme.

A mile or so northeast of Castletown is Ronaldsay, the island's principal airport. Adjacent to the airport and open weekends only, the **Manx Aviation and Military Museum** presents the story of the island's wartime and civil aviation history in the 20th century.

Nearby, in the village of Ballasulla, is **Rushen Abbey** – the most substantial medieval religious site in the Isle of Man. This ancient Cistercian monastery now has an interpretive centre that explains the abbey's past importance and illustrates the daily life of the monks.

A couple of miles further along the A5 road towards Douglas, visitors should look out for the **Fairy Bridge**. For centuries, Manx people have taken no chances when it comes to the little people and it is still customary to wish the fairies who live under the bridge a "Good Morning" when crossing.

LOCATOR MAP

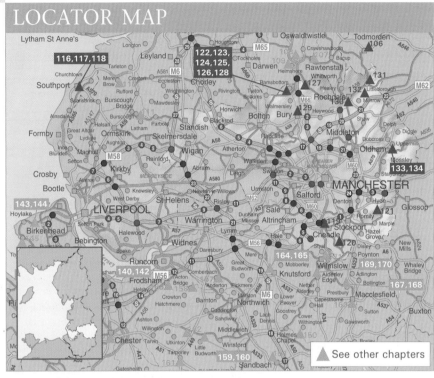

ADVERTISERS AND PLACES OF INTEREST

The Local Government Act of 1972 (effective 1974) involved the creation of Merseyside and Greater Manchester. Greater Manchester took a major chunk from Lancashire and a smaller part from Cheshire, while Merseyside took another section of Lancashire and the northern part of The Wirral from Cheshire.

The metropolitan county of Merseyside comprises the districts of Liverpool, Knowsley, St Helens, Sefton and The Wirral (places of interest in The Wirral will be found in the Cheshire chapter). Merseyside is centred round Liverpool, one of the country's leading cities, and recently announced as the European City of Culture for 2008. After decades of neglect and under-investment the city has been transformed and has become one of the most vibrant and exciting in the land. Liverpool first began to show a different face to the world at the time of the Merseybeat Era in the 1960s.

Liverpool has two magnificent cathedrals, both of which should be on the itinerary of any visitor to the city. Football fans will be sure to visit the grounds of Liverpool or Everton. There are many organised walks and tours covering all aspects of city life, and the Mersey ferry is a favourite way of admiring the city's transformed waterfront. Aintree is the home of the world's most famous steeplechase, the Grand National, and Merseyside has another major racecourse in Haydock Park at Newton-le-Willows.

Outside the city, Merseyside has its share of grand houses and rural attractions. Notable among these are Croxteth Hall & Country Park, Knowsley Safari Park and the National Trust's Speke Hall. The Trust also has the care of a stretch of coast at Formby, an internationally important site for wildlife and home of the famous Formby red squirrels. The whole stretch of coastline from the Mersey Estuary to north of Southport, is a haven for birdwatchers. Southport itself is a delightful spot that combines Victorian elegance with all the amenities of a popular seaside resort and a generous supply of culture.

The metropolitan county of Greater Manchester comprises the districts of Bolton, Bury, Manchester, Oldham, Rochdale, Salford, Stockport, Tameside, Trafford and Wigan. Manchester, like Liverpool, has been transformed over the past few years, and is notable for many fine buildings; some, like the Town Hall and the Cathedral, have long been city landmarks, while the new generation of buildings include Trinity Bridge and the City of Manchester Stadium. Manchester's museums and galleries are the most numerous and diverse outside the capital, ranging from the Museum of Science & Industry to the John Rylands Library and the Whitworth Gallery. And even in the post-Beckham era, the Manchester United Museum in Trafford is a magnet for football fans from all over the world. In Salford, the Lowry is a stunning cultural complex overlooking the Manchester Ship Canal.

Visitors to Manchester do not have to travel far to be in the country: Tameside, for example, offers country parks, woodland, moorland and reservoirs. It was the 3rd Duke of Bridgewater who commissioned the first canal in the country, linking his coal mines with Manchester and Liverpool. By 1850, 4,000 miles of canals transported 30 million tonnes of freight throughout the country

Liver Building, Liverpool

each year. They have long since ceased to fulfil their original role, but many stretches have been restored to become a splendid leisure amenity. Several canals run through Greater Manchester, including the Ashton Canal, the Bridgewater Canal, the Leeds & Liverpool Canal, the Rochdale Canal and the Manchester Ship Canal.

The main towns of Greater Manchester - Bolton, Bury, Oldham, Rochdale, Stockport, Wigan - have all retained a great sense of history with restored old industrial buildings and a variety of museums, and careful, public-spirited planning has ensured that they all offer plenty of green spaces for walking and leisure activities. Among the finest of the attractions outside the towns are Bramall Hall, a wonderful old 'magpie' house near Cheadle Hulme, Haigh Hall & Country Park near Wigan, and Hall I' th' Wood near Bolton.

LIVERPOOL

Liverpool has been completely transformed in recent years, is currently gearing up for its role as the European City of Culture for 2008. The title is awarded by the European Union to celebrate the cultural identity of Europe's greatest cities and alternates annually among the member states. The most striking example of this transformation is **Albert Dock**, a painstakingly restored masterpiece of Victorian architecture. Designed by Jesse Hartley and built to hold the biggest sailing ships of the day, it was opened by Prince Albert in 1846. By the end of the 19th century steam had largely replaced sail and the Dock was in decline. It finally closed in 1972 and stood derelict for some years. 1984 saw the start of its rebirth, and now the Dock is among the country's most popular heritage attractions, with some four million visitors a year. Behind the giant cast-iron columns and huge brick facades are dozens of visitor attractions, shops and retail outlets, restaurants, cafés, offices, TV studios and luxury apartments.

In modern times, it was the Beatles who really put the city on the map worldwide, and the Fab Four are still responsible for a large proportion of the millions of tourists who now flock here each year. The annual Beatle Week is by far the busiest time to visit Liverpool, and 2003 saw its 20th anniversary. **The Beatles Story** is the city's major tribute to its four most famous sons, a walk-through experience that recreates the sights and sounds of the Merseybeat era. The National Trust is responsible for two of the Beatles' homes. **Mendips** was the childhood home of John Lennon, where he lived with his Aunt Mimi and Uncle George, while **20 Forthlin Road** was the terraced home of Paul McCartney during the early years of the Beatles. Here they composed and rehearsed their earliest songs. Visits to these houses start from Albert Dock or Speke Hall.

Albert Dock's many other visitor attractions include **Tate Liverpool** which is the largest gallery of modern and contemporary art outside London and specialises in works from 1900 to the present day. Spread over four floors, it is one of four Tates, the others being Tate Britain and Tate Modern in London and Tate St Ives in Cornwall. Tate Liverpool hosts regular special exhibitions and has a year-round programme of tours, informal gallery talks, study days and Sunday family events.

Merseyside Maritime Museum is three museums in one - the Maritime Museum with its Transatlantic Slavery Gallery, the Museum of Liverpool Life and HM Customs & Excise National Museum.

Liverpool has many other notable architectural gems apart from Albert Dock. Among these are **Liverpool Museum**, whose collections cover archaeology, ethnology and the natural and physical sciences; the **Walker**, with 600 years of art including masterpieces by Rubens, Rembrandt, Poussin, Gainsborough and Hogarth; and St George's Hall, one of the finest neo-classical buildings in the world.

Liverpool boasts two spectacular cathedrals, one Anglican, the other Roman Catholic. The Anglican **Liverpool Cathedral** is an amazing 20th century Gothic-style masterpiece, begun in 1904 when the foundation stone was laid by King Edward VII and completed in 1978, when Queen Elizabeth II attended the celebrations. Even through two world wars, work never ceased, and, though the city was assailed repeatedly by enemy bombs, the cathedral escaped

The Metropolitan Cathedral of Christ the King, Liverpool

in 1967, but in the previous century there was a scheme to build a cathedral second only in size to St Peter's. Only the crypt was built, and that can be visited on a guided tour.

The **Liverpool Football Club Museum & Tour Centre** celebrates all things Liverpool, past, present and future, including a re-creation of the standing Kop. The tour takes in the dressing room, the team dug-out and the tunnel, and displays in the museum cover the whole history of the club. Fans of The Toffees will make for Goodison Park for a tour of **Everton Football Club**.

AROUND LIVERPOOL

SEFTON PARK
3 miles SE of Liverpool City Centre

The beautifully restored centrepiece of the park is the **Palm House**, opened in 1896 and rescued from a dilapidated state in the early 1990s. Re-opened in 2002, The Grade II* listed octagonal three-tiered structure houses plants from around the world in the Liverpool Botanical Collection and stages a year-round programme of events and concerts.

SPEKE
8 miles SE of Liverpool City Centre off the A561

Dating from 1490, **Speke Hall** is one of the greatest half-timbered houses in the country, set in splendid gardens and woodland that belie its location in the Liverpool suburbs close to the airport. The interior spans the centuries, from the Tudor Great Hall to Jacobean plasterwork and the Victorian oak parlour and kitchens. Other attractions include the restored Home Farm building, a children's play area and a

serious damage. Designed by Giles Gilbert Scott and built mainly of locally quarried sandstone, the cathedral abounds in superlatives: the largest Anglican cathedral in Europe; the largest church organ in the world, with 9,765 pipes; the highest and heaviest ringing peal of bells in the world.

The **Metropolitan Cathedral of Christ the King** is a dramatic modern masterpiece, its focal point being a circular nave of glass and concrete, the work of Sir Frederick Gibberd. The Lantern Tower of the nave contains the world's largest stained-glass window, designed by John Piper and Patrick Reyntiens. This cathedral was completed giant maize maze. The Hall also hosts a programme of events from Easter onwards.

KNOWSLEY

5 miles E of Liverpool City Centre off the A580

Easily reached from the city, via the A580 and the M57 (Junction 2), **Knowsley Safari Park** brings visitors face to face with the great outdoors and creatures of the wild. A five-mile safari drive gets close to baboons, lions, tigers, zebras, elephants, rhinos, bison, ostriches, camels, wildebeest and many other creatures. In the walkabout area are a reptile house, children's lake farm, otter pools, giraffes and meerkats, performing sea lions and parrots, as well as a restaurant and snack bar and over 20 rides, including dodgems, a pirate ship and a mini railway.

Heavy Horses at Sefton Park

The only one of its kind in the UK, the **National Wildflower Centre** in Court Hey Park is a peaceful place where visitors can learn about the huge variety of colourful wildflowers native to this country.

ST HELENS

12 miles E of Liverpool City Centre

St Helens was once a centre of the glass industry, a heritage that is illustrated in the fascinating displays in the **World of Glass**. Here, visitors can learn about the history and the techniques, both through interactive displays and through regular demonstrations by the resident glass artists.

NEWTON-LE-WILLOWS

15 miles E of Liverpool on the A580

One mile from Junction 23 of the M6, Haydock Park is the region's premier year-round racecourse, with 30 days racing on the flat and over the jumps. Highlights of the year include the Peter Marsh Chase and Swinton Hurdle under National Hunt rules and the Stanley Leisure Sprint Cup on the flat. Newton-le-Willows was the site of the first fatal railway accident. William Huskisson, MP for Liverpool, alighted from a carriage on the opening day of the Manchester & Liverpool Railway and was struck by a train hauled by George Stephenson's *Rocket*.

WEST DERBY

4 miles NE of Liverpool City Centre close to the M57/A580 junction

Croxteth Hall & Country Park is the Edwardian country estate of the Earl of Sefton, a place with many attractions for all ages. The Hall itself - elegant, opulent and beautifully maintained - stands in a

500-acre estate that includes a working farm, a lovely walled garden and a country park with woodland, wildlife, an adventure playground and a riding centre. Special events staged throughout the year include flower shows, family-fun days and murder mystery nights.

AINTREE

3 miles N of Liverpool City Centre on the A59

One of the most popular sporting attractions around Liverpool is the **Grand National Experience** at Aintree racecourse. The tours, which take place at 11am and 2pm on Tuesday and Friday, take in the museum and picture gallery, the weighing room, parade ring, stables, stewards room, a simulated race of champions, a virtual reality ride, Red Rum's statue, Red Rum's grave, a tour of the actual racecourse, souvenir shop, coffee shop and picnic area. Red Rum's record in the world's greatest steeplechase is one that will probably never be equalled: three times a winner (1973, 1974 & 1977) and twice runner-up (1975 & 1976).

Year by year, the facilities for spectators at the Grand National are improving, and there are other meetings apart from the three-day Grand National fixture: Ladies night May evening meeting, Family Day meeting in October, Becher Chase Day in November. The Visitor Centre at the course is open Tuesday to Friday late May to late October, and at other times by appointment.

SEFTON

5 miles N of Liverpool off the A59

This quiet old village stands at the edge of a rich and fertile plain of farmland that lies just behind the West Lancashire coast. It formed part of the estate of the Earls of Sefton (descendants of the Molyneux family) right up until 1972. The village has a pub, a 16th century corn mill and a delightful church, **St Helen's**, with a 14th century spire. Inside, there's a beautifully restored ceiling with bosses and moulded beams, 16th century screens, well-preserved box pews, two medieval effigies of knights, and an elaborately carved pulpit of 1635. A series of brasses recounts the history of the Molyneux family from their arrival in Britain with William the Conqueror. Though this is a small village, its name has also been given to the large metropolitan district of north Merseyside which stretches from Bootle to Southport.

INCE BLUNDELL

6 miles N of Liverpool off the A565

The village takes part of its name from the Blundell family who have for centuries exerted much influence on the village and surrounding area. Ince comes from the Celtic word 'Ynes' which means an island within a watery meadow and it would have perfectly described the village's situation before the surrounding land was drained.

The annual candlelight service at the village **Church of the Holy Family** is an ancient custom that appears to be unique to this county. The people of the parish decorate the graves in the cemetery with flowers and candles before holding a service there. Common in Belgium, this custom was brought to the village at the beginning of the 20th century.

LYDIATE

7 miles N of Liverpool on the A5147

This is another pleasant old village bordering the flat open farmland created from the West Lancashire mosses. Lydiate itself means an enclosure with a gate to stop cattle roaming and, though the age of the settlement here is uncertain, the now ruined **St Katharine's Chapel** dates from the 15th century. However, the most frequented building in the village is **The Scotch Piper**, a lovely cruck-framed house with a thatched roof that has the reputation for being the oldest pub in the region.

FORMBY

12 miles N of Liverpool off the A565

Like Ormskirk, Formby has a connection with potatoes. It's said that sailors who had travelled with Sir Walter Raleigh to Virginia brought back potatoes with them and grew them in the fields around what was then a small village. There are still many acres of potato fields being cultivated in the area. To the west of the town, **Formby Point** and Ainsdale National Nature Reserve form the most extensive dune system in Britain, 450 acres of wood and duneland. Formby Point was the site of Britain's first lifeboat station, built in 1776 and still to be seen.

The origins of this small coastal town lie in the time of the Vikings and the name Formby comes from the Norse Fornebei meaning Forni's town. Between the Norman Conquest and the time of the Dissolution in 1536, there were a succession of landowners but, by the mid-16th century, the Formby and Blundell families emerged as the chief owners. Formby Hall, built for William Formby in 1523, occupies a site that was first developed in the 1100s.

Today, Formby is perhaps better known as a quiet and desirable residential area and also the home of an important red squirrel sanctuary at the National Trust **Freshfield Nature Reserve** and pine

Sand Dunes at Freshfield, Formby

forest. From the shoreline there are magnificent views over the Mersey estuary and, on a clear day, the hills of Wales and of Lakeland are also visible. The whole stretch of this coastline is filled with birding sites, from Seaforth Nature Reserve on the Mersey Estuary to Marshside RSPB Reserve north of Southport.

AINSDALE

17 miles N of Liverpool on the A565

Towards the sea, from the centre of the village, lies what was Ainsdale-on-Sea with its old Lido and the more modern Pontin's holiday village. Between here and Formby, further down the coast, the sand dunes form part of the **Ainsdale National Nature Reserve**, one of the most extensive dune systems in the country. It's also one of the few

Freshfield

Distance:	3.7 mile (5.9 kilometres)
Typical time:	120 mins
Height gain:	0 metres
Map:	Explorer 285
Walk:	ww.walkingworld.com ID:257
Contributor:	Jim grindle

Access Information:

The walk starts at Freshfield station on the Southport /Liverpool line. Access by road is from the A565. Follow the tourist signs to Formby Point (National Trust). The route crosses the railway line where there is parking. Alternatively, park in the National Trust reserve and start the walk from Waymark 10.

Description:

The walk follows the railway line to a crossing and then goes through a golf course. An extensive plantation of Corsican Pine is entered on a track leading to the beach. You turn into the National Trust property and through the woods again before a short road walk to the station.

Additional Information

There are several shops by the station where you can buy food and drink. The Freshfield Hotel can be found by turning left at the crossroads 200m inland from the level crossing. There are toilets suitably concealed inside a man-made sand dune in the National Trust reserve. There are usually ice-cream vans here also.

The reserve is one of the remaining strongholds of the red squirrel in England and they can be seen throughout the woods. The place where you would be unlucky not to see one would be in the area near the Warden's hut shown at waymark 10. These woods are also the first place recorded in Britain where the collared dove nested after it spread from its traditional habitat in central Europe in the '50s. On the beach, but more particularly in winter, are thousands of waders and sea birds.

Overhead you may see some of the huge flocks of pink-footed geese that winter here from Iceland. From the beach you can usually see the North Wales coast with the Clwydian hills (highest point Moel Famau) to the left and the Carneddau to the right. In the other direction, the Lake district can also be seen but usually needs colder air; Blackpool Tower is often visible, however.

Features:

Sea, Pub, Toilets, National Trust/NTS, Wildlife, Birds, Flowers, Great Views, Good for Wheelchairs

Walk Directions:

1 On leaving the platform turn left and left again at the telephone box. Walk past this row of shops and then the station car park.

2 At the end of the car park you can continue on the road or branch left onto the bridleway - they join up again further on. The tarmac ends at the last house and becomes a gravelled track.

3 Take the fork left on the wider track, following the railway line as far as a level crossing.

4 Go over the railway line and follow the track through a golf course, until you reach a metal gate at the entrance to the National Nature Reserve.

5 Take the left fork, which takes you for 1km between the golf course on the left and the reserve on the right. White-topped posts indicate the right way, but you have only to keep to the broad, gravelled track. Go through a more open area where the pines give way to birch, willows and sea-buckthorn with orange berries. There is a last stand of pine and you reach a junction by the sand dunes. This is as far as you can go in a wheelchair but it is very pleasant - reverse your outward route.

6 Take the fork left which winds between buckthorn, with the woods to the left and the sea behind the dunes to the right. After 1km the path leads to the beach. Again there are white-topped posts.Ahead of you is the Welsh coast.

7 Keeping in the same direction, i.e. the sea on your right, walk along the beach. Paths off the beach are marked by 2m-high posts with yellow tops and a name. Go as far as the fourth of these, marked 'Victoria Road South'.

8 Turn left and climb by the fence to the top of the dunes.

9 A board walk leads down into the car park. Keep going right through (past the coach in the photograph) and onto a concrete road leading to the Wardens' hut and the exit from the National Trust property. Just before this hut you will find the toilets and also drinking water for dogs. Look on the right for 'Squirrel Walk' - this is the best place to see them. The wardens sell food that will tempt the squirrels to eat out of your hand.

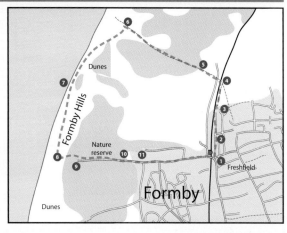

10 Keep straight on and the concrete road gives way to tarmac - Victoria Road.

11 You can check that you are on Victoria Road at the postbox. It is less than 1km back to the station, directly down this road.

remaining habitats of the endangered natterjack toad which breeds in the shallow pools that form in the sand dunes. This quirky creature is the only species of toad that walks rather than hops. As well as supporting the toads, the salt pools are the natural habitat for a variety of rare dune plants, including Dune Helleborine, Grass of Parnassus and Round-Leaved Wintergreen.

SOUTHPORT

Besides offering a step back in time, the broad promenades of Southport, its elegant tree-lined streets, and its superb shopping still makes this one of the most visited towns in this region.

The fashion for sea-bathing is usually reckoned to have originated with George III's regular dips at Weymouth in the late 1700s, but at Southport they'd already been doing it for generations. Only once

a year though, on St Cuthbert's Eve, the Sunday following August 20th. The holiday became known as 'Bathing Sunday, when folk travelled some distance to throw off their clothes and frolick naked in the sea'. The tradition was associated with the legend, or fact, that St Cuthbert had once been shipwrecked but had miraculously been able to swim to the shore and safety.

Southport's history as an all-year, rather than a one-day-a-year resort began in 1792 when its first hotel was built. A local man, 'Duke' Sutton, went to the beach, gathered all the driftwood he could find, nailed it together, put in the minimum of furniture, and opened for business.

Within a few years other houses and hotels had sprung up among the dunes and by 1802 'Duke' Sutton felt confident enough to rebuild his makeshift, if environmentally-friendly hotel, in stone.

FORGE BRASSERIE

Queen Anne Street, Southport,
Lancashire PR8 1EH
Tel: 01704 500522 Fax: 01704 546359
e-mail: forgebrasserie.co.uk
website: www.forgebrasserie.co.uk

Tucked away in one of Southport's little known streets, yet close to the centre of town, is a real hidden gem. The Forge Brasserie has established a far-reaching reputation for being one of the northwest's finest steak and seafood restaurants. It was taken over in 2000 by Barry and Maureen Wilkinson who run the place together with head chef Gary Moyses and second chef John Boardman.

The restaurant is housed in what was originally a blacksmith's – hence the name – although over the years it has been used as a fire station and a printing company. Today, the interior remains simple yet stylish, retaining some of its original character with the blacksmith's fireplace still apparent. There are seating areas downstairs and upstairs with the bar located in a light and airy courtyard. One

of the highlights is the open plan kitchen where customers can watch the chefs in action and be seduced by the sights, smells and sounds of the busy goings-on.

The restaurant is open at lunchtime and evenings, Monday to Saturday, and its extensive menus give pride of place to fish, seafood and steaks, although there is much more to tempt the appetite as well. Everything is freshly prepared to order using only the freshest of ingredients and you can choose your own fish or lobster prior to cooking. The à la carte selection includes such delights as Boston clam chowder, oysters, hot duck salad and the Famous Forge money bags – filo pastry parcels stuffed with spinach, blue cream cheese and spring onions – and that's just for starters.

The main course choices include chicken, lamb, the finest steaks and some classic fish dishes such as Coquilles Saint-Jacques and Lobster Thermidor. At lunchtime, the menu places more emphasis on lighter meal selections, with other more traditional dishes available. An early evening fixed price menu is served Tuesday to Friday, and there's a two-course special menu on Monday evenings. Tuesday is Steak Promotion Night when 11 steak dishes are greatly reduced in price; on Fridays, it's the turn of 19 fish dishes to be offered at these not-to-be-missed prices.

Booking is advisable at all times to avoid disappointment, especially at weekends and for the special themed evenings in the week. Major credit cards are accepted and party bookings are welcome.

Lord Street, Southport

lands of the two neighbouring lords of the manor. A superb shopping street today, the exceptionally wide pavements, with gardens along one side and an elegant glass-topped canopy along most of the other side, make this one of the most pleasant places to shop in the country. Many of the town's classical style buildings are found along its length and it has been designated a conservation area. Off Lord Street, there is one of the town's several covered arcades – **Wayfarers Arcade**, built in 1898 and a fine example of these popular shopping malls. The modest entrance opens out into a beautiful cast-iron and glass conservatory with a first floor gallery and splendid central dome. Originally named the Leyland Arcade after the town's Member of Parliament, it took its present name in 1976 after the arcade's most successful leaseholder.

Over-confident as it turned out. The following year he was thrown into Lancaster gaol for debt and later died a pauper.

Southport though continued to thrive and by the 1860s was by far the most popular seaside resort in Lancashire. The town's only problem was that its main attraction, the sea, was getting further and further away as silt from the Ribble estuary clogged the beach. The town council's response was to build the second-longest pier in the country, complete with a miniature railway which is still operating, create numerous parks and gardens, and construct elegant boulevards such as Lord Street. All that activity in Victorian times imbued the town with an appealingly genteel atmosphere which, happily, it still retains.

The town's central, main boulevard, **Lord Street**, is a mile long road that was built along the boundary bordering the

In a central position along Lord Street stands Southport's rather modest **Town Hall**. Built in 1852 and of a classical design, its facade includes a beautiful carving in bold relief of the figures of Justice, Mercy, and Truth picked out in white against a Wedgwood blue background. Further along, the Atkinson Central Library was built in 1879 as the premises of the Southport and West Lancashire Bank. The original ceiling of the banking hall can still be seen as can its fireplace. On the first floor is the **Atkinson Art Gallery**, which contains collections of British art and Chinese porcelain. In Shakespeare Street, the **British Lawnmower Museum** is a

PHILLIP GODFREY DESIGNER GOLDSMITH

6 Bold Street, Southport,
Merseyside PR9 0DD
Tel: 01704 544817
e-mail: godfreyphillip@hotmail.com
website: www.phillipgodfrey.biz

Designer and goldsmith **Phillip Godfrey** and his wife Elizabeth run their eponymous shop in smart premises just off Lord Street – the main shopping street of Southport. Apprenticed as a goldsmith in 1973 in his native Birmingham, Phillip became a master of his profession, building a lofty reputation for superb design and craftsmanship in precious

metals.

The shop, which he opened 17 years ago, has attractive window displays and a ground floor showroom. An ever-changing 'off-the-shelf' selection of jewellery is available at prices ranging from £10 to £10,000 and combines well with his own designer range. Phillip has built up a large clientele who regularly travel from London and beyond to seek out his distinctive designs. To complement these, he has added the popular jewellery ranges 'Pistachio' and Gecko's 'Concepts'. For late 2005, Phillip designed a range of unusual colour and shaped freshwater pearls mounted in precious metals.

The demand for Phillip's hand-made platinum rings and bespoke commissions has grown hugely during 2005 and appointments are now a necessity.

tribute to the gardening machinery industry, with an unrivalled collection of machines, many from the Victorian and Edwardian eras, as well as lawnmowers once owned by such celebrities as Princess Diana and Vanessa Feltz.

Not all the notable buildings in Southport are Victorian and the Top Rank Bingo Club, originally called the Garrick Theatre, was held to be the finest theatre when it was opened in 1932. With much of its exterior as it would have appeared when it first opened, it is a wonderful example of the Art Deco style. Finally, Lord Street is also home to the town's war memorial, **The Monument**. Opened on Remembrance Day 1923 by the Earl of Derby, this is a large and grand memorial that remains the town's focal point. Its design was the subject of a competition and the winning entry was submitted by Garyson and Barnish, designers of the famous Royal Liver Building in Liverpool. The central obelisk is flanked by twin colonnades on which the names of the town's more than 1,000 dead are inscribed.

Every self-respecting Victorian resort had a **Promenade** and Southport's is a typical example, flanked by grand hotels on the land side and a series of formal gardens on the other. Here you'll also find the **Model Railway Village** set in beautifully landscaped and sheltered gardens.

As the silting up of the Ribble estuary progressed unchecked the **Marine Lake** was constructed at the northern end of the promenade. At over 86 acres, this man-made lake is the largest in Britain and as well as being an attractive site and a place for the pursuit of all manner of watersports it is also host to an annual 24-hour yacht race.

From the centre of the promenade

BRITISH LAWNMOWER MUSEUM

106-114 Shakespeare Street, Southport, Lancashire PR8 5AJ
Tel: 01704 501336 Fax: 01704 500564
e-mail: info@lawnmowerworld.co.uk
website: www.lawnmowerworld.co.uk

The **British Lawnmower Museum**, located in the picturesque Victorian seaside holiday resort of Southport, houses a collection of pristine exhibits of special interest built up over a period of over 50 years and is now a tribute to the garden machinery industry which has developed over the past 170 years. Many of the machines have been rescued from the scrap yard and restored to their present very high standard. In addition to early grass cutting and garden machines dating from the 1830s, the exhibition houses the largest collection of vintage toy lawnmowers and games in the world.

The lawnmower was invented in 1830 by Edwin Budding of Gloucester, thought of as a madman testing the strange contraption at night. Originally designed to trim the nap from cloth, the cylinder machine he devised has not changed in principle since that date and has been the only traditional lawnmower for formal lawns used throughout Great Britain.

Included in this unique national collection are manufacturers not normally associated with the garden industry, names such as Rolls Royce, Royal Enfield, Daimler, Hawker Sidley, Perkins Diesel, British Leyland and many more. A lot of the exhibits, memorabilia and industrial artifacts are from the Victorian and Edwardian era and have been restored and keep a small part of British engineering heritage alive. In addition there are many examples previously owned by the rich and famous.

extends Southport's **Pier** which, at 1,460 yards long was the longest pier in the country until 1897. Following a fire in 1933 it was shortened but it remains the second longest in the country. Looking at the pier today it is hard to imagine that at the end of the last century pleasure steamers were able to depart from here to Barrow in Cumbria, Bangor, Wales, and the Isle of Man. Along the shore line, and opened in the spring of 1998, the new sea wall and **Marine Drive** is a wonderful modern construction, the length of Southport's sea front, that blends well with the town's Victorian heritage.

The normal attractions of a seaside resort have not been forgotten and **Pleasureland** is the obvious choice for those seeking thrills and hair-raising rides; the 100+ rides and attractions include the country's tallest, fastest looping coaster, go-karts, kids' quad bikes and bumper boats. Keen gardeners will know Southport for its splendid annual Flower Show, second only to Chelsea, and golfers will be familiar with the name of Royal Birkdale Golf Course, just south of the town centre. Southport has one more sporting association of which it is justly proud. From behind a car show room in the 1970s, Ginger McCain trained Red Rum on the sands of Southport to a record breaking three magnificent wins in the Grand National run at Aintree. A statue of the great horse can be seen in Wayfarers Arcade.

AROUND SOUTHPORT

CHURCHTOWN

1 mile NE of Southport on the A5267

This charming village, complete with thatched cottages, has retained much of its village feel and is certainly worthy of exploration in its own right.

Considerably predating the seaside resort, Churchtown is, as its name suggests, centred around its church. Since it is dedicated to St Cuthbert, it is possible that while fleeing from the Danes, the monks of Lindisfarne rested here with the remains of their famous saint.

However, it is likely that the village was, for many years, known by the name of North Meols and a chapel of Mele is mentioned in the *Domesday Book*. Derived from the Norse word 'melr' meaning sand dune, there was certainly a thriving fishing village here in the early 1100s. In 1224, Robert de Coudrey granted the village the right to hold a market, the likely place for which is the cross standing opposite the church in the heart of the village.

As the settlement lay on a crossroads and at the start of a route over the sands of the Ribble estuary, it was a place of considerable importance. It was also here that the tradition of sea bathing in this area began, when, in 1219 St Cuthbert's Eve was declared a fair day, which later became known as Bathing Sunday.

There is still plenty to see in this small village. The present **Meols Hall** dates from the 17th century but its appearance today is largely thanks to the work carried out by the late Colonel Roger Fleetwood Hesketh in the 1960s. When the colonel took over the house in the late 1930s, the older and larger part of the hall had been demolished in 1733 and the remaining building was rather nondescript. Taking the gabled bay of the late 17th century, extensions were added to give the house a varied roofline and a three dimensional frontage.

The hall is the last home of the Hesketh family who at one time had owned most of the coastal area between Southport and Heysham. Originally, the manor had been granted to Robert de

Coudrey, coming into the Hesketh family by marriage in the late 16th century. There has been a house on this site since the 13th century. Occasionally open to visitors, the hall has a fine art collection and, in the entrance hall, are three carved chairs that were used in Westminster Abbey during the coronation of

Urbis, Manchester

Charles II. During World War I, Moels Hall was used as a military hospital.

Planned on the site of the old Churchtown Strawberry Gardens in 1874, the **Botanic Gardens**, restored in 1937, are beautifully maintained and present a superb example of classic Victorian garden design. With magnificent floral displays, a boating lake, wide, twisting paths, and a fernery, little has changed here since the day the gardens were first opened by the Rev Charles Hesketh. Built in 1938, following the gardens' restoration, the **Botanic Bowling Pavilion** mimics the style of the late Regency architect Decimus Burton. Here, too, is the Botanic Gardens Museum, with its fine exhibition on local history and its gallery of Victoriana.

MANCHESTER

Like Liverpool, Manchester has seen an urban renaissance as new buildings and open spaces have been developed, transforming the face of the city.

Santiago Calatrava's Trinity Bridge, Bridgewater Hall, home of the Hallé Orchestra, and the City of Manchester Stadium take their places as landmarks alongside the splendid Town Hall, the Cathedral and the Baroque Church of St Ann with its rare glass by William Peckitt of York. The Victorian **Town Hall**, perhaps the finest in the country, is the work of Alfred Waterhouse; its many treasures include a wealth of stained glass and mosaic, and Ford Madox Brown's murals in the Great Hall.

Manchester's museums and art galleries are the most impressive and diverse outside London. All repay lengthy visits, and in particular the **Museum of Science & Industry**, telling the story of the world's first major industrial city; the **Jewish Museum** housed in the city's oldest purpose-built synagogue; **Manchester Museum** in the University, famed for its Egyptian collections; the ultra-modern **Urbis** with interactive displays exploring life in different cities of the world; the **Manchester United Museum** in Trafford; the **City Art Gallery**; the

Whitworth Gallery, best known for its British watercolours; and the **John Rylands Library**, built by Basil Champneys to house the library of the cotton magnate.

Four miles to the north of the city centre, **Heaton Park** is the largest of Manchester's open spaces. Its 640 acres nestle in the foothills of the Pennines and over the last few years its rolling landscape has been restored to its original character when it was part of the estate surrounding Heaton Hall, home of the Earls of Wilton. The hall itself was rebuilt from 1772 onwards by the architect James Wyatt and is a striking example of neo-classical decoration. The newly restored Orangery is also open to the public and a popular venue for wedding celebrations and receptions.

Victoria Building and Mariners Canal Bridge, Salford Quays

Seven miles to the east of Manchester is the district of **Tameside**, much of which is open land comprising moorland, country parks, reservoirs and woodland. At Portland Basin, where three canals meet, is a new heritage centre that hosts special events throughout the year, including the Tameside Canals Festival.

AROUND MANCHESTER

SALFORD

4 miles W of Manchester city centre off the M602

Salford's major attraction is undoubtedly **The Lowry**, located in the fashionable Salford Quays. A stunning modern complex overlooking the Manchester Ship Canal, The Lowry houses two theatres and an exciting children's activity gallery as well as the eponymous Lowry collection. L S (Laurence Stephen) Lowry, noted for his distinctive paintings

of Northern industrial landscapes, spent some time as a rent collector. He was granted the freedom of Salford in 1965 and is buried in Manchester Southern Cemetery, which is also the final resting place of Sir Matt Busby, for 50 years intimately associated with Manchester United. A footbridge to the Trafford side of the canal leads from The Lowry to the **Imperial War Museum North**, a fantastic aluminium-clad building whose three metal 'shards' represent conflict on air, sea and land. Its exhibits are dedicated to ordinary people and their stories whether far from home in a battle zone or growing up in the midst of war.

Also within the Quays complex is the **Salford Museum & Art Gallery** which houses art from the 19th century to the present day; a fine collection of statuary; a unique reconstruction of a Victorian cobbled street and hands-on displays of local history. Another museum, **Ordsall Hall**, occupies Salford's oldest building, a superb black and white timbered structure dating from Elizabethan times. Within this Grade I listed building, exhibits cover more than 600 years of the town's history.

Just minutes from the town centre are two great lungs: Blackleach Country Park, reclaimed from former industrial land to become a scenic oasis; and Clifton Country Park which has been imaginatively developed from what was the Wet Earth Colliery, one of the first deep mines to be sink in the Irwell Valley and established around 1740.

ALTRINCHAM

8 miles SW of Manchester on the A560

The writer Thomas de Quincey visited Altrincham in the early 1800s and thought its bustling market "the gayest scene he ever saw". The market was established by Royal Charter in 1290 is still very active, although the old houses that de Quincey also noted have sadly gone. The market is now centred on a Victorian hall opened in 1880, and the range of stalls is splendidly diverse (though the goods for sale do not now run to wives - it is recorded that in 1823 a man sold his wife by auction for the equivalent of 7½p!). A modern bustling town, Altrincham nevertheless has a long history, with clear evidence that there was a settlement beside the River Bollin some 6,000 years ago. Even older than that is the prehistoric body

preserved in peat discovered on Lindow Common nearby. From Victorian times, Altrincham has been a favoured retreat for Manchester businessmen and the town is well supplied with inns and restaurants.

STOCKPORT

6 miles SE of Manchester on the A6

Nearly 50 percent of the borough is green space, so visitors will find plenty of opportunities for walking and enjoying the countryside. One of the town's most fascinating attractions is the **Hat Works**, located in the restored Wellington Mill. It is the country's first and only museum dedicated to hats and hat-making, and visitors can learn about Stockport's historic links with hatting (more than 4,500 people were employed in the industry here at the end of the 19th century), see the original machinery and enjoy an amazing display of hats of all shapes and sizes, from miniature hats made by apprentices to the world's tallest topper. Close by are **Stockport Museum** – one of the first purpose built museums in the UK and located in the delightful Victorian Vernon Park, and the **Air Raid Shelters** which provide a trip back in time to the Second World War, when tunnels were built into the red sandstone rock to accommodate thousands of people seeking refuge from air raids.

Only recently opened to the public,

STOCKPORT AIR RAID SHELTERS

61 Great Underbank, Stockport, Cheshire SK1 1NE
Tel: 0161 474 1940

Stockport's unique **Air Raid Shelters** have been carved into the natural sandstone cliffs in Stockport town centre and are the largest purpose built Second World War civilian underground air raid shelters. They were boarded up after the war and rediscovered a few years ago, since when they have been imaginatively restored to give visitors the feel of wartime Britain.

Visitors can explore the labyrinth of underground passages and wander through the reconstructed Warden's post, Toilets, First Aid Room, Canteen Tool Stores, Benches and Bunkers that once housed over 5,000 people during a night in the Blitz.

BRAMALL HALL

Bramhall Park, Bramhall, Stockport, Cheshire SK7 1NK
Tel: 0845 8330974

Bramall Hall is known as one of "England's treasures". It is a magnificent black and white Tudor manor house with Victorian additions set in 70 acres of beautiful parkland, which is landscaped in the style of Capability Brown. Take a tour of this beautiful house and you'll discover the spectacular Tudor plaster pendant ceiling, a wonderful 16th century embroidered table carpet and the wonderful wall paintings discovered by the Victorian owner.

The new costumed interpretation will give you a feel of the household in Bramall in 1890, with glimpses of the family from upstairs and the staff from downstairs. After a tour around this beautiful house, relax in the tearoom or restaurant and be tempted by delicious cakes, scrumptious light refreshments or a three-course lunch. Bramall Hall provides a pleasurable learning experience with a fascinating day out.

Staircase House in the Market Place is a beautifully restored medieval town house which is famous for its rare cage newell staircase. Visitors journey through time from the building's humble beginnings as a cruck-framed structure to the splendour of the 17th century town house.

A few miles east of Stockport is another fascinating building, the **Chadkirk Chapel**. Set in the heart of Chadkirk Country Estate, this immaculately restored 14th century chapel has associations with the 7th century missionary St Chad. Visitors can relax in the peace of the chapel, then take a walk through woodlands and along the scenic Peak Forest Canal to Etherow Park.

CHEADLE HULME

7 miles S of Manchester on the A34

Developed in Victorian times as a commuter town for better-off workers in Manchester, Cheadle Hulme is a busy place with a fine park on its eastern edge in which stands one of the grandest old 'magpie' houses in Cheshire, **Bramall Hall**. This eye-catching, rambling perfection of black and white timbered buildings overlooks some 62 acres of exquisitely landscaped woods, lakes and formal gardens. The oldest parts of the Hall date from the 14th century: for five of the next six centuries it was owned by the same family, the Davenports. Over the years, the Davenport family continually altered and extended the originally quite modest manor house. But whenever they added a new Banqueting Hall, 'Withdrawing Room', or even a Chapel, they took pains to ensure that its design harmonised happily with its more ancient neighbours. Along with Little Moreton Hall and Gawsworth Hall, Bramall represents the fullest flowering of a lovely architectural style whose most distinctive examples are all to be found in Cheshire.

THE PANHANDLE

The narrow finger of land pointing up to West Yorkshire was chopped off from Cheshire in the 1974 Local Government redrawing of boundaries and put into Greater Manchester, but more than 30 years on most of its population still consider themselves Cheshire folk. At its northern end lie Longdendale and Featherbed Moss, Pennine scenery quite unlike anywhere else in the region.

MARPLE

10 miles SE of Manchester on the A626

Marple's most famous son is probably the poet and novelist Christopher Isherwood, who was born at Marple Hall in 1904 and could have inherited it from his grandfather had he so wished. Instead, the author of *Mr Norris Changes Trains* and *Sally Bowles* (the source material for the musical *Cabaret*) renounced the life of a country squire for the more sybaritic attractions of California. But Marple made a great impression on him as is evident in his book *Kathleen and Frank,* based on the letters and diaries of his parents.

Peak Forest Canal, Marple

Isherwood revels in the wildness of the Goyt Valley, not just its scenery but also its weather - "it never really dries out,"

NEEDHAMS FARM

Uplands Road, Werneth Low, Gee Cross, nr Hyde, Cheshire SK14 3AG
Tel: 0161 368 4610 Fax: 0161 367 9106
e-mail: charlotte@needhamsfarm.co.uk
website: www.needhamsfarm.co.uk

Set in idyllic rural surroundings, nestling beneath Werneth Low and Etherow Country Parks, **Needhams Farm** was originally built in 1662 and still retains its stone fireplaces and exposed beams. It is now the home of Charlotte and Ian Walsh, both of whom hail from Edinburgh and now welcome bed & breakfast guests. They moved to Werneth Low in 1984, taking over the 30-acre farm and bred cattle until 2000 when they ceased farming – but they still have Fred, their pet goat, and various sheep are to be found in the surrounding areas.

Charlotte, a former nurse, is an accomplished cook and, in addition to providing hearty breakfasts,

is also happy to serve home-cooked evening meals based on locally produced ingredients. Meals are served in the cosy dining room and Needhams Farm has a residential licence so you can enjoy a drink with your meal. Accommodation comprises four doubles, one family, and one single, all with en suite facilities, plus a twin room with private bathroom. All the bedrooms enjoy panoramic views over the Derbyshire and Cheshire countryside, and all are equipped with remote control colour TV, direct dial telephone, radio/clock alarm, hairdryer and hospitality tray.

Isherwood wrote.

Marple is also famous for its flight of 16 locks on the Peak Forest Canal and the mighty three-arched aqueduct that carries the canal over the River Goyt. At Marple, the Peak Forest Canal is joined by the Macclesfield Canal and there are some attractive towpath walks in both directions.

STALYBRIDGE

6 miles E of Manchester on the A57

Set beside the River Tame and with the North Pennine moors stretching for miles to the east, Stalybridge was one of the earliest cotton towns and its mill workers among the most radical and militant during the Chartist troubles of the 1840s. Oddly, one of their leaders was a former Methodist minister, the Rev. Joseph Rayner Stephens, who had broken away from the Wesleyan ministry and established his own 'Stephensite' chapels – one in King Street, Stalybridge, the other in the sister town across the Tame, Ashton under Lyme. He campaigned tirelessly against the long hours worked in the factories and the policy, introduced in 1834, of refusing poor relief outside the workhouse.

When in 1842 the mill-owners tried to impose reductions in pay, the workers' embryonic trade union closed all the mills in north Cheshire and south Lancashire. Stephens was tried and sentenced to 18 months in Chester gaol. On his release, he continued his efforts to improve the workers' pay and conditions for another 38 years. His funeral was attended by thousands and the workers erected a granite obelisk to his memory in Stalybridge's attractive Stamford Park. On it is inscribed a quotation from the speech he delivered at his trial: "The only true foundation of Society is the safety, the security and the

happiness of the poor, from whom all other orders of Society arise".

MERSEYSIDE AND GREATER MANCHESTER

Before the Industrial Revolution this was a sparsely populated region of remote hillside farms and cottages that relied, chiefly, on sheep farming and the wool trade. Many of the settlements date back to before the Norman Conquest and although little may have survived the rapid building of the 19th century there are three surprisingly wonderful ancient houses to be seen here: Smithills Hall and Hall-i'-th'-Wood at Bolton and Turton Tower, just to the north.

However, there is no escaping the textile industry. Lancashire's ideal climate for cotton spinning and weaving – damp so that the yarn does not break – made it the obvious choice for the building of the mills. There are numerous valleys with fast flowing rivers and streams and then the development of the extensive coalfields around Wigan supplied the fuel to feed the power hungry machinery. Finally, there was a plentiful supply of labour as families moved from the hill top sheep farms into the expanding towns and villages to work the looms and turn the wheels of industry.

In a very short time, smoke and soot filled the air and the once clear streams and rivers became lifeless valleys of polluted squalor. There are many illustrations in the region of the harsh working conditions the labourers had to endure and the dirt and filth that covered much of the area. Now that much of this has been cleaned up, the rivers running once again fast, clear, and supporting wildlife, the lasting legacy of those days is the splendid Victorian architecture of which every town has at least one example.

BOLTON

Synonymous with the Lancashire textile industry, Bolton is also an ancient town that predates its expansion due to cotton by many centuries. First settled during the Bronze Age, by the time of the Civil War, this was a market town supporting the surrounding villages. The town saw one of the bloodiest episodes of the war when James Stanley, Earl of Derby, was brought back here by Cromwell's troops after the Royalists had been defeated. In a savage act of revenge for the massacre his army had brought on the town early in the troubles, Stanley was executed and his severed head and body, in separate caskets, were taken back to the family burial place at Ormskirk. Whilst in captivity in the town, Stanley was kept prisoner at Ye Olde Man and Scythe Inn which, dating from 1251, is still standing in Churchgate today and is the town's oldest building.

Bolton is fortunate in having two particularly fine old mansions, both on the northern edge of the town. **Hall-i'-th'-Wood**, is a delightful part-timbered medieval merchant's house dating from 1530 to 1648. A fine example of a wealthy merchant's house, Hall i'th'Wood was saved from dereliction by Lord Leverhulme in 1900 and has been restored and furnished with displays of fine 17th and 18th century furniture along with interesting items of local importance. The hall has a second claim to fame since, for a number of years one of several tenants here was Samuel Crompton, the inventor in 1799 of the

Town Hall, Bolton

spinning mule. Naturally, the hall has a replica of Crompton's mule on display.

Bolton's second grand house, **Smithills Hall**, stands on an easily defended hill and was built in the 1300s as a pele, or fortified dwelling. It was extended over the years and this superb Grade I listed building now displays some of the best examples of medieval, Tudor and Victorian Arts & Crafts architecture in the region. The hall was bought by Bolton Corporation in the late 1930s and has been beautifully restored. In addition to the impressive collection of furniture and artifacts on display, the hall also hosts changing exhibitions throughout the year. As well as seeing one of the oldest and best preserved fortified manor houses in the county, visitors can also wander along the hall's wooded nature trail.

Close to Smithills Hall, in Moss Bank Park, is **Animal World & Butterfly House** which provides a safe habitat for a variety of animals and birds ranging from farm animals to chipmunks, from wildfowl and tropical birds. In the tropical atmosphere of the Butterfly House, are free-flying butterflies and moths as well as insects, spiders, reptiles and tropical plants.

The centre of Bolton is a lasting tribute to the wealth and prosperity generated by the spinning of high quality yarn for which the town was famous. The monumental **Town Hall**, opened in 1873, is typical of the classical style of buildings that the Victorian town fathers favoured – tours are available. The hall is still the town's central point and it is now surrounded by the recently refurbished pedestrianised shopping malls, market hall, and the celebrated **Octagon Theatre**. The town's excellent **Museum, Art Gallery & Aquarium** is one of the largest regional galleries in the northwest with excellent collections of fine and decorative art, including examples of British sculpture and contemporary ceramics. There are collections of natural history, geology, and Egyptian antiques here as well as some fine 18th and 19th century English watercolours and some contemporary British paintings and graphics.

Bolton's most recent major attraction is the state-of-the-art **Reebok Stadium**, home of Bolton Wanderers, one of the world's oldest football clubs. Visitors can take a look behind the scenes at one of Europe's finest stadiums, seeing everything from the players' changing-rooms to the bird's eye vantage point of the Press Box.

On the northwestern edge of the town is **Barrow Bridge Village**, a small model village built during the Industrial Revolution to house workers at the two six-storey mills that used to operate here. Small bridges cross a picturesque stream and a flight of 63 steps leads up the hillside to the moors. Barrow Bridge village was the inspiration for Benjamin Disraeli's famous novel *Coningsby*.

AROUND BOLTON

TURTON BOTTOMS
4 miles N of Bolton off the B6391

Turton Tower near Bolton was built both for defensive purposes and as a residence. In 1400, William Orrell erected his sturdy, four-square pele (fortified dwelling) in search of safety during those lawless and dangerous years. Some 200 years later, in more settled times, a lovely, half-timbered Elizabethan mansion was added. Successive owners made further additions in a charming motley of architectural styles. Quite apart from its enchanting appearance, Turton is well worth visiting to see its display of old weapons and a superb collection of vintage furniture, outstanding amongst which is the sumptuously carved Courtenay Bed of 1593.

RAMSBOTTOM
6 miles NE of Bolton on the A676

Ramsbottom is a no-nonsense stone-built Pennine hill town with steep roads leading out of town to the east and west. One of these leads to the **Peel Tower** which dominates the surrounding countryside. Erected in 1852 to commemorate the life of the area's most famous son, Sir Robert Peel, the tower is some 128 feet high. Now restored, the tower itself is occasionally open to the public and provides some spectacular views.

Peel Tower, Ramsbottom

In the Market Place is the Grant Arms, which commemorates two chief bigwigs

of the town in the early 1800s. The Grant brothers were immortalised by Charles Dickens as the Cheeryble brothers in *Nicholas Nickleby*. These generally philanthropic mill owners made sure of the profits of their pub by paying their workforce in tokens that could only be redeemed in the Grant Arms.

Ramsbottom is placed on the Irwell Sculpture Trail and in the Market Place is the wonderful *Tilted Vase* by Edward Allington. This two ton sculpture is

RAMSONS

18 Market Place, Ramsbottom, Lancashire BL0 9HT
Tel: 01706 825070
e-mail: chris@ramsoms.org.uk
website: www.ramsoms.org.uk

Back in 1985, chef Ros Hunter and her partner Chris Johnson opened a little restaurant in Ramsbottom. Their high profile menus featuring strictly seasonal and organic produce were well ahead of their time and quickly attracted the attention of national food writers. Twenty years later **Ramsons** has become something of a local institution as a place of celebration. Whilst Chris "continues to amuse and abuse the customers", Ros has retired from the stove which is now in the capable hands of Abdulla Naseem and Amy Bicknell who were complimented in the *Good Food Guide 2005* for their "heartfelt directness…translating prime

raw materials into simple straightforward ideas, with an intelligent streak". They describe their menus as "Italian-influenced" – a refined but simple cuisine that is fiercely respectful of the seasons and the pedigree of the ingredients. Ramsons beautiful food is complemented by a unique list of 200 Italian wines, all sourced directly from passionate small-scale winemakers, and also on sale in the basement "Hideaway" – a wine shop where simple everyday food is served in the style of an Italian Enoteca. Ramsons is open for lunch and dinner, Wednesday to Saturday; lunchtime only on Sundays.

THE CULTURED BEAN

9e Bridge Street, Ramsbottom, Lancashire BL0 9AB
Tel: 01706 825232

When Sharon Canavan and her daughter Leanne Entwistle opened **The Cultured Bean** in 2004, their aim was – and is – to serve the finest quality coffees, chocolate drinks and teas, supported by a light lunch, dessert and patisserie menu. "We are proud of our menu with regards to diversity and quality," says Sharon, "and we refuse to pay homage to the fast food industry." As well as the range of coffees which are fresh roasted and ground in house, the menu offers a choice of quality teas and hot chocolates, and refreshing soft drinks.

Eatables include speciality sandwiches, light dishes and

salads such as nicoise, and some wonderful desserts and pastries. To complement your meal, there's a good choice of mostly European wines at reasonable prices, and a selection of beers. It's not just the food and drink here that pleases. The décor of the Cultured Bean is a delight to the eye with its marble-topped tables and high-backed chairs with leather upholstery, all from Italy. Halogen lighting picks out the striking art works created by local artists that decorate the light-coloured walls. Finally, on the first Thursday evening of each month they feature cuisine and wine from a different country.

TASTE FINE FOODS

76 Bridge Street, Ramsbottom, Bury, Lancashire BL0 9AG
Tel: 01706 822175
e-mail: virginia@newton4432.freeserve.co.uk

The frontage of **Taste Fine Foods** looks very inviting with its high-arched Victorian style windows displaying just a few of the culinary treats to be found inside. Ginny Newton took over an existing delicatessen here in 2001, completely revamped the premises and greatly extended the choice of items on offer. On the ground floor you'll find an excellent selection of olives including Italian back and green ones, stuffed with garlic, pimento or almonds; pesto sauces; sun-dried tomatoes, pickled hot chillies and much, much more. Chocoholics can indulge themselves with the selection of French and English hand-made chocolates.

There's an extensive range of organic foods of every kind, beers from all around the world along with a small selection of wines, including organic ones. Spanish foods are well-represented along with Italian cheeses and salamis. A particularly popular item is the English Lakes ice cream from Cumbria with a choice of 16 different flavours. Also on sale are freshly-cut sandwiches made with locally-baked bread. From the ground floor a central wooden staircase leads down to The Big Cheese – an enticing display of some 40 or 50 varieties of cheese.

IMELDA'S

9 Square Street, Ramsbottom, Lancashire BL0 9BE
Tel: 01706 829829
e-mail: sales@imeldas.biz

It was said of Imelda Marcos that, "They searched her wardrobe for skeletons but only found fabulous shoes". Named after this most famous shoe collector of all time, **Imelda's** in Ramsbottom's town centre stocks an astonishing array of stunning footwear along with some superb handbags and other accessories. The boutique, with its distinctive cream canopy, was established in 2003 by Deana Stannard who had previously been working at Harrods in London. Deana travels twice a year to Milan, Paris and Spain to seek out the most striking quality footwear she can find. She also seeks out gorgeous hand-made handbags (mostly Italian) and accessories from such leading names as Rodo, Gardenia, Givenchy, Emilio Pucci and other select houses.

Back in Lancashire, these stunning creations are cleverly displayed with minimalist panache – a single shoe, for example, on its separate glass shelf. Subdued lighting and unobtrusive background music all add to the atmosphere of a shrine to the shoe. Deana and her knowledgeable and friendly staff provide a very personal service and Deana even offers an out-of-hours service if required. No wonder discerning shoppers travel from all over the northwest to marvel at the shoe's Imelda's displays.

COUNTRY CHIC

23 Bolton Street, Ramsbottom, Bury, Lancashire BLO 9HU
Tel: 01706 827090
e-mail: sarah@countrychic.co.uk
website: www.countrychic.co.uk

Opened in September 2003, **Country Chic** specialises in beautiful gifts for the home and garden. The first thing you notice in the shop is the wonderful aroma emanating from the gorgeous scented candles made locally in Waddington. The ground floor contains lots of lovely hand-made lavender-filled hearts, stainless steel tableware from Culinary Concepts which make fabulous gifts. Hand-painted mugs and jugs, locally-made hand-embroidered wall hangings, books, stationary and contemporary silver jewellery by Pistachio. In the potting shed at the rear you will find great garden gift ideas such as anti bug mugs, wallsconces, planters, plants in a bag and fabulous painted iron garden furniture.

The stock is displayed on French and Gustavian-style painted furniture (which is also for sale), alongside smaller pieces that Sarah paints herself using the Malabar paint range stocked in the shop. The first floor houses a magnificent Bordeaux-style bed, wonderful cotton quilted bedspreads and woollen throws, and a small range of fabrics, pretty table lamps and cushions. Also upstairs is the kitchen area with colourful enamelware from Garden Trading and Chandlers, and superb accessories such as bright ironing board covers, peg bags and laundry bags from Greengate and Cally & Co.

FISHERMAN'S RETREAT

Riding Head Lane, Turn-cum-Shuttleworth,
nr Ramsbottom, Lancashire BL0 0HH
Tel: 01706 825314   Fax: 01706 821815
e-mail: info@fishermansretreat.com
website: www.fishermansretreat.com

Set in 70 acres of beautiful countryside, the **Fisherman's Retreat** is an outstanding pub and restaurant with an interesting history. Back in 1981, Hervey and Susan Magnall purchased Twine Valley with their house funds. At that time, the 25-acre valley contained four fishing lodges and the remains of old stone buildings including a tumbledown mill for bleachers and dyers where Hervey's great-grandfather had once worked. His father and grandfather had played in the valley as children.

Hervey and Susan introduced a herd of South Devon and Longhorn cattle but it became evident that the valley needed to pay for itself in a more substantial way. The existing lodges were used to start up a trout fishery rearing rainbow trout for the purpose of stocking the 4.5-acre fly fishing lodge. Local people were soon travelling up the road for 'fresh trout'.

It was around 1990 that Hervey Snr overheard two cold and hungry fishermen debating where to go for a bite to eat and a bit of warmth. The idea for a 'Fisherman's Retreat' was born. It was built in 1992 using 90% reclaimed materials: the outer stone came from the dilapidated old mill buildings in the valley; the inside walls used reclaimed bricks from the old bus station in Ramsbottom. The beams also came from the bus station; wood from Prestwich hospital chapel was used to make the window frames, and much of the seating is provided by old pews from around the country.

Today, this popular restaurant offers an extensive menu of home-made and freshly prepared wholesome food. The Magnalls pride themselves on sourcing and supporting local producers. Their own three lakes provide the trout for dishes like the Fresh Twine Valley fillet of trout pan-fried with bacon and almonds, while their herd of Charollais cattle provides much of the beef served here. All the beef joints are left to hang for a minimum period of four weeks, an ageing process that improves the tenderness and flavour of the meat.

Other items on the menu include hot sandwiches and burgers, salads, and smaller meals suitable for children. And if you give one week's notice, you can even have a whole roast suckling pig which will feed six hungry people. Food is served every day from noon until 9pm. To accompany your meal, there's an extensive choice of wines, beers and more than 200 single malt whiskies.

MUSE WOMENSWEAR

10 Market Place, Ramsbottom, Bury, Lancashire BL0 9HT
Tel: 01706 827627
e-mail: enquiries@musewomenswear.co.uk
website: www.musewomenswear.co.uk

Launched in February 2005 by North West fashion entrepreneur Amanda Heath, Muse Womenswear offers the discerning shopper an unrivalled showcase of designer collections from the leading international fashion houses.

Positioned in the centre of Ramsbottom, Muse has a gently sophisticated yet welcoming atmosphere with Amanda presenting collections in a very personal way. The striking, stylish interior of the shop has the ambience of a chic Parisienne boutique, with two floors offering high fashion for day and evening wear from such leading names as Alice Temperley, Nicole Farhi, Day Birger et Mikkelson, Paul & Joe, John Smedley, and more. Customers can also purchase exquisite designer jewellery from Les Nereides and Dyrberg Kem.

Amanda's natural creative flair, once illustrated in her dancing years when she performed as a Royal ballet dancer, is now teamed with her fashion savvy to make Muse a unique shopping experience. Customers from around the county have been flocking to discover the delights of this fashion lover's haven, and Muse Womenswear has rapidly earned a reputation as the region's most influential designer boutique.

classical in shape to reflect the surrounding buildings but also bolted together to reflect the old industries.

BURY

6 miles E of Bolton on the A58

There was a settlement at Bury in Bronze Age times, but as late as 1770 it was still just a small market town, surrounded by green fields. That was the year a man named Robert Peel established his Ground Calico Printing Works, the first of many mills that would follow. The opening of the works along with the subsequent mills, print and bleach works so dominated this part of the Irwell Valley that not only did they transform the landscape but also heavily polluted the river. At the height of the valley's production it was said that anyone falling into the river would dissolve before they had a chance to drown. Today, thankfully, the valley towns are once again clean and the river clear and fast flowing.

With the family fortune gleaned from those prosperous mills, Robert Peel junior, born in the town in 1788, was able to fund his illustrious career in politics, rising to become Prime Minister in 1841. Famous for the repeal of the Corn Laws, Robert Peel was also at the forefront of the setting up of the modern police force – hence their nickname 'Bobbies'. A statue of Bury's most distinguished son stands in the Market Square and there's an even grander memorial near the village of Holcombe, a few miles to the north.

Another of Bury's famous sons was John Kay, inventor of the Flying Shuttle. Sadly, Kay neglected to patent his invention. He moved to France where he died a pauper and is buried in an unmarked grave. The people of Bury, however, remembered him. In his

Clock Tower, Bury

memory, they created the delightful **Kay Gardens** in the town centre and erected a splendidly ornate clock-house tower.

A short walk from Kay Gardens, **The Met** is a lively arts centre which puts on performances to suit all tastes, from theatre and children's shows to rock nights and world music. The Met also organises Bury's Streets Ahead Festival each May, a colourful street carnival which attracts artistes from around the world.

This part of town has become known as the "Culture Quarter", since Bury's **Art Gallery & Museum** is also located here. Reopened in 2005 after extensive refurbishment, the gallery has a fine collection of paintings, including works by Turner, Constable and Landseer, and the outstanding Thomas Wrigley collection of Victorian oil paintings. The building also houses

EAST LANCASHIRE RAILWAY

Bury - Ramsbottom - Rawtenstall
Tel: 0161 764 7790

The **East Lancashire Railway** offers visitors an opportunity to step back in time to the age of steam and travel along this delightful stretch of track. Your journey can be broken at Ramsbottom or Irwell Vale stations where you could enjoy a lineside picnic.

On Platform 2 at Bury Bolton Street Station, the period tearooms offer views of the locomotives arriving or departing from the station, while you enjoy a meal in the pleasant surroundings. Snacks and meals are available and the rooms can be pre-booked for special occasions.

A wide variety of events take place throughout the year, including Santa Specials, a Day out with Thomas and Friends, 1940s Wartime weekend and Steam Enthusiasts Weekend - ring for current details. Adults can actually drive a steam or deisel locomotive on the 'Footplate Experience' or an entire train can be hired for a special occasion or event. Facilities for the disabled are extremely good with access at all the stations, toilets at the main stations and a specially adapted carriage with wide doors and hydraulic lift.

the Bury Archives Service which makes available local records dating from 1675 to the present day.

The town has a real treat for those who thrill to the sight, sound and smell of steam locomotives. Bolton Street Station is the southern terminus of the **East Lancashire Railway** which operates regular services along a nine-mile scenic route through the lovely Irwell Valley to Rawtenstall. For the really smitten, there's the opportunity to actually drive one of the steam or diesel locomotives. Serious devotees of transport history will also want to explore the **Bury Transport Museum**, just across the road from the station. The museum houses a wonderful collection of vintage road and rail vehicles, ranging from a 19th century steam road-roller to a "Stop Me and Buy One" ice-cream vendor's tricycle.

Another museum of interest is the **Lancashire Fusiliers Museum** which tells the story of Lancashire's famous regiment from its foundation in 1688 and has an outstanding collection of medals and period uniforms.

A major shopping centre for the northwest, Bury is also proud of its ancient **Market** which has been operating since 1440. Held on Wednesdays, Fridays and Saturdays, the market is now the largest in the north with more than 370 stalls offering a huge choice of some 50,000 different product lines. Don't leave without purchasing one of Bury's famous black puddings.

Looking at Bury today it seems hard to imagine that at one time this typical Lancashire mill town had a castle. A settlement probably existed here in the Bronze Age and there is certainly evidence that the Romans passed through this area. By the 12th century, the town was the manor of the Norman de Bury family and, in the mid-14th century, the land came under the ownership of the Pilkingtons. It was dismantled following the Battle of Bosworth in 1485 at which Henry VII defeated Richard III. Unlucky Thomas Pilkington had backed the wrong side.

ROCHDALE PIONEERS MUSEUM

31 Toad Lane, Rochdale OL12 ONU
Tel: 01706 524920
e-mail: museum@co-op.ac.uk
website: www.co-op.ac.uk

The Rochdale Pioneers Museum is regarded as the home of the world wide co-operative movement. It's the perfect place to come and see how your ancestors did their shopping.

In Toad Lane on December 21st 1844 the Rochdale Equitable Pioneers Society opened their store selling pure food at fair prices and honest weights and measures, starting a revolution in retailing.

See the recreation of the original shop with its rudimentary furniture and scales. Here the basic needs of daily life such as butter, sugar, flour and oatmeal first went on sale over 150 years ago.

Journey back in time with early advertising, packaging and retailing artifacts, Co-operative postage stamps, commemorative china and rare dividend coins and commodity tokens. See the development of 'dividend' and the Co-op's success.

The foundations of the castle have recently been excavated and form the centrepiece of Castle Square.

On the outskirts of the town lies **Burrs Country Park** which, as well as offering a wide range of activities, also has an interesting industrial trail around the historic mill site.

WALMERSLEY

2 miles NE of Bolton on the A56

Hidden away in the village of Walmersley, just north of Bury, is **Hark to Dandler**, an attractive pub dating from the mid-19th century that is thought to have originally been a vicarage. During a recent refurbishment a very old child's coffin was found, full of early 19th-century artefacts, behind the cellar walls and, along with the two resident ghosts, this certainly adds an air of mystery to the pub. The name though is more easily explained as it is named after a lead dog of the local hunt.

TOTTINGTON

4 miles N of Bolton on the B6213

Tottington's pub is also named after a dog. The **Hark to Towler**, in the centre of the town, is very much a local's pub that happily welcomes visitors. Dating back to the 1800s, this imposing red brick pub's unusual name means call - hark - to the lead dog of the hunt - Towler.

An unspoilt farming town on the edge of moorland, Tottington escaped the industrialisation of many of its neighbours due to its, then, isolated position and it is still an attractive place to visit.

ROCHDALE

Lying in a shallow valley formed by the little River Roch, the town is surrounded,

to the north and east, by the slopes of the Pennines that are often snow covered in winter. With its origins in medieval times, the town, like so many others in Lancashire, expanded with the booming cotton industry and its magnificent Victorian **Town Hall** (1871) rivals that of Manchester in style if not in size. There are tours of the grand building with its spectacular Grand Staircase, hammer-beamed Great Hall, stained glass, statuary, ceramics and paintings. There's a scheduled tour every Friday afternoon; at other times by arrangement.

However, it is not textiles for which Rochdale is most famous but for its role as the birthplace of the Co-operative Movement in 1844. In carefully restored Toad Lane, to the north of the town centre, is the world's first Co-op shop, now the **Rochdale Pioneers Museum**. Today, the Co-op movement represents a staggering 700 million members in 90 countries around the world and the celebration of its 150th anniversary in 1994 focused attention on Rochdale. The story of the Rochdale Pioneers and other aspects of the town's heritage are vividly displayed in the Arts & Heritage Centre, **Touchstones**. The restored Grade II listed building of 1889 was originally a library but now contains interactive high-tech exhibitions, five art galleries, the Tourist Information Centre, a local studies centre, with free Internet access, café/bar, bookshop and performance studio.

As well as the Pioneers, Rochdale was home to several other famous sons and daughters, amongst them the 19th century political thinker, John Bright, the celebrated singer Gracie Fields (who now has a theatre here named after her), and Cyril Smith, Rochdale's former Liberal Member of Parliament.

The town's most distinctive church is **St John the Baptist Catholic Church** which has a beautiful dome modelled on the Byzantine Santa Sofya in Istanbul. The church is unique in England because of its huge mosaic of Italian marble depicting the Resurrection of Christ.

Running from the southeast corner of the town, the **Rochdale Canal** is a brave piece of early-19th century civil engineering that traversed the Pennines to link the River Mersey with the Calder and Hebble Navigation. Some 32 miles in length and with 91 locks, it must be one of toughest canals ever built and, though the towpath can still be walked, the last commercial boat passed through the locks in 1937. The canal was officially abandoned in 1952, but exactly half a century later the entire 32-mile long waterway was re-opened to full navigation. Together with the newly restored Huddersfield Narrow Canal it allows a complete circuit of the South Pennine Ring.

Between Rochdale and Littleborough lies Hollingworth Lake, originally built as a supply reservoir for the canal, but for many years a popular area for recreation known colloquially as the 'Weavers' Seaport', as cotton workers unable to afford a trip to the seaside came here. Now part of the **Hollingworth Lake Country Park** and with a fine visitor centre, there are a number of pleasant walks around its shores.

NORTH OF ROCHDALE

WHITWORTH

4 miles N of Rochdale on the A671

This pleasant town, of cottages and farms, lies on Pennine moorland above Rochdale. Between here and Bacup, a distance of only seven miles, the railway line, another feat of Victorian engineering, climbs over 500 feet. Not surprisingly, there were many problems during its construction, such as frequent landslides, but once constructed this was a picturesque line with attractive station houses with neat well-tended gardens along the route. The line, like so many, fell to the extensive railway cuts of the 1960s.

HEALEY

1 mile N of Rochdale on the A671

Lying in the valley of the River Spodden, this old village, now almost engulfed by the outer reaches of Rochdale, is an area rich in wildlife as well as folklore. Nearby is Robin Hood's Well, one of a number of springs feeding the river. Here, it is said, sometime in the 12th century the Earl of Huntingdon was lured to the well by a witch pretending to be his nursemaid. Once at the well, the witch told the young man that he would never inherit his earldom unless he had her magic ring

HOLLINGWORTH LAKE B&B

164 Smithy Bridge Road, Littleborough, Rochdale, Lancashire OL15 0DB
Tel: 01706 376583

"Everything you would expect from a top class hotel at B&B prices," is the proud claim made by Chris Firth about the accommodation at **Hollingworth Lake B&B**. The North West Tourist Board seems to agree and has awarded a five-Diamonds rating. Guests stay either in the main house or in separate rooms in the lovely garden area with its patio, balcony terrace and fish-filled pond. The five rooms (one single; one twin; two doubles and one family room) are all en suite, non-smoking, and immaculately furnished and decorated. A full English breakfast is included in the tariff; children and pets are welcome.

SWING COTTAGE GUEST HOUSE & CRAFT STUDIO

31 Lakebank, Hollingworth Lake,
Littleborough, Lancashire OL15 0DQ
Tel: 01706 379094 Fax: 01706 379091
e-mail: swingcottage@aol.com
website: www.hollingworthlake.com

Occupying a lovely position on the edge of Hollingworth Lake and surrounded by the breathtaking Pennine hills, **Swing Cottage Guest House & Craft Studio** offers the unusual combination of craft shop, tearoom and bed & breakfast accommodation. The three enterprises are owned and run by John Howarth and Amanda Healey who took over here in the autumn of 2002. The businesses are housed in an attractive building parts of which date back to 1810.

The flag-stoned Craft Studio displays a wonderful variety of crafts, all of them hand crafted and most of them made by local craftspeople. There's a huge range of pottery items, mirrors, lamps, vases, clocks, wooden toys, jigsaws, costume jewellery, baby knitwear, soft toys and cushions, walking sticks and even rocking horses. The walls are almost covered with an extensive range of limited edition prints and paintings, and the Studio also stocks a large selection of soaps and scented candles, traditional confectionery, jams and marmalades, and much, much more. And if you want a name or number plaque for your house, the Studio can do that too.

Next door to the Craft Studio and overlooking the lake, is the guest house where John and Amanda make every effort to ensure that their guests enjoy a comfortable stay with everything they would normally expect of a first class B&B with some extra little touches. A non-smoking establishment, Swing Cottage has a four-diamond rating from the English Tourism Council and in 2005 received the Greater Manchester Best B&B Award. There are four bedrooms (three doubles; one twin) which are also available for single and family occupancy. All rooms are en suite, tastefully decorated to a very high standard and three of them have beautiful lake views. Each room is centrally heated with its own thermostat and tea/coffee-making facilities are provided.

Breakfast is served in Winnie's Teapot, a traditional tea room with a warm and friendly atmosphere that serves a wide choice of home-baked meals, (including vegetarian options), 4-egg omelettes, snacks, afternoon teas, cakes and sticky buns. Beverages include Fair Trade coffee with free refills, herbal teas and soft drinks.

Swing Cottage is just a short walk from the Smithy Bridge train station on the main line from Manchester to York. Manchester city centre is just a 15-minute train journey which makes city centre shopping very accessible.

as a means of identification. Gazing into the well, Robin got such a fright that he fainted and the witch took off on her broomstick. Emerging from the well, the King of the Fairies gave the lad his own ring and told him to go up into Healey Dell and interrupt the witches whilst they were hatching their next spell. Doing as he was instructed Robin entered the coven and threw the ring into their cauldron whereupon there was a great flash of light and the witches were reduced to evil-looking fairies destined to live forever in the Fairy chapel.

Opened in 1972, **Healey Dell Nature Reserve** does not promise visitors sightings of either witches or fairies but there is a wealth of wildlife to be discovered along the nature trails. This is an ancient area which has only been invaded by the construction of the commercially non-viable Rochdale to Bacup railway in the late 19th century. The oak and birch woodland on the northern river bank is all that remains of a prehistoric forest and, whilst the owners of Healey Hall made some impact, little has changed here for centuries.

LITTLEBOROUGH

3 miles NE of Rochdale on the A58

Occupying a Grade I listed building dating from the late 1700s, the **Littleborough Coach House and Heritage Centre** hosts regular exhibitions by local artists and has arts and crafts for sale.

This small town lies beside the River Roch and on the main route between Lancashire and Yorkshire first laid down by the Romans. Known as the Roman Causey, it was an impressive structure 16 feet 6 inches wide, cambered and with gutters at each side. In the middle of the road is a shallow groove which has been

the subject of endless controversy – no-one has yet come up with a satisfactory explanation of its purpose. The road cuts across the bleak Pennine moors by way of **Blackstone Edge** where some of the best preserved parts of the Roman structure can still be seen. At the summit is a medieval cross, the **Aigin Stone**, which offers spectacular views over Lancashire right to the coast.

To the south of Littleborough, **Hollingworth Lake Water Activity Centre** offers sailing, canoeing, windsurfing, rowing and, during the summer months, lake trips on the *Lady Alice*.

SUMMIT

5 miles NE of Rochdale off the A6033

At Summit, the Rochdale to Halifax railway line dives into a tunnel that runs for a mile and a half under the Summit Ridge of the Pennines before emerging in Yorkshire. This extraordinary feat of engineering, the longest tunnel in the world when it was completed in 1844, is as remarkable in its way as the Roman Causey which follows a similar route on top of the hills.

SOUTH OF ROCHDALE

MILNROW

2 miles E of Rochdale on the A640

One of the finest examples of a giant steam Mill Engine in the country and other steam-powered plant can be seen at the **Ellenroad Engine House** next to Junction 21 of the M62. The 3,000-horsepower twin engines *Alexandra* and *Victoria* were once used to power the Ellenroad Cotton Spinning Mill which closed long ago but the Engine House with its steam-raising plant and 220ft chimney have been carefully preserved. The engines are in steam on the first

MILLYARD GALLERY

97 The Square, Uppermill, Saddleworth,
Lancashire OL3 6BD
Tel/Fax: 01457 870410
e-mail: joan@millyardgallery.fslife.co.uk
website: www.millyard-gallery.co.uk

Occupying two floors of a fine old millstone grit building,
the **Millyard Gallery** hosts four major exhibitions each
year featuring established artists with work in international
collections. These alternate with ongoing exhibitions of
oils, pastels, watercolours and etchings by artists with national reputations. Landscapes in oils, pencil
and watercolours by Saddleworth artists are always available. The spacious rooms provide an excellent
setting for displays of unique sculptures in stone, ceramics and glass, along with innovative work in

textiles and embroidery, and exciting, vibrant
contemporary art.

The Gallery can also supply giclée silkscreen prints
and limited editions from leading Fine Art publishers.
The Gallery is also home to Saddleworth Picture
Framing, a high quality, bespoke framing service for oils,
watercolours, photographs, needlework, tapestries,
sporting and family memorabilia, with all work
undertaken on the premises. The Gallery, which is open
daily, is a member of both the Fine Art Guild and the
Guild of Master Craftsmen, and operates the Arts
Council's interest-free loan scheme.

OLDFIELD COTTAGE ANTIQUES

Queen Anne Gallery, 64 High Street, Uppermill,
Saddleworth, Oldham, Lancashire OL3 6HA
Tel: 01457 874728 Fax: 01457 872690
website: www.oldfieldcottageantiques.co.uk
e-mail: info@oldfieldcottageantiques.co.uk

In business for more than 20 years, **Oldfield Cottage
Antiques** has built up a huge clientele both locally and from
far and wide. It's located in the centre of the village of
Uppermill opposite the park and occupies what used to be
the village Co-op shop. Inside, alongside kitchen wares, pottery, handicrafts and a giftware gallery,
there's an extensive range of interior decoration products – baskets from willow, rattan, sea grass or
rush; candles; glassware; vases; candle holders; wine racks and more. Old and restored pine furniture
fills the shop and the gallery showroom upstairs, as well as locally crafted pieces which are designed
and made to order.

There are more than 250 new, exclusive and imaginatively
designed products together with the Oldfield Kitchen Design
showroom. Owner Jenny Meadows says, "The showroom gives a
platform for what we think is comfortable, beautiful and functional
in kitchen design, and fitting for any home." Also on display are a
fantastic range of traditional handmade wooden toys and games,
as well as Danish white porcelain tableware in the Galzone range,
including dinner plates, jugs, bowls, cookware and mugs. And if
all that browsing makes you feel in need of refreshment, there's a
café upstairs with a warm Yorkshire welcome and hospitality.

Sunday of every month except January.

It was to this small industrial town in the foothills of the Pennines that John Collier came as the schoolmaster in 1729. Collier is perhaps better known as Tim Bobbin, the first of the Lancashire dialect poets. Collier remained in Milnrow for the rest of his life and, drinking rather more than he should, he earned extra money by selling his verse and by painting pub signs. The local pub which dates back to the early 1800s is, appropriately, named after him.

SHAW

3 miles SE of Rochdale on the A633

A typical mill town, founded on the wealth of the cotton trade, this was also a market town for the surrounding area. Closed since 1932, Jubilee Colliery, to the northeast of the town centre, has been reclaimed as a nature reserve and it is now an attractive haven for wildlife in the Beal Valley.

DELPH

7 miles SE of Rochdale on the A6052

Taking its name from the old English for quarry, this is probably a reference to the bakestone quarries found to the north of the village. Also close by, high on a hill above the village, lies **Castleshaw**, one of a series of forts the Romans built on their military road between Chester and York. The banks and ditches give visitors an excellent indication of the scale of the fort and many of the items found during recent excavations are on show in the Saddleworth Museum.

DOBCROSS

7 miles SE of Rochdale off the A6052

This attractive Pennine village, once the commercial heart of the district of Saddleworth, retains many of its original weavers' cottages, clothiers, and merchants' houses, and little has changed around the village square in the last 200 years. Used as the location for the film *Yanks*, Dobcross is also notable as the birthplace of the giant Platt Brothers Textile Machinery business which was, in the latter part of the 19th century, the largest such machine manufacturing firm in the world.

UPPERMILL

8 miles SE of Rochdale on the A62

Of the 14 villages that make up Saddleworth parish, Uppermill is the most central. It is certainly home to the area's oldest building, **Saddleworth Parish Church** which was originally built in the 12th century by the Stapletons as their family chapel. Extended over the years, it has several interesting features including a gravestone to commemorate the Bill's

Viaduct at Uppermill

o'Jack's murders. In 1832, the people of Saddleworth were stunned to learn that the landlord of the Bill's o'Jack's Inn and his son had been bludgeoned to death. Several thousand people turned out for the funeral but the case was never solved. The tombstone relates the whole story.

Almost a century-and-a-half later, the whole country was horrified by the "Moors Murderers", Ian Brady and Myra Hindley, who buried four of their victims on Saddleworth Moor.

The story of this once isolated area is illustrated at the **Saddleworth Museum**, housed in an old mill building on the banks of the Huddersfield Canal. There is a reconstruction of an 18th century weaver's cottage as well as a collection of textile machinery, local history gallery and local art exhibitions.

Also in Uppermill is the **Brownhill Visitor Centre**, which not only has information on the northern section of the Tame Valley but also exhibitions on local wildlife and the area's history.

DIGGLE

8 miles SE of Rochdale off the A62

Above the village, on **Diggle Moor** lies Brun Clough Farm where, it is said, the cries of child slaves who were ill-treated in the early days of the textile mills can still be heard coming from the outhouses. Part of the **Oldham Way** footpath, a 30-mile scenic walk through the countryside on the edge of the Peak District National Park, crosses the moorland.

Much of the village itself is a conservation area, where the pre-industrial weaving community has been preserved along with some of the traditional skills. However, Diggle Mill, which used to operate the second largest waterwheel in the country, no longer exists.

The Huddersfield Narrow Canal, completed in 1811, is one of the three canals that crossed the difficult terrain of the Pennines and linked Lancashire with Yorkshire. The entrance to the **Standedge Canal Tunnel**, the longest and highest canal tunnel in Britain, lies in the village. The last cargo boat passed through the tunnel in 1921 and following a long period of closure, it has now been re-opened.

DENSHAW

5 miles SE of Rochdale on the A640

In the moorland above the village is the source of the River Tame which flows through the Saddleworth area and eventually joins the River Goyt at Stockport. A charming 18th century village, Denshaw's Scandinavian name would suggest that there has been a settlement here for many centuries.

Until 1974, the Saddleworth area was part of the West Riding of Yorkshire and residents of the parish are still eligible to play for the Yorkshire cricket team. Cricket has always been a passion here. One 19th century mill owner built 'Cricketers Row' near Denshaw to house his team and the terrace even includes a residence for the 12th man.

Cheshire has received a bad press recently from writers such as Jeremy Clarkson and AA Gill who have portrayed the county as a kind of *Footballer's Wives* territory packed with Porsches, bloated with bling and mindlessly devoted to conspicuous consumption. It's certainly true that more millionaires live in this captivating corner of the country than anywhere else in England. Britain's richest peer, the Duke of Westminster, with an estimated wealth of £5,600 million, lives on a large estate just south of Chester. And more champagne is quaffed here than anywhere else in Britain.

But that's only a tiny part of the county's 2,000-year-long story which effectively begins with the arrival of the Romans. But even before the 20th Legion established the garrison of Deva in 70AD, Cheshire was famous for its salt mines. By the time of the *Domesday Book*, the salt towns, or "wiches" – Nantwich, Northwich, Middlewich – were firmly established. The process at that time involved pumping the salt brine to the surface and boiling it to produce granular salt. In 1670, huge deposits of rock salt were discovered and these are still being mined, mostly for use in keeping the country's roads free from ice.

Another local product with a long history is Cheshire cheese which has been famous for generations. John Speed, the famous Elizabethan map-maker and a Cheshire man himself, noted: "The soil is fat, fruitful and rich....the Pastures make the Kine's udders to strout to the pail, from whom the best Cheese of all Europe is made". Later, some enthusiasts even promoted the idea that the name Cheshire was actually short for cheese-shire.

Both these historic industries, along with Macclesfield's once famous silk factories, have been overtaken in the 20th century by tourism. Chester, with its long history, varied and fascinating "magpie" architecture, and huge range of shops, restaurants and inns, is now the fourth most visited location in England after the "golden triangle" of London, Stratford and Oxford. One small disappointment, though. Visitors don't get to see the county's best known character, the grinning Cheshire Cat. The phrase "To

Shropshire Union Canal at Chester

LOCATOR MAP

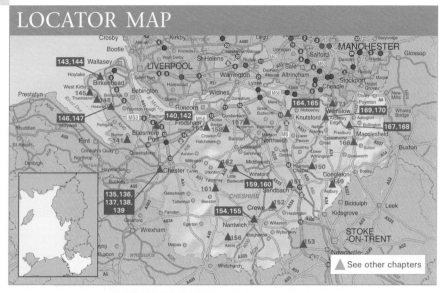

ADVERTISERS AND PLACES OF INTEREST

grin like a Cheshire cat" was in use long before Lewis Carroll adopted it in *Alice in Wonderland*. Carroll spent his childhood in the Cheshire village of Daresbury and would have regularly seen the local cheeses moulded into various animal shapes, one of which was a grinning cat.

Further east again is the charming riverside town of Doncaster, which was established by the Romans and today has the air of a pleasant market town. However, this was once one of the country's most important centres of steam locomotive manufacture and it is famous for having created the *Mallard*, which still holds the record for the top speed attained by a steam train. Today, though, Doncaster is best known as the home of the St Leger, Britain's oldest classic horse race.

Elsewhere in the county visitors can discover the delights of Roche Abbey, a 12th-century Cistercian house, Conisbrough Castle, which boasts the oldest stone keep in England, and the faded Victorian grandeur of Brodsworth Hall.

CHESTER

The city's strategic position on the River Dee close to the Welsh border was important even before the Romans arrived in AD70. They based a large camp, or *caster*, here and called it Deva after the Celtic name for the river. It was during this period that the splendid city walls were originally built – two miles round, and still the most complete in the country.

In Saxon times "Ceastre" became the administrative centre of a shire, and was the last major town in England to fall to William the Conqueror during his dreadful Harrowing of the North. William pulled down half of Chester's houses and re-inforced the message of Norman domination by building a castle overlooking the Dee.

Subsequent Earls of Chester (the present Prince of Wales is the current one, incidentally) were given a free, and very firm hand, in dealing with the local Saxons and with the still-rebellious Welsh who continued to make a nuisance of themselves right through the Middle Ages. In return for its no-

nonsense dealing with these problems Chester received a number of royal privileges: borough status, a licence for a market and, around 1120, the first commission in England for a Sheriff – long before his more famous colleague in Nottingham received his. And the Mayor of Chester can still claim the medieval title of "Admiral of the Dee".

The problem with the Welsh was finally resolved in 1485 when a Welsh-based family, the Tudors, defeated Richard III at Bosworth Field and Owen Tudor claimed the throne as Henry VII. For more than 150 years Chester enjoyed an unprecedented period of peace and prosperity. Then came the Civil War. Chester supported the King but Charles I had the galling experience of watching from the city walls as his troops were defeated at nearby Rowton Moor. For two long years after that rout, the city was under seige until starvation finally forced its capitulation. **The King Charles Tower** on the wall is now a small museum with displays telling the story of that siege.

Seventy years later, in the course of his *Tour through the Whole Island of Great*

NICHOLS HOME

8 Godstall Lane, Chester CH1 1LN
Tel/Fax: 01244 343027
website: www.nicholshome.co.uk

Opened in May 2002, **Nichols Home** has quickly become
the first port of call for anyone looking for distinctive
quality pieces to enhance their home. This stylish shop
is owned and run by Jean Myles and Ronnie Nichols –
Jean has a fashion degree from Liverpool University and
was a visiting lecturer at the Glasgow School of Art;
Ronnie has wide experience in retail management. They
specialise in vintage furniture such as farmhouse tables, pine cupboards, wooden and tin travelling
trunks as well as old mirrors. Seasonally they carry a beautiful and unusual collection of Christmas
decorations. Their extensive range also includes Newgate clocks, china, enamelware, French soaps
and a good selection of practical wicker baskets.

There's still more: costume jewellery, melt candles hand
made in Clitheroe, and gilt letters (which have proved very
popular) are just some of the hundreds of items on display.
A great place to browse – and to find those tricky Christmas
presents. The shop stands on Godstall Lane, one of only
four medieval lanes to have survived within the city walls.
The lane led to the Abbey of St Werburgh – now Chester
Cathedral – and its name means 'God's Place' which is
believed to refer to a hermit who lived near here in the 1100s.

GALERIJA SILVERBIRCH

51 Watergate Street, Chester CH1 2LB
Tel: 01244 351115
e-mail: karyn@libecans.freeserve.co.uk

Located in the heart of this historic city, **Galerija
Silverbirch** was opened by Karyn Libecans in
October 2004 and offers an outstanding selection
of art works of every kind. The gallery occupies an
interesting building with a vaulted ceiling that is
believed to have been part of a 14th century
monastery that stood here. Subdued lighting
accentuates the white walls and highlights the imaginatively displayed pieces around the gallery;
contemporary music plays softly in the background. There's a good choice of modern paintings, both
originals and framed prints.

Some truly striking sculptures are carefully positioned
for maximum effect. Smaller items include hand-made
jewellery in silver and precious stones, especially Baltic
Amber; hand-made wooden lamps and decorative pieces
such as toadstools and mushrooms, and mirrors in
wooden frames. The gallery also stocks a superb range of
furniture, hand-made using English woods such as oak
and elm – chests, dressers, coffee tables, chairs – all in
delightfully original designs; and a range of colourful
ceramics. A great place to visit if you are looking for gifts
with something very special about them.

Britain, Daniel Defoe came to Chester by the ferry over the River Dee. He liked the city streets, "very broad and fair"; admired the "very pleasant walk round the city, upon the walls", and disliked its cathedral, "built of red, sandy, ill looking stone". However, he had nothing but praise for its "excellent cheese".

James Boswell, Dr Johnson's biographer, visited Chester in the 1770s and wrote, "I was quite enchanted at Chester, so that I could with difficulty quit it". He was to return again, declaring that "Chester pleases my fancy more than any town I ever saw". Modern visitors will almost certainly share his enthusiasm.

Probably the best introduction to this compact little city is to join one of the frequent sightseeing tours conducted by a Blue Badge guide. These take place every day, even Christmas Day, and leave from the **Chester Visitor Centre**. The Centre can also provide you with a wealth of information about the city, including a full calendar of events that range from the **Chester Regatta**, the oldest rowing races in the world and **Chester Races**, the oldest in Britain, to the **Lord Mayor's Show** in May and the **Festival of Transport**, featuring an amazing parade of vintage cars, in August.

Towering above the city centre is **Chester Cathedral**, a majestic building of weathered pink stone which in 1992 celebrated its 900th birthday. It was originally an abbey and is one of very few to survive Henry VIII's closure of the monasteries in the 1540s. The cloisters are regarded as the finest in England and the monks' refectory is still serving food although nowadays it is refreshments and lunches for visitors. There's a fine

The Cross and The Rows, Chester

14th century shrine to St Werbergh, the princess/abbess who founded the first church on this site in Saxon times, and some intricately carved Quire stalls almost 800 years old which are reckoned to be the finest in Britain. It was at Chester Cathedral, in 1742, that George Frederick Handel personally conducted rehearsals of his oratorio *The Messiah* before its first performance in Dublin: a copy of the score with annotations in his own hand remains on display.

Chester is famous for its outstanding range of museums. At the **Dewa Roman Experience** you can re-live the sights, sounds and even the smells of daily life in Roman Chester. A superb display of artefacts from Chester and elsewhere in the Roman Empire are on display and kids love dressing up in replica suits of Roman armour. "Dewa" incidentally is not a mis-spelling of the Roman name

THE CHEESE SHOP

116 Northgate Street, Chester CH1 2HT
Tel: 01244 346240 Fax: 01244 314659
e-mail: carole@chestercheeseshop.co.uk
website: www.chestercheeseshop.com

With more than 200 varieties of regional British cheeses on offer, **The Cheese Shop** has something to suit every palate. This 'temple dedicated to cheese' was established some 20 years ago by Carole Faulkner, Cheshire born and Cheshire bred, and so, she says, "Strong in t'arm and thick in t'ead!" Carole trained as a cheesemaker at the Reaseheath Agricultural College in Nantwich and then travelled throughout Europe furthering her knowledge of cheese and other foods.

Following her marriage to Malcolm, a quantity surveyor, she lived in Singapore and Hongkong before they returned to England and opened their own restaurant. They found it very difficult to

obtain a suitable variety of cheeses so decided to open their own cheese shop in the heart of historic Chester. Shaded by a blue and white striped awning, the shop was built in the 1800s as a butcher's and the hooks for hanging meat still protrude from the cellar ceiling.

Carole and Malcom buy their cheeses direct from local farms, transport them in their own chilled transport, and then store them in the Victorian temperature-controlled cellars beneath the shop. The cheeses are turned every day so that the moisture does not

settle at the bottom. The 200 varieties on sale range from red, white and blue Cheshire to a huge selection of goats, ewes and unpasteurised cheeses. Carole's own favourites are the ewes' milk varieties – hence the excellent choice.

As well as cheese, the shop also stocks a delicious selection of regional foods such as dry-cured bacons, eggs, home-cooked ham, hand-made chutneys, pâtés, fruit wines and liqueurs. From further afield come Dorset soups, and olive oils and hand-made pastas from Tuscany.

Well-informed staff are always happy to help make any mealtime an occasion to cherish; there are free tastings of Carole's favourite local cheeses, and if you are looking for an unusual gift, how about a delightful pottery cheese bell or locally made salt pig?

It's not surprising to discover that The Cheese Shop has been winner of the Produce Shop of the Year Award three times in succession and in 2005 was given the Outstanding Achievement Award at the Chester Food & Drink Festival. Enough to keep anyone busy you'd think, but Carole also makes time to exercise her four rescue dogs and to raise money for North Clwyd Animal Rescue.

for Chester but is how Romans of the time pronounced "Deva". The **Grosvenor Museum** has furnished period rooms, a Timeline gallery travelling back through the city's history, a gallery of paintings by local contemporary artists, crafts and other artefacts connected with Chester. The **Chester Heritage Centre** tells the city's story from the Civil War siege to the present day. **On The Air** broadcasting museum chronicles the world of radio and TV from the pioneering days of BBC radio to satellite and digital TV, while the **Chester Toy & Doll Museum** is a nostalgic treasure-house of antique playthings. Recently re-opened after a major redevelopment, the Cheshire Military Museum which recounts the story of the county's military history using computers, tableaux and hands-on exhibits to present the soldier's life through the last 300 years.

Quite apart from its historical attractions, Chester is also one of the major shopping centres for the north west and north Wales. All the familiar High Street names are here, often housed in much more appealing buildings than they usually inhabit, along with a great number of specialist and antique shops. For a unique shopping experience, you must visit the world-famous, two-tiered galleries of shops under covered walkways known as **The Rows** which line both sides of Bridge Street. The Rows are an architectural one-off: no other medieval town has anything like them. Many of the black and white, half-timbered frontages of The Rows, so typical of Chester and Cheshire, are actually Victorian restorations, but crafted so beautifully and faithfully that even experts can have difficulty distinguishing them from their 13th century originals.

THE RIVERSIDE TEA GARDENS

The Groves, Chester CH1 1SD
Tel: 01244 314440 Mobile: 0771 8891916
Fax: 01824 704653
e-mail: henshall1.btinternet.com

What nicer way to enjoy tea on a sunny summer afternoon than sitting on the terrace of **The Riverside Tea Gardens** watching the leisurely traffic on the River Dee passing by? Built in the early 1800s as two houses, the tea rooms are located on the Chester side of the Queen's Park suspension bridge. If you're unlucky with the weather, there's plenty of room inside in a large, very comfortable room with an open fire, settees and armchairs – it's more like having tea in a friend's sitting room than in a tea room.

Paula Henshall – born and bred in Chester – took over these delightful tea rooms in 2000 and has made them the place to take tea in the city. Her menu offers a great choice of teatime treats such as the Chester cream tea served with freshly baked scones, and some wonderful cakes many of which are made by members of the Ruthin Women's Institute, (Ruthin is Paula's home town and where she breeds Great Danes). Also on the menu is a good selection of light meals including home-made soup, jacket potatoes, freshly-made sandwiches, and a dish called 'War of the Roses' described as 'Lancashire hot pot meets Yorkshire pudding!'

Close by is the **Eastgate Clock**. It was erected in 1897 to celebrate Queen Victoria's Diamond Jubilee, a beautifully ornate construction which is probably the most photographed timepiece in the world. If *your* timing is right and you arrive hereabouts at 12 noon in the summer, you should see, and certainly hear, the **Town Crier** delivering some stentorian civic message.

A few steps bring you to Chester's famous **City Walls** which were originally built by the Romans to protect the fortress of Deva from attacks by pesky Celtic tribes. Nowadays, the two-mile long circuit – an easy, level promenade, provides thousands of visitors with some splendid views of the River Dee, of the city's many glorious buildings and of the distant Welsh mountains. Here, during the summer months, you may come across Caius Julius Quartus, a Roman Legionary Officer in shining armour conducting a patrol around the fortress walls and helping to re-create the life and times of a front-line defender of the Empire. At one point, the wall runs alongside St John Street, which has a curious history. In Roman times it was the main thoroughfare between the fortress and the **Amphitheatre**, the largest ever

Eastgate Clock, Chester

uncovered in Britain, capable of seating 7,000 spectators. During the Middle Ages however this highway was excavated and turned into a defensive ditch. Over the years, the ditch gradually filled up and by Elizabethan times St John Street was a proper street once again.

No visit to Chester would be complete without a trip to **Chester Zoo** on the northern edge of the city. Set in 110 acres of landscaped gardens, it's the

CHESHIRE MILITARY MUSEUM

The Castle, Chester CH1 2DN
Tel: 01244 327617

The **Cheshire Military Museum** is a registered museum with stunning displays and collections telling the story of Cheshire's military history. The Soldiers of Cheshire is an interactive exhibition where 300 years of history of the soldier's life is shown through computers, tableaux and hands-on exhibits.

Here you can meet Sergeant Shipp at Bhurtpore and walk a length of trench at Ypres. Enjoy the 'With Love' feature and much more for all the family. Facilities include a small shop, toilet and access for the disabled. Open daily 10am-5pm (last entry 4.30pm) except for two weeks over Christmas.

largest zoo in Britain, caring for more than 5,000 animals from some 500 different species. The Zoo also provides a refuge for many rare and endangered animals which breed freely in near-natural enclosures. What's more, it has the UK's largest elephant facility and is the only successful breeder of Asiatic elephants in this country – to date four youngsters have been born here. The Zoo has more than a mile of overhead railway providing a splendid bird's-eye view of the animals and the Roman Garden. Other attractions include the Rare Penguin Breeding Centre with windows enabling visitors to see the birds "flying" underwater; a Forest Zone with spacious homes for Buffy Headed Capuchin monkeys; and special enclosures for the black rhinos and red pandas. Offering more than enough interest for a full day out, the Zoo is open every day of the year except Christmas Day.

AROUND CHESTER

MOULDSWORTH

10 miles NE of Chester on the B5393

Housed in a wonderful 1930s Art Deco building, **Mouldsworth Motor Museum** contains a unique collection of more than 60 vintage, classic and sports cars, motorcycles and old bicycles. The museum also has displays of old toys and teapots.

TARVIN

5 miles E of Chester off the A54 or A51

In the *Domesday Book* Tarvin is recorded as one of the larger manors in Cheshire and by the 1300s was the centre of an extensive parish. The present church was begun at this time and boasts the oldest surviving timber roof in Cheshire. The

village came to prominence in the Civil War when Gen. Sir William Brereton made it his headquarters during the siege of Chester. In August 1644 there was fighting around the church and bullet marks can still be seen around its west door. One of them even penetrated a brass by the chancel in memory of a former mayor of Chester and remained there for many years until a Victorian sightseer prised it out and made off with it. Just over a century after that skirmish, a major fire in 1752 destroyed much of Tarvin but one fortunate result of the conflagration was that the rebuilding of the village left it with an abundance of handsome Georgian buildings.

Tarvin is about halfway along the **Baker Way**, which runs from Chester Station to Delamere Station at the edge of Delamere Forest Park. The trail follows the Shropshire Union Canal from Chester to Rowton Bridge, thence to Hockenhull Platts, Tarvin, Ashton, Brines Brow and Delamere Forest.

GATESHEATH

8 miles SE of Chester off the A41

Occupying a Victorian farmhouse in Gatesheath, the Country Centre at New Russia Hall is a quite unique attraction. To begin with, there's the Orchard Paddock, a magnet for children with its appealing collection of farm animals and pets, swings and crazy golf. Anyone interested in flower arranging can watch the staff of the Dried Flower Workshop creating unique arrangements which can be bought, or you can buy all the materials to make your own. You can also see them creating painted plant pots, boxes and small pieces of furniture. There is a comprehensive display of greeting cards and gifts, a tea room, and Uncle Peter's Fudge Kitchen where you can try the superbly tasty fudge.

Incidentally, the name New Russia Hall has nothing to do with Muscovy or the "Evil Empire" but comes from a corruption of "rushes" which once grew abundantly in the marshy ground nearby and provided the basic materials for local basketmakers.

TATTENHALL

8 miles SE of Chester off the A41

Tattenhall is a fine old village within sight of the twin castles of Beeston and Peckforton perched atop the Peckforton Hills. There are some attractive old houses and a Victorian church with a graveyard which gained notoriety during the 19th century because of the activities of a gang of grave-robbers. They lived in caves in the hills nearby and, once they had disposed of the bodies to medical gentlemen, used the empty coffins to store their booty from more conventional thieving. At that time Tattenhall was a busy little place. The Shropshire Union Canal passes close by and the village was served by two railway stations on different lines. Today, only one railway line survives (and no stations), the canal is used solely by pleasure craft, but the village is enjoying a new lease of life as a desirable community for people commuting to Chester, a short drive away.

Small though it is, Tattenhall has entertained some distinguished visitors. No less a personage than King James I once stayed at The Bear & Ragged Staff. This attractive hostelry was then a modest one-storey building with a thatched roof but later became an important coaching inn, (the old mounting steps still stand outside. The pub's unusual name suggests some connection with the Earls of Warwick whose crest it is. (The first Earl supposedly strangled a bear, the second Earl clubbed a giant to death).

Brown tourist signs on the A41 point the way to **Cheshire Ice Cream Farm**, where real dairy ice cream is made in over 30 different flavours, including rhubarb and custard, Cointreau and orange, and a seasonal sherry trifle. Visitors can watch the cows being milked, and a video shows the whole process of making ice cream 'from cow to cone'. Young visitors can romp in the Playbarn, and the farm is home to many rare breed animals (alpacas, miniature donkeys, pygmy goats, Jacob sheep) and rescued birds of prey and hedgehogs.

BELGRAVE

4 miles S of Chester on the B5445

Belgrave is hardly large enough to qualify as a hamlet but it has given its name to the London area known as Belgravia. Both are owned by the Duke of Westminster, Britain's richest landowner, whose family home, Eaton Hall, stands beside the River Dee a couple of miles west of the village. The Duke's family, the Grosvenors, were well established in Cheshire by the 1300s but it was acquisition by marriage of a large estate to the west of London that brought them huge riches. As London expanded westwards during the 18th and 19th centuries, their once rural estate was developed into elegant squares and broad boulevards, many with names reflecting the Duke's Cheshire connections – Eaton Square, Eccleston Square, Grosvenor Place and Chester Row.

The Grosvenor's vast Victorian mansion suffered badly when it was occupied by the military during the Second World War. In the 1970s it was demolished and replaced by a more modest concrete structure which has divided architectural opinion as to its merits – one writer described it "as modern as a 1970s airline terminal". The house is not open to the public but its gardens occasionally are.

SALTNEY

2 miles SW of Chester off the A5104

For centuries, the ferry boat from Saltney on the south side of the River Dee provided a vital link for travellers from north Wales making their way to the great city of Chester. Modern roads put the ferrymen out of business a long time ago but their memory is honoured at the Saltney Ferry public house.

THE WIRRAL (PARTLY IN MERSEYSIDE)

Two Old English words meaning heathland covered with bog myrtle gave The Wirral its name and well into modern times it was a byword for a desolate place. The 14th century author of *Sir Gawayne and the Green Knight* writes of:

> *"The wilderness of Wirral: few lived there*
> *Who loved with a good heart either*
> *God or man"*

The Wirral's inhabitants were infamous for preying on the shipwrecks tossed on to its marshy coastline by gales sweeping off the Irish Sea. The 19th century development of shipbuilding at Birkenhead brought industry on a large scale to the Mersey shore but also an

influx of prosperous Liverpool commuters who colonised the villages of the Caldy and Grange Hills and transformed the former wilderness into a leafy suburbia. The 1974 Local Government changes handed two thirds of The Wirral to Merseyside leaving Cheshire with by far the most attractive third, the southern and western parts alongside the River Dee. Tourism officials now refer to The Wirral as the "Leisure Peninsula", a fair description of this appealing and comparatively little-known area. One of its major attractions is **Ness Gardens**, a 64-acre tract of superbly landscaped gardens on the banks of the River Dee. The gardens are run by the University of Liverpool as an Environmental and Horticultural Research Station and are planned to provide magnificent displays all year round. There are children's play and picnic areas, well-marked interest trails, and licensed refreshment rooms.

ELLESMERE PORT

8 miles N of Chester on the A5032

An interesting 8½-mile trail for walkers and cyclists runs along the Shropshire Union Canal between Chester and Ellesmere Port. It passes through communities and countryside, and along its route are 10 sculptures that mark important gateways to the Canal. Local artist Stephen Hitchin designed

THE BOAT MUSEUM

South Pier Road, Ellesmere Port CH65 4FW
Tel: 0151 355 5017 Fax: 0151 355 4079
website: www.boatmuseum.org.uk

Experience life afloat as you climb aboard the historic narrow boats, or step back in time to the period dockworkers cottages along Porters Row. With exhibitions of working steam diesel engines, colourful displays of canal ware and the fascinating history of canal development, Britain's industrial and social heritage is brought vividly to life at **The Boat Museum**. The 7.5 acre site is right by J9 of the M53, provides a great day out for all the family, and has a gift shop, café and free car park.

GORDALE GARDEN CENTRE

Chester High Road, Burton, South Wirral,
Cheshire CH64 8TF
Tel: 0151 336 2116 Fax: 0151 336 8152
e-mail: jill@gordale.co.uk
website: www.gordale.co.uk

Easy to find on Chester High Road midway between
Chester and Heswall, **Gordale Nursery & Garden
Centre** has been a leader in its field for more than 50
years. Attention to detail puts Gordale head and
shoulders above the rest, and owners Jill and Peter
Nicholson never stop looking for ways to make a top-notch business even better. Superbly laid out in
extensive purpose-built premises that cover 12 acres, the centre stocks everything connected with
gardens, and a great deal more besides, and each department is run by a highly trained manager (some
of these have more than 20 years' service).

The range of plants for sale is second to none with plants sourced from leading nurseries across
Europe. Traditional roses, rhododendrons, azaleas, alpines, heathers, climbers, perennials, fruit and
conifers sit alongside the increasingly fashionable
tree ferns, bamboos, ferns, palms, citrus and
grasses. Bedding and houseplants are kept in
climatically controlled greenhouses ensuring the
best quality whatever the season and staff are
always on hand to provide advice. Birdbaths,
sundials, traditional and modern sculptures from
the stoneware department and wonderful pots
provide talking points for a garden.

The range of garden furniture and accessories
is as wide as you'll find anywhere, with tables
and chairs in wood, resin, metal and glass, indoor
cane furniture for conservatories, sunloungers,
side tables and footstools, parasols and cushions,
garden lighting, gas and charcoal barbecues, and
picnic ware in all styles. Other departments provide books, clothes, speciality foods, ceramics, fresh
and silk flowers, and a huge selection of gifts for birthdays, weddings and other special occasions as
well as the departments you would expect to find in a traditional garden centre such as bulbs, seeds,
composts, tools, garden care and watering equipment. The 180-seat coffee shop is open throughout
the day for coffees, teas, home-made cakes and light meals.

The children's play area, combined with the extensive landscaped grounds, wild fowl, ducks and
peacocks make the centre a worthwhile day trip for the entire family, and its regular programme of
promotional events including a bulb weekend and the annual summer garden party provide interest
throughout the seasons. But it is at Christmas time
when the centre takes on a magical quality. With
regular demonstrations by leading florists, late night
shopping, Santa's grotto and one of the best
Christmas displays in the North West, they have
everything you need under one roof to complete
your Christmas shopping.

Gordale Garden Centre has recently won Retail
Outlet of the Year 2005 from the Horticultural
Trades Association, and was also winner of Pan
Britanic Industries 2004 award for Britain's Best
Garden Retailer.

each sculpture to reflect the character of its location and to provide directions along the route. Among the places of interest on the route are the Backford Gap, marking the southern end of the Wirral Peninsula, and Caughall Bridge, constructed by Thomas Telford. The northern end of the Canal lies within the Mersey Community Forest, a network of small woodlands with public access. The first part of the Shropshire Union Canal was completed in 1779, linking Chester to Nantwich. The link between Chester and Netherpool (soon to become better known as Ellesmere Port) was opened in 1795, and passengers could take the boat from Chester to Liverpool, changing at Ellesmere Port, for 7½d first class (about 3p).

Warehouse Basin, Ellesmere Port

Railways gradually replaced the canals in the 19th century, and the Shropshire Union had more or less ceased its working life by the 1920s. Since the

BLUE PLANET AQUARIUM

Cheshire Oaks, Ellesmere Port, Cheshire CH65 9LF
Tel: 0151 357 8800
e-mail: info@blueplanetaquarium.co.uk
website: www.blueplanetaquarium.com

The award-winning **Blue Planet Aquarium** is Britain's largest all weather aquarium attraction and has two floors of interactive displays and exhibits. Take a journey of adventure through the waters of the world, from the misty northern streams to the shark-inhabited waters of the exotic Caribbean. Take a peek at the array of some of the most scary and poisonous creatures in the world. Watch one of the largest collections of sharks in Europe pass inches from your face, as you walk through the breathtaking underwater tunnel, which at 230ft, is one of the longest in the world. An otter enclosure has been carefully constructed to create the perfect environment for its inhabitants and friendly sea creatures can be seen in the Rockpool area, where there are crabs, rays, starfish and lots more.

Tasty meals are available at the Caribbean themed restaurant and fantastic souvenirs can be purchased at the gift shop. For those over 18, there is a chance to dive with the sharks. The fee includes two hours training and safety briefing, equipment hire, a 30 minute dive in the main exhibit with the expert team of divers and a certificate. Qualified divers can also have night dive sessions.

BAGS OF INSPIRATION

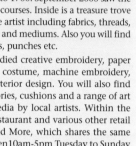

The Courtyard, Carr Farm Garden Centre, Birkenhead Road,
Meols, Wirral CH47 9RE
Tel: 0151 632 5883
website: www.bagsofinspiration.com

After several years of supplying textiles and art materials to colleges
and universities, proprietor Hilary Naghashi, a mixed media artist and
designer, was given the opportunity to restore the farmhouse in the
rustic courtyard of Carr Farm Garden Centre, part of which dates back to 1700. September 2005 saw the
opening of **Bags of Inspiration**, a retail shop and workshops for craft courses. Inside is a treasure trove
of basic, as well as some of the more unusual, products for the creative artist including fabrics, threads,
beads, natural and hand-dyed silk fibres, knitting wools, various paints and mediums. Also you will find
a range of card making materials, handmade papers, buttons, peel-offs, punches etc.

The staff have a wealth of knowledge between them having studied creative embroidery, paper
craft, textile decorative techniques, bead needle weaving, theatrical costume, machine embroidery,

passementerie, upholstery and interior design. You will also find
within the shop jewellery, accessories, cushions and a range of art
work, both textile and mixed media by local artists. Within the
Garden Centre, you will find a restaurant and various other retail
outlets including Glass Galore and More, which shares the same
building. Bags of Inspiration is open 10am-5pm Tuesday to Sunday
and 11am-5pm Monday. Free parking and disabled access. It is a
short drive from the M53; leave at junction 2 and follow the signs
to Moreton, Hoylake and West Kirby. The Garden Centre is on the
left.

GLASS GALORE & MORE

The Courtyard, Carr Farm Garden Centre, Birkenhead Road,
Meols, Wirral CH47 9RE
Tel: 0151 632 0637
e-mail: Glassgalore0637@aol.com
website: www.glassgalore.co.uk

Situated adjacent to Carr Farm Garden Centre on the Wirral
Peninsula between Meols and Moreton on the A553, Glass Galore
& More shares a traditional farmhouse which in part dates back to the 18th century. Within this
quaint building you will find authentic oak beams and a hint of life as it used to be. A variety of items
are on sale here such as Victorian and Edwardian stripped pine furniture, chosen for its character and
rustic charm, as well as other quality wooden furniture; antique and contemporary glassware (including
a range of paperweights) from fine cut glass to substantial modern pieces; collectables with famous
names such as Beswick, Coalport and Royal Worcester; old and new jewellery including costume and
precious pieces, and cushions and curtains among the soft furnishings.

Proprietor Jill Owen has been selling antiques and collectables
for the past four years and relocated to Carr Farm over two-and-a-
half years ago, expanding into selling stripped pine furniture.
Proving successful is a service Jill provides which involves selling
for clients on a commission basis and she will also search for items
on request. It is an ideal place to browse around at leisure and
discover that perfect present or that special item of furniture for
the home. Also within the courtyard are other retail outlets and
inside the comprehensive Garden Centre is a very popular
restaurant. Glass Galore & More is open 10am-5pm every day.

1960s this and many other canals have found a new role supporting the leisure industry. The history of the Canal can be explored at the **Boat Museum** (see panel on page 273), set in Ellesmere Port's historic dock complex. The Museum has the world's largest floating collection of canal craft, along with working exhibitions of restored steam, diesel and gas engines in the Power Hall and Pump House. Porters Row recreates the dockworkers' cottages of 1840, 1900, 1930 and 1950. Boat trips run most days throughout the summer. Ellesmere Port's other major attraction is **Blue Planet** (see panel on page 275), billed as Britain's biggest and best aquarium adventure. On the moving walkway that runs through the underwater safari tunnel visitors can see rays, sharks and over 1,000 other fish and marine life at close quarters. The piranha exhibit is one of the largest in Europe, and among the many other attractions are a display of amphibians, shark feeding and regular special events.

EASTHAM

10 miles NW of Chester off the A41

Eastham Woods Country Park is a 76-acre oasis of countryside amidst industrial Merseyside and enjoys considerable status amongst bird-watchers as one of few northern woodlands with all three species of native woodpecker in residence. Just a mile or so from the Park is Eastham village, another little oasis with a church and old houses grouped around the village green. The venerable yew tree in the churchyard is reputed to be the oldest in England.

BEBINGTON

12 miles NW of Chester off the A41

Much of the Wirral's Merseyside is heavily industrialised but a dramatic exception is **Port Sunlight** near

Bebington. This model village was created in 1888 by William Hesketh Lever, later 1st Viscount Leverhulme, to house the workers in his soap factory and was named after his most famous product, Sunlight Soap. Leverhulme wanted to provide "a new Arcadia, ventilated and drained on the most scientific principles". Some 30 architects were employed to create the individually designed rows of rustic cottages and the whole village is now a Conservation Area. The history of the village and its community is explored at the Port Sunlight Heritage Centre where there are scale models of the village, a Victorian port and Sunlight House, original plans for the building and displays of period advertising and soap packaging. A major attraction is the **Lady Lever Art Gallery** which houses a magnificent collection of pre-Raphaelite paintings by Millais and Rosetti, portraits by Gainsborough and Reynolds, dramatic landscapes by Turner and Constable, an impressive Wedgwood collection and some superb pieces of 18th century furniture. The gallery also has a gift shop and a popular tea room, the Lady Lever Café. Lord Leverhulme and his wife are buried in the graveyard of Christ Church.

BIRKENHEAD

20 miles NW of Chester off the M53

If you were asked, "Where is the largest group of Grade I listed buildings in England?", Birkenhead would probably not be your first guess. But you can find these buildings in Hamilton Square where you'll also find the **Old Town Hall**, although that only merits a Grade II rating. It now houses an exhibition telling the story of the famous Cammell Laird shipyard, a model of the Woodside area in 1934 when King George V opened the Queensway road tunnel under the Mersey, and a collection of delightful Della Robbia pottery. Also within the Town Hall are an art gallery, theatre, cinema and concert hall.

The **Birkenhead Heritage Trail** guides visitors around the town's various attractions and includes trips on a genuine Hong Kong tram and a beautifully restored Birkenhead tram of 1901. The trail takes in the Shore Road Pumping Station with its "Giant Grasshopper" steam pump. It was one of several used to extract water from the Mersey railway tunnel – Europe's very first underwater rail tunnel. Other attractions along the trail include an Edwardian Street scene display, a unique historic transport collection and a visit to the Pacific Road Arts and Exhibition Centre. Just along from Pacific Road is Egerton Bridge which offers a bird's eye

view over the docklands. Moored alongside East Float Dock Road are two historic warships, now museums. Both the frigate *HMS Plymouth* and the submarine *HMS Onyx* served during the Falklands War and are now preserved as they were in the 1980s.

HMS Plymouth saw action throughout the campaign and while carrying out a lone daylight bombardment was hit by four bombs. *HMS Onyx* was the only non-nuclear submarine to take part in the conflict. She carried 20 men from the SAS and SBS in addition to her own full crew, and was so crowded that she fully deserved her nickname *'The Sardine's Revenge'*. Also on display is a German U-boat, *U534*, whose sinking marked the end of the Battle of the Atlantic in May 1945. The submarine was recovered after lying for 50 years on the seabed. The latest addition to the Birkenhead fleet is *HMS Bronington*, a 'Ton' class minesweeper launched in 1953. The 'Tons', the last wooden warships built for the Royal Navy were all named after towns and villages listed in the *Domesday Book* whose names ended with 'ton'. HRH Prince Charles commanded *HMS Bronington* from February 1976 until December 15th of that year, the final day of his active service in the Royal Navy.

Birkenhead Priory, a Benedictine monastery

Town Hall, Birkenhead

established around 1150, is the oldest standing building on Merseyside. The site contains museum displays, concert space and a chapel dedicated to *HMS Conway*. A climb up St Mary's is rewarded with magnificent views across Birkenhead to the Welsh Hills and across the Mersey to Liverpool.

Birkenhead Park, to the east of the town centre, is a remarkable example of an early Victorian urban park with two lakes, rockery, Swiss bridge and formal gardens. This vast parkland was designed by Sir Joseph Paxton, architect of London's Crystal Palace, who also designed the spectacular main entrance which is modelled on the Temple of Illysus in Athens. Interestingly, it became the model for an even more famous park – Central Park in New York.

Just out of town is the purpose-built **Williamson Art Gallery & Museum** which exhibits a wealth of local and maritime history, a permanent display of Victorian oil paintings, tapestries by Lee and English watercolours. The gallery also hosts a full programme of temporary exhibitions.

WEST KIRBY

18 miles NW of Chester on the A540

Set beside the Dee estuary and looking across to the Welsh mountains, West Kirby was just a small fishing village until the railway link with Liverpool was established in the 1880s. Today, it's a bustling seaside town with some 28,000 inhabitants. A big attraction here is the **West Kirby Marine Lake**, a 52-acre man-made saltwater lake. With a maximum depth of 5ft it offers a degree of safety unobtainable on the open sea. Courses in sailing, windsurfing and canoeing are available at the Wirral Sailing Centre.

West Kirby is well-known to bird-watchers and naturalists because of the

PALMS FINE FOODS

22 Banks Road, West Kirby, Wirral, Cheshire CH48 0RD
Tel: 0151 625 6776

Established more than 25 years ago, **Palms Fine Foods** is well known throughout the area for the quality of produce on sale here. Debbie Williams took over the business in 2004 and has continued to extend the variety and range of items on offer. A superb choice of fresh bread and cakes are available and the shelves are stocked with a colourful

array of preserves. Cheese lovers will find a huge choice to ponder over, along with an extensive selection of meats and vegetarian products. Many of the items are organic and quite a few of them are not available in supermarkets.

Debbie and her helpful staff are always on hand to assist customers find exactly what they want amongst the enormous range of products on sale.

Hilbre Island

Distance:	5.0 mile (8.0 kilometres)
Typical time:	120 mins
Height gain:	25 metres
Map:	Explorer 266
Walk:	ww.walkingworld.com ID:1738
Contributor:	Jim Grindle

Access Information:

Merseyrail to West Kirby Station. There is a large car park at the rear of the leisure centre next to the station.

Description:

The walk from West Kirby to Hilbre is not exacting but can be done only if there is sufficient time between tides. It is also quite a bracing place to visit, so you need to wrap up warm on most occasions. The rewards are an open vista of the estuary and the nearby Welsh hills, seabirds and waders and grey Atlantic seals; highly recommended.

Additional Information

All the facilities are on the mainland; there are no toilets or cafe and very little shelter on the islands, although a visitor centre is promised. You can ring the Ranger Service for information about the tides on 0151 648 4371.

It is advised that you leave the islands three hours before high water. The three islands form part of the Dee Estuary SSSI which is one of the ten most important estuaries in Europe for the overwintering of wildfowl and waders and as a resting-place for other birds on migration. The bright red rock is Bunter sandstone, which also forms Thurstaston Hill on the mainland.

Many flint arrowheads and other artefacts from Neolithic times have been found on the islands, while a bronze axe-head and a burial urn show occupation during the Bronze Age. The Romans had a signal station here and there is written evidence of the Normans' presence. In 1864 a burial slab with four skeletons beneath was discovered, while a cross head dating from about 1000 AD has also been found (you will find what looks like a grave carved out of the stone as you approach Waymark 8).

The Dean and Chapter of Chester Cathedral owned and leased out the islands for many years in a period when they were visited by passengers waiting to embark for Ireland. At that time there was a public house on Hilbre. Later still, there was a telegraph signal station and a lifeboat station.

Features:

River, Sea, Pub, Toilets, Play Area, Church, Wildlife, Birds, Flowers, Great Views, Cafe, Gift Shop, Food Shop, Good for Kids, Mostly Flat, Public Transport, Nature Trail, Restaurant, Tea Shop

Walk Directions:

1 Turn to the right outside the station and in a few moments you will see the ornate Barclays Bank building on the other side of the road. If unsure ask anybody to direct you to Safeway.

2 Turn left here, pass Safeway and you will come to the shore.

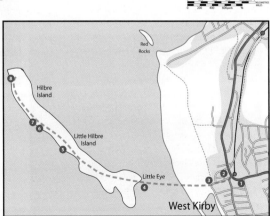

3 Just to the left there are toilets and more important, a notice-board with good advice for anybody about to make the crossing. It is important that you follow the instructions. Do not attempt to go half-right directly to Hilbre, but go out at right angles towards the first, smaller island.

4 This is Little Eye. Here you turn right and make for the next island.

5 It isn't Hilbre though, but Middle Eye (or Little Hilbre). You can go around it on either side but it is much easier to climb onto it. There are some steps towards the left-hand side. Go the whole length of the island, climb down the easy rocks on the far side and make for Hilbre itself.

6 Head for the left where you will find a ramp.

7 Go up this onto the island and walk the whole length, passing a number of buildings, including what is expected be a visitor centre. At the far end are the remains of a lifeboat station, which is as far as you can go.

8 The buildings ahead are the old lifeboat station. From here retrace your steps back to West Kirby.

Hilbre Islands, part-time islands that can be reached at low tide across Dee Sands. Permits (free) from the Wirral Borough Council are required to visit the main island where there is a resident warden. Two smaller islands, Middle Eye and the tiny Little Eye, do not require permits. The latter is notable for its impressive number of wader roosts.

West Kirby is also the starting point for the **Wirral Way**, a 12-mile long linear nature reserve and country park created mostly from the trackbed of the old West Kirby to Hooton railway. When it was opened in 1973 it was one of the first Country Parks in Britain. The local council has also produced a series of circular walks based around the former stations along the line. One of these, **Hadlow Road Station**, a short distance from the centre of Willaston, is especially interesting. The station hasn't seen a train since 1962 but everything here is spick and span, the signal box and ticket office apparently ready for action, a trolley laden with milk churns waiting on the platform. Restored to appear as it would have been on a typical day in 1952, the station's booking office still has a pile of pre-decimal change at the ready, including silver sixpences, half-crowns and eight-sided threepenny pieces.

Brimstage

14 miles NW of Chester via M53 and A5137

The most striking building in this tiny hamlet is **Brimstage Hall**, a medieval pele, or fortified tower. It's not known why such a tower, more appropriate to the lawless border regions, should have been built in peaceful Cheshire. Another mystery is the date of its construction – estimates range from 1175 to 1350 and a raft of human bones found at the bottom of a long-forgotten well in 1957 failed to resolve any of these questions. There is another puzzle too. Could the stone carving of a smirking domestic cat in the old chapel (now a gift shop) be the original of Lewis Carroll's "Cheshire Cat" which had a notorious habit of disappearing leaving only its smile behind? Today, the old courtyard is home to a cluster of craft and speciality shops, and an excellent tea room and restaurant.

Heswall

14 miles NW of Chester on the A540

Set on a steep hillside, Heswall was an important port before the silting up of the River Dee. After decades of decline, the town flourished again as a choice retreat for Liverpool commuters following the opening of the railway tunnel under the Mersey in 1888. If you take the road down to the beach from

THE VILLAGE GALLERY

Village Road, Heswall, Wirral CH60 0BX
Tel: 0151 352 7672
e-mail: valwolff@tiscali.co.uk
website: www.village-gallery.co.uk

The Village Gallery in Heswall occupies a small sandstone single storey building that was originally the Post Office and has an unusual crenellated frontage. The gallery was established by Val Wolff in 1989 and moved to its present premises in 2001. Inside, you'll find a wide choice of goods ancient and modern – antique chairs in bold and striking modern fabrics, oils and watercolours traditional, contemporary and abstract; and oil paintings of musicians by revered artist Dorothy Bradford.

There's also studio pottery by master potters and Val also looks out for what she calls "any strikingly different objets d'art from any age and any culture". Her aim, she says, "is to offer to the public unusual, unique and sometimes quirky decorative items which make life interesting and individual. How satisfying it is to possess original works by gifted artists and craftsmen which are unique and escape the sameness of mass-produced objects. Those who dare to be different and do not wish to follow the herd are welcome with open arms!" The gallery also offers a quality framing and upholstery service.

DEE FINE ARTS

182 Telegraph Road, Heswall, Wirral CH60 0AJ
Tel/Fax: 0151 342 6657
e-mail: sales@deefinearts.com
website: www.deefinearts.com

In November 2005 Dee Fine Arts celebrated its 25th Birthday. Deirdre Waite started the business working from home in partnership with her husband John. They specialise in contemporary paintings and prints, and mount regular exhibitions, including one-man shows. The work of local artists such as Heswall-born Matthew Snowden, known for his evocative local landscapes, and well-known artists such as Anne Bridges, Lynda Roberts and George Thompson, have all had exhibitions in the Gallery. Complimenting the artwork is an excellent selection of pottery from local potters and small bronze animal sculptures from Midland-based sculptors.

A key aspect in Dee Fine Art's success is its excellent framing service. They stock what is probably the best selection of frames on Merseyside with a choice of nearly 400 in metal, wood, ovals and swepts. There are also nearly 350 different coloured mounts available. "We frame anything from simple prints to 3D items including, recently, a football signed by Wayne Rooney," says Deirdre. Other services provided by Dee Fine Arts include restoration of oils and watercolours; washlining of mounts and calligraphy. Stretching of tapestries and needleworks are two other specialities.

the town centre there are outstanding views across the Dee estuary to the hills of Wales. Heswall's most famous son is the cricketer Ian Botham.

THORNTON HOUGH

14 miles NW of Chester via the A540 and B5136

The huge village green at Thornton Hough, covering some 14 acres and surrounded by half-timbered black and white houses, was one of the most picturesque spots in Cheshire until it was relocated to Merseyside in 1974. Much of the village was built by Lord Leverhulme after he established his soap factory at Port Sunlight a few miles to the north and his grandson lives at Thornton Manor (private). The village boasts two churches, one of which has no fewer than five clocks – the fifth was installed by Joseph Hirst, a Yorkshire mill owner who also built houses here and wished to see a church clock from his bedroom window.

PARKGATE

12 miles NW of Chester via the A540 and B5134

After Neston port became unusable, maritime traffic moved along the Dee Estuary to Parkgate which, as the new gateway to Ireland, saw some notable visitors. John Wesley, who made regular trips to Ireland, preached here while waiting for a favourable wind, and George Frederick Handel returned via Parkgate after conducting the very first performance of *The Messiah* in Dublin. J.M.W. Turner came to sketch the lovely view across to the Flintshire hills. A little later, Parkgate enjoyed a brief spell as a fashionable spa. Lord Nelson's mistress, Lady Hamilton (who was born at nearby Ness where you can still see the family home, Swan Cottage) took the waters here in an effort to cure an unfortunate skin disease. Another visitor was Mrs Fitzherbert, already

CHURCH FARM ORGANICS

Church Farm, Church Lane, Thurstaston, Wirral, Cheshire CH61 0HW
Tel: 0151 648 7838 Mobile: 07801 087483
Fax: 0151 648 9644
e-mail: sales@churchfarm.org.uk
website: www.churchfarm.org.uk

Taking over an old cattle farm in 1992, Steve and Brenda Ledsham have created and built up **Church Farm Organics** to be one of the very best sources of organic produce in the whole area. Their achievement has been recognised by their receiving the accolade of Farm Shop of the Year in both 2001 and 2004. The fruit and vegetables on sale in the farm shop are all organic and most of them are grown on the 60-acre farm, along with bedding and herbaceous plants. Among hundreds of organic lines, including meat and fish, the owners also sell their own honey and free range eggs, vital elements in their commitment to selling local food to local people, and to contributing to the local community in whatever ways they can.

This ethos manifests itself in many ways: the coffee shop on the premises is a favourite meeting place, and among other services are a box scheme and home delivery service, pick-your-own facilities in season (including a wonderful maze of lavender), and a livery yard. The shop is closed on Mondays; open Tuesday, 10am-7pm; Wednesday to Friday, 10am-5.30pm; Saturday 9am-5.30pm; and Sunday, 11am-5pm.

secretly married to the Prince Regent, later George IV. When Holyhead developed into the main gateway to Ireland, Parkgate's days as a port and watering-place were numbered. But with fine Georgian houses lining the promenade, this attractive little place still retains the atmosphere of a gracious spa town.

NESTON

11 miles NW of Chester off the A540

Right up until the early 19th century, Neston was the most significant town in The Wirral, one of a string of small ports along the River Dee. In Tudor times, Neston had been one of the main embarkation points for travellers to Ireland but the silting up of the river was so swift and inexorable that by the time the New Quay, begun in 1545, was completed, it had became useless. Visiting Neston in the late 1700s, Anna Seward described the little town set on a hill overlooking the Dee Estuary as "a nest from the storm of the ocean".

THE WELSH BORDERS

Awake or asleep, the medieval Lords of the Marches made sure their swords were close at hand. At any time, a band of wild-haired Welshmen might rush down from the hills to attack the hated Normans who had dispossessed them of their land. A thousand years earlier their enemies had been the Romans and the centuries-old struggle along the Marches would only end when one of their own people, Henry Tudor, defeated Richard III in 1485 and ascended the throne as Henry VII. Conflict was to flare up again during the Civil War when the Welsh supported the Royalist forces against mainly Parliamentary Cheshire but nowadays the valley of the Dee is a

peaceful and picturesque area, and nowhere more so than around Farndon on the Denbighshire border.

FARNDON

7 miles S of Chester off the B5130

Built on a hillside overlooking the River Dee, Farndon is literally a stone's throw from Wales. Most travellers agree that the best approach to the principality is by way of this little town and its ancient bridge. Records show that building of the bridge began in 1345 and it is one of only two surviving medieval bridges in the county, the other being in Chester. From Farndon's bridge, riverside walks by the Dee extend almost up to its partner in Chester. During the Civil War, Farndon's strategic position between Royalist North Wales and parliamentarian Cheshire led to many skirmishes here. Those stirring events are colourfully depicted in a stained glass window in the church, although only the Royalist heroes are included.

One Farndon man who deserves a memorial of some kind but doesn't have one is John Speed, the famous cartographer, who was born here in 1542. He followed his father's trade as a tailor, married and had 18 children, and was nearly 50 before he was able to devote himself full time to researching and producing his beautifully drawn maps. Fortunately, he lived to the age of 87 and his 54 Maps of England and Wales were the first really accurate ones to be published.

Close to Farndon, and well signposted from the A534, stands **Stretton Watermill**, a working corn mill in a lovely peaceful setting.

MALPAS

14 miles S of Chester on the B5069

With its charming black and white

cottages and elegant Georgian houses Malpas is one of the most delightful old villages in Cheshire though its Norman-French name implies that it once lay in difficult terrain – "mal passage". Of the Norman castle that once protected this hill-top border town only a grassy mound behind the red sandstone church survives. Approached through 18th century gates attributed to Vanbrugh, **St Oswald's Church** is lavishly decorated with a striking array of gargoyles but is most notable for the splendour of its interior. The nave roof is brilliant with gilded bosses and winged angels, all created around 1480, and there are two magnificent chapels separated from the nave by delicately carved screens. The Brereton chapel dates from 1522 and contains an alabaster effigy of Sir Randal Brereton, in the armour of a medieval knight, together with his lady. Across the aisle, the Cholmondeley chapel commemorates Sir Hugh Cholmondeley who died in 1605.

The Cholmondeley family owned huge estates around Malpas and it was they who built the town's attractive old almshouses and a school in the 18th century. They lived at Cholmondeley Castle, a few miles to the north-east. The Gothic-style castle is not open to the public but the 800 acres of **Cholmondeley Castle Garden** are. The gardens are planted with a variety of acid-loving plants including rhododendrons, hydrangeas, magnolias, camellias, dogwoods, mahonias and viburnums. There's a lovely Temple Garden with a rockery, lake and islands, and a Silver Garden planted with distinctive silver-leafed plants as a commemoration of Elizabeth II's Silver Jubilee. The paddocks are home to rare breeds of farm animals, including llamas and African pygmy goats.

ROSSETT
6 miles S of Chester off the A483

In Rossett, a pleasant village beside the River Alyn, and about a mile across the border into north Wales, is The Golden Grove inn. Here, history strikes as an almost tangible force when you enter the inn's portals for the first time. The entrance and reception area of what is now the bar, (including a tiny snug bar) was the original 13th century inn in its entirety. The low oak beams and ornate carved dark wood bar were additions during the 1600s. Naturally, such an ancient establishment has its own ghost, one James Clarke who actually expired at the inn on April 21st, 1880. James was generally believed to be the landlady's lover; certainly, she had him buried in the courtyard and erected a headstone to his memory.

HIGHER KINNERTON
8 miles SW of Chester off the A55/A5104

One of the oldest and most picturesque coaching inns in north Wales, the Royal Oak, also boasts a resident ghost and stands where one of most famous trees in the country once towered. Here in September 1644 King Charles I, fleeing Cromwell's troops after his defeat at Chester, evaded his pursuers by hiding amidst the branches of the Kinnerton Oak. Derek Thompson, an accomplished artist who runs the Royal Oak together with his wife Lee, has inscribed this romantic tale around the walls of the old beamed snug. It's just one of the many charming features here, along with the inglenook crackling with log fires and the fascinating collection of old pots and water jugs.

CHESHIRE PEAKS & PLAINS

To the east rise the Peak District hills,

THE PLOUGH AT EATON

Macclesfield Road, Eaton, Congleton,
Cheshire CW12 2NH
Tel: 01260 280207 Fax: 01260 298458
e-mail: theploughinn@hotmail.co.uk
website: www.plough-eaton.co.uk

The Plough at Eaton has a long history going
back to the 1600s when it was built as a
coaching inn. In those days, the beer used to
be brought up from the cellar in large jugs and
served to travellers in the lamp-lit bar and cosy
snug. The inn has been modernised in recent
years but the ancient oak beams, small alcoves
and blazing open hearth fires are still in place and make this a cosy, intimate place for a quiet drink or
a meal. Food is also served in the Old Barn Restaurant which is full of character with its gallery and
wealth of exposed timbers. Although it looks as if it has always been here, the barn is originally from
Wales where it watched over the Welsh hills for more than 300 years. It arrived at Eaton in hundreds
of pieces rather like a huge jigsaw puzzle waiting to be assembled. Since its change of address the barn
fulfils a new role as a luxurious restaurant rather than as a winter store for cattle feed.

As well as the popular menu, specials which change regularly, are served in both the non-smoking
Old Barn and the pub. It includes traditional
favourites such as steak & kidney pudding,
and imaginative, original dishes created by
the experienced team of chefs. All the dishes
are freshly prepared from natural ingredients
and served by attentive and helpful staff. In
2004, the restaurant was runner-up in *High
Life* magazine's North West Restaurant of the
Year Award; made its first entry into the *Good
Pub Guide*, and received a four-Diamond
rating from the RAC.

If you are planning to stay in this
attractive corner of the county, close to the
Peak National Park and historic attractions
such as Gawsworth Hall, the Plough offers
some impressive accommodation. In 1985,
the garages at the rear of the pub were converted into eight double en suite rooms. The bedrooms were
created by top London designer Michael Priest of Belgravia who also created the interior design for
Raymond Blanc's Le Manoir aux Quat' Saisons
and Inverlockie Castle. The bedrooms were
inspired by traditional Royal Doulton china
ranges and feature matching key fobs and door
nameplates. A further nine rooms are currently
nearing completion, all offering the same
sumptuous comfort and some with disabled
facilities.

The Plough is also licensed to hold civil
ceremony marriages and its delightful garden
provides a perfect setting for those all-
important wedding photographs.

westwards gently undulating pastures and woods drop down to the Cheshire Plain. This is an area of sudden and striking contrasts. Within half a mile you can find yourself travelling out of lowland Cheshire into some of the highest and wildest countryside - acres of lonely uplands with rugged gritstone crags, steep valleys watered by moorland streams. Here too is the old salt town of Middlewich, and Sandbach with its famous Saxon crosses, along with a host of quiet, attractive villages. The busy M6 cuts through the area, north to south, but you have only to drive a few miles off the motorway to find yourself wandering along winding country lanes between fertile fields. The two major towns of South Cheshire are Nantwich, with a history stretching back beyond Roman times, and Crewe, with no history at all until 1837. That was when the Grand Junction Railway arrived and five years later moved all its construction and repair workshops to what had been a green field site. We begin our survey of this varied region at Congleton, set amongst the foothills of the Pennines.

CONGLETON

Some residents have dubbed this thriving old market town the "Venice of the North" because of the number of nearby man-made lakes such as Astbury Mere and Brereton Country Park which both offer a wide range of recreational activities. Set in the foothills of the Pennines, Congleton was an inhabited place as long ago as the Stone Age. The remains of a 5,000-year-old chambered tomb known as **The Bridestones** can be seen beside the hill road running eastwards from the town to the A523 road to Leek.

In Elizabethan times, the townspeople of Congleton seem to have had a passion

for bear baiting. On one occasion, when the town bear died they handed 16 shillings (80p) to the Bear Warden to acquire another beast. The money had originally been collected to buy a town bible: the disgraceful misappropriation of funds gave rise to the ditty: *"Congleton rare, Congleton rare, sold the bible to buy a bear"*. Known locally as the "Bear Town", Congleton was the very last town in England to outlaw the cruel practice of bear baiting but the town's emblem is still an upright chained bear. A more attractive distinction is the fact that it is also one of only four towns in Cheshire where the medieval street pattern has remained intact and the only town where the curfew bell is still rung each night at 8pm.

One of the oldest buildings in Congleton is **The Lion & Swan Hotel**, a 16th century coaching inn on the old Manchester to London route. This grand old building with its superb black and white half-timbered frontage has been fully restored to its Tudor glory, with a wealth of exposed, dark oak beams and elaborately carved fireplaces, as well as the oldest window in town, dating from 1596. Another ancient hostelry is **Ye Olde Kings Arms** whose pink-washed half-timbered frontage leans picturesquely to the left as if exhausted with the weight of years.

Congleton's impressive Venetian Gothic style **Town Hall**, built in 1864, contains some interesting exhibits recalling the town's long history, including some fine civic regalia. There are displays recording the work of such ancient civic officials as the swine-catcher, the chimney-looker and the ale-taster, and aids to domestic harmony like the "brank" – a bridle for nagging wives which used to be fastened to a wall in the market place. Other exhibits include a prehistoric log boat, coin hoards from

THE SWETTENHAM ARMS

Swettenham Village, nr Congleton,
Cheshire CW12 2LF
Tel: 01477 571284
e-mail: info@swettenhamarms.co.uk
website: www.swettenhamarms.co.uk

Located just four miles from Junction 18 of the M6, Swettenham village sits beside the River Dane in an Area of Outstanding Natural Beauty. At the heart of the village are the 700-year-old parish church and, just across the road, the **Swettenham Arms**, a stunning 16th century inn, as picturesque an old hostelry as you could find. It began life as a nunnery where the sisters would provide weary travellers with much needed rest and sustenance. That ancient tradition is maintained by the current owners, Jim and Frances Cunningham, who have garnered a shelf full of awards for their outstanding inn. The AA featured it in their Pick of the Pubs 2006; CAMRA named it as Summer Pub (Macclesfield & East Cheshire) 2005; in the same year it was also declared Best Dressed Country Pub in Great Britain and a Free House of the Year Finalist ....the roll of honour stretches back to 1996 when it was also a Freehouse of the Year finalist.

A major attraction at the Swettenham Arms is the superb home-cooked food which is based almost exclusively on the freshest of local produce and served seven days a week, at lunchtime and in the evenings, against the backdrop of old timbers and open fires. The menu offers a blend of traditional fare and imaginative alternatives such as grilled goat's cheese with toasted walnuts and peaches amongst the starters, and Thai green chicken curry with scented jasmine rice as one of the main courses. To complement your meal, a wide range of high quality beers is available.

Jim and Frances are very much 'hands on' hosts, ensuring extra little touches such as fresh flowers and welcoming fires on cooler days. They have also produced an interesting little booklet detailing leisurely walks and days out around the Swettenham Arms. These include the Lavender and Sunflower Meadow which they created adjacent to the inn. It will be in full flower for the summer of 2006 and Jim and Frances expect it will prove a wonderful attraction for brides who choose the inn's Lovell Suite for their wedding. The suite is one of the most charming in Cheshire and provides an idyllic setting for a romantic civil wedding ceremony.

the Civil War, and more recent acquisitions covering the Industrial Revolution and the Second World War.

During the 18th century Congleton developed as an important textile town with many of its mills involved in silk manufacture, cotton spinning and ribbon weaving. In Mill Green near the River Dane, you can still see part of the very first silk mill to operate here.

ASTBURY

2 miles SW of Congleton on the A34

The pretty little village of Astbury, set around a triangular village green, was once more important than neighbouring Congleton which is why it has a much older church, built between 1350 and 1540. Arguably the finest parish church in the county, **St Mary's** is famous for its lofty recessed spire (which rises from a tower almost detached from the nave), and the superb timber work inside: a richly carved ceiling, intricate tracery on

Little Moreton Hall, near Astbury

the rood screen, and a lovely Jacobean font cover.

But just three miles down the A34 is an even more remarkable building. Black and white half-timbered houses have almost become a symbol for the county of Cheshire and the most stunning example is undoubtedly **Little Moreton Hall** (National Trust), a "wibbly wobbly" house which provided a memorable location for Granada TV's adaptation of *The Adventures of Moll Flanders*. The only bricks to be seen are in the chimneys, and the hall's huge overhanging gables, slanting walls, and great stretches of leaded windows, create wonderfully complex patterns, all magically reflected in the still flooded moat. Ralph Moreton began construction in 1480 and the fabric of this magnificent house has changed little since the 16th century. A richly panelled Great Hall, parlour and chapel show off superb Elizabethan plaster and wood work. Free guided tours give visitors a fascinating insight into Tudor life, and there's also a beautifully reconstructed Elizabethan knot garden with clipped box hedges, a period herb garden and a Yew Tunnel.

About a mile south of Little Moreton Hall is the Rode Hall estate. It was an 18th century owner of the estate, Randle Wilbraham, who built the famous folly of **Mow Cop** (National Trust) to enhance the view from his mansion. This mock ruin stands atop a rocky hill 1,100ft above sea level, just yards from the Staffordshire border. On a clear day, the views are fantastic: Alderley Edge to the north, the Pennines to the north-east, south to Cannock

Chase and Shropshire, and westwards across Cheshire. **Rode Hall** itself, home of the Wilbraham family since 1669, is a fine early 18th century mansion standing within a park created by three of England's most notable landscape designers. Humphry Repton drew up the plans for the landscape and Rood Pool in 1790; between 1800 and 1810 John Webb constructed the Pool, a 40-acre lake, along with the terraced rock garden and grotto. In 1860 William Nesfield designed the formal garden, which remains much as he planned it to this day.

Biddulph Grange Gardens

BIDDULPH

5 miles SE of Congleton on the A527

Biddulph Grange Gardens are imaginatively divided into a series of enclosed areas bounded by massive rock structures, hedges, stumps, roots and moulded banks. A trail leads through a superb Chinese garden to an enchanting Scottish glen while other areas reproduce the magic of Egypt or the tranquillity of rural America. The shop is packed with gardening books, Victorian plants, cards and quality souvenirs, and there's also a pleasant tearoom offering local specialities and home-made cakes.

SANDBACH

1 mile SW from Junction 17 of the M6

Sandbach's former importance as a stopping place for coaches (both stage and motor) is evident in the attractive old half-timbered inns and houses, some of them thatched, which line the main street. Sandbach's handsome market square is dominated by its two famous

stone crosses, 16 and 11 feet tall. These superbly carved crosses (actually only the shafts have survived) were created some time in the 9th century, and the striking scenes are believed to represent the conversion of Mercia to Christianity during the reign of King Penda. A plaque at their base notes that they were restored in 1816 "after destruction by iconoclasts" – i.e. the Puritans. The restorers had to recover fragments from here and there: some had been used as street paving, cottage steps or in the walls of a well. Somehow they fitted the broken stones together, like pieces of a jigsaw, and the result is immensely impressive.

HOLMES CHAPEL

5 miles N of Sandbach on the A50/A54

In the mid-18th century, the little village of Holmes Chapel was stirred by two important events. In 1738, John Wesley came and preached outside St Luke's Church. Fifteen years later, on July 10th, 1753, a disastrous fire swept through the village. When the flames were finally

La Casa Vecchia

4 Old Market Square, Sandbach, Cheshire CW11 1AT
Tel: 01270 761077
e-mail: info@lacasavecchia.co.uk
website: www.lacasavecchia.co.uk

In Italian **'La Casa Vecchia'** means The Old House which is a faithful description of the Grade II listed 16th century building in which you'll find this outstanding restaurant. It was established in 1989 by Hazel Warr who says she took inspiration from her Italian relatives and maintained the ethos of the restaurant's origins by providing a wide range of freshly cooked Italian food – pizzas, pastas, veal, chicken and steak dishes. Hazel has achieved her high standards by employing professional Italian chefs and waiters, and this strong Italian connection has made La Casa Vecchia one of the most genuine Italian dining establishments outside Italy.

Adding greatly to the truly Mediterranean atmosphere are the walls covered by a colourful mural of a Venetian seascape. "The team's objective," says Hazel "is for the customer to have a value-for-money eating experience and to thoroughly enjoy their visit to the restaurant." The menus are changed each month to ensure that every visit brings a new dining experience and every dish on the menu is made on the premises in keeping with the authentic Italian diet. This includes the wonderful desserts which make for a perfect finale.

quenched, only two buildings had survived the blaze: St Luke's Church and The Old Red Lion alongside.

About three miles southeast of Holmes Chapel, **Brereton Heath Country Park** is a popular beauty spot where the heath land and flower meadows are crisscrossed by a network of many footpaths. The former sand quarry provides a congenial habitat for a range of species details of which can be obtained from the park ranger at the Visitor Centre. The lake here is used for angling, canoeing and windsurfing.

Goostrey

6 miles NE of Middlewich on minor road off A50

The village of Goostrey is a quiet little place on a minor road just north of Holmes Chapel but famous for its annual gooseberry shows where competitors vie to produce the plumpest berries. The name of the village has nothing to do with gooseberries but derives from a personal name, Godhere, and the Saxon word for tree.

Lower Withington

7 miles NE of Middlewich on the B5392

Visible from miles around, the huge white dish of the world famous **Jodrell Bank** radio telescope has a good claim to being the most distinctive building in the county. The Observatory came into service in 1957 and was used by both Americans and the Soviets in their exploration of space. In November 2002, following an upgrading, the radio telescope re-entered service with a capacity 30 times that of the original. Jodrell bank's Science Centre offers visitors a wonderful array of hands-on exhibits, including a 25ft telescope, while its Planetarium travels through the heavens, explaining the secrets of Rocky Dwarfs and Gassy Giants along the way.

DELIKATESSA

4 Heath Street, Crewe, Cheshire
Tel: 01270 253444
e-mail: tom@delikatessa.co.uk
website: www.delikatessa.co.uk

Opened in December 2002 and located just three doors along from the Lyceum Theatre, **Delikatessa** is a family-owned and run quality delicatessen, café and coffee bar. Everything here is done with great style with lots of stained glass, light-coloured oak, ceramic tiles and modern lighting. The delicatessen area is on the ground floor and is stocked with a vast range of products. Amongst the speciality cheeses are Mrs Appleby's Cheshire Cheese and Blue Cheshire, along with Irish and Italian varieties. Then there are the olives, sun-dried tomatoes, artichokes and balsamic onions; a

wide selection of meats including Italian and Polish salamis; and a daily changing selection of 'Patchwork Pâtés' such as duck liver, apricot and brandy.

From the ground floor, a fine oak staircase leads to the first floor coffee bar which serves an appetising choice of salads (salami, brie & cranberry, perhaps), sandwiches and filled croissants and bagels, along with freshly ground coffee and a variety of teas. Everything on the menu is prepared to order, attractively presented and served with a smile. And if you are having a special occasion or function in the near future, Delikatessa can supply you with a really tasty and interesting selection of food.

THE OLD SWAN RESTAURANT

Crewe Road, Madeley Heath, Crewe, Cheshire
CW3 9LD
Tel: 01782 751199
website: www.theoldswaninmadeleyheath.com

After working for the Roux brothers, Antonio Carluccio and many of the well known restaurants in London, as well as running his own restaurant in Tuscany, chef Luca Nervi returned to England in 2005 with his wife Joanna and opened **The Old Swan Restaurant** in Madeley Heath. Formerly a public house, it has been renovated to become a fine dining restaurant while maintaining the cosiness of a typical English pub. A formal à la carte menu that changes with the seasons is served in the evenings, and a more informal lunch menu is served in the bar.

A typical menu might feature Lancashire blue souffle with poached pear and caramelised walnuts or confit of rabbit ravioli with truffle flavoured leeks amongst the starters; main dishes such as roasted monkfish with saffron sauce, rosti potato, braised red cabbage and glazed carrots, or fillet steak with truffle sauce. All dishes are cooked to order, vegetarians are always catered for, and half portions are available for children. To accompany your meal, the wine list features some fine Tuscan wines which are directly imported from small producers. The Old Swan is non-smoking; credit cards are accepted; closed all day on Tuesdays.

The dynamic duo of Albert Einstein and Isaac Newton are at hand to guide visitors on this fascinating exploration of the Universe. Outside, there's a superb 35-acre arboretum planted with 2,000 species of trees and shrubs, each one helpfully labelled, and an Environment Discovery Centre which explains the importance of trees to the natural environment. The site also contains a picnic area, play area, café and shop.

In the nearby village of Lower Withington, old farm buildings have been sympathetically converted to provide an attractive setting for **Welltrough Dried Flowers** which boasts one of the largest selections of dried and silk flowers in the North. There are literally hundreds of different kinds and shapes, and the seven separate showrooms include a permanent Christmas Room, a Dickensian Street and a demonstration room where Day Workshops are held.

MIDDLEWICH

2 miles W of Junction 18 of the M6

The Romans called their settlement here Salinae, meaning saltworks. Excavations have revealed outlines of their long, narrow, timber workshops, brine pits and even a jar with the word AMYRCA scratched on it. (Amurca was the Latin name for brine waste which was used throughout the Empire as a cleansing agent). Middlewich Town Council publishes an informative leaflet detailing the **Roman Middlewich Trail,** a one-mile circular walk that reveals the history and layout of the Roman town and shows how Middlewich would have looked in those days.

In modern times, it was the need for Cheshire's salt manufacturers to get their cumbersome product to markets in the Midlands and the south which gave a great impetus to the building of canals in the county. Middlewich was particularly well-provided for with its own Middlewich Branch Canal linking the town to both the Shropshire Union and the Trent & Mersey canals. Today, most of the canal traffic comprises traditional narrow boats which can also be hired for holiday trips.

During the Civil War, Middlewich witnessed two of the bloodiest battles fought in the county. In March 1644, Royalists trapped Cromwell's men in the narrow lanes and alleys of the town and slaughtered 200 of them. A few managed to find refuge in **St Michael's Church.** The church has changed greatly since those days but still has some notable old carvings and a curiosity in the form of a carved coat of arms of the Kinderton family of nearby Kinderton Hall. Their crest shows a dragon eating a child, a reference to the occasion on which Baron Kinderton killed a local dragon as it was devouring a child. The incident apparently took place at Moston, near Sandbach, and a lane there is still called Dragon Lane.

CREWE

In 1837 the Grand Junction Railway arrived and five years later moved all its construction and repair workshops to what had been a green field site. A workforce of 900 had to be housed so the company rapidly built cottages, each one shared by four of the lowest paid workers, and detached "mansions" which accommodated four families of the more highly skilled. At one time, seven out of every 10 men in Crewe worked on the railways.

Later, in 1887, the railway company also provided the town with one of the most splendid parks in the north of England, **Queens Park**, some 40 acres of lawns and flowerbeds together with an ornamental lake. Rolls Royce's engineering works brought further prosperity to the town, but it is as a railway centre that Crewe is best known. Even today, the station offers a choice of six different routes to all points of the compass. The **Railway Age** museum offers a fascinating insight into Crewe's place in railway history with hands-on exhibits, steam locomotive rides, model railway displays and a children's playground. Also worth a visit is the **Lyceum Theatre**, built in 1902 and with its glorious Edwardian opulence undimmed.

A couple of miles north of Crewe, **Lakemore Country Park Animal Kingdom** is home to a wide variety of animals – wallabies, llamas, miniature donkeys, owls and many other unusual and rare breeds. Children can feed that farm animals, visit the pets corner and enjoy both the indoor and outdoor play areas. Within the 36-acre site are five fishing lakes and there's also a log cabin coffee shop.

A pleasant country walk using footpaths, towpaths and old drovers' roads starts at Moss Bridge, on the western outskirts, of Crewe, and takes in **Sandbach Flashes**, one of the best places for birdwatching in Cheshire. Waders and wildfowl gather in large numbers in winter, attracting predators such as

merlin and sparrowhawks, and the salty conditions resulting from the local industry are ideal for plants usually only found in coastal areas, such as sea club-rush, lesser sea-spurrey and sea aster. Further along the walk, Winterley Pool is a refuge favoured by mute swans.

ENGLESEA BROOK

4 miles SE of Crewe off the A500

In the hamlet of Englesea Brook an early 19th century 'Ranter' Chapel now houses the **Museum of Primitive Methodism** which gives an insight into the working class religion of that era with the help of a video, museum and children's costumes.

NANTWICH

4 miles SW of Crewe on the A51

The most disastrous event in the long history of Nantwich was the Great Fire of 1583 which consumed some 600 of its thatched and timber-framed buildings. The blaze raged for 20 days and the townspeople's terror was compounded when some bears kept behind the Crown Hotel escaped. (Four bears from Nantwich are mentioned in Shakespeare's comedy *The Merry Wives of Windsor*). Queen Elizabeth contributed the huge sum of £2,000 and also donated quantities of timber from Delamere Forest to assist in the town's rebuilding.

JULIE AT RUTH RAE

56 Hospital Street, Nantwich, Cheshire CW5 5RP
Proprietor: Julie Clewlow
Tel/Fax: 01270 624555
e-mail: Julie@ruthrae.co.uk

Established for 40 years **Julie at Ruth Rae** specialises in clothes of distinction for the 40+ age group, sizes 10-26. Experienced sales assistants are available to advise and an in house alteration service is provided with no charge on new stock.

A grateful citizen, Thomas Cleese, commemorated this royal largesse with a plaque on his new house at No. 41, High Street. The plaque is still in place and reads: "God grant our ryal Queen in England longe to raign / For she hath put her helping hand to bild this towne again".

The most striking of the buildings to survive the conflagration, perhaps because it was surrounded by a moat, is the lovely black and white house in Hospital Street, known as **Churche's Mansion** after the merchant Richard Churche who built it in 1577. Astonishingly, when the house was up for sale in 1930, no buyer showed any interest and the building was on the point of being transported brick by brick to America when a public-spirited local doctor stepped in and rescued it. The ground floor is now an antiques centre.

The Great Fire also spared the stone-built 14th century church. This fine building, with an unusual octagonal tower, is sometimes called the **Cathedral of South Cheshire** and dates from the period of the town's greatest prosperity as a salt town and trading centre. Of exceptional interest are the magnificent chancel and the wonderful carvings in the choir. On the misericords (tip-up seats) are mermaids, foxes (some dressed as monks in a sharp dig at priests), pigs, and the legendary Wyvern, half-dragon, half-bird, whose name is linked with the River Weaver, 'wyvern' being an old pronunciation of weaver. An old tale about the building of the church tells of an old woman who brought ale and food each day from a local inn to the masons working on the site. The masons discovered that the woman was cheating them by keeping back some of the money they put "in the pot" for their refreshment. They dismissed her and

INGLENOOK FINE ARTS

31 Pillory Street, Nantwich, Cheshire CW5 5BQ
Tel: 01270 611188 or 0800 652 1071
e-mail: inglenookfinearts@yahoo.co.uk

A professional artist and picture restorer, Jill Bagshaw established **Inglenook Fine Arts** in 1993 although she and her husband Gerry have been restoring paintings for some 30 years. They offer a one-stop shop service for all aspects of fine art restoration, cleaning and bespoke picture framing to conservation and museum standards if required. Services include cleaning, lining and relining damaged or torn canvasses, making good paint loss, varnish stripping of oil

paintings on canvas and panels, from ancient to modern, and also all kinds of frame restoration.

Also available is a bespoke swept frame-making service with a choice of more than 800 mouldings. It's not just paintings to be framed, Inglenook also frames tapestries, embroideries, batiks, decoupages, medals, football shirts, Javan marriage necklaces – in fact, just about anything you can think of! On display in the shop is a wide range of open and limited edition prints and Jill is happy to take commissions for paintings of landscapes, portraits of your favourite view, person or pet. All the services available at Inglenook are also provided by Gerry at his Greenends Gallery in Whitchurch.

took revenge by making a stone carving showing the old woman being carried away by Old Nick himself, her hand still stuck in a pot. A plaque in the church remembers the Rev Joseph Priestley (1733-1804), who was a minister here. A writer on education, philosophy, government and science, he is best known today as the discoverer of oxygen.

During the Civil War, Nantwich was the only town in Cheshire to support Cromwell's Parliamentary army. After several weeks of fighting, the Royalist forces were finally defeated on 25th January, 1644 and the people of Nantwich

Nantwich Church

celebrated by wearing sprigs of holly in their hair. As a result, the day became known as **"Holly Holy Day"** and every year, on the Saturday closest to January 25th, the town welcomes Cromwellian pikemen and battle scenes are re-enacted by members of the Sealed Knot. There are records of the Civil War in the **Nantwich Museum** in Pillory Street which also has exhibitions about the town and its dairy and cheese-making industries.

But it was salt that had once made Nantwich second only in importance to Chester in the county. The Romans had mined salt here for their garrisons at Chester and Stoke where the soldiers received part of their wages in "sal", or salt. The payment was called a "salarium", hence the modern word "salary". Nantwich remained a salt producing town right up to the 18th century but then it was overtaken by towns like Northwich which enjoyed

better communications on the canal system. But a brine spring still supplies Nantwich's outdoor swimming pool.

Within a few miles of the town are two notable gardens. A major attraction, a mile south of the town off the A51, is **Stapeley Water Gardens** which attracts nearly 1.5 million visitors each year. The 64-acre site includes the National Collection of Nymphaea – more than 350 varieties of water lilies, a Tropical Oasis with exotic flowers and pools stocked with piranhas and huge catfish, and a comprehensively equipped garden centre. Other attractions within the landscaped grounds include a restaurant, two cafés and a gift shop. The Zoo room is home to a family of cotton top tamarin monkeys, water dragons, box tortoises, scorpions, tarantulas and a cayman crocodile. There are frogs of all kinds - poison arrow frogs, tree frogs, South American cane toads - in the

World of Frogs, while in the tropical house piranhas, catfish and pacus are shaded by the enormous leaves of the Giant Amazon water lily. The Stingray Pool, the Tunnel of Underwater Life and the blacktip reef sharks are other attractions not to be missed at this brilliant family venue, which is open throughout the year.

About six miles further south along the A51 and straddling the Staffordshire border, **Bridgemere Garden World** provided the location for BBC TV's *Gardeners' Diary*. This is just one of 22 different gardens, amongst them a French rose garden, a woodland setting, a cottage garden and a rock and water area. The extensive glasshouses contain houseplants of every description and the garden centre is stocked with everything a gardener could possibly need. There's also an aquatics house with some splendid fish, a specialist food hall, a

flower arrangers' centre, a bookshop, restaurant and coffee shop.

A few miles south of Nantwich, just off the A530 Whitchurch road, is **Hack Green Secret Nuclear Bunker**. For 50 years this vast underground complex remained secret, built as the centre of regional government in the case of a nuclear war, but it was declassified in 1993 and is now a unique attraction open to the public. Visitors pass through the massive blast doors into the chilling world of the Cold War, including the Minister of State's office, life support area, communications centre and decontamination facilities. Cinemas show once secret films, and children can have fun as secret agents, following the Soviet Spy Mouse Trail. A trip can end with a visit to the bunker's NAAFI-style canteen to pick up survival rations, and a browse through the shop for a souvenir.

THE DUSTY MILLER

Cholmondeley Road, Wrenbury, Nantwich, Cheshire CW5 8HG
Tel: 01270 780537
website: www.dustymiller-wrenbury.co.uk

The Dusty Miller occupies an idyllic location beside the Llangollen branch of the Shropshire Union Canal and close to one of the unusual lift bridges that are unique to this waterway. The pub's name is appropriate since it was originally a mill, built in the 1700s, and owner Mark Sumner's grandfather actually worked here as a miller. Mark, as chef/proprietor, leads a team of six in preparing the dishes on the imaginative and appetising menu which is based on fresh ingredients, many of them from the Cheshire area.

Amongst the starters you may find gravadlax (cured at Fleetwood) or Morecambe Bay potted shrimps, whilst main courses include baked chicken stuffed with Bury black pudding and pasta, roast tomatoes and rocket in a Cheshire cheese & double cream sauce. A selection of light bites (Lancashire pork sausage & egg, perhaps) and daily specials extend the choice even further. To accompany your meal, choose from the concise wine list or sample one of the excellent ales on tap, amongst them some real ales. Booking is essential on Saturday evenings and advisable at other times – don't forget to ask for a window table so you watch the activity on the canal.

AOUND NANTWICH

BEESTON

8 miles NW of Nantwich on minor road off the A49

A craggy cliff suddenly rising 500ft from the Cheshire Plain, its summit crowned by the ruins of **Beeston Castle** (English Heritage), Beeston Hill is one of the most dramatic sights in the county. The castle was built around 1220 but didn't see any military action until the Civil War. On one rather ignominious occasion during that conflict, a Royalist captain and just eight musketeers managed to capture the mighty fortress and its garrison of 60 soldiers without firing a shot. A few years later, Cromwell ordered that the castle be "slighted", or partially destroyed, but this "Castle in the Air" is still very imposing

with walls 30ft high and a well 366ft deep. An old legend asserts that Richard II tipped a hoard of coins, gold and jewels down the well, but no treasure has yet been discovered. The castle hill is a popular place for picnics, and it's worth climbing just to enjoy the spectacular views which extend across seven counties and over to a "twin" castle. **Peckforton Castle** looks just as medieval as Beeston but was, in fact, built in 1844 for the first Lord Tollemache who spared no expense in re-creating features such as a vast Great Hall and a keep with towers 60ft tall. The architect Gilbert Scott later praised Peckforton as "the very height of masquerading". Its authentic medieval appearance has made the castle a favourite location for film and TV companies, and on Sundays and Bank Holidays during the season the Middle Ages are brought to life here with mock battles and tournaments. The castle also offers guided tours, refreshments and a speciality shop.

WILLASTON

2 miles E of Nantwich between the A534 and A500

It was in the village of Willaston that one of the most unusual world records was established in 1994. Some 200 competitors had gathered at the Primary School here for the annual **World Worm Charming Championships**. The prize goes to whoever induces the greatest number of worms to poke their heads above a nine-square metre patch of playing field, aided only by a garden fork. Each contestant is allowed half an hour and the current world

Beeston Castle

champion charmed 511 out of the ground – a rate of more than 17 wrigglies a minute. The secret of his wonderful way with worms has not been revealed.

WYBUNBURY

5 miles S of Crewe on the B5071

South Cheshire's answer to the Leaning Tower of Pisa is the 100ft high tower of **St Chad's Church** in Wybunbury. It was built in 1470 above an unsuspected ancient salt bed. Subsidence has been the reason for the tower's long history of leaning sideways by as much as four feet and then being straightened up, most recently in 1989. It now rests on a reinforced concrete bed and is unlikely to deviate from the vertical again. The tower stands alone: the body of the church, once capable of holding a congregation of 1,600, collapsed on no fewer than five occasions. In 1972, the villagers finally decided to abandon it and build a new church on firmer ground.

Starting from the old tower a pleasant walk takes in **Wybunbury Moss National Nature Reserve** (see page 300), where the mossland habitat is home to rare plants such as sundew, bog asphodel and bog rosemary. The boggy area at the western end of the Moss is what remains of the well that supplied Wybunbury in the Middle Ages.

NORTH WEST CHESHIRE

The northwestern part of the county contains the pleasant rural area known as the Vale Royal, and the more industrial environs of Warrington and Runcorn. It was Prince Edward, later Edward I, who gave the area its name and who founded the great Abbey of Vale Royal in fulfilment of a solemn vow made in dramatic circumstances. He was returning from the Crusades when his ship was struck by a violent storm. The Prince made a pledge to the Virgin that if his life were spared he would found an Abbey for 100 monks. Lo! the ship was tossed ashore, and the Prince and his companions waded through the surf to safety. In 1277, Edward, now king and with his young wife Eleanor of Castile by his side, honoured his vow by placing the first stone of Vale Royal Abbey. "No monastery," he decreed, "shall be more royal than this one in liberties, wealth and honour, throughout the whole world." Vale Royal Abbey, about three miles south of Northwich, indeed became the largest and most powerful Cistercian Abbey in England, a building reputedly even more glorious than Tintern or Fountains. Unlike those abbeys, however, barely a stone of Vale Royal now remains in place. The abuse by the medieval abbots of their vast wealth, and of their unfettered power of life and death over the inhabitants of the Vale, may partly explain why their magnificent building was so quickly and completely destroyed after Henry VIII's closure of the monasteries. Over the centuries, the county has lost many fine buildings unnecessarily, but the deliberate destruction of Vale Royal Abbey must take prime place in the litany of crimes against wonderful architecture.

NORTHWICH

The Vale Royal is now a district borough centred on the old salt town of Northwich. Even before the Romans arrived, Cheshire salt was well known and highly valued. But production on a major scale at Northwich began in 1670 when rock salt was discovered in nearby Marston. Salt may seem an inoffensive sort of product, but its extraction from the Keuper marl of the Cheshire Plain

Wybunbury

Distance:	3.0 mile (4.8 kilometres)
Typical time:	90 mins
Height gain:	0 metres
Map:	Explorer 257
Walk:	ww.walkingworld.com ID:370
Contributor:	Robin and Christine Jones

Access Information:

Wybunbury is situated off the A500 Stoke to Nantwich road. Parking is available at the rear of the Swan Inn.

Description:

This is quite an intriguing walk, around Wybunbury Moss which is a nature reserve set up to protect one of the best floating bogs in Europe. A word of warning - please keep to the paths as it is dangerous to enter the Moss. If you are lucky, as we were, on returning to the Tower you may get the conducted tour. Plenty to see in this, one of Cheshire's oldest villages.

Additional Information

Please keep to the paths as it is DANGEROUS to enter the Moss. Wybunbury Moss consists of a thick bed of peat floating on water. The peat is covered by sphagnum moss and supports numerous rare bog plants including the insectivorous sundew and several very rare insect species. Wybunbury Tower was built in the 15th century. This is all that is left of the many churches built on this unstable site and eventually moved to a better one. The Tower had a lean but is now stabilised. The Moat is mentioned on the maps of the area and refers to two medieval moated houses, one built by the Bishop of Lichfield. Wybunbury is mentioned in the Doomsday Book; the oldest house is the Elizabethan cottage next door to the Swan Inn.

Features:

Pub, Church, Wildlife, Birds, Flowers, Great Views

Walk Directions:

1 Leave the car park, turn right in front of the pub and walk up the main street.

2 At Kiln Lane turn right and walk down the drive. At the stile in the hedge cross, turn left and walk along the field edge. Cross this stile and continue in the same direction. Cross this stile and enter the grounds of a large house. Keep straight ahead, aiming for the round flowerbed on the far side of the drive.

3 Walk round the circular bed; the path is on the far side.

4 At this junction of paths turn right to walk round The Moss. At this point take the left-hand gate and continue on the path.

5 Join the road and continue ahead. As the road turns left keep straight ahead into the grassy lane. Cross this stile and continue along the defined path which follows the field edge.

6 As the path turns to the right follow it through this gate. Follow the path to this stile, cross it and turn right along the field edge. Cross this stile and follow the path now heading for the church tower. Follow the track leading up to a gate in the wall of the churchyard.

7 Walk through the graveyard and through this gate at the foot of the tower. Should you see this gentleman on your travels he may (as he did with us) give you a tour of the tower. Go through the gate and turn left to follow the path round the tower. Go through this gate and descend the steps - take care, they can be slippery.

8 When the path reaches the lane turn left and walk along the road.

9 At this farm drive on the right, turn right and follow the drive round to the left. Cross this stile on the right of the drive (I like it when there is no fence, just a stile). Now walk up the slope towards the hedge. Go over this stile and follow the grassy path up the hill to the next stile. Cross this stile and turn sharp right yo follow the path along the field edge.

10 Cross over this stile and go down a short "green lane" to the road. Go over the stile and turn right to walk down the road. At this junction take the right fork, heading back towards the church tower.

11 At this lane junction turn left and walk down the lane towards Brook House.

12 Just before the gates to Brook House turn right over this stile and descend towards the stream. Cross the footbridge and follow the defined path up the hill over the next field. Go over this stile, ascend the steps and walk along the edge of the playing-field. Walk across the car park and up a short drive.

13 On meeting the main road, turn right and walk back to the start and the car park.

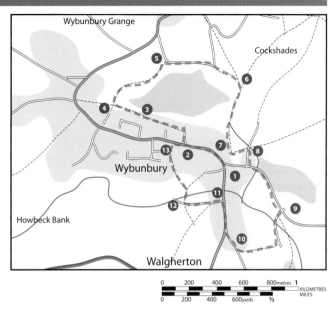

Wybunbury Grange

Cockshades

Wybunbury

Howbeck Bank

Walgherton

```
0    200   400   600   800metres  1
                                      KILOMETRES
                                      MILES
0    200   400   600yards    ½
```

has produced some quite spectacular side-effects. In Elizabethan times, John Leland, recorded that a hill at Combermere suddenly disappeared into underground workings, and Northwich later became notorious for the number of its buildings leaning at crazy angles because of subsidence. Even today, the White Lion Inn in Witton Street lies a complete storey lower than its original height. The arrival in the 19th century of new processes of extraction brought different problems. In 1873, John Brunner and Ludwig Mond set up their salt works at Winnington on the northern edge of the town to manufacture alkali products based on brine. The ammonia process involved cast an appalling stench over the town and devastated vegetation for miles around. On the other hand, Brunner and Mond were model employers. They paid their workforce well, built houses for them and were amongst the first firms in the country to give their employees annual holidays with pay.

The long involvement of Northwich and Cheshire with salt production is vividly recorded at the **Salt Museum**, the only one of its kind in Britain. It stands about half a mile south of the town centre in London Road (A533) and occupies what used to be the Northwich Workhouse which, like so many of those dreaded institutions, is an exceptionally handsome late-Georgian building, designed by George Latham, the architect of Arley Hall. With its unique collection of traditional working tools, and lively displays which include working models and videos, the Salt Museum recounts the fascinating story of the county's oldest industry. Not only can ancient remains such as Roman evaporating pans and medieval salt rakes be seen, but there is also much to remind visitors of the vital part that salt plays in the modern chemical industry.

The **Water Heritage Trail** concentrates on the industrial archaeology and water heritage of Northwich, and takes visitors to docks, locks, bridges and warehouses. One of the highlights is the **Dock Road Edwardian Pumping Station**, a fully restored sewage pumping station where the noise and splendour of the working machinery create an atmosphere of power and tradition.

AROUND NORTHWICH

ANDERTON
1 mile N of Northwich off the A533

One of the most stupendous engineering feats of the canal age was the **Anderton Boat Lift**, built in 1875 and recently restored. This extraordinary construction was designed to transfer boats from the Trent & Mersey Canal to the Weaver Navigation 50ft below. Two barges would enter the upper tank, two the lower, and by pumping water out of the lower tank, the boats would exchange places. Thousands of visitors come every year to marvel at this impressive structure which was conceived and designed by Edward Leader Williams who later went on to engineer the Manchester Ship Canal.

About a mile north of Anderton, **Marbury Country Park** (see panel opposite) was formerly part of a large country estate but the area is now managed by Cheshire County Council whose wardens have created a variety of habitats for plants, trees and animals. The Park lies at the edge of Budworth Mere and there are attractive

walks and bridleways around the site where you'll also find an arboretum, picnic area and garden centre.

CUDDINGTON
5 miles SW of Northwich off the A49

Cuddington is at the western end of the **Whitegate Way**, a pleasant rural walk of about five miles which follows the trackbed of the old railway that used to carry salt from the Winsford mines. There is a picnic site and car park at the former Whitegate Station.

SANDIWAY
5 miles SW of Northwich on the A49

A popular attraction at Blakemere Craft Centre on Chester Road is the **Cheshire Waterlife Aquatic and Falconry Centre**. Falconers fly several different species of birds of prey, supplying a running commentary on each bird, and visitors can also take a guided tour of the aviary complex - home to several species of rare owls - and take lessons in bird handling and falconry. The centre has a pets corner, with rabbits, guinea pigs, hamsters and caged birds, and also

Anderton Boat Lift

MARBURY COUNTRY PARK

Comberbach, Northwich,
Cheshire CW9 6AT
Tel: 01606 77741

Marbury Country Park was once part of a large country estate whose history dates back to around 1200 AD. Marbury itself means a fortified or stockaded dwelling by the mere or water. The first family took the name Marbury and lived there until 1684. When the last male heir died the estate was bought by Richard Earl Rivers who never lived there. On his death in 1714 it was bought by his son-in-law James, the 4th Earl of Barrymore. It was the Barry family who shaped the park with extensive landscaping and the building of the hall.

A succession of owners and uses then followed, culminating in the hall being demolished in 1968 due to rot. In 1975, 196 acres was leased from the owners, ICI, by Cheshire County Council and restoration work was begun. Further land was later aquired and today it is managed by the Countryside Management Service to benefit wildlife and visitors.

Each habitat is carefully managed to encourage different plants and animals, so there is always plenty to see at all times of the year. In spring the woodland is covered by a spectacular carpet of wildflowers and willow warblers, chiffchaffs and blackcaps herald the arrival of summer. Autumn shows the colours of the trees off to their best and in winter, the Mere becomes a focus for many birds including goldeneye and greylag geese.

houses marine fish and invertebrates, koi carp and tropical fish.

HATCHMERE

8 miles W of Northwich on the B5152

In medieval times the village of Hatchmere was surrounded by the Forest of Delamere, the largest of Cheshire's three woodlands. It stretched from the Mersey to Nantwich and although there were small areas of pasture and arable land, its status as a royal forest meant that the prime duty of those in charge of it was the preservation of the "beasts of the chase". It was not until 1812 that Delamere was officially "disafforested" and today Delamere Forest covers little more than an area about two miles long and one mile deep. From Hatchmere, attractive trails lead through the woods and around Hatch Mere, the sizeable lake that gives the village its name.

CROWTON

4 miles W of Northwich on the B5153

Crowton has many times been voted the Best Kept Village in Cheshire and its 18th century hostelry, the Hare & Hounds enjoys a particularly scenic position in this appealing village.

ACTON BRIDGE

4 miles W of Northwich off the A49

The bridge here crosses the River Weaver, a waterway whose scenic merits have been largely unsung. The Vale Royal Council has developed the **Weaver Valley Way** which allows walkers to enjoy some lovely stretches, particularly those between Weaver Bridge and Saltersford Locks, and the 6-mile route from Northwich to Winsford Marina.

During World War I, Acton Bridge made an unusual contribution to the war

ASH HOUSE FARM

Acton Bridge, Northwich, Cheshire CW8 3QS
Tel: 01606 852717 Fax: 01606 853752
e-mail: sue_schofield40@hotmail.com
website: www.ashhousefarm.co.uk

Standing in beautiful well-stocked gardens with superb
views of the rolling Cheshire countryside, **Ash House Farm**
is an impressive creeper-clad Georgian farmhouse which
was previously owned by Alexander Carlton Greg who
gave Quarry Bank Mill in Styal to the National Trust. Sue
and Fred Schofield came here in 1991 and since then have
extended the farm to 220 acres and expanded their herd of cows to about 110. They have also planted
a large quantity of shrubs and roses in the immaculate garden which is overlooked by both the guest
lounge, with its log-burning stove, and the dining room.

Sue and Fred have been welcoming bed & breakfast
guests here since 1993 and the warm, homely atmosphere
of the house makes this a very relaxing place to stay. There
are just two very comfortable guest bedrooms, one family
and one twin, both very attractively furnished and
decorated. Sue provides a full farmhouse or continental
breakfast, served on decorative china and at times to suit
everyone's timetable. Sue will also cater for any special
dietary requirements. For evening meals there are several
good pubs within easy reach and a microwave and fridge
are available for the use of guests.

effort. Near the village was a plantation
of hazel pear trees whose fruit is quite
inedible but whose juice provided the
khaki dye for soldiers' uniforms.

MARSTON

1 mile NE of Northwich on a minor road

In Victorian times, the Old Salt Mine at
Marston was a huge tourist attraction.
About 360 ft deep and covering 35 acres, it
even brought the Tsar of Russia here in
1844. Ten thousand lamps illuminated the
huge cavern as the Emperor sat down to
dinner here with eminent members of the
Royal Society. By the end of the century,
however, subsidence caused by the mine
had made some 40 houses in the village
uninhabitable, and one day in 1933 a hole
50ft wide and 300ft deep suddenly
appeared close to the Trent & Mersey
Canal. Happily, the village has now
stabilised itself, and at the **Lion Salt Works
Museum** on most afternoons you will find

volunteer workers keeping alive the only
surviving open pan salt works in Britain.

ANTROBUS

5 miles N of Northwich off the A559

Just a couple of miles from the
magnificent Arley Hall and its world-
famous gardens, is the pleasing little
village of Antrobus, the only place in
Britain to bear this name. Even the
Oxford Dictionary of English Place Names
is baffled by Antrobus: "Unexplained" it
says curtly, adding as its excuse, "Hardly
English".

GREAT BUDWORTH

3 miles NE of Northwich off the A559

A charming small village nowadays,
"Great" Budworth was accorded that
designation at a time when it was the
largest ecclesiastical parish in all
Cheshire, the administrative centre for
some 35 individual communities. The

imposing church on the hill, built in the 14th and 15th centuries, reflects its importance during those years. **St Mary & All Saints** attracts many visitors to its host of quaint carvings and odd faces that peer out at unexpected corners: some with staring eyes, others with their tongues poking out. There's a man near the pulpit who appears to be drowsing through some interminable sermon. Under the roof of the nave you'll find a man with a serpent, another in mid-somersault, and a minstrel playing bagpipes. The distinguished 17th century historian, Sir Peter Leycester, is buried in the Lady Chapel, and in the Warburton Chapel there is a finely carved Tudor ceiling and 13th century oak stalls – the oldest in Cheshire. During the 19th century, Great Budworth was part of the Arley Hall estate and it is largely due to the energetic Squire Egerton-Warburton, a "conservationist" well ahead of his time, that so many of the attractive old cottages in the village are still in place.

Great Budworth

There are many grand houses in Cheshire, and many fine gardens, but at **Arley Hall and Gardens** you will find one of the grandest houses and one of the finest gardens in perfect harmony. The present Hall was completed in 1845, a few years after Rowland Egerton-Warburton arrived at Arley with his new bride, Mary Brooke. The newly-married couple took possession of a dilapidated old mansion, infested with rats and with antiquated drains from which an unbearable stench drifted through the house. Understandably, Rowland and Mary soon demolished the old hall and in its place rose a sumptuous early-Victorian stately home complete with (bearing in mind those drains) such state-of-the-art innovations as "Howden's Patent Atmospheric Air Dispensers". Rowland and Mary were both ardent gardeners and it was they who master-minded the magnificent panoramas of today's Arley Gardens. Rowland is credited with creating what is believed to be the first herbaceous border in England; his descendant, the present Viscount Ashbrook, has continued that tradition by cultivating "The Grove", an informal woodland garden planted with spring bulbs, flowering shrubs and exotic trees, a pleasing contrast to the more formal

THE RED LION

Vicarage Lane, Little Budworth, Cheshire CW6 9BY
Tel/Fax: 01829 760275
e-mail: theredlionlittlebud@tiscale.co.uk

The first landlord at **The Red Lion** served his first customer way back in in 1797; many others have succeeded him. One of them, Fanny Worsley, was landlady here for more than 40 years, from 1879 to 1921. The inn stands next to the parish church in the delightful village of Little Budworth and is now in the capable hands of landlady Julie Wardle, a friendly and welcoming host. It enjoys a great reputation for its traditional, freshly prepared home-cooked food

with a menu that offers all the popular favourites like steaks or fish & chips along with a selection of vegetarian dishes and salads.

The well-kept ales include real brews such as Robinson's Unicorn. As well as the separate non-smoking dining room, there's an open plan bar with a snug and open coal fire. This is a lively pub which supports no fewer than three bowls teams and has its own bowling green as well as a secluded beer garden for fair-weather days. A recent addition to The Red Lion's amenities is its quality accommodation – four comfortable guest bedrooms all attractively decorated and with en suite facilities.

THE HOLLIES FARM SHOP

Forest Road, Little Budworth, Cheshire CW6 9ES
Tel: 01829 760414
e-mail: mail:theholliesfarmshop.com
website: www.theholliesfarmshop.com

Set in the heart of the Cheshire countryside, just four miles from the village of Tarporley, **The Hollies Farm Shop** is a family-run business established more than 30 years ago. During that time the Cowap family have built up one of the most comprehensive rages of products in the county – a complete alphabet of culinary delicacies and gourmet foods from asparagus to zucchini. As well as carefully selected fresh produce from local suppliers, the shop stocks a wide selection of international specialities.

In their search for quality products, the family has often visited the producers' farms, kitchens and vineyard. As Philip Cowap says, "It is by getting to know more about them, their production methods and their ambitions that gives us the confidence to offer these products to our customers, safe in the knowledge that they have surpassed our demanding standards." In addition to the edibles on offer, the shop also has an extensive choice of flowers which the staff are always happy to hand-tie into beautiful bouquets. And in the nursery area you'll find a great range of bedding plants and shrubs, hanging baskets (empty or ready-planted) and patio containers.

design of the main gardens.

Other attractions at Arley include a tea room housed in a beautifully converted 16th century barn and a plant nursery offering a wide selection of herbaceous and other plants.

Also within the Arley estate, **Stockley Farm** is a 400-acre organic dairy farm that provides a great family day out. A visit begins with a tractor and trailer ride to the farm where there are always baby animals for children to handle and feed. Adult animals include an 18-hand shire horse, Star, a lovely big pig called Olive, and Kate, the Highland cow. There are miniature tractors to ride, pony rides, an adventure play area, a souvenir shop and a Country Café.

PICKMERE

6 miles NE of Northwich on the B5391

The delightful village of Pickmere commands superb views of the Cheshire Plain, extending from the Dee estuary to the Pennine hills. The nearby **Pick Mere**, from which the village takes its name, is popular with wind surfers and yachtsmen, and boats are available for hire.

LACH DENNIS

4 miles SE of Northwich on the B5082

The small village of Lach Dennis derives its name from the Old English *laecc*, meaning a bog, and the Dennis family which once had an estate here. A mile or so to the east, **Shakerley Mere Nature Reserve** is host to a diverse range of wildlife with Canada Geese, herons, mute swans and mallards a common sight. Cormorants fly here from their breeding grounds on the coast to feast on the fish and more exotic species arrive at different times of the year. There's a pleasant 1.5 mile walk around the mere.

WINSFORD

6 miles S of Northwich on the A54

Winsford is another of the Cheshire salt towns which expanded greatly during the 19th century, swallowing up the old villages of Over and Wharton on opposite banks of the River Weaver. Two legacies of those boom years should be mentioned. One is Christ Church which was specifically designed so that it could be jacked up in the event of subsidence. The other is Botton Flash, a sizeable lake caused by subsidence but now a popular water recreation area for the town.

LITTLE BUDWORTH

7 miles SW of Northwich off the A49 or A54

Little Budworth Common Country Park is a pleasant area of heathland and woods, ideal for picnics and walking. The nearby village enjoys splendid views over Budworth Pool but will be better known to motor racing enthusiasts for the Oulton Park racing circuit a mile or so to the south.

COTEBROOK

7 miles SW of Northwich on the A49

The **Cotebrook Shire Horse Centre** is home to the internationally renowned Cotebrook Shire Horse Stud. In addition to these mighty beasts, the Centre has miniature Shetland ponies, pigs, goats, ducks and hens, foxes, red deer, red squirrels and birds of prey. Open daily all year, the Centre also has a nature trail, picnic area and gift shop.

TARPORLEY

12 miles SW of Northwich on the A51/A49

In the days when most of this area was part of Delamere Forest, Tarporley was the headquarters of the verderers or forest wardens. It was from Tarporley in the early 17th century that John Done,

David Alexander

56B High Street, Tarporley, Cheshire CW6 0AG
Tel: 01829 733557
e-mail: dwalton74@aol.com

David Alexander is very much a family business with husband, wife and daughter all involved in the enterprise. David Alexander Walton has been a diamond setter for some 35 years, having trained in the world-famous Hatton Garden. He and his family opened their shop in Tarporley's High Street in November 2003 after 10 years running the business in Davenham, Cheshire.

David's wife, Denise, and daughter Emma are responsible for buying and sales while his own expertise in is directed to making, cleaning, repairing, re-modelling and restoring jewellery. He is happy to accept commissions for pieces such as wedding or engagement rings and you'll probably see him at work since his workshop at the rear of the premises is visible from the shop. Housed in what are believed to be early-19th century cottages, the shop stocks a wide variety of jewellery but specialises in silver and diamonds. It is an agent for the Hot Diamonds range that includes bracelets, earrings, brooches, chains, pendants and cuff-links. The shop also stocks an elegant range of gifts and items such as the gleaming range of silver picture frames.

Fox & Barrel

Forest Road, Cotebrook, Tarporley, Cheshire CW6 9DZ
Tel: 01829 760529 Fax: 01829 760192
e-mail: info@foxandbarrel
website: www.foxandbarrel.com

Designated Cheshire Dining Pub of the Year in 2003 by the *Good Pub Guide*, and National Best Pub of the Year 2000, the **Fox and Barrel** is a lively traditional hostelry with a reputation for serving outstanding food. The pub stands beside the A49 north of Tarporley surrounded by unspoilt Cheshire countryside and derives its name from the occasion when a former landlord allowed a pursued fox to escape to the cellar. The interior of the inn is very inviting with its huge open log fire, old beams, panelled walls, china ornaments and jugs, wooden floor with rugs, and wondrously carved chair overlooking the bar area.

Daily newspapers are always available and there are bookshelves filled with leather bound volumes. In the non-smoking restaurant, chef Peter Cunningham Ward offers an inventive and appetising regular menu as well as daily specials. Bar snacks, sandwiches and baguettes are served in the bar, and Sunday lunch is served from noon until 3pm. There's a good selection of wines – more than a dozen of them available by the glass; real ales on tap; a secluded patio for fairweather dining; and live jazz sessions the 1st Monday evening in the month, with musical entertainment on most other Monday evenings.

Chief Forester and Hereditary Bow-bearer of Delamere, entertained King James to a hunt. The chase was, he reported, a great success: *"deer, both red and fallow, fish and fowl, abounded in the meres"*. A gratified King rewarded his host with a knighthood.

The village boasts an impressive survivor in the Tarporley Hunt Club which is primarily a dining club and still holds an annual banquet in the town. Founded in 1762, it is now the oldest Hunt Club in the country.

Uᴛᴋɪɴᴛᴏɴ

10 miles SW of Northwich off the A49 or A51

During the Middle Ages, the verderers had their own courts in which they meted out rough justice to offenders against the forest laws. One such court was at Utkinton, just north of the town, and in an old farmhouse there stands a column formed by an ancient forest tree, its roots still in the ground. When the court was in session, the wardens would place on this tree the symbol of their authority, the Hunting Horn of Delamere. The farmhouse is not open to the public but the horn, dating from around 1120, has survived and can be seen at the Grosvenor Museum in Chester.

Aꜱʜᴛᴏɴ

8 miles E of Chester on the B5393

A couple of miles to the northeast of Ashton stretch the 4,000 acres of **Delamere Forest**, a rambler's delight with a wealth of lovely walks and many picnic sites, ideal for a peaceful family day out. In Norman times, a "forest" was a part-wooded, part-open area, reserved as a hunting ground exclusively for royalty or the nobility. There were savage penalties for anyone harming the deer, even if the deer were destroying

crops, and household dogs within the forest had to be deliberately lamed to ensure that they could not harass the beasts. By the early 1600s, many of the great oaks in the forest had already been felled to provide timber for ship-building – as well as for Cheshire's familiar black and white half-timbered houses. Since the early 1900s, Delamere Forest has been maintained by the Forestry Commission which has undertaken an intensive programme of tree planting and woodland management. Delamere is now both an attractive recreational area and a working forest with 90% of the trees eventually destined for the saw mills.

WARRINGTON

Lying on an important bridging point of the River Mersey, Warrington claims to enjoy Britain's most convenient location. It stands midway between the huge conurbations and ports of Manchester and Liverpool and on a nodal point of communications close to where the M6, M62 and M56 motorways intersect, and where the electrified West Coast main line links London and Scotland.

Warrington is North Cheshire's largest town – an important industrial centre since Georgian and Victorian times and with substantial buildings from those days to prove it. Its imposing **Town Hall** was formerly Lord Winmarleigh's country residence, built in 1750 with all the appropriate grandeur: windows framed in expensive copper, and elaborately-designed entrance gates 25ft high and 54ft wide. Along with its park, it provides a dignified focus for the town centre. A major Victorian contribution to the town is its excellent **Museum and Art Gallery** in Bold Street, dating from 1857 and one of the earliest municipal museums. The exhibits are remarkably varied: amongst them are shrunken heads, a unique china teapot collection, a scold's bridle, Egyptian mummies, a Roman actor's mask and other Roman artefacts discovered in nearby Wilderspool. There are some fine paintings as well, most of which are Victorian watercolours and oils, and a rare Vanous still life.

In the Old Market Square is a granite sculpture by Edwin Russell of the **Mad Hatters Tea Party**. This statue was unveiled by the Prince and Princess of Wales in 1984 and commemorates the area's connection with Lewis Carroll, who lived in nearby Daresbury. The **River of Life** in Bridge Street is a memorial to the victims of the 1993 terrorist bomb: artist Stephen Broadbent worked with local children to design 12 bronze plaques, each with an inscription chosen by the children – self-control, joy, peace, forgiveness, encouragement, reconciliation, patience, justice, love, hope, friendship and faithfulness.

Also worth visiting is **St Elphin's Church** with its 14th century chancel and memorials celebrating the Butler and Patten families.

The town's premier leisure site is Victoria Park, purchased by the Corporation in 1897 and named to commemorate Queen Victoria's jubilee. The park is a good starting point for exploring the area, following the Mersey Way along the river or joining Black Bear Park and the Trans-Pennine Trail.

An interesting curiosity at Bridge Foot nearby is a combined telephone kiosk and letter box. These were quite common in the early 1900s, but Warrington's is one of the few survivors. Also associated with the town are two prominent entertainers: the TV presenter Chris Evans was born here, and the durable comedian and ukelele player George Formby is buried in the Catholic section of the town's cemetery.

AROUND WARRINGTON

DARESBURY
5 miles SW of Warrington on the A558

All Saints' Church in Daresbury has an absolutely unique stained glass window. There are panels depicting a Gryphon and a Cheshire Cat, others show a Mock Turtle, a March Hare and a Mad Hatter. This is of course the **Lewis Carroll Memorial Window**, commemorating the author of *Alice in Wonderland*. Carroll himself is shown at one side, dressed in clerical garb and kneeling. His father was Vicar of Daresbury when Carroll was born here in 1832 and baptised as Charles Lutwidge Dodgson. The boy apparently enjoyed an idyllic childhood at Daresbury until his father moved to another parish when Charles/Lewis was 11 years old.

WIDNES
6 miles SW of Warrington on the A557

Described in the 1860s as a "quiet industrial village", Widnes now has a population of around 60,000. It stands on the north shore of the Mersey, linked to Runcorn by a remarkably elegant road bridge. A popular attraction is **Spike Island** which has recently had a makeover by the local council and now provides a landscaped walk from which the superstructures of ships passing along the Manchester Ship Canal can be seen gliding past. Widnes also has a popular family attraction in the **Catalyst Science Discovery Centre**, where three interactive galleries and more than 100 hands-on exhibits make sense of the world of science. Recent additions include a hi-tech Discovery Lab, a state of the art Virtual Theatre, and a World of Opportunities careers gallery.

RUNCORN
7 miles SW of Warrington on the A557

Runcorn is one of Britain's best known post-war new towns, developed around a much older town bearing the same name. Here, **Norton Priory** is always a delightful and intriguing place for a family outing, whatever the weather. Despite being situated close to Junction 11 of the M56, it lies in a peaceful oasis with 16 acres of beautiful woodland gardens running down to the Bridgewater Canal. The Augustinian priory was built in 1134 as a retreat for just 12 "black canons", so named because they wore a cape of black woollen cloth over a white linen surplice. Recent work by the Norton Priory Museum Trust has uncovered the remains of the church, chapter house, cloisters and dormitory, and these finds are informatively explained in an audio-visual presentation. The Museum is open every day from noon, all year; the gardens, which include a charming walled garden, are open from April to October.

LYMM
6 miles E of Warrington on the A56

During the stage coach era, Eagle Brow was notorious, a dangerously steep road that dropped precipitously down the hillside into the village of Lymm. To bypass this hazard, a turnpike was built (now the A56), so conserving the heart of this ancient village with its half-timbered houses and well-preserved village stocks. The Bridgewater Canal flows past nearby and the church is reflected in the waters of Lymm

Dam. Popular with anglers and bird-watchers, the dam is a large man-made lake, part of a lovely woodland centre which is linked to the surrounding countryside and the canal towpath by a network of footpaths and bridleways. The village became an important centre for the fustian cloth (corduroy) trade in the 19th century but is now best known simply as a delightful place to visit.

Lymm stands on the sides of a ravine and its streets have actually been carved out of the sandstone rock. The same rock was used to construct Lymm's best-known landmark, the ancient cross crowned with a huge cupola that stands at the top of the High Street.

DUNHAM MASSEY
9 miles E of Warrington on B5160

Dunham Massey Hall and Park (National Trust) has 250 acres of parkland where fallow deer roam freely and noble trees planted in the late 1700s still flourish. There's a restored water-mill which is usually in operation every Wednesday, and there are splendid walks in every direction. The Hall, once the

Bridgewater Canal, Lymm

home of the Earls of Stamford and Warrington, is a grand Georgian mansion of 1732 which boasts an outstanding collection of furniture, paintings and Huguenot silver. The Hall is open most days from April to October: the Park is open every day.

HELSBY

8 miles NE of Chester on the A56

There are seven Iron Age forts scattered across Cheshire, but only the one at Helsby, maintained by the National Trust, is open to the public. The climb out of the village along pretty woodland paths to the red sandstone summit is quite steep but the views across the marshes to the Mersey Estuary and Liverpool repay the effort.

FRODSHAM

10 miles NE of Chester on the A56

This is an attractive town with a broad

High Street lined with thatched cottages and spacious Georgian and Victorian houses. During the 18th and early 19th centuries, Frodsham was an important coaching town and there are several fine coaching inns. Built in 1632, The Bear's Paw with its three stone gables recalls the bear-baiting that once took place nearby. Of the Earl of Chester's Norman castle only fragments remain, but the **Church of St Laurence** (an earlier church here was recorded in the *Domesday Book*) is noted for the fine 17th century panelling in its exquisite north chapel. The Vicar here from 1740 to 1756 was Francis Gastrell, a name that is anathema to all lovers of Shakespeare. Gastrell bought the poet's house, New Place, at Stratford and first incensed the towns-people by cutting down the famous mulberry tree. Then, in order to avoid paying the Corporation poor rate, he pulled the house itself down. The outraged citizens

THE COTTAGE TEA SHOP

121 Main Street, Frodsham, Cheshire WA6 7AF
Tel: 01928 733673

Occupying two 300-year-old cottages on Frodsham's main street, **The Cottage Tea Shop** is a delightful traditional tea room owned and run by Graham and Louise Nickson, both of whom were born and grew up in the town. Customers can enjoy their refreshments either in the light and airy conservatory at the rear, in the cosy, cottage-style tea rooms inside, or at tables on the pavement outside. As well as teatime treats such as cream teas, home-made cakes, freshly baked scones,

toasted crumpets or tea cake, the extensive menu also offers a breakfast selection, served from 10am until 2.30pm, hot savouries such as stilton & mango rarebit or spicy tomatoes on toast, home-made soup, jacket potatoes and a wide choice of sandwiches. There's a special menu for children up to 10 years old.

Everything on the menu is locally sourced wherever possible and freshly prepared to order. The tea room is licensed, with wine served by the glass and bottled beer available, and private functions are catered for. Graham and Louise also own The Toy Box, next but one to the tea room, where you'll find a fascinating collection of traditional wooden toys, birth and christening gifts.

of Stratford hounded him from the town and he returned to the parish at Frodsham that he had neglected for years.

KNUTSFORD

Knutsford and its people were the heroes of one of the most durable of Victorian novels, Elizabeth Gaskell's *Cranford*. This gently humorous, sympathetic but sharply-observed portrait of the little Cheshire town, and the foibles and pre-occupations of its citizens, was first published in 1853 and is still delighting readers today. Elizabeth was scarcely a month old when she came to Knutsford. Her mother had died shortly after her birth and her father sent her here to be brought up by an aunt who lived in a road which has now been re-named Gaskell Avenue. The motherless child grew up to be both strikingly beautiful and exceptionally intelligent. Early on she evinced a lively interest in the town's characters and its history: she was intrigued, for example, to find that in the house next door to her aunt's had once lived a notorious highwayman, Edward Higgins, hanged for his crimes in 1767; she wrote a story about him. Marriage to William Gaskell, a Unitarian pastor in Manchester, took her away from Knutsford, although she returned often and for long periods, and after her death in 1865 she found a resting place in the grounds of the Unitarian Chapel; here, too, lie her husband and two of her four daughters.

The Knutsford that Elizabeth Gaskell knew so well and wrote about so vividly has expanded a great deal since those days of course, but in its compact centre, now designated an Outstanding Area of Conservation, the narrow streets and cobbled alleys still evoke the intimacy of

HOLLY TREE FARM SHOP

Chester Road, Knutsford, Cheshire WA16 0EU
Tel: 01565 651835 Fax: 01565 654522
e-mail: hollytreefarmshop@tiscali.co.uk
website: www.hollytreefarmshop.co.uk

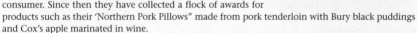

Conveniently located just a quarter of a mile from junction 19 of the M6, **Holly Tree Farm Shop** was established in 1992 by Karol and Michael Bailey with the dream of supplying quality produce, reared and prepared on their farm, direct to the consumer. Since then they have collected a flock of awards for products such as their 'Northern Pork Pillows" made from pork tenderloin with Bury black puddings and Cox's apple marinated in wine.

Their gluten-free British Bulldogs and Sicilian lamb sausages have also received awards. Karen was also runner-up in the Woman Farmer of the Year competition; the business won the Made in Cheshire Rural Enterprise Award 2002/2003 and, perhaps the most prestigious accolade of all, they were acclaimed by Rick Stein as one of his Food Heroes. In addition to their own meats, which are all free from routine drugs, growth promoters and other additives, the farm shop stocks produce from other local suppliers who maintain the same high standards of animal welfare. A recent addition to the farm shop's amenities is Mother Goose's Tea Room which offers an appetising choice that includes scrumptious home-made scones and soups, light meals and delicious cakes.

a small Victorian town. Two parallel roads, Toft Street and King Street, form a rectangle surrounding the old town. But Mrs Gaskell would surely be astonished by the building erected in King Street to her memory by Mr Richard Harding Watt in 1907. A gifted entrepreneur, Mr Watt had made a huge fortune in Manchester as a glove manufacturer, but what really aroused his enthusiasm was the flamboyant architecture he had seen during his travels through Spain, southern Italy and the Near East.

On his return, he spent lavishly on trying to transform Knutsford in Cheshire into Knutsford-on-the-Med. At the north end of the town, he built a laundry complete with Byzantine domes and a minaret. A vaguely Ottoman style of architecture welcomed serious-minded artisans to his Ruskin Reading Rooms. In Legh Road, he erected a series of villas whose south-facing frontages are clearly in need of a really hot sun. And in King Street, as homage to the town's most famous resident, Richard Watt spent thousands of Victorian pounds on the Gaskell Memorial Tower. This tall, blank-walled building seems a rather incongruous tribute to the author who was herself so open and so down-to-earth.

But it is eccentrics like Richard Watt who make English architecture as interesting as it is. He was so proud of his contribution to the town's new buildings that, travelling on his coach to the railway station, he would rise to his feet and raise his hat to salute them. As he did so, one day in 1913, his horse suddenly shied, the carriage overturned, and Richard Watt was thrown out and killed. What other changes he might have made to this grand old town, had he lived, we can only imagine.

An unusual exhibition and well worth visiting is the **Penny Farthing Museum**, located in the Courtyard Coffee House off King Street. These bizarre machines were in fashion for barely 20 years before the last model was manufactured in 1892. The collection includes a replica of the famous Starley Giant with a front wheel seven feet in diameter, and a sign outside the coffee house promises a free tea to anyone arriving on a penny-farthing.

Close by, in Tatton Street, is the **Knutsford Heritage Centre**. Knutsford is a town with a long history – Edward I granted the town a Charter in 1262, and at the same time a local landowner, William de Tabley, was given a money-making licence to control the market. The Heritage Centre is housed in a restored 17th century timber-framed building which in Victorian times was a smithy. During the restoration the old forge and bellows were found in a remarkable state of preservation. The

wrought-iron gate in front of the centre was specially created for the Centre and depicts dancing girls taking part in Knutsford's famous Royal May Day celebrations – Royal because in 1887 the Prince and Princess of Wales honoured the festivities with their presence. Every May Day the town centre streets are closed to all traffic except for the May Queen's procession in which colourful characters such as Jack in Green, Highwayman Higgins and Lord Chamberlain, Morris dancers, Maypole dancers and many others take part. One curious tradition whose origins are unknown is the practice of covering the streets and pavements with ordinary sand and then, using white sand, creating elaborate patterns on top. A colourful Knutsford character was Trumpet Major Smith, who sounded the Charge into the Valley of Death at the Battle of Balaclava. He is buried in the grounds of the Georgian parish church.

Tatton Park, near Knutsford

AROUND KNUTSFORD

Sweeping up to the very edge of Knutsford are the grounds of **Tatton Park**, 2,000 acres of exquisite parkland landscaped in the 18th century by the celebrated Humphry Repton. This lovely park, where herds of red and fallow deer roam freely, provides a worthy setting for the noble Georgian mansion designed by the equally celebrated architect Samuel Wyatt. The combination of the two men's talents created a house and park that have become one of the National Trust's most visited attractions. Tatton's opulent state rooms, containing paintings by artists such as Canaletto and Van Dyck along with superb collections of porcelain and furniture, provided the television production of *Brideshead Revisited* with a sumptuous setting for Marchmain House.

More than 200 elegant pieces of furniture were commissioned from the celebrated cabinet-makers, Gillow of Lancaster. Particularly fine are the superb bookcases in the library, constructed to house the Egerton family's collection of more than 8,000 books. By contrast, the stark servants' rooms and cellars give a vivid idea of what life below stairs was really like. The Egerton family built Tatton Park to replace the much earlier **Tudor Old Hall**, which nestles in a wood in the deer park and dates back to around 1520. Here, visitors are given a guided tour through time from the late Middle Ages up to the 1950s. Flickering light from candles reveals the ancient timber roof of the Great Hall, supported by ornate quatrefoils, while underfoot, the floor is strewn with rushes, providing a warm place for the medieval Lord of the Manor and his servants to sleep. There's much more: Home Farm is a working farm, working as it did in the 1930s, complete with vintage machinery. Traditional crafts (including pottery), stables and many farm animals provide a complete picture of rural life some 60 years ago. Tatton's famous gardens include a Victorian maze, an orangery and fernery, a serene Japanese garden, American redwoods, and a splendid Italian terraced garden. There's also a busy programme of educational activities for children, an adventure playground, shops, and a restaurant. You can even get married in the sumptuous mansion and hold your reception either in the house itself, in the Tenants Hall which can cater for parties of up to 430, or in a marquee in the magnificent grounds. With so much on offer it is small wonder that Tatton Park has been described as the most complete historic estate in the country.

Just west of Knutsford, on the A5033, is **Tabley House**, home of the Leicester family from 1272 to 1975. Mrs Gaskell often came to picnic in the grounds of the last of their houses, a stately Georgian mansion designed by John Carr for the first Lord de Tabley in 1761. This Lord de Tabley loved paintings and it was his son's passion for art, and his hunger for others to share it, that led to the creation of London's National Gallery. His personal collection of English pictures, on display in Tabley House, includes works by Turner (who painted the house several times), Lely, Reynolds, Opie and Martin Danby, along with furniture by Gillow, Bullock and Chippendale, and fascinating family memorabilia spanning three centuries.

Through various activities, the Friends of Tabley House raise funds for the restoration and refurbishment of the house; recent undertakings have included the redecoration of the grand entrance hall and the restoration and rehanging of the 18th hall lantern. The 17th century chapel next to the house looks perfectly in place but it was originally built on an island in Tabley Mere and only moved to its present site in 1927.

Also in Tabley, at the Old School, is the **Tabley Cuckoo Clock Collection.** Brothers Roman and Maz Piekarski are well-known horologists and clock restorers and over the last 25 years they have sought out and renovated some of the rarest and most notable examples of this 300-year-old craft. Also on display are some mid-19th century cuckoo clocks which include complex musical movements to reproduce popular tunes of the day.

MERE

3 miles NW of Knutsford on the A50/A556

One of the **Kilton Inn**'s more notorious guests, back in the 18th century, was Dick Turpin. This intrepid highwayman made the inn the base from which he plundered travellers along the Knutsford to Warrington road (now the comparatively safe A50). After one such robbery (and murder) Turpin, on his famous horse Black Bess, "galloped to the Kilton and, altering the clock, strolled on to the bowling green and proved an alibi by the short time he took to cover the four miles".

MOBBERLEY

2 miles E of Knutsford on the B5085

The main glory of this scattered village is the spectacular woodwork inside the church: massive roof beams with striking winged figures and one of the finest rood screens in the country, dated 1500. The screen is covered with a rich tracery of leaves and fruit, coats-of-arms, and religious symbols. Two generations of the Mallory family held the rectorship here, one of them for 53 years. He is commemorated in the east window. Another window honours his grandson, George Mallory, the mountaineer who perished while making his third attempt to climb Mount Everest in 1924.

At the Whitsun Bank Holiday each year steam traction enthusiasts from all across the country descend on the village for the **Mobberley Steam Party** hosted by the Bull's Head Inn.

LOWER PEOVER

4 miles S of Knutsford on the B5081

The village of Lower Peover (pronounced Peever) is effectively made up of two hamlets. One is grouped around the village green on the B5081, the other is at the end of a cobbled lane. It's a picturesque little group. There's a charming old coaching inn, The Bells of Peover, which during World War II numbered Generals Patton and Eisenhower among its customers. The American flag still flies here alongside the Union Jack. Nearby are a handsome village school founded in 1710, and a lovely black and white timbered church, more than 700 years old, with a massive Perpendicular tower

built in 1582. **St Oswald's** is notable as one of the few timber-framed churches in the country still standing, and is probably the oldest. Inside, there is a wealth of carved wood – pews and screens, pulpit and lectern, and a massive medieval chest made from a single log of bog oak. At one time local girls who wished to marry a farmer were required to raise its lid with one hand to demonstrate they had the strength to cope with farm life.

About three miles east of Lower Peover is **Peover Hall**, very much hidden away at the end of a winding country road but well worth tracking down. During World War II, General George Patton lived for a while at the Hall, which was conveniently close to his then headquarters at Knutsford. There's a memorial to him in the church nearby,

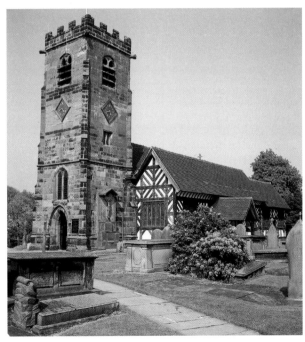

St Oswald's Church, Lower Peover

Over Peover

Distance:	4.5 mile (7.2 kilometres)
Typical time:	150 mins
Height gain:	0 metres
Map:	Landranger 118
Walk:	ww.walkingworld.com ID:214
Contributor:	Robin and Christine Jones

Access Information:

Bus services available from Macclesfield, Knutsford and Northwich to Over Peover (peever). No train services. Access by car from M6 Motorway - leave at Junction 19 - for Knutsford town centre - take the A50 South - for Stoke and Holmes Chapel for 2.1/2 miles. Turn left into Stocks Lane at the Whipping Stocks Inn. Parking is available on the roadside just after the road bends to the left in a small lay-by.

Description:

This walk is in a figure-of-eight, starting at one of the entrance drives to the Peover Hall Estate. The Hall itself dates from 1585, and is still occupied as a residence. To the west is the Jodrell Bank Radio Telescope, which is open to visitors all year. The river, known as the Peover Eye, gives its name to the village. Peover is an Anglo-Saxon word meaning "bright water". Parts of the Church of St Lawrence featured in the walk are 550 years old, but most was rebuilt about 200 years ago.

Features:

River, Pub, Church, Stately Home, Wildlife, Birds, Flowers, Great Views

Walk Directions:

1 Walk to the Four Lane Ends junction and follow the lane with the footpath markers. Carry straight on along the drive past the village hall and through the gates. Cross the stile and continue along the avenue of trees. A word of warning: you may find horses and riders crossing this path, where the fences have been modified for cross-country events.

2 Over the stile, cross the footbridge and through the gate. On the right is Peover Pool, a conservation area. Walk straight ahead following the direction of the yellow waymark arrows on the gate. On arrival at the main gates of Peover Hall , cross the stile and turn left away from the house.

3 At the lane turn right - do not go up the path labelled 'Church'. We go to see the church later.

4 At this stile on the left-hand side of the lane, proceed along the field edge in the direction of the wood. Turn right on reaching the wood and proceed along the field edge to the corner of the wood. On reaching the corner of the wood, take the marked footpath on the left leading downhill into the wood.

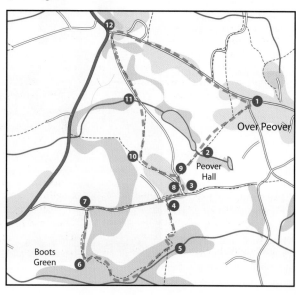

5 On reaching the river (The Peover Eye) turn right and follow the path along the riverbank. Do not cross the river. As the path ascends into Spinney Wood, follow the path to the left, going in the same direction as before. The path is marked by white spots painted on the trees.

6 The path will lead you to a white gate. Turn right through the gate and follow the field edge to walk alongside the greenhouses.

7 Where the farm drive meets the lane at the end of the glasshouses, turn right along a bridleway. Follow the path until it joins the lane again in front of the cottages.

8 Proceed along the lane passing Waymark 4, to arrive back outside the gates to Peover Hall. Walk to the left of the gates in front of the old stable block. At the end of the stables go through the white gates and turn right.

9 At the main junction of the path, turn right to go up to the church. Of interest here is the pets' cemetery.

10 Follow this path up to the church - unfortunately mostly closed - and then turn left to rejoin the main path. Cross this stile and turn left. Go to the next stile and turn right, following the path through the meadow. Follow the path through the old gateway.

11 Cross this stile and then turn left along the drive, which is more distinct once you cross the cattle grid. On reaching the end of the drive, proceed through the white gates and turn right onto the road.

12 Refreshments are available at the Whipping Stocks Inn. Now it's just a gentle stroll down Stocks Lane back to the to where the car is parked.

but many more to the Mainwaring family, whose fine monuments crowd beside each other in both the north and south chapels.

MACCLESFIELD

Nestling below the hills of the High Peak, Macclesfield was once an important silk manufacturing town. Charles Roe built the first silk mill here in 1743, beside the River Bollin, and for more than a century and a half, Macclesfield was known as *the* silk town. It's appropriate then that Macclesfield can boast the country's only **Silk Museum** (see panel on page 320) where visitors are given a lively introduction to all aspects of the silk industry, from cocoon to loom. The museum is housed within the Heritage Centre, built in 1813 as a Sunday school to provide education for the children who worked in the silk mills. An award-winning audio-visual programme traces the development of the silk industry in Macclesfield and there are fascinating exhibitions on the Silk Road across Asia,

on silk cultivation, fashion and other uses of silk. The Heritage Centre itself has some interesting displays on Macclesfield's rich and exciting past.

The silk theme continues at nearby **Paradise Mill**. Built in the 1820s and in commercial use until 1981, it is now a working museum demonstrating silk weaving on 26 Jacquard hand looms. Exhibitions and restored workshops and living rooms capture the working conditions and lives of mill workers in the 1930s. It is also possible to buy locally-made silk products here.

In pre-Saxon times, Macclesfield was known as Hameston – the homestead on the rock, and on that rock is set the church founded by King Edward I and Queen Eleanor. From the modern town, a walk to the church involves climbing a gruelling flight of 108 steps. **St Michael and All Angels** was extended in the 1890s but its 14th century core remains, notably the Legh Chapel built to receive the body of Piers Legh, who had fought at Agincourt and died at the Siege of Meaux. Another chapel contains the famous Legh Pardon brass, which recalls the medieval practice of selling pardons for sins past, and even more conveniently for sins not yet committed. The inscription on the brass records that in return for saying five Paternosters and five Aves the Legh family received a pardon for 26,000 years and 26 days. The Savage Chapel and other parts of the church contain many memorials to the illustrious Savage family, whose numbers included Sir Thomas, who became Archbishop of York towards the end of the 15th century.

One of the Macclesfield area's most famous sons is Charles Frederick Tunnicliffe, the celebrated bird and wildlife artist, who was born at the nearby village of Langley in 1901. He studied at the Macclesfield School of Art and first came to public attention with his illustrations for Henry Williamson's *Tarka the Otter* in 1927. A frequently changing collection of Tunnicliffe's striking oil paintings, watercolours and etchings can be seen at the **West Park Museum** in a public park on the northwestern edge of town. This

purpose-built museum, founded in 1898 by the Brocklehurst family, also includes exhibits of ancient Egyptian artefacts acquired by Marianne Brocklehurst during visits to Egypt between 1873 and 1891. The collection features a mummy case, and the afterlife displays examine the process of mummification and the objects buried with the dead. Incidentally, the park boasts what is thought to be the largest bowling green in England.

A less well-known figure is William Buckley, who was born in Macclesfield around 1780 and later became a soldier. He took part in a mutiny at Gibraltar against the Rock's commanding officer, the Duke of York, father-to-be of Queen Victoria. The mutiny failed and Buckley was transported to Australia. There he escaped into the outback and became the leader of an aboriginal tribe who took this giant of a man, some six feet six inches tall, as the reincarnation of a dead chief. For 32 years Buckley never saw a white man or heard a word of English. When the explorer John Bateman, on his way to what is now Melbourne,

MACCLESFIELD SILK MUSEUMS

Silk Museum, Park Lane, Macclesfield, Cheshire SK11 6TJ
Tel: 01625 612045 Fax No: 01625 612048
website: www.silk-macclesfield.org

Macclesfield Silk Museums, based on three listed sites, tells the story of silk with particular reference to Macclesfield, once known as the silk capital of England and associated with silk for 400 years.

The Silk Museum is housed within the Heritage Centre, a former Sunday School built in 1814 to educate the children who worked in the mills. There is an-award winning audio visual programme whilst silk costume and textiles illustrate the importance of silk to fashion and its use for special occasions. The Mulberry Tree coffee shop offers light snacks

and a fuller menu. Just a short walk away new displays have been developed in the former School of Art and Design exploring the properties of silk, design education and Macclesfield's diverse textile industries. Archive footage accompany displays of historic textile machinery. Experience what life was like in a typical silk mill by taking a guided tour with one of the museum's knowledgeable and entertaining guides. Exhibitions and room sets illustrate life in the 1930s.

discovered him, Buckley had virtually forgotten his mother tongue. He was pardoned, given a pension and died at Hobart at the age of 76.

AROUND MACCLESFIELD

PRESTBURY

3 miles N of Macclesfield via the A523/A538

A regular winner of the Best Kept Village title, Prestbury is a charming village where a tree-lined main street runs down to a bridge over the River Bollin, ancient stocks stand against the church wall, and old coaching inns and black and white buildings mingle with the mellow red brickwork of later Georgian houses. The Church of St Peter, dating from the 13th century, still maintains a tradition which began in 1577. Every autumn and winter evening at 8pm a curfew bell is rung,

The Priest's House, Prestbury

ARTIZANA

The Village, Prestbury,
Cheshire SK10 4DG
Tel/Fax: 01625 827582
e-mail: art@artizana.co.uk
website: www.artizana.co.uk

A showcase for the very best in contemporary British design, **Artizana** was opened in 1984 and shortly afterwards it was selected for quality by the Crafts Council, an honour bestowed annually on just a handful of galleries. It was also one of only two private craft galleries in the UK to be invited by the Queen to a

reception for the arts in 1998 to celebrate the completion of the renovation of Windsor Castle by world-renowned craftsmen. In its Prestbury show-room, Artizana displays a dazzling collection of ceramics, glass, wood, silver, sculpture and furniture.

In addition to the work on display, Artizana has undertaken a number of prestigious commissions for private individuals and public institutions, including Lyme Park in Stockport for the National Trust, St Mungo's Museum in Glasgow, the City Art Gallery in Manchester, the Harris Museum in Preston, the White House Restaurant in Prestbury, as well as commissions for private households throughout Britain and abroad. There's no substitute for visiting Artizana's showroom but you can view current displays as well as past exhibitions and commissions on its comprehensive website.

ARTIZANA SUITE

The Village, Prestbury,
Cheshire SK10 4DG
Tel/Fax: 01625 827582
e-mail: suite@artizana.co.uk
website: www.artizana.co.uk/suite

Adjoining the Artizana gallery, renowned for contemporary British crafts and furniture, (see previous page), the **Artizana Suite** is the ultimate townhouse accommodation in the heart of Prestbury village. Exquisitely furnished and decorated, the suite is fully serviced and offers privacy, convenience and elegance for the discerning tourist or business visitor. The Artizana Suite is the only accommodation in the area that has been awarded the highest rating (five-Diamonds) by the English Tourist Board. More than just a hotel, it is truly a home away from home.

Centrally heated, the Artizana Suite has an elegantly furnished living room (with TV, stereo and broadband), a fully equipped kitchen with an informal dining area, a large bedroom with a double kingsize bed, a study which can be made into a child's room if required, and a bath room with bath tub and shower. A personal laundry service is also available, and guests have their own private parking space in the courtyard.

with the number of chimes corresponding to the date of the month. Close by is a building known as the **Norman Chapel** with a striking frontage carved with the characteristic Norman zig-zags and beaked heads. Even older are the carved fragments of an 8th century Saxon cross preserved under glass in the graveyard. Opposite the church is a remarkable magpie timber-framed house which is now a bank but used to be the vicarage. During the Commonwealth, the rightful incumbent was debarred from preaching in the church by the Puritans. Undaunted, the priest addressed his parishioners from the tiny balcony of his vicarage.

ADLINGTON

4 miles N of Macclesfield off the A523

Adlington boasts a fine old house, **Adlington Hall**, which has been the home of the Legh family since 1315 and is now one of the county's most popular attractions. Quadrangular in shape, this magnificent manor house has two distinctive styles of architecture: black and white half-timbered buildings on two sides, later Georgian additions in warm red brick on the others. There is much to see on a tour of the Hall, with beautifully polished wooden floors and lovely antique furnishings enhancing the air of elegance and grandeur. The Great Hall is a breathtaking sight, a vast room of lofty proportions that set off perfectly the exquisitely painted walls. The beautifully preserved 17th century organ here has responded to the touch of many maestros, none more famous than George Frederick Handel, who visited the Hall in the 1740s.

BOLLINGTON

4 miles NE of Macclesfield on the B5091

In its 19th century heyday, there were 13

cotton mills working away at Bollington, a little town perched on the foothills of the High Peak. Two of the largest mills, the Clarence and the Adelphi, still stand, although now adapted to other purposes. The Victorian shops and cottages around Water Street and the High Street recall those busy days. A striking feature of the town is the splendid 20-arched viaduct which once carried the railway over the River Dean. It is now part of the **Middlewood Way**, a 10-mile, traffic-free country trail that follows a scenic route from Macclesfield to Marple. The Way is open to walkers, cyclists and horse riders and during the season cycles are available for hire, complete with child seats if required. Just as remarkable as the viaduct, although in a different way, is **White Nancy**. This sugarloaf-shaped, whitewashed round tower stands on Kerridge Hill, more than 900 feet above sea level. It was erected in 1817 to commemorate the Battle of Waterloo and offers sweeping views in all directions.

SUTTON
2 miles S of Macclesfield off the A523

This small village, close to the Macclesfield Canal, is honoured by scholars as the birthplace of Raphael Holinshed, whose famous *Chronicles of England, Scotland & Ireland* (1577) provided the source material for no fewer than 14 of Shakespeare's plays. As well as drawing heavily on the facts in the Chronicles, the Bard wasn't above adopting some of Holinshed's happier turns of phrase.

BOSLEY
6 miles S of Macclesfield on the A523

To the east of Bosley town

centre runs the **Macclesfield Canal**, one of the highest waterways in England, running for much of its length at more than 500 feet above sea level. Thomas Telford was the surveyor of the 26-mile route, opened in 1831, which links the Trent and Mersey and the Peak Forest canals. Between Macclesfield and Congleton, the canal descends over 100 feet in a spectacular series of 12 locks at Bosley, before crossing the River Dane via Telford's handsome iron viaduct. Other unusual features of this superbly engineered canal are the two 'roving bridges' south of Congleton. These swing from one bank to the other where the towpath changes sides and so enabled horses to cross over without the tow-rope having to be unhitched.

GAWSWORTH
3 miles SW of Macclesfield off the A536

Gawsworth Hall is a captivating sight with its dazzling black and white half-

Gawsworth Hall

timbered walls and lofty three-decker Tudor windows. The Hall was built in 1480 by the Fitton family, one of whose descendants, the celebrated beauty Mary Fitton, is believed by some to be the Dark Lady of Shakespeare's sonnets. The Bard would no doubt approve of Gawsworth's famous open-air theatre, where performances range from his own plays to Gilbert and Sullivan operas, with the Hall serving as a lovely backdrop. Surrounded by a huge park, Gawsworth, to quote its owner Timothy Richards, is "the epitome of a lived-in historic house". Every room that visitors see (which is virtually every room in the house) is in daily use by him and his family. And what wonderful rooms they are. Myriad windows bathe the rooms in light, the low ceilings and modest dimensions radiate calm, and even the richly-carved main staircase is conceived on a human scale. The beautifully sited church, and the lake nearby, add still more to the appeal of this magical place. The Hall was the scene - in 1712 - of a famous duel when Lord Mohun and the Duke of Hamilton fought over the estates; both were killed. The country's last professional jester, a certain Samuel Johnson, lived in the house and is buried in a nearby spinney.

CAPESTHORNE HALL

5 miles W of Macclesfield on the A34

The home of the Bromley-Davenport family for generations, Capesthorne Hall dates back to 1719, when it was designed by the Smiths of Warwick. It was altered in 1837 by Blore, and following a fire in 1861 it was remodelled and extended by the celebrated architect Anthony Salvin. The present building presents a magnificent medley of Elizabethan-style turrets and towers, domes and cupolas, while inside the house is a wealth of

portraits and artefacts collected by family members during the course of their Grand Tours throughout Europe, America and the Far East. The Queen Anne Room features a monumental fireplace, while the Box Room has a fascinating collection that ranges from a Victorian oak letterbox to antique hat boxes and cigar boxes. In medieval times the head of the Bromley-Davenport family held the post of Chief Forester of Macclesfield Forest, which gave him authority to mete out summary justice to anyone who transgressed the savage forestry laws. As a reminder of their power, the family crest includes the severed head of a felon. One of these crests, on the main staircase built in the 1860s, was commissioned by the staunchly Conservative Bromley-Davenport of the time and the felon's head is instantly recognisable as the Liberal leader of the day, William Ewart Gladstone. In the grounds, near the Georgian family chapel, the 18th century Italian gates open on to lakeside gardens.

NETHER ALDERLEY

6 miles NW of Macclesfield on the A34

Nether Alderley Mill is a delightful 15th century watermill that has been restored by the National Trust. The red sandstone walls are almost hidden under the huge sweep of its stone tiled roof. Inside is the original Elizabethan woodwork and Victorian mill machinery which is still in working order, with two tandem overshot wheels powering the mill. The 14th century church of St Mary is almost a private mausoleum for the Alderley branch of the Stanley family: monuments to dead Stanleys are everywhere. Living members of the family were provided with an unusual richly carved pew, set up on the wall like an opera box and reached by a flight of steps outside.

ALDERLEY EDGE

6 miles NW of Macclesfield on the A34

Alderley Edge

Alderley Edge takes its name from the long, wooded escarpment, nearly two miles long, that rises 600 feet above sea level and culminates in sandy crags overlooking the Cheshire Plain. In Victorian times, this spectacular area was the private preserve of the Stanley family and it was only under great pressure that they grudgingly allowed the 'Cottentots' of Manchester access on occasional summer weekends. Nowadays, walkers can roam freely along the many footpaths through the woods, one of which will take them to **Hare Hill Gardens**, one of the lesser-known National Trust properties. These

HENRY D. JOHNSTONE JEWELLERS

51a London Road, Alderley Edge, Cheshire SK9 7DY
Tel: 01625 583565 Fax: 01625 583673
e-mail: henryjohnstone@btconnect.com

It was a school trip to the historic Kimberley diamond mine when Henry Johnstone was a child in South Africa that inspired his passion for jewellery. Later, as a manager for the prestigious Watches of Switzerland group and as general manager at Cheshire-based Cottrills, he extended his knowledge of precious metals and stones. Now, as owner-manager of the **Henry D. Johnstone Jewellers**, his wide experience as a watch and jewellery specialist provides outstanding expertise. He specialises in hand-made wedding rings, diamond rings and jewellery, as well as a comprehensive range of pre-owned quality wristwatches.

The extensive displays include Fuurer Jacot Swiss wedding rings; Anonimo writstwatches from Florence, Italy; Autore South Sea pearls; hand-made Italian jewellery from Marco Bicego and many other leading brands. There's a jewellery workshop on the premises which, using computer-aided design, provides bespoke jewellery design and a fast, efficient service. The workshop also undertakes specialist and general jewellery repairs, as well as watch and clock repairs, and also offers a valuation service. And if you are looking for great savings on a comprehensive range of new or previously owned wristwatches, you'll find a great selection of Rolex, Cartier, Patek Philippe, Omega and all quality Swiss wristwatches on sale here.

THE LAVENDER TREE

105 Brook Lane, Alderley Edge, Cheshire SK9 7RU
Tel: 01625 599532 Fax: 01625 586269
e-mail: info@thelavendertree.com
website: www.thelavendertree.com

If you are thinking of brightening up your interior décor, the place to seek out is **The Lavender Tree** at Alderley Edge where you'll find innovative and distinctive designs to reflect your lifestyle. The combined experiences of partners Sarah McCall and Emma Bolton include many years within the fashion, floral and interior design industries. They decided to use their knowledge and solid backgrounds to create a venue for relaxation – "an inspirational place that uses beauty and solace to gently calm and massage the soul". On display are floral designs, soft furnishings, full interior designs, carpets, floorings, paint effects, candles and an array of desirable gifts.

Sarah and Emma offer a personal design consultancy to help you bring your design dreams into reality with everything made-to-measure and fitted to a very high standard. If they don't have a particular item, they will source it from elsewhere or have it made to your specification. Many clients also use their floral design service to give reception desks and offices an exceptionally pleasing focal point. To balance your lifestyle, Sarah and Emma also offer holistic therapies which include reflexology, Reiki, aromatherapy and baby/toddler massage – as they put it: "everyone should experience the contentment of pure relaxation".

Victorian gardens include fine woodland, a walled garden themed in blue, white and yellow flowers, and huge banks of rhododendrons.

WILMSLOW

6 miles NW of Macclesfield off the A34

The oldest building in Wilmslow is **St Bartholomew's Church**, built between 1517 and 1537, and notable for its magnificent ceiling, some striking effigies, and for the fact that Prime Minister-to-be Gladstone worshipped here as a boy. A hamlet in medieval times, Wilmslow mushroomed as a mill town in the 18th and 19th centuries, and is now a busy commuter town offering a good choice of inns, hotels and restaurants.

Claiming to be the smallest tourist attraction in the country, **Romany's Caravan**, or Vardo, stands in its own

Romany's Caravan, Wilmslow

APPAREL

16 Water Lane, Wilmslow, Cheshire SK9 5AA
Tel: 01625 536825 e-mail: enquiries@apparel-cheshire.co.uk
Fax: 01625 536826 website: www.apparel-cheshire.co.uk

Customers visiting **Apparel**, in Wilmslow's town centre, enter a world of indulgence, style and glamour, and discover a unique shopping experience in a relaxed and friendly atmosphere. Within its two floors of modern displays, this popular boutique offers a wide range of designer labels to ensure you 'dress to impress'. It stocks collections by Armani, D&G, Cavalli, Nolita, Velvet, Liu Jo, Custo, Guru, and Sass & Bide, and also brings to the northwest the latest fashions from Milan and Paris. These collections are complemented by a delightful choice of accessories, shoes and boots.

special Memorial Garden in Wilmslow. Its interior has been restored to what it was like when used by traveller Romany and his family when on holiday in his beloved north country. It is open to the public on the second Saturday of the month during May, June, July and September.

STYAL

7 miles NW of Macclesfield off the B5166

Cared for by the National Trust, **Styal Country Park** is set in 250 acres of the beautifully wooded valley of the River Bollin and offers many woodland and riverside walks. The Park is open to the public from dawn to dusk throughout the year and is a wonderful place for picnics. Lying within the Park is **Quarry Bank Mill**, a grand old building erected in 1784 and one of the first generation of cotton mills. It was powered by a huge iron waterwheel fed by the River Bollin. Visitors follow the history of the mill through various galleries and displays within the museum, including weaving and spinning demonstrations, and can experience for themselves, with the help of guides dressed in period costume, what life was like for the 100 girls and boys who once lived in the Apprentice House. The Mill stages a full programme of events throughout the year. Also within the park is the delightful **Styal Village**, which was established by the mill's original owner, Samuel Greg, a philanthropist and pioneer of the factory system. He took children from the slums of Manchester

Quarry Bank Mill, Styal

to work in his mill, and in return for their labour provided them with food, clothing, housing, education and a place of worship.

DISLEY

8 miles SE of Stockport on the A6

The small town of Disley lies close to the Macclesfield Canal and little more than half a mile from **Lyme Park Country Park**. At the heart of the spectacular 1,400-acre moorland park where red and fallow deer roam freely, stands Lyme Park (National Trust), home of the Legh family for more than 600 years. The elegant Palladian exterior of this great house encloses a superb Elizabethan mansion. Among the many treasures on show are carvings by Grinling Gibbons, tapestries from Mortlake, and a unique collection of English clocks. The house featured many times in the BBC's 1995 production of *Pride and Prejudice* when it represented the exterior of Pemberley, the home of Elizabeth Bennett's curmudgeonly lover, Mr Darcy. It also appeared in Granada's *The Forsyte Saga*, and some of the costumes from that production are on display. Amenities at the park include two shops, a restaurant, tea room and a children's play area. From Easter to October, Lyme Park hosts a varied programme of events, from plant fairs and outdoor performances of plays to art exhibitions and a Morris Minor Owners Club Rally.

TOURIST INFORMATION CENTRES

CHESHIRE

ALTRINCHAM
20 Stamford New Road
Altrincham
Cheshire
WA14 1EJ
Tel: 0161 912 5931 or 0161 912 5932
Fax: 0161 912 5954
e-mail: tourist.information@trafford.gov.uk

CHESTER (TOWN HALL)
Town Hall
Northgate Street
Chester
Cheshire
CH1 2HJ
Tel: 01244 402111 or 01244 402385
Fax: 01244 400420
e-mail: tis@chester.gov.uk

CHESTER VISITOR CENTRE
Chester Visitor Centre
Vicars Lane
Chester
Cheshire
CH1 1QX
Tel: 01244 402111 or 01244 351609
Fax: 01244 403188
e-mail: tis@chester.gov.uk

CONGLETON
Town Hall
High Street
Congleton
Cheshire
CW12 1BN
Tel: 01260 271095 or 01260 285257
Fax: 01260 298243
e-mail: tourism@congleton.gov.uk

ELLESMERE PORT
Unit 22b
McArthur Glen Outlet Village
Kinsey Road
Ellesmere Port
Cheshire
CH65 9JJ
Tel: 0151 356 7879
Fax: 0151 356 1005
e-mail: cheshireoaks.cc@visitor-centre.net

KNUTSFORD
Council Offices
Toft Road
Knutsford
Cheshire
WA16 6TA
Tel: 01565 632611 or 01565 632210
Fax: 01565 652367
e-mail: ktic@macclesfield.gov.uk

MACCLESFIELD
Macclesfield
Town Hall
Macclesfield
Cheshire
SK10 1DX
Tel: 01625 504114 or 01625 504115
Fax: 01625 504116
e-mail: informationcentre@macclesfield.gov.uk

NANTWICH
Church House
Church Walk
Nantwich
Cheshire
CW5 5RG
Tel: 01270 610983
Fax: 01270 610880
e-mail: touristi@crewe-nantwich.gov.uk

NORTHWICH
Information Centre
1 The Arcade
Northwich
Cheshire
CW9 5AS
Tel: 01606 353534 or 01606 353500
Fax: 01606 353516
e-mail: tourism@valeroyal.gov.uk

RUNCORN
6 Church Street
Runcorn
Cheshire
WA7 1LT
Tel: 01928 576776
Fax: 01928 569656
e-mail: tourist.info@halton-borough.gov.uk

WARRINGTON

The Market Hall
Academy Way
Warrington
Cheshire
WA1 2EN
Tel: 01925 632571
Fax: 01925 654593
e-mail: informationcentre@warrington.gov.uk

WILMSLOW

The Information Centre
Rectory Fields
Wilmslow
Cheshire
SK9 1BU
Tel: 01625 522275 or 01625 504114
Fax: 01625 549684 or 01625 504116
e-mail: i.hillaby@macclesfield.gov.uk

CUMBRIA

ALSTON MOOR

Town Hall
Front Street
Alston
Cumbria
CA9 3RF
Tel: 01434 382244 or 01768 867466
Fax: 01434 382255
e-mail: alston.tic@eden.gov.uk

AMBLESIDE

Central Buildings
Market Cross
Ambleside
Cumbria
LA22 9BS
Tel: 015394 32582 or 015394 32602
Fax: 015394 34901
e-mail: amblesidetic@southlakeland.gov.uk

APPLEBY-IN-WESTMORLAND

Moot Hall
Boroughgate
Appleby-in-Westmorland
Cumbria
CA16 6XE
Tel: 017683 51177
Fax: 017683 51090
e-mail: tic@applebytown.org.uk

BARROW-IN-FURNESS

Forum 28
Duke Street
Barrow-in-Furness
Cumbria
LA14 1HU
Tel: 01229 894784
Fax: 01229 894703
e-mail: touristinfo@barrowbc.gov.uk

BOWNESS

Glebe Road
Bowness-on-Windermere
Cumbria
LA23 3HJ
Tel: 015394 42895
Fax: 015394 88005
e-mail: bownesstic@lake-district.gov.uk

BRAMPTON

Moot Hall
Market Place
Brampton
Cumbria
CA8 1RW
Tel: 016977 3433
Fax: 016977 3433
e-mail: ElisabethB@CarlisleCity.gov.uk

BROUGHTON-IN-FURNESS

Town Hall, The Square
Broughton-in-Furness
Cumbria
LA20 6JF
Tel: 01229 716115
Fax: 01229 716115
e-mail: e-mail@broughton-tic.fsnet.co.uk

CARLISLE

Old Town Hall
Greenmarket
Carlisle
Cumbria
CA3 8JE
Tel: 01228 625600
Fax: 01228 625604
e-mail: tourism@carlisle-city.gov.uk

COCKERMOUTH

Town Hall
Market Street
Cockermouth
Cumbria
CA13 9NP
Tel: 01900 822634
Fax: 01900 822603
e-mail: e-mail@cockermouth-tic.fsnet.co.uk

CONISTON
Ruskin Avenue
Coniston
Cumbria
LA21 8EH
Tel: 015394 41533
Fax: 015394 41802
e-mail: Conistontic@lake-district.gov.uk

EGREMONT
12 Main Street
Egremont
Cumbria
CA22 2DW
Tel: 01946 820693
e-mail: e-mail@egremont-tic.fsnet.co.uk

GRANGE-OVER-SANDS
Victoria Hall
Main Street
Grange-over-Sands
Cumbria
LA11 6DP
Tel: 015395 34026
Fax: 015395 34331
e-mail: grangetic@southlakeland.gov.uk

GRASMERE
Redbank Road
Grasmere
Cumbria
LA22 9SW
Tel: 015394 35245
Fax: 015394 35057
e-mail: Grasmeretic@lake-district.gov.uk

HAWKSHEAD
Main Car Park
Hawkshead
Cumbria
LA22 0NT
Tel: 015394 36525
Fax: 015394 36349
e-mail: hawksheadtic@lake-district.gov.uk

KENDAL
Town Hall
Highgate
Kendal
Cumbria
LA9 4DL
Tel: 01539 725758 or 01539 721780
Fax: 01539 734457
e-mail: kendaltic@southlakeland.gov.uk

KESWICK
Moot Hall
Market Square
Keswick
Cumbria
CA12 5JR
Tel: 017687 72645
Fax: 017687 75043
e-mail: keswicktic@lake-district.gov.uk

KILLINGTON LAKE
Killington Lake Services
M6 South
Nr Kendal
Cumbria
LA8 0NW
Tel: 015396 20138
Fax: 015396 21071
e-mail: killingtonlake@blackpool.gov.uk

KIRKBY LONSDALE
24 Main Street
Kirkby Lonsdale
Cumbria
LA6 2AE
Tel: 015242 71437
Fax: 015242 71437
e-mail: kltic@southlakeland.gov.uk

KIRKBY STEPHEN
Market Street
Kirkby Stephen
Cumbria
CA17 4QN
Tel: 017683 71199
Fax: 017683 72728
e-mail: ks.tic@eden.gov.uk

MARYPORT
Maryport Town Hall
Senhouse Street
Maryport
Cumbria
CA15 6BH
Tel: 01900 812101 or 01900 822634
Fax: 01900 811211 or 01900 822603
e-mail: maryporttic@allerdale.gov.uk

MILLOM
Station Building
Station Road
Millom
Cumbria
LA18 5AA
Tel: 01229 774819
e-mail: millomtic@copelandbc.gov.uk

PENRITH

Middlegate
Penrith
CA11 7PT
Tel: 01768 867466
Fax: 01768 891754
e-mail: pen.tic@eden.gov.uk

RHEGED

Rheged Tourist Information Centre
Rheged
Penrith
CA11 0DQ
Tel: 01768 860034
Fax: 01768 868002
e-mail: tic@rheged.com

SILLOTH-ON-SOLWAY

Solway Coast Discovery Centre
Liddel Street
Silloth-on-Solway
Cumbria
CA7 4DD
Tel: 016973 31944 or 01900 812101
Fax: 016973 31944
e-mail: sillothtic@allerdale.gov.uk

SOUTHWAITE

M6 Service Area
Southwaite
Carlisle
Cumbria
CA4 ONS
Tel: 016974 73445
Fax: 016974 73445
e-mail: southwaitetic@visitscotland.com

ULLSWATER

Main Car Park
Glenridding
Penrith
Cumbria
CA11 0PD
Tel: 017684 82414
Fax: 017684 82414
e-mail: ullswatertic@lake-district.gov.uk

ULVERSTON

Coronation Hall
County Square
Ulverston
Cumbria
LA12 7LZ
Tel: 01229 587120
Fax: 01229 582626
e-mail: ulverstontic@southlakeland.gov.uk

WHITEHAVEN

Market Hall
Market Place
Whitehaven
Cumbria
CA28 7JG
Tel: 01946 852939
Fax: 01946 852954
e-mail: tic@copelandbc.gov.uk

WINDERMERE

Victoria Street
Windermere
Cumbria
LA23 1AD
Tel: 015394 46499
Fax: 015394 47439
e-mail: windermeretic@southlakeland.gov.uk

WORKINGTON

21 Finkle Street
Workington
Cumbria
CA14 2BE
Tel: 01900 606699
Fax: 01900 606699
e-mail: workingtontic@allerdale.gov.uk

GREATER MANCHESTER

BOLTON

Central Library Foyer
Le Mans Cres
Bolton
Greater Manchester
BL1 1SE
Tel: 01204 334321
Fax: 01204 398101
e-mail: tourist.info@bolton.gov.uk

BURY

The Met Arts Centre
Market Street
Bury
Greater Manchester
BL9 0BN
Tel: 0161 253 5111
Fax: 0161 253 5919
e-mail: touristinformation@bury.gov.uk

MANCHESTER AIRPORT (TRM 1)
International Arrivals Hall Terminal 1
Manchester Airport, Manchester
Greater Manchester
M90 3NY
Tel: 0161 436 3344 or 0161 489 6412 (am)
Fax: 0161 489 8831 or 0161 489 6413 (am)
e-mail: airportTIC@marketing-manchester.co.uk

MANCHESTER AIRPORT (TRM 2)
International Arrivals Hall Terminal 2
Manchester Airport, Manchester
Greater Manchester
M90 4TU
Tel: 0161 489 6412 or 0146 436 3344
Fax: 0161 489 6413 or 0161 489 8831
e-mail: airportTIC@marketing-manchester.co.uk

MANCHESTER VISITOR INFORMATION CENTRE
Manchester Visitor Centre
Town Hall Extension, Lloyd St
Manchester
Greater Manchester
M60 2LA
Tel: 0161 234 3157 or 0161 234 3158
Fax: 0161 236 9900
e-mail:
    manchester_visitor_centre@notes.manchester.gov.uk

OLDHAM
12 Albion Street
Oldham
Greater Manchester
OL1 3BD
Tel: 0161 627 1024
Fax: 0161 911 3064
e-mail: ecs.tourist@oldham.gov.uk

SADDLEWORTH
Saddleworth Museum
High Street, Uppermill
Saddleworth, Oldham
Greater Manchester
OL3 6HS
Tel: 01457 870336
Fax: 01457 870336
e-mail: ecs.saddleworthtic@oldham.gov.uk

SALFORD
The Lowry, Pier 8 Salford Quays
Salford
Greater Manchester
M50 3AZ
Tel: 0161 848 8601
Fax: 0161 872 3848
e-mail: christine.ellis@salford.gov.uk

STOCKPORT
Staircase House
30 Market Place
Stockport
Greater Manchester
SK1 1ES
Tel: 0161 474 4444
Fax: 0161 429 6348
e-mail: tourist.information@stockport.gov.uk

WIGAN
62 Wallgate
Wigan
Greater Manchester
WN1 1BA
Tel: 01942 825677
Fax: 01942 776477
e-mail: tic@wlct.org

ISLE OF MAN

DOUGLAS
Sea Terminal Buildings
Douglas
Isle of Man
IM1 2RG
Tel: 01624 686766
Fax: 01624 627443
e-mail: tourism@gov.im

LANCASHIRE

ACCRINGTON
Town Hall
Blackburn Road
Accrington
Lancashire
BB5 1LA
Tel: 01254 872595
Fax: 01254 380291
e-mail: tourism@hyndburnbc.gov.uk

ASHTON-UNDER-LYNE
Council Offices
Wellington Road
Ashton-Under-Lyne
Lancashire
OL6 6DL
Tel: 0161 343 4343
Fax: 0161 342 2822
e-mail: tourist.information@mail.tameside.gov.uk

BARNOLDSWICK
The Council Shop
Fernlea Avenue
Barnoldswick
Lancashire
BB18 5DL
Tel: 01282 666704
Fax: 01282 666704
e-mail: tourist.info@pendle.gov.uk

BLACKBURN
50-54 Church Street
Blackburn
Lancashire
BB1 5AL
Tel: 01254 53277
Fax: 01254 683536
e-mail: visit@blackburn.gov.uk

BLACKPOOL
1 Clifton Street
Blackpool
Lancashire
FY1 1LY
Tel: 01253 478222
Fax: 01253 478210
e-mail: tic@blackpool.gov.uk

BURNLEY
Burnley Bus Station
Croft Street
Burnley
Lancashire
BB11 2EF
Tel: 01282 664421 or 01282 423125
Fax: 01282 454086
e-mail: tic@burnley.gov.uk

CLEVELEYS
Victoria Square
Thornton
Cleveleys
Lancashire
FY5 1AU
Tel: 01253 853378
Fax: 01253 866124
e-mail: cleveleystic@btopenworld.com

CLITHEROE
12-14 Market Place
Clitheroe
Lancashire
BB7 2DA
Tel: 01200 425566 or 01200 442226
Fax: 01200 414488
e-mail: tourism@ribblevalley.gov.uk

FLEETWOOD
Old Ferry Office, The Esplanade
Fleetwood
Lancashire
FY7 6DL
Tel: 01253 773953
Fax: 01253 876656
e-mail: ferrytic@btopenworld.com

GARSTANG
Council Offices, Discovery Centre
High Street
Garstang
Lancashire
PR3 1FU
Tel: 01995 602125
Fax: 01995 604325
e-mail: garstangtic@btopenworld.com

LANCASTER
29 Castle Hill
Lancaster
Lancashire
LA1 1YN
Tel: 01524 32878 or 01524 582393
Fax: 01524 382849 or 01524 847472
e-mail: lancastertic@lancaster.gov.uk

LYTHAM ST ANNES
Visitor & Travel Information Centre
67 St Annes Road West
Lytham St Annes
Lancashire
FY8 1SL
Tel: 01253 725610
Fax: 01253 640708
e-mail: touristinformation@fylde.gov.uk

MORECAMBE
Old Station Buildings, Marine Road Central
Morecambe
Lancashire
LA4 4DB
Tel: 01524 582808
Fax: 01524 832549
e-mail: morecambetic@lancaster.gov.uk

PENDLE HERITAGE CENTRE
Park Hill
Barrowford
Nelson
Lancashire
BB9 6JQ
Tel: 01282 661701
Fax: 01282 661701
e-mail: heritage.centre@pendle.gov.uk

PRESTON
The Guildhall
Lancaster Road
Preston
Lancashire
PR1 1HT
Tel: 01772 253731 or 903215/6/7
Fax: 01772 903214
e-mail: tourism@preston.gov.uk

RAWTENSTALL
41-45 Kay Street
Rawtenstall
Rossendale
Lancashire
BB4 7LS
Tel: 01706 244678 or Fax: 01706 226590
e-mail: tourism@rossendalebc.gov.uk

ROCHDALE
Touchstones
The Esplanade
Rochdale
Lancashire
OL16 1AQ
Tel: 01706 864928
Fax: 01706 864215
e-mail: tic@rochdale.gov.uk

MERSEYSIDE

BIRKENHEAD
Tourist Information Centre
Woodside Ferry Terminal
Birkenhead
Merseyside
CH41 6DU
Tel: 0151 647 6780 or 0151 666 3188
Fax: 0151 666 2448 or 0150 691 8188
e-mail: touristinfo@wirral.gov.uk

LIVERPOOL JOHN LENNON AIRPORT
Arrivals Hall, South Terminal
Liverpool John Lennon Airport
Speke Hall Avenue
Liverpool
Merseyside
L24 1YD
Tel: 09066806886 or 0151 709 5111
Fax: 0151 907 1056 or 0151 707 0986
e-mail: info@visitliverpool.com

LIVERPOOL (MARITIME MUSEUM)
Merseyside Maritime Museum
Albert Dock
Liverpool
Merseyside
L3 4AQ
Tel: 0906 680 6886 or 0151 709 5111
Fax: 0151 478 4552
e-mail: tic@liverpoolmuseums.org.uk

LIVERPOOL (QUEEN SQUARE)
Queen Square
Roe Street
Liverpool
Merseyside
L1 1RG
Tel: 0906 680 6886
(Calls charged at 25 pence per minute).
Fax: 0151 707 0986 or 0151 708 0204
e-mail: info@visitliverpool.com

SOUTHPORT
112 Lord Street
Southport
Merseyside
PR8 1NY
Tel: 01704 533333
Fax: 01704 500175
e-mail: info@visitsouthport.com

ST HELENS
The World of Glass
Chalon Way East
St Helens
Merseyside
WA10 1BX
Tel: 01744 755150
Fax: 01744 616966
e-mail: info@sthelenstic.com

INDEX OF ADVERTISERS

JEWELLERY

David Alexander, Tarporley   p308
Henry D. Johnstone Jewellers,
    Alderley Edge   p325
The Linden Tree, Cockermouth   p74
Phillip Godfrey Designer Goldsmith,
    Southport   p238

PLACES OF INTEREST

Abbot Hall Art Gallery & Museum, Kendal   p13
The Aquarium of the Lakes, Lakeside   p25
The Armitt Museum, Ambleside   p31
The Beacon, Whitehaven   p70
Blue Planet Aquarium, Ellesmere Port   p275
The Boat Museum, Ellesmere Port   p273
Bramall Hall, Stockport   p244
Brantwood, Coniston   p53
British Lawnmower Museum, Southport   p239
Cheshire Military Museum, Chester   p270
Dalemain Historic House, Penrith   p111
The Dock Museum, Barrow-in-Furness   p47
East Lancashire Railway, Bury   p254
Helmshore Mills Textile Museum,
    Helmshore   p196
High Head Sculpture Valley, Ivegill   p128
Lakeland Wildlife Oasis, Hale   p12
Lakeland's Woodland Heritage Exhibition,
    Backbarrow   p44
Lancaster Castle, Lancaster   p137
Lancaster Maritime Museum, Lancaster   p139
Macclesfield Silk Museums, Macclesfield   p320
Manx Electric Railway, Douglas   p212
Marbury Country Park, Comberbach   p303
Maryport Maritime Museum, Maryport   p80
Muncaster Castle, Ravenglass   p64
North Pennines Heritage Trust, Nenthead   p106
Rochdale Pioneers Museum, Rochdale   p255
Rossendale Museum, Rawtenstall   p194
Ruskin Museum, Coniston   p53
Stockport Air Raid Shelters, Stockport   p243
Threlkeld Mining Museum, Keswick   p87
Towneley Hall Art Gallery & Museums,
    Burnley   p184

Windermere Steamboats & Museum,
    Windermere   p23
WWT Martin Mere, Rufford   p206

SPECIALIST FOOD AND DRINK

Airey's Farm Shop, Ayside   p24
Cartmel Sticky Toffee Pudding Co. Ltd,
    Cartmel   p40
The Cheese Shop, Chester   p268
Cheesie Tchaikovsky, Clitheroe   p161
Church Farm Organics, Thurstaston   p283
Country Cuts Organic Meats, Santon Bridge   p68
Delikatessa, Crewe   p292
The Hollies Farm Shop, Little Budworth   p306
Holly Tree Farm Shop, Knutsford   p313
Kitridding Farm Shop, Lupton   p11
The Laird's Larder, Carlisle   p123
Lucy's of Ambleside, Ambleside   p30
Mansergh Hall Farm Shop, Kirkby Lonsdale   p8
Palms Fine Foods, West Kirby   p279
The Pie Mill, Threlkeld   p88
Taste Fine Foods, Ramsbottom   p250

INDEX OF WALKS

Looking for more walks?

The walks in this book have been gleaned from Britain's largest online walking guide, to be found at *www.walkingworld.com*.

The site contains over 2000 walks from all over England, Scotland and Wales so there are plenty more to choose from in this book's region as well as further afield - ideal if you are taking a short break as you can plan your walks in advance. There are walks of every length and type to suit all tastes.

Want more detail for the walks in this book? Next to every walk in this book you will see a Walk ID. You can enter this ID number on Walkingworld's 'Find a Walk' page and you will be taken straight to the details of that walk.

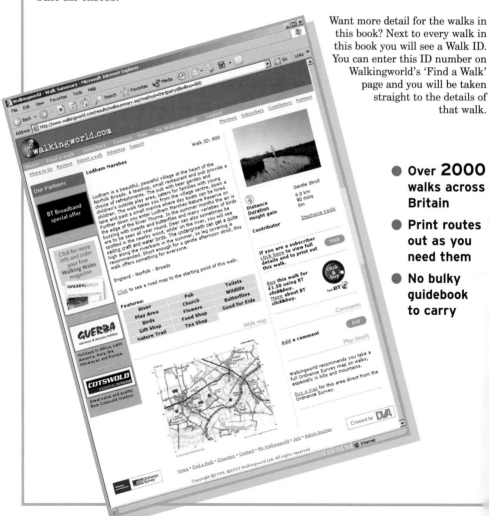

- Over **2000** walks across Britain

- Print routes out as you need them

- No bulky guidebook to carry

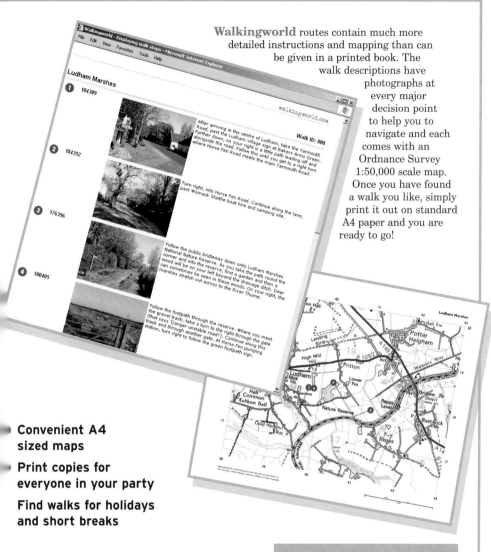

Walkingworld routes contain much more detailed instructions and mapping than can be given in a printed book. The walk descriptions have photographs at every major decision point to help you to navigate and each comes with an Ordnance Survey 1:50,000 scale map. Once you have found a walk you like, simply print it out on standard A4 paper and you are ready to go!

- Convenient A4 sized maps
- Print copies for everyone in your party
- Find walks for holidays and short breaks

A modest annual subscription gives you access to over 2000 walks, all in Walkingworld's easy to follow format. The database of walks is growing all the time and as a subscriber you gain access to new routes as soon as they are published.

Visit the Walkingworld website at *www.walkingworld.com*

ORDER FORM

To order any of our publications just fill in the payment details below and complete the order form. For orders of less than 4 copies please add £1 per book for postage and packing. Orders over 4 copies are P & P free.

Please Complete Either:

I enclose a cheque for £ [_____] made payable to Travel Publishing Ltd

Or:

Card No: [_____]   Expiry Date: [_____]

Signature: [_____]

NAME: [_____]

ADDRESS: [_____]

TEL NO: [_____]

Please either send, telephone, fax or e-mail your order to:
Travel Publishing Ltd, 7a Apollo House, Calleva Park, Aldermaston, Berkshire RG7 8TN
Tel: 0118 981 7777   Fax: 0118 982 0077 e-mail: info@travelpublishing.co.uk

	PRICE	QUANTITY		PRICE	QUANTITY
HIDDEN PLACES REGIONAL TITLES			**COUNTRY PUBS AND INNS**		
Cornwall	£8.99	....	Cornwall	£5.99	....
Devon	£8.99	....	Devon	£8.99	....
Dorset, Hants & Isle of Wight	£8.99	....	Sussex	£7.99	....
East Anglia	£8.99	....	Yorkshire	£8.99	....
Gloucs, Wiltshire & Somerset	£8.99	....	Wales	£8.99	....
Heart of England	£8.99	....	**COUNTRY LIVING RURAL GUIDES**		
Hereford, Worcs & Shropshire	£8.99	....	East Anglia	£10.99	....
Lake District & Cumbria	£8.99	....	Heart of England	£10.99	....
Lancashire & Cheshire	£8.99	....	Ireland	£11.99	....
Northumberland & Durham	£8.99	....	North East	£10.99	....
Peak District	£8.99	....	North West	£10.99	....
Sussex	£8.99	....	Scotland	£11.99	....
Yorkshire	£8.99	....	South of England	£10.99	....
HIDDEN PLACES NATIONAL TITLES			South East of England	£10.99	....
England	£11.99	....	Wales	£11.99	....
Ireland	£11.99	....	West Country	£10.99	....
Scotland	£11.99	....			
Wales	£11.99	....			
HIDDEN INNS TITLES					
East Anglia	£7.99	....			
Heart of England	£7.99	....	**Value** [_____]		
North of England	£7.99	....			
South	£7.99	....	**Postage and Packing** [_____]		
South East	£7.99	....			
Wales	£7.99	....			
West Country	£7.99	....	**Total Value** [_____]		
Yorkshire	£7.99	....			

READER REACTION FORM

The *Travel Publishing* research team would like to receive reader's comments on any visitor attractions or places reviewed in the book and also recommendations for suitable entries to be included in the next edition. This will help ensure that the *Country Living series of Guides* continues to provide its readers with useful information on the more interesting, unusual or unique features of each attraction or place ensuring that their visit to the local area is an enjoyable and stimulating experience. To provide your comments or recommendations would you please complete the forms below and overleaf as indicated and send to:

**The Research Department, Travel Publishing Ltd,
7a Apollo House, Calleva Park, Aldermaston, Reading, RG7 8TN.**

Your Name:

Your Address:

Your Telephone Number:

Please tick as appropriate:

Comments ☐   Recommendation ☐

Name of Establishment:

Address:

Telephone Number:

Name of Contact:

READER REACTION FORM

COMMENT OR REASON FOR RECOMMENDATION:

....
....
....
....
....
....
....
....
....
....
....
....
....
....
....
....
....
....
....

READER REACTION FORM

The *Travel Publishing* research team would like to receive reader's comments on any visitor attractions or places reviewed in the book and also recommendations for suitable entries to be included in the next edition. This will help ensure that the *Country Living series of Guides* continues to provide its readers with useful information on the more interesting, unusual or unique features of each attraction or place ensuring that their visit to the local area is an enjoyable and stimulating experience. To provide your comments or recommendations would you please complete the forms below and overleaf as indicated and send to:

**The Research Department, Travel Publishing Ltd,
7a Apollo House, Calleva Park, Aldermaston, Reading, RG7 8TN.**

Your Name:

Your Address:

Your Telephone Number:

Please tick as appropriate:

Comments ☐   Recommendation ☐

Name of Establishment:

Address:

Telephone Number:

Name of Contact:

READER REACTION FORM

COMMENT OR REASON FOR RECOMMENDATION:

INDEX TO TOWNS & PLACES OF INTEREST